21st Century African Development Strategies

"A book that interrogates Africa's development challenges from several different angles is rare. One that builds on the analytical competences of mathematics, economics, and other social sciences, and then proceeds to map out a pathway to long-term, self-sustaining, development, is even rarer. Haider Khan and the two Sonkos have succeeded where previous efforts failed. Their multidisciplinary approach has enabled them to interrogate Africa's contemporary challenges holistically, prior to coming up with innovative solutions."

—Professor M J Balogun, *former Director-General, Administration Staff College of Nigeria, (ASCON) and Adviser to the President of the United Nations General Assembly*

"This is a unique book, combining impressive 'big picture' reflections on ethics, history, and political economy with fine-grained analyses of individual sectors, including education, innovation, and Islamic finance. It is a very important contribution to the debate on the future of a most complex continent that will play an increasingly important role in the global economy and society."

—Professor Ha-Joon Chang, *SOAS University of London*, author of *Edible Economics*

"Achieving economic transformation in a fast-changing world of technological disruption and geopolitical shifts is a fundamental challenge facing Africa today. *21st Century African Development Strategies: Facing Challenges with Innovative Approaches* is a bold contribution to unpacking and prioritizing the policy responses that are required. This book is a must-read for anyone interested in Africa's future."

—David Luke Professor in Practice & Strategic Director, *Firoz Lalji Institute for Africa, London School of Economics and Political Science.*

"This book brings together three passionate voices to explore how Africa can tackle its biggest challenges and unlock new opportunities in the 21st century. Covering topics like business, finance, and social progress, it offers fresh, practical ideas grounded in a wealth of empirical evidence and experience. For those who share the authors' goal for a better, stronger future for Africa, this is a must-read."

—Dr Daouda Sembene, *CEO of AfriCatalyst and Former IMF Executive Director*

"The book offers a sweeping and bold assessment of the economic, social and political challenges confronting Africa. It also profers solutions that are innovative and original. It is a must-read for all those seeking to grasp the complexities and potentials of the continent."

—His Excellency Omar Alieu Touray, *Ph.D, President of the ECOWAS Commission*

Karamo N. M. Sonko • Haider A. Khan
Mariama Sonko

21st Century African Development Strategies

Facing the Challenges With Innovative Approaches

palgrave
macmillan

Karamo N. M. Sonko
Heeno International
Banjul, The Gambia

Mariama Sonko
Heeno International
Banjul, The Gambia

Haider A. Khan
Josef Korbel School of
International Studies
University of Denver
Denver, CO, USA

ISBN 978-3-031-93078-2 ISBN 978-3-031-93079-9 (eBook)
https://doi.org/10.1007/978-3-031-93079-9

This Palgrave Macmillan imprint is published by the registered company Springer Nature Switzerland AG.
The registered company address is: Gewerbestrasse 11, 6330 Cham, Switzerland

Dedicated to the hardworking people of Africa, especially those who are protecting the sanctity of the family, catering for the poor and vulnerable, and educating, feeding and healing our people!

Foreword

It is not easy to find a book that is both academic and policy-oriented, theoretical and practical, secondary and first-hand, contemporary and historical, multidisciplinary and technical, but the authors of this book have succeeded in providing one through this publication.

The Topics

The selected topics covered in the book show its relevance:

1. Whither Africa?
2. Purposeful education for development;
3. Markets and the state;
4. Ignored but fundamental social issues, such as ethnicity and migration;
5. New opportunities in one of Africa's biggest development constraints—resource mobilization;
6. Resilience in the post-COVID African economy;
7. Innovation and technology;
8. Agriculture; and
9. Health.

The Approach

1. The authors approach Africa's problems as challenges and aim to be relevant, as much as possible, to a varied potential readership in Africa and to all those interested in Africa from outside the continent;
2. They provide relevant case studies in the book;
3. The study is multidisciplinary, reflecting the academic backgrounds of the three authors (mathematics, economics, finance, political science, public administration, and sociology); and
4. The book is rigorous and evidence-based with relevant mathematical models and statistical analysis.

In some ways, the book may be unique because:

1. The authors reflect the varied and three-generational experiences of the three writers (Professor Haider Khan, his student Karamo N.M. Sonko and his daughter Mariama Sonko). Thus, the publication integrates their diverse academic and professional experiences (since the 1980s) in academia, business, governments and international organizations;
2. It is critical but constructive;
3. Very interesting case studies from Africa and Asia are presented; and
4. It addresses a number of key areas of interest and reveals new concepts which are not yet commonly found in the existing academic literature on Africa's development.

Based on the contents and wealth of knowledge it offers, this book should be of interest to:

African leaders and policy makers;
Diplomats and aid officials from the developed countries;
Multilateral development finance institutions;
NGOs involved in development activities in Africa; and
Academic institutions, scholars and students.

The co-authors of this book recognize the importance of unity, human-centred development, peace and stability in Africa. They clearly demonstrate that we (Africans) cannot do anything for our people without peace and stability. Therefore, they stress the need and urge us for deeper and better thinking and correctly defined alliances at all times across our continent that are practical, beneficial and respected by all Africans. As the dedication shows, the book honours the African people, especially those who are working hard in protecting the sanctity of the family, providing for the weak and vulnerable, and educating, feeding and healing our people! This is more than a simple dedication, because it captures the true spirit of the book through what the first author once told me, "My heart and pocket are in Africa"! The heart means love for our people and the pocket means readiness to invest in our people. These commitments are reflected in the book but go beyond it as shown by the conferment on him of the "Africa Humanitarian Award in Education" by the Global Skills Hub (United Kingdom) and Lion Outreach International (United States) at the Third Africa Education Summit, organized by these two and their distinguished partners, hosted by the government of Zimbabwe in Victoria Falls, April 3–5, 2025. Therefore, this book also illustrates an interface between academia and development practice, with an inspirational commitment for all Africans.

Congratulations to the authors.

Riyadh, Saudi Arabia
April 4, 2025

Sidi O. Tah

Preface

Africa is a continent with numerous challenges, calling for numerous solutions! As a result, many scholars have attempted to offer explanations, formal theories and solutions to these challenges. To be realistic no single attempt or publication can claim to address them all. Yet, it can be done in a sufficiently broad manner which captures the most important of the challenges by looking at key areas of Africa's development, the fundamental causes of the challenges, and seeking innovatives. In the process, one should also look at emergent opportunities and strategies that have either not been addressed at all in the existing literature or not addressed adequately or enough. This is what this book intends to achieve. In summary, the authors have attempted to produce a publication for a diverse readership about African development strategies in the twenty-first century. We deal with crosscutting sectors, in chapters that synergistically outline Africa's challenges and solutions through multidisciplinary and technical analyses. The work covers many of the key and latest relevant concerns and interests in business, economic development, finance, and other areas in contemporary African affairs of the twenty-first century.

The authors are very grateful to all those who have supported and encouraged us. These include, first and foremost, our families who have morally and materially stood by us throughout the days and nights we have spent writing the book. Then there are those who commented on the work. These include: The Honourable Dr Sidi O. Tah, President and CEO of the Arab Bank for Economic Development in Africa (BADEA) who wrote the foreword; His Excellency Dr Omar Alieu Touray, President of the ECOWAS Commission; Professor M. J. Balogun, former Special

Adviser to the President of the General Assembly of the United Nations and Director-General, the Administrative Staff College of Nigeria; Professor Ha-Joon Chang, SOAS University of London, formerly at the University of Cambridge; Professor David F. Luke of the London School of Economics and Political Science; Dr Daouda Sembene, CEO of AfriCatalyst and former IMF Executive Director; and others we might have forgotten. We are also grateful to the Palgrave Macmillan acquisition editors for all their pre-publication efforts, including the time spent on reviewing our proposal internally and externally.

Banjul, The Gambia	Karamo N. M. Sonko
Denver, CO, USA	Haider A. Khan
Banjul, The Gambia	Mariama Sonko

Contents

List of Figures

List of Tables

CHAPTER 1

Whither Africa? An Introduction to Africa's Challenges and This Book

1.1 Introduction

Africa is a continent with numerous challenges, calling for numerous solutions! As a result, many scholars have attempted to offer explanations, formal theories and solutions to these challenges. To be realistic no single attempt or publication can claim to address them holistically. Yet, it can be done in a sufficiently broad manner which captures the most important of the challenges by looking at key areas of African development, the fundamental causes of the challenges and seeking innovative solutions. In the process, one has to also look at emergent opportunities and strategies that have either not been addressed at all in the existing literature or not addressed adequately. This is what our book seeks to achieve. In summary, our attempt is to produce a book for a diverse readership about African development strategies in the twenty-first century. It deals with crosscutting sectors, in chapters that synergistically outline Africa's challenges and solutions through multidisciplinary and technical approaches. It concisely covers key and latest relevant concerns and interests (not necessarily all!) in business, economic development, finance and socio-economic issues in contemporary Africa of the twenty-first century. We seek to provide refreshing approaches to old and new challenges, with visions for the future emanating from the perspectives of three authors, spanning three generations and representing the two genders. We seek to also provide evidence-based and very pertinent research for policy and action. The

K. N. M. Sonko et al., *21st Century African Development Strategies*,
https://doi.org/10.1007/978-3-031-93079-9_1

views of the authors on the issues covered may not be uniform, but our good will and love for Africa are the same. In this introductory chapter we summarize some of the most urgent challenges and how to address them before presenting the structure of the book.

1.2 Growth with Shocks

Africa is growing at a rapid pace. Since the beginning of the twenty-first century, the continent has witnessed demographic, economic and political transformations. Some of these transformations have been voluntary and some involuntary, some internaly caused, some externally generated. As its economies grow and its demographic and cultural landscapes evolve, the challenges in African societies will inevitably present more significant challenges and opportunities in the future.

Despite multiple shocks, the continent remains the second-fastest growing region in the world, and a number of African countries tend to be on the recovery path after decades of setbacks, although structural transitions and sustainability on this path are yet to be fully determined. Africa's real GDP growth was expected to increase to 3.7% in 2024 and 4.3% in 2025, surpassing the expected global average. Seventeen African economies were projected to grow by more than 5% in 2024. Nevertheless, the recovery is slow and fragile, necessitating greater resilience for African countries against future shocks (African Development Bank Group, 2024[1]). For Sub-Saharan Africa (SSA) the IMF reports growth rates of 4.0% in 2024 and forecasts of 4.0%, and 4.3% in 2025 and 2026 respectively (IMF, World Economic Outlook Update, July 2025).

1.3 Population

One of our first observations is that Sub-Saharan Africa's (SSA) population will double by 2050, potentially making it one of the most dynamic regions in a rapidly ageing world. However, this can be a boon or a bane. Growth and employment tomorrow require action today—specifically that children across the continent have access to a quality education and other opportunities (Chap. 2).

[1] African Development Bank. 2024. *Africa's Macroeconomic Performance and Outlook*. Abidjan, Côte d'Ivoire: African Development Bank.

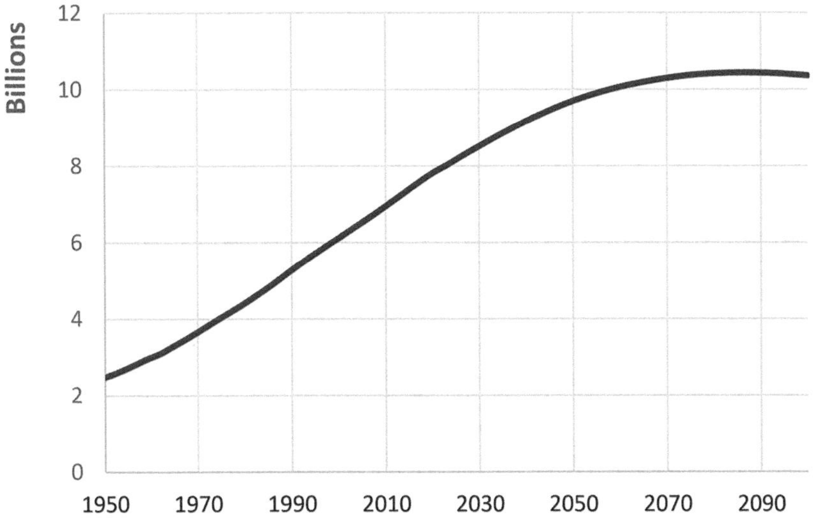

Fig. 1.1 Dynamics of the world population—empirical estimates (until 2022) and the medium forecast of the UN Population Division until 2100. (Data source: UN Population Division, 2022, United Nations Department of Economic and Social Affairs, Population Division (2022). World Population Prospects 2022: Summary of Results. UN DESA/POP/2022/TR/NO. 3)

In spite of the regressions in population in Western nations, the dynamics of worldwide demographic growth will continue to rise for quite a long time. Although this population growth in the second half and the last third of the twenty-first century is expected not to be a "population explosion" or "population bomb", the population of the earth can still increase, from the current level, by two to three billions. Here, Tropical Africa and several countries from Asia (like Yemen, Afghanistan) will be the main source of the growth (see Figs. 1.1, 1.2, and 1.3).

The reasons for the increase in population are from traditional and religious perspectives, and a number of other factors preventing active entry into the second phase of the demographic transition in Tropical Africa. In most countries of this part of the continent, fertility is declining rather slowly.[2] The overall historical trend globally is that the less developed the

[2] See, for example, Kebede, E., Goujon, A., & Lutz, W. (2019), "Stalls in Africa's fertility decline partly result from disruptions in female education," *Proceedings of the National Academy of Sciences*, 116 (8), 2891–2896. https://doi.org/10.1073/pnas.1717288116, retrieved April 12, 2025; and Andrey Korotayev, and Julia Zinkina, and Sergey Shulgin,

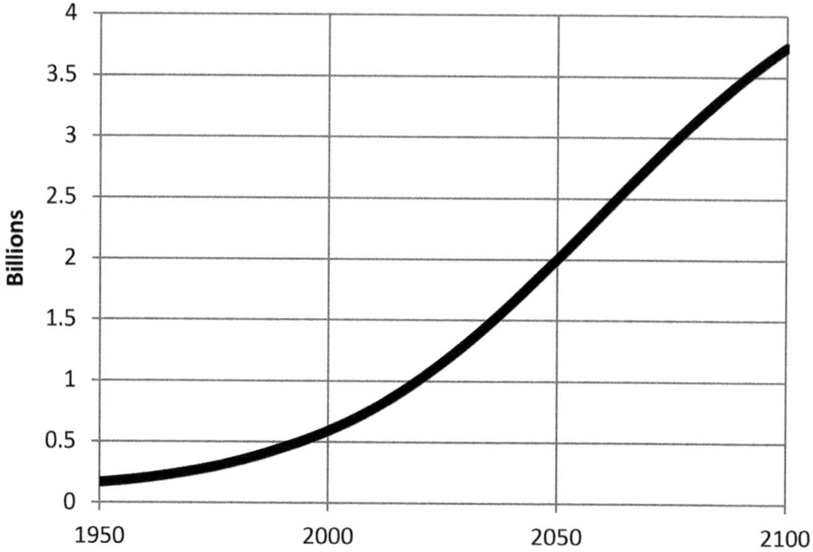

Fig. 1.2 Dynamics of the population of Tropical Africa for the period 1950–2020 with a projection to 2100 (UN medium projection). (Data source: UN Population Division, 2022, United Nations Department of Economic and Social Affairs, Population Division (2022). World Population Prospects 2022: Summary of Results. UN DESA/POP/2022/TR/NO. 3)

country, the lower the level of prevalence of modern education and urbanization in it, and the higher the birth rate. Hence, as Tropical African countries develop, some argue that a reduction in the birth rate is likely to be inevitable, but it is not clear at what speed this will happen. However, the overall growth of the earth's population at any given moment in the forthcoming decades will depend on the African growth rate. Meanwhile, every nation will continue to have the rights to their own policies and practices regarding population. Peoples' right to have children and independently maintain their religious and traditional values must be respected,

"Explaining Current Fertility Dynamics in Tropical Africa from an Anthropological Perspective: A Cross-Cultural Investigation," Volume 50, Issue 3, 2015, https://doi.org/10.1177/1069397116644158; and Grinin, Leonid, and A. Korotayev, "Africa—The Continent of the Future. Demographic and Economic Challenges and Opportunities," *World Futures The Journal of General Evolution*, February 2024, DOI: 10.1080/02604027.2024.2315262.

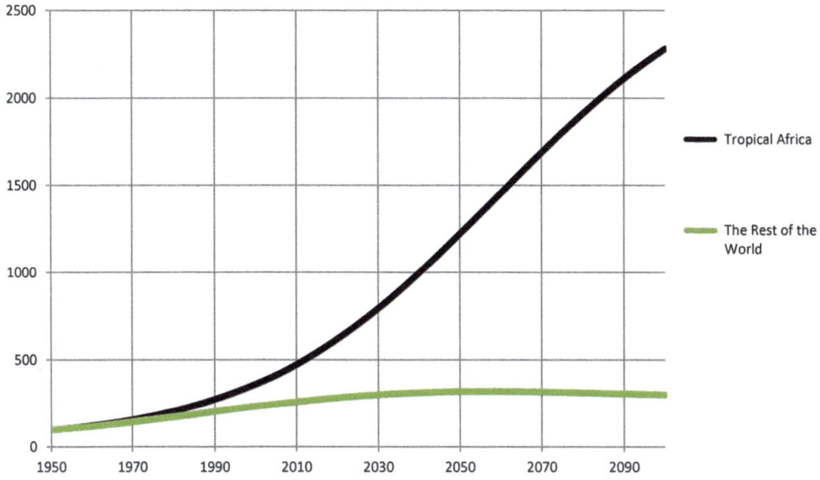

Fig. 1.3 Relative dynamics of the population of Tropical Africa and the rest of the world for 1950–2020 projected to 2100 (UN medium projection), 100=1950 level. (Data source: UN Population Division, 2022, United Nations Department of Economic and Social Affairs, Population Division (2022). World Population Prospects 2022: Summary of Results. UN DESA/POP/2022/TR/NO. 3)

although the biggest challenges for Africa and other fast-growing populations are how to create jobs and maintain social stability (Chap. 4).

On the other hand, high-income countries in the world are facing decreasing birth rates. The African labour force can be seen as an advantage and a potential source of human capital to assist in resolving the issue of labour shortages worldwide. Africa is experiencing economic growth, despite which the high population growth will continue, at least for now, particularly in its urban population. This future projected growth can become valuable as a contributing factor to global economic growth, which is slowly dwindling as developed economies face a slowdown in their economic growth rates. Africa is faced with a real opportunity to become the world's "skills basket" if it can seize this opportunity. As countries such as China, Indonesia and India show, big populations can be boons at national and global levels, and we attempt to clearly show how this can be done by Africa in the various chapters of this book.

1.4 Minerals and Energy

Another angle to consider is how African can benefit from the shortage of natural resources in a world that is hungry for the green energy transition. Africa could present a very valuable source of supply in new energy sources such as lithium, cobalt and others referred to as rare earth elements (REEs) or critical minerals. Among these, Africa holds about 50% of the world's known cobalt reserves, about 60% of manganese reserves and significant shares of others such as lithium and platinum group metals.[3] In this vein, if the continent does not play its cards well it could easily become a pawn in the competition between superpowers (notably through Russian, American, European and Chinese companies) to access its critical minerals needed for a green energy transition. This is also called the Green Energy Revolution, and it includes some rare earth minerals which are critical for the overall objective of switching from coal, oil and gas to renewable or clean energy.

Among the powers above, the Chinese have already secured mining contracts across Sub-Saharan Africa (SSA) and produces about 58% of all REEs worldwide. It has become the main importer of minerals from Africa, with mineral exports from Sub-Saharan Africa to China totalling about US$10 billion in 2019, for example. More recently, in 2024, about $7.8 billion went into mining in Africa from the Chinese government.[4] China's authority and domination of the global rare earths market is due to policies and politics that are welcomed by decision makers in the host countries. It is clear that China knows what it wants and how to get along with those who have them. However, for China's critics the country's success is due to its adoption of an import strategy that is not in abidance with World Trade Organization (WTO) guidelines. China, like other countries, who do not believe that the world trading system is fair enough, does not agree.[5] This resulted in the EU, United States, United Kingdom along

[3] U.S. Geological Survey (USGS) Mineral Commodity Survey World Data 2025.

[4] Savage, Rachel, and Duncan Miriri, "Post-COVID, China is back in Africa and doubling down on minerals," Reuters, May 29, 2024, https://www.reuters.com/markets/commodities/post-covid-china-is-back-africa-doubling-down-minerals-2024-05-28/, retrieved April 13, 2025.

[5] Ironically, the United States, under President Trump, is one of those countries that are very critical of the world trading system, and Trump in his second term has moved very fast with tariffs to demonstrate that. These tariffs which were universally imposed at differential rates are considered to be the most sweeping in world trade in a century, and some have predicted that they would lead to a world trade war and worse.

with other industrialized countries in the West creating a "Minerals Security Partnership (MSP)" in June 2022. This partnership is aimed at countering what they perceive as the Chinese mineral dominance, through discussions with African nations with rich mineral resources, such as Democratic Republic of Congo (DRC), Angola, Mozambique, South Africa, Botswana, Tanzania, Uganda and Zambia. African countries can and should take advantage of the competition for critical minerals through their dominance in the supply of such minerals in the face of the rapid demand for them in world markets. Again, they should choose what are in their best interests!

So far, foreign direct investment (FDI) in rare earth production tends to be confirming the "pollution haven" hypothesis about the environmentally harmful effects of FDI flowing into the affected countries. Although the full potential of rare earths in SSA has remained largely untapped due to low exploration, the dark side of the energy transition is becoming increasingly visible. These include pollution of soil, air and water as well as inadequate disposal of toxic residues and intensive water and energy use, occupational and environmental risks, child labour and sexual abuse as well as corruption and armed conflicts. For instance, in August 2023, Nigeria, Africa's largest economy, suspended certain Chinese mining activities within its borders, including the activities of Ruitai Mining Company due to what the government reported to be their involvement in illegal titanium ore mining. Namibia and the Democratic Republic of Congo (DRC) followed suit.

Africa's significant reserves and production of critical or transition minerals are key for the global energy transition and achieving the "net zero" emissions goal (Diene 2022), (https://publication.aercafricalibrary.org/server/api/core/bitstreams/4359d28a-5d62-4ab5-8132-d27616695dd1/content) To take advantage of the global demand for these minerals and technologies, Africa requires significant investments. The continent still suffers from significant investment financing gaps, receiving only about 2% of global investments in renewable energy.[6] Figure 1.4 shows that between 2003 and 2018, globally Sub-Saharan Africa, in particular, received the least capital investment in renewable energy-related industry clusters (environmental technology, ICT and electronics, transportation

[6] IRENA, *Renewable Energy Market Analysis: Africa and its Regions,* January 2022, https://www.irena.org/publications/2022/Jan/Renewable-Energy-Market-Analysis-Africa, retrieved April 13, 2025.

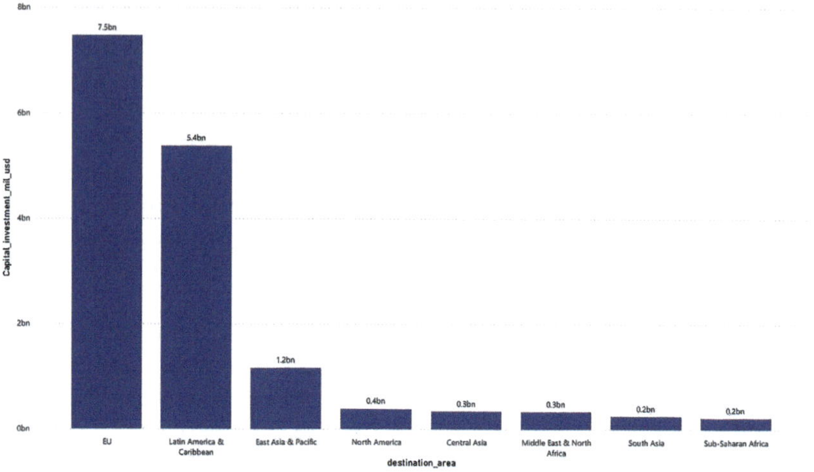

Fig. 1.4 Capital investments across regions (2003–2018). (Source: Antonio Andreoni and Elvis Avenyo, 2023, Antonio Andreoni and Elvis Avenyo, Critical Minerals and Routes to Diversification in Africa: Linkages, Pulling Dynamics and Opportunities in Medium-High Tech Supply Chains, Background paper commissioned by the UNCTAD secretariat for the 2023 edition of the Economic Development in Africa Report, 2023, https://unctad.org/system/files/non-official-document/edar2023_BP1_en.pd, retrieved April 12, 2025)

equipment, etc.). However, the availability of investments in natural resources is one thing, another critical chalenge is for Africa to stop the seemingly chronic problem of exporting raw materials and importing finished products. In natural resources, the continent's vast endowments can only be sustainably beneficial if these resources can be processed and utilized locally (not only exported) to enhance Africa's industrialization and energy transition, among many other reasons.

1.5 Impediments to Growth and Development

In Africa, the main impediments to growth and development include poverty and food insecurity, unemployment, limited realized opportunities, gender inequity and inefficient use of natural resources and land. These challenges are in combination with economic recessions and climate and biodiversity crises. However, there is an opportunity for African countries to capitalize on their strengths, learn from the mistake of others and themselves and succeed in promoting sustainable development and innovation. Despite, or perhaps because of, its challenges, Africa is struggling in its efforts to become a hub for sustainable innovation and growth.

1.6 Inclusive Development: A Challenge to African Democracy

Inclusive development remains a challenge in Africa. After independence, many countries underscored the need for development and economic growth. However, several challenges hinder the attainment of development that embraces inclusivity. Let us take South Africa, for instance (detailed case study in Chap. 5). Despite the end of apartheid and the implementation of multiparty politics in South Africa, the country continues to encounter numerous challenges that impede equitable growth. As of 2022, an estimated population of over 18.2 million individuals, out of a total population of about 62 million South Africans, resided in abject poverty, defined by a poverty threshold of only US$1.90 per day.[7] This resulted in an estimated increase of 123,000 individuals falling below the poverty line, compared to the previous year (2021). Additionally, it is projected that by this year (2025), more than 18.5 million individuals residing in South Africa will be living on a daily income not exceeding US$1.90.[8]

This is a general problem across Africa, not limited to South Africa alone. In recent years, many African countries have gone to the ballot box and celebrated the achievement or consolidation of the democratic process, without enough progress on the economic side and inclusive development. This has contributed to setbacks to the democratic process in a number of countries, calling for deep reflections on whether democracy should come before or after development or whether they can go in tandem in Africa. If they cannot go in tandem, then we should decide which one to go for first and, in any case, decide whether to go for imported democracy or our own customized or home-grown "Africracy" as we would call it! An exploration of the possibility of "Africracy" should take into account African cultural values, traditional methods of governance,

[7] Cowling 2023 https://www.statista.com/statistics/1263737/national-poverty-line-in-south-africa/; Stats SA 2023 https://www.statssa.gov.za/publications/P03101/P031012023.pdf.

[8] Cowling 2023 https://www.statista.com/statistics/1263737/national-poverty-line-in-south-africa/; Stats SA 2023 https://www.statssa.gov.za/publications/P03101/P031012023.pdf.

and the needs for social and political stability and economic progress. Whatever answer one may have, and has the right to have, it is clear that our people cannot dance on empty stomachs and to the beat of the ballot box alone. More and objective scholarly work is needed to make the right recommendations for Africa on this subject. Such recommendations should draw on African realities and the historical experiences of the developed industrialized countries. They should also look at other countries doing well in catering for the needs of their people, with or without imported democracy. In the end, Africa must go for what is in Africa's best interest! [9]

1.7 Droughts and Poverty

In relation to the above, currently over 36 million people in East Africa alone are being impacted by the worst drought in decades. There is a severe shortage of both food and water, and millions of children are acutely malnourished. Other factors, such as political instability, extreme poverty and poor infrastructure, are also contributing to the increasingly severe impacts of extreme weather in East Africa and other parts of Africa. In the wake of droughts, social changes and poverty, violence against children is also increasing in Africa. Many children are being forced into work at an early age to help put food on the table. Girls are more likely to be victims, including getting them married young so that the family will have one less mouth to feed.

[9] Some recent surveys on democracy in Africa may be worth reading: Bratton, Michael, "Poor people and democratic citizenship in Africa," Afro Barometer Working paper WP56, 1 Jan 2006; Africa Barometer Network, "Africans want more democracy, but their leaders still aren't listening," *Afrobarometer Policy Paper* No. 85, January 2023, https://www.afrobarometer.org/wp-content/uploads/2023/01/PP85-PAP20-Africans-want-more-democracy-but-leaders-arent-listening-Afrobarometer-Pan-Africa-Profile-18jan23.pdf, retrieved May 13.2025; Africa Barometer Network, "African democracy update: Democratic satisfaction remains elusive for many," 11 Sep 2015, https://www.afrobarometer.org/articles/democracy-day-2015/, retrieved May 13, 2025; and Afro Barometer, "Popular opinions on democracy," 10 November 2015, https://www.afrobarometer.org/event/popular-opinions-democracy/, retrieved May 13, 2025.

1.8 Rapid Increase in Hunger, Undernourishment and Stunting

The number of people experiencing hunger in Africa increased by 11 million in 2022, rising from 270.6 million in 2021 to 281.6 million in 2022 and by a staggering 61 million since the outbreak of the COVID-19 pandemic in 2020. In 2022, 340 million Africans lacked stable food access. (? For a detailed discussion of the situation of food insecurity/deprivation in Africa and its causes, the interested reader may refer to David Luke (ed.), How Africa Eats Trades, LSE Press, 2023, David Luke (ed.), How Africa Eats. Trade, Food Security and Climate Risks, LSE Press, 2025, and https://www.google.com/search? q=David+Fashole+Luke+How+Africa+trades&sca_esv=602bc0460517bd79&source=hp&ei=-W_yaJ7JHJiTkdUP2Jm4sAQ&iflsig=AOw8s4IAAAAAaPJCREi3Hog6QjPDy1Q7IF7qHn5Tstd& ved=0ahUKEwjeqeHo1KuQAxWYSaQEHdgMDkYQ4dUDCBs&oq=David+Fashole+Luke+How+Africa+trades&gs_lp=Egdnd3M-td2l6IiREYXZpZCBGYXNob2xlIEx1a2UgSG93IEFmcmljYSB0cmFkZXNIk5oBUABYuowBcAB4AJABAJgBlAWgAblUqgELMi0yMi4xMC4xLjO4AQzIAQD4AQGfpstate=ive&vld=cid:a5ea24ed,vid:T2O2zuG7Q_E,st:0). The adverse trend in hunger has been associated with drought and conflict resulting in increased food insecurity, undernourishment and stunting. The prevalence of undernourishment (PoU) increased from 19.4% in 2021 to 19.7% in 2022, while one out of every three children (under five years of age) is stunted as of 2022. Of Africa's population 60% experienced moderate or severe food insecurity in 2022, up from 45.5% in 2015. Similarly, in 2022, 80% of Africa's population was unable to afford healthy food while an estimated 145 million children, under five years, experienced food poverty. A recent World Health Organization Report indicates this, even as the food situation improves in other regions.[10]

[10] FAO, AUC, ECA and WFP, *Africa – Regional overview of food security and nutrition. Statistics and trends,* 2023, https://openknowledge.fao.org/server/api/core/bitstreams/c6c81d5f-e337-4b3e-8330-555c9ed0e741/content#:~:text=In%202022%2C%20nearly%20282%20million,since%20the%20COVID%2D19%20pandemic.&text=An%20estimated%20868%20million%20people,%E2%80%93%20were%20severely%20food%2D%20insecure, retrieved April 12, 2025; UNDP, *Africa Sustainable Development Report, 2024,* Reinforcing the 2030 Agenda and Agenda 2063 and Eradicating Poverty in Times of Multiple Crises: The Effective Delivery of Sustainable, Resilient and Innovative Solutions, https://www.undp.org/africa/publications/2024-africa-sustainable-development-report,

Central Africa and East Africa subregions experience the highest proportions of undernourished people, with 29.1% and 28.5% of their populations undernourished, respectively. This distressing hunger crisis is anticipated to significantly worsen by 2030. As the African Development Bank (AfDB) observed, Africa is the world's hungriest continent and for many "hunger has become a way of life". (https://afdb.africanewsroom.com/press/african-development-bank-to-join-world-leaders-at-the-g20-leaders-summit-prioritizing-global-solutions-to-end-hunger?lang=en#:~:text=In%20Africa%20over%20280%20million,human%20dignity%2C%E2%80%9D%20he%20said; and https://www.afdb.org/fr/news-and-events/its-time-nourish-africa-once-and-all-50645#:~:text=Africa%27s%20food%20systems%20are%20failing,hunger%20in%20all%20its%20forms)

Food insecurity in Africa is arising from several sources, including those already discussed above. In 2021 it stood at 57.9%, showing a 2 percentage point increase over that of 2020 and a 5.5 percentage point increase prior to the outbreak of the COVID-19 pandemic (Fig. 1.5). The rise in

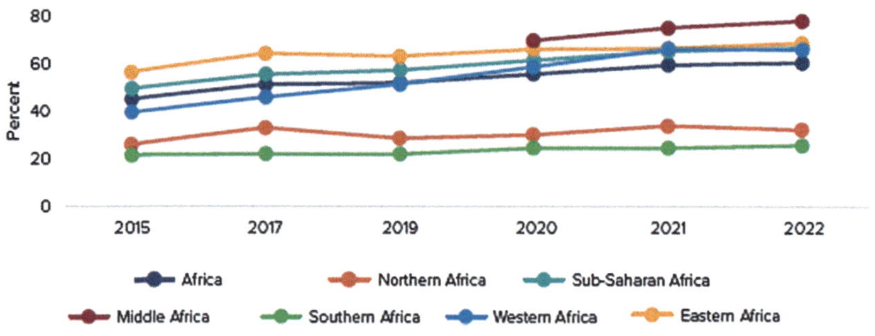

Fig. 1.5 Prevalence of moderate or severe food insecurity in Africa. Source: Africa Sustainable Report, 2024, Africa Sustainable Development Report (2024). Reinforcing the 2030 Agenda and Agenda 2063 and eradicating poverty in times of multiple crises: the effective delivery of sustainable, resilient and innovative solutions)

retrieved April 12, 2025; and FAO, Chapter 2: "Food Security and Nutrition around the World, " in *The State of Food Security and Nutrition in the World 2023*, https://openknowledge.fao.org/server/api/core/bitstreams/f1ee0c49-04e7-43df-9b83-6820f4f37ca9/content/state-food-security-and-nutrition-2023/food-security-nutrition-indicators.html.

the prevalence of moderate or severe food insecurity in the region is particularly prominent in the East and Central Africa subregions. It is attributed to a combination of factors including but not limited to major droughts, conflicts and civil unrest, high levels of inflation (food, fuel and fertilizers) and general economic slowdown in many countries in these subregions.

1.9 High Food Costs

Much of the African region is experiencing abnormally high food costs. This is due to macroeconomic difficulties and exacerbated by domestic grain shortages and changes in global food and fuel supplies. The situation increases the risks of diseases such as dehydration, waterborne diseases (including cholera), skin infections and malnutrition. The irony is that Africa is vastly endowed with fertile and unused land. Furthermore, in spite of recurrent drought in some countries, others such as the Sudan have no water issues, either underground or surface.

1.10 Increasing Risks to Children

As indicated earlier, drought continues to have far-reaching consequences in Africa. The lack of food and water is a direct threat to children, in particular, and their families. Many people in the region depend on their livestock and make a living through agriculture. Due to the drought, animals die and crops are repeatedly destroyed. Families are then forced to move to other regions to access food and water. This has a detrimental impact on children's school attendance, safety and security, in addition to the other consequences already mentioned.

1.11 Conflict and Pandemic Aftershocks

The ongoing drought is also causing conflicts over resources. The consequences of the civil upheaval in Ethiopia, Kenya, Sudan and poor relations between some countries are all worsened by the drought or dispute over land and water. In short, the drought further aggravates the suffering of the population. At the global level, the war in Ukraine has contributed to a shortage of grains and a rise in the prices of many essential items, including the cost of fuel. This comes at a time when many countries in Africa are still recovering from the economic impacts of COVID-19 even after its official ending (Chap. 5).

1.12 Africa, the Lowest per Capita Contributor to Global Carbon Emissions but the Biggest Victim

Africa represents 17% of the global population, yet it accounts for less than 4% of global carbon emissions. South Africa, Nigeria and North African countries account for most of Africa's emissions (Figs. 1.6 and 1.7). Africa's per capita carbon emissions of 1 tonne compares favourably with North America's (15 tonnes), G20 countries' (6.14 tonnes), East Asia and the Pacific's (6.61 tonnes), and the European Union's (6.25 tonnes). Even in terms of greenhouse gases from all sources and all uses, Africa's per capita share remains the lowest. Nevertheless, Africa is shown to bear the brunt of the climate crisis. Therefore, Africa is demanding climate financing support. Africa received $30 billion per year for climate adaptation while its needs are $277 billion per year, leaving a huge financing gap.[11]

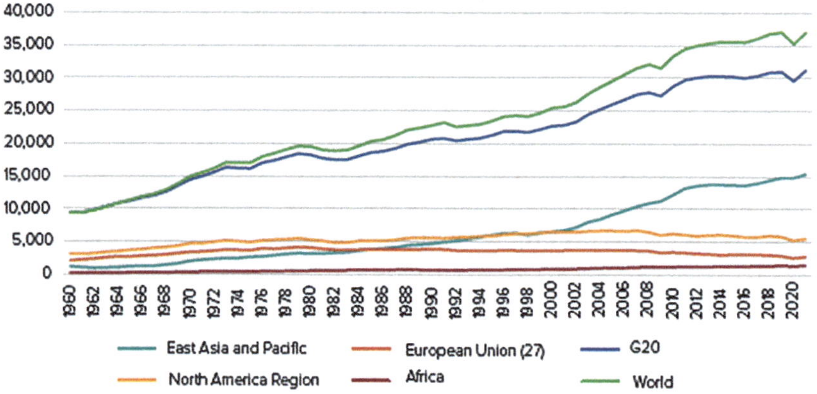

Fig. 1.6 Total greenhouse gas emissions (megatonnes). (Source: Global Carbon Budget, 2024, Global Carbon Budget (2024); Population based on various sources (2024) – with major processing by Our World in Data. "Annual CO_2 emissions (per capita) – GCB" [dataset]. Global Carbon Project, "Global Carbon Budget"; Various sources, "Population" [original data]. https://ourworldindata.org/co2-and-greenhouse-gas-emissions)

[11] African Development Bank. 2024. *Africa's Macroeconomic Performance and Outlook.* Abidjan, Côte d'Ivoire: African Development Bank.

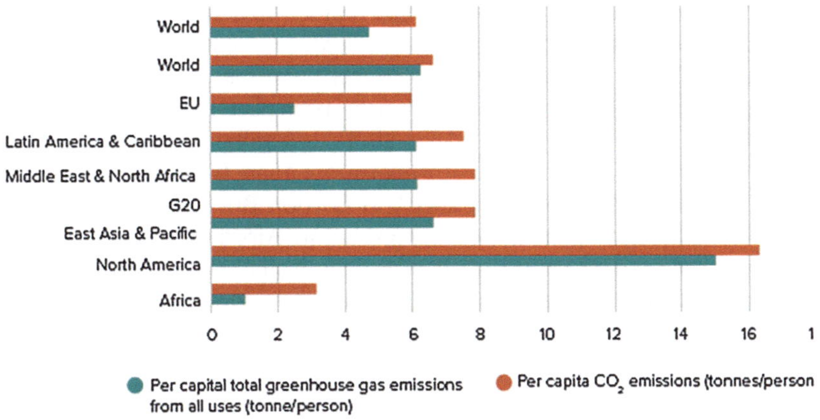

Fig. 1.7 Per capita total greenhouse gas emissions and per capita CO_2 emission. (Source: Global Carbon Budget, 2024, Global Carbon Budget (2024); Population based on various sources (2024)—with major processing by Our World in Data. "Annual CO_2 emissions (per capita) – GCB" [dataset]. Global Carbon Project, "Global Carbon Budget"; Various sources, "Population" [original data]. https://ourworldindata.org/co2-and-greenhouse-gas-emissions)

1.13 Navigating Climate Challenges

As mentioned in the preceding section, Africa is bearing the brunt of the global climate crisis. Escalating climate threats are jeopardizing the continent's agricultural productivity and food security. Climate projections suggest an exacerbation of extreme weather events, including droughts, floods and heatwaves in Africa. Such events disrupt farming activities, exacerbate land degradation and escalate food insecurity, particularly in vulnerable regions.[12] Climate change is a real and increasing threat to Africa's agriculture and to African economies. In East Africa, the increasing frequency of drought is already becoming evident. Since 1999, poor rainy seasons have happened every two to three years, compared with once every five to six years pre-1999.

[12] United Nations Secretary-General, 2023. Also refer to Karamo NM Sonko, and Mariama Sonko, Chapter *Demystifying ESG: Charting the ESG Course in Africa*, Palgrave Macmillan, London and New York, 2023.

Increasing temperatures and rainfall pattern changes are leading to an increase in the intensity and frequency of extreme weather occurrences in Africa, with grave consequences. Indeed, natural disasters including droughts and floods have increased at a faster pace in Africa now compared with the rest of the world. In 2020, 1.2 million Africans were displaced by floods and tropical storms—more than twice the amount of people displaced by violent conflict.[13] A Carbon Brief analysis of disaster records finds that extreme weather events in Africa have killed at least 4,000 people and affected a further 19 million since the start of 2022.[14]

The Intergovernmental Panel on Climate Change projects that Africa will experience a combination of warming and increased heavy precipitations. This pattern has been predicted to lead to "dry gets drier and wet gets wetter" scenarios. Wet regions along the equator are forecast to witness a 30% increase in rainfall, while already dry regions are expected to experience a 20% decrease. These most unfortunate changes, if proven correct, would exacerbate prolonged periods of drought and flooding across the continent.

As for the impact on agriculture, the International Panel on Climate Change reports a 34% reduction in agricultural productivity growth since 1961 due to climate change, surpassing declines in any other region. Future warming will further strain food systems by shortening growing seasons and increasing water stress. A global warming of 2°C above pre-industrial levels will lead to yield reductions for staple crops, with a projected 9% decline in maize yield in West Africa and a 20–60% decline in wheat yield in Southern and North Africa compared with 2005 yields.

To mitigate the adverse impacts of climate change on food systems and livelihoods, the continent must urgently prioritize climate adaptation measures, including resilient crop varieties, water management strategies, sustainable land use and sustainable finance.

Growth prospects in agriculture (Chap. 3) are promising in spite of the numerous challenges. For instance, resilient agroforestry and

[13] International Monetary Fund (2020), "Adapting to Climate Change in Sub-Saharan Africa", in Regional Economic Outlook: Sub-Saharan Africa, April, Washington D.C. Mounir Bari and Sébastien Dessus (2022), "Adapting To Natural Disasters In Africa: What's in it for the Private Sector?", International Finance Corporation, World Bank Group, November 2022. https://www.researchgate.net/publication/365297748_ADAPTING_TO_NATURAL_DISASTERS_IN_AFRICA_What's_in_it_for_the_Private_Sector

[14] Aruna Chandrasekhar 2023. 'Timeline: The 60-year history of carbon offsets', Carbon Brief, 25 September. See: https://interactive.carbonbrief.org/carbon-offsets-2023/timeline.html

climate-smart agricultural practices, including those using traditional methods such as flood-recession farming or recessional agriculture, have boosted food security. To some extent, business-oriented nutrition models have helped communities to diversify food sources, improve nutrient intake, increase productivity and boost incomes. With about 65% of the world's arable land in Africa, the continent has the potential to fully nourish its population and become the "world's food basket". However, as in several other areas, such as its growing youth population, this depends on the continent's ability to transform potential into reality through progress.

1.14 Conflict-Related Deaths, Disputes and Wars

Over the past decade, the world has experienced a rise in the number of armed conflicts.[15] Armed conflicts here constitute interstate, intrastate, extra-systemic, non-state conflicts, and one-sided violence that took place (Uppsala Conflict Data Program, 2023[16]). Africa stands out with relatively high numbers of conflicts compared to other regions over the past two decades. In 2022, Africa's armed conflicts (98) constituted about 53.8% of global conflicts (182). Worldwide, fragile and conflict-affected states (FCS) are home to 1.3 billion people trying to survive amid profound challenges. Out of 39 FCS, 18 are in Sub-Saharan Africa, with a total population of more than 670 million people.[17]

Therefore, peace and security must remain part of Africa's priorities, since they are prerequisites for sustainable growth and resilient development. Notwithstanding the high number of conflicts, the continent has seen a fall in the number of conflict-related deaths, but very far from being

[15] See Figure 37 "Number of conflicts worldwide in 1989–2022 by region" in Uppsala Conflict Data Program, 2023, Uppsala Conflict Data Program and Peace Research Institute Oslo (2024) – processed by Our World in Data. "One-sided violence" [dataset]. Uppsala Conflict Data Program and Peace Research Institute Oslo, "Armed Conflict version 24.1"; Uppsala Conflict Data Program, "Georeferenced Event Dataset v24.1" [original data].

[16] Uppsala Conflict Data Program and Peace Research Institute Oslo (2024) – processed by Our World in Data. "One-sided violence" [dataset]. Uppsala Conflict Data Program and Peace Research Institute Oslo, "Armed Conflict version 24.1"; Uppsala Conflict Data Program, "Georeferenced Event Dataset v24.1" [original data].

[17] IMF, " Pushed to the Brink: Fragility and Conflict in Sub-Saharan Africa," file:///C:/Users/karamo.sonko/Downloads/FCSNote%20(3).pdf; and https://www.elibrary.imf.org/view/journals/068/2025/002/article-A001-en.xml.

enough. Agenda 2063's First Ten-Year Implementation Plan sets a score of conflict-related deaths which comprise the aggregate results of analyses of 15 country reports (per 100,000 persons). Substantial progress has been achieved as the figure dropped drastically from 202 in 2013 to 144 in 2020. Additionally, the score indicates that 2021 targets (121 conflict-related deaths) and 2023 targets (101 conflict-related deaths) have been surpassed.[18] This improvement aligns with the generally peaceful security situation observed across the continent in recent years, albeit the persistence of some exceptions and unpleasant shocks in certain areas. Some countries have taken steps to maintain peace and stability. For instance, the Kenyan government established peace committees at both the county and cross-border levels to support peace and security initiatives. Additionally, the Nyumba Kumi initiative promotes community policing at the household level to combat crime and enhance peace and security.[19]

On the other hand, in 2022, Africa witnessed significant conflict-related fatalities, painting a sobering picture of the human cost of these conflicts. These developments highlight the severe impact of conflict on human life across the continent. The economic impact of violence also surged by 17%, amounting to $17.5 trillion or 13% of combined African GDP.[20]

Despite the progress made from 2013 to 2020, it is crucial to address the ongoing insecurity that persists in different subregions of Africa. These challenges not only hinder socio-economic development, but also pose a threat to the progress achieved, risking both lives and livelihoods.

Africa needs peace and stability. We cannot do anything for our people (including achieving sovereignty) without peace and stability! We need deep and good thinking and correctly defined alliances across Africa that are practical and respected by all Africans.

[18] African Union Commission and African Union Development Agency – NEPAD (2022). AUC & AUDA-NEPAD Second Continental Report on the Implementation of Agenda 2063. AUC & AUDA-NEPAD, Midrand, South Africa.

[19] African Union (2023) "The AU Peace and Security Council Handbook 2022: Guide on the Council's Procedure, Practice and Traditions", African Union Commission and New Zealand Crown, https://au.int/en/handbook

[20] African Union (2023) "The AU Peace and Security Council Handbook 2022: Guide on the Council's Procedure, Practice and Traditions", African Union Commission and New Zealand Crown, https://au.int/en/handbook

1.15 High Illicit Financial Flows

Illicit financial flows (IFFs) pose significant challenges to global efforts to achieve the SDGs. These flows consist of illegally earned, transferred or utilized money across borders, often involving activities such as corruption, tax evasion, money laundering and illegal trade. IFFs deprive countries of much-needed revenue that could otherwise be invested in infrastructure, healthcare, education and poverty reduction initiatives. This undermines efforts to achieve SDG 1 (no poverty), SDG 2 (zero hunger), SDG 3 (good health and well-being), SDG 4 (quality education) and SDG 8 (decent work and economic growth). Some sources of IFFs, such as illegal logging, wildlife trafficking and illegal fishing, contribute to environmental degradation and biodiversity loss. This undermines efforts to achieve SDG 13 (climate action), SDG 14 (life below water) and SDG 15 (life on land).

The total value of inward and outward IFFs remains substantial and continues to undermine efforts to achieve the SDGs. A report by Global Financial Integrity (2014) estimated that illicit outflows from developing countries reached approximately $1.3 trillion in 2020, while illicit inflows amounted to around $1.1 trillion during the same period.[21]

Africa is particularly vulnerable because of poverty and other causes. A report on the governance performance in Africa notes that IFFs "erode the revenue for public investment and social spending, hence weakening governance and institutions" (African Peer Review Mechanism and African Governance Architecture, 2019).[22] Furthermore, citing a report by the United Nations Conference on Trade and Development (UNCTAD), the African Peer Review Mechanism notes that Africa loses about US$88.6 billion annually, representing 3.7% of its GDP in IFFs. In 2021, the High-level Panel on International Financial Accountability, Transparency and Integrity for Achieving the 2030 Agenda (the FACTI Panel) remarked that IFFs divert resources away from sustainable development as well as

[21] Spanjers, Joseph, and Dev Kar, "Illicit Financial Flows from Developing Countries: 2003–2012," Global Financial Integrity, December 16, 2014, https://gfintegrity.org/report/2014-global-report-illicit-financial-flows-from-developing-countries-2003-2012/, retrieved April 13, 2025.

[22] African Union, "The African Peer Review Mechanism," https://au.int/en/aprm

And African Union, About AGA (African Governance Architecture), https://au.int/en/aga/about, retrieved April 13, 2025.

worsen inequalities, fuel instability, undermine governance, and damage public trust in African countries.[23]

Addressing the issue of IFFs requires coordinated efforts at the national, regional and international levels, including enhanced regulatory frameworks, improved transparency and accountability measures, strengthened law enforcement and increased international cooperation. By combating IFFs, African countries can unlock resources to advance sustainable development and build more inclusive, resilient and prosperous societies.

1.16 Wide Variation Among Countries in Expenditures

The variations in government expenditures constitute an indicator which provides insights into how government resources are allocated and utilized across different sectors, reflecting the priorities and commitments of a nation towards achieving development. It is essential for transparency and accountability in public financial management, enabling stakeholders to monitor and evaluate the effectiveness of government spending in Africa. According to recent data,[24] expenditures as proportions of the original budgets vary widely across countries. Several countries, such as Sudan, Zimbabwe and Zambia, have very high expenditure levels compared to their original budgets. This may indicate issues with fiscal discipline, budget planning or economic challenges leading to overspending. Countries like Algeria, Angola, Benin and Botswana have expenditure levels ranging from around 90 to 100% of their original budgets. While still relatively high, these countries appear to have better control over their expenditures compared to the high-expenditure countries. On the other hand, countries like Rwanda, Guinea-Bissau, Kenya and Lesotho have lower expenditure levels, ranging from around 60 to 80% of their original budget.[25]

[23] High-level Panel on International Financial Accountability, Transparency and Integrity, *Financial Integrity for Sustainable Development. Report of the High Level Panel on International Financial Accountability, Transparency and Integrity for Achieving the 2030 Agenda,* February 2021, https://factipanel.org/docpdfs/FACTI_Panel_Report.pdf, retrieved April 13, 2025.

[24] UN DESA, Figure 41 Government expenditures as a proportion of original approved budget, by sector (most recent years) in "United Nations E-Government Survey 2024", Department of Economic and Social Affairs, Accelerating Digital Transformation for Sustainable Development.

[25] Global Financial Integrity, December 16, 2014, https://gfintegrity.org/report/2014-global-report-illicit-financial-flows-from-developing-countries-2003-2012/, retrieved April 13, 2025.

High expenditure levels relative to the original budget may lead to fiscal imbalances, debt accumulation and macroeconomic instability if not properly managed.[26] On the other hand, low expenditure levels could indicate conservative fiscal policies, difficulties in executing planned expenditures, underinvestment in critical sectors or inefficiencies in budget execution and resource mobilization. Both macroeconomic conditions call for alignment of budgets, spending and development goals in Africa.

Policy makers in countries with high expenditure levels may need to focus on improving fiscal discipline, enhancing budget transparency and strengthening oversight mechanisms to ensure sustainable public finances. Conversely, countries with low expenditure levels may need to prioritize investments in key sectors while ensuring efficient use of resources.

Africa's public finances expose, in the clearest manner, Africa's incongruous status as perhaps the richest but poorest continent in the world. Apart from its always talked-about natural resources, Africa does not seem to properly manage even what it has or can have financially. These can be seen in the idle resources sitting in national pension funds and massive financial or resource leakages through a variety of sources. According to a recent estimate, the continent can mobilize $1.43 trillion of additional revenue from tax and nontax sources by curbing, for instance, illicit financial flows, corruption, profit shifting and high interest payments (African Development Bank, African Economic Outlook, 2025).

[26]The IMF has observed that levels in Sub-Saharan Africa are elevated and vulnerabilities are high.

Public debt ratios, for instance, remain elevated compared to pre-COVID levels and interest payments as a share of revenues are considerably higher than in other regions, with the median interest-to-revenue ratio exceeding 12% in 2024 (IMF, *Breaking the Trend: Debt Stabilization in Sub-Saharan Africa*, April 2025), https://www.imf.org/en/Publications/REO/SSA/Issues/2025/04/25/regional-economic-outlook-for-sub-saharan-africa-april-2025?cid=sm-com-fb-SM2025-REOAFRAPR2025001#, retrieved May 15, 2025. Yet, this is only a small part of the larger concern of total external debt ratios, which in the case of debt-to-GDP are between 50% to more than 100% for many African countries. In 2023, for instance, African countries owed US685.5 billion to external creditors, which was equivalent to 24.5% of their combined GDP in 2023 (World Bank, "How much do African Countries Owe?" https://data.one.org/analysis/african-debt, retrieved May 29, 2025). The alarm bell for debt-distressed countries was rang by Pope Francis who set up the Jubilee Commission to come up with a blueprint for tackling the debt and development crises and creating the financial foundations for a sustainable people-centered global economy. The Commission observed that "To meet obligations to their external creditors, debt-distressed countries are sacrificing investments in education, healthcare, infrastructure, and climate resilience. Core aspects of national sovereignty are put into question as econom ic policy serves creditors rather than citizens. National politics is delegitimized if fiscal and financial policies are in the service of finance rather than in the service of development" (https://www.pass.va/content/dam/casinapioiv/pass/pdf-booklet/2025_jubilee_report.pdf).

1.17 Corruption, a Significant Challenge Across Many Countries

Corruption globally presents a complex and pervasive issue that significantly impacts socio-economic development. The 2023 Corruption Perceptions Index by Transparency International, which ranks 180 countries and territories by their perceived levels of public sector corruption, reveals that over two-thirds of countries score below 50, highlighting serious corruption problems, globally.

The report further indicates that most African countries are either stagnant or failing to make progress in the fight against corruption. It ranks many of the African countries poorly in terms of perceived levels of corruption, with most of the countries scoring below 50 out of 100, indicating the high levels of perceived corruption.

The proportion of persons who reported to have paid a bribe to a public official at least once or were asked for a bribe in the preceding 12 months increased dramatically from 9.5% in 2013 to 31.4% in 2021. This poor performance calls for greater efforts to strengthen operationalization of the norms of the African Union (AU) Convention on Preventing and Combating Corruption and the African Charter on Values and Principles of Public Service and Administration in the management of public affairs.[27]

Notwithstanding the poor performance at the continental level, a number of African countries have put legislative and regulatory measures in place to establish and maintain strong institutions and transformative leadership at all levels. Senegal, for example, created a national office in 2014 to fight corruption and fraud and to enhance capacity building. The country also adopted strategies for public procurement and increasingly modernizing the legal system. Tunisia established an anti-corruption body to formulate policies on fighting against corruption and protecting whistleblowers. Namibia is integrating the SDGs, Agenda 2063 and other African development agendas into their national development plans. Specifically,

[27] African Union, "*Convention on Preventing and Combating Corruption*," adopted by the 2nd Ordinary Session of the Assembly of the Union, Maputo, Mozambique, 11 July 2003, https://au.int/sites/default/files/treaties/36382-treaty-0028_-_african_union_convention_on_preventing_and_combating_corruption_e.pdf; and African Union Commission, *African Charter on Values and Principles of Public Service and Administration*, Adopted by the 16th Ordinary Session of the of Heads of State and Government of the AU Addis Ababa, Ethiopia - 31st January 2011 Entered into force on 23rd July 2016, https://au.int/sites/default/files/treaties/36386-treaty-charter_on_the_principles_of_public_service_and_administration.pdf; both retrieved April 13, 2025.

they established a framework of engagement for civil societies, implemented an open-door policy at grassroots level and established policies on methodologies for public institutions to work with civil society activists. Malawi established an integrity committee for every public institution, coordinated by an anti-corruption bureau, and commits at least 1% of the budget from each public institution to the integrity committee.[28] Nevertheless, challenges still remain continent-wide in implementing these and other measures effectively. Africa still continues to face challenges and experience failures in dealing with corruption. It is often criticized for its inability or inadequate seriousness in dealing with corruption.

1.18 African Challenges: Role of the African Union

The Organisation of African Unity (OAU) existed from 1963 to 2002. It had the noble objectives of uniting African countries from all parts of the continent and promoting peace among them. The African Union succeeded it, with more explicit economic objectives, the pursuit of which has led to the African Continental Free Trade Area (AfCFTA), a decision taken by the 18th Ordinary Session of Assembly of Heads of State and Government, held in Addis Ababa, Ethiopia, in January 2012. Because of its market size of 1.4 billion people and combined GDP of $3.4 trillion the AfCFTA is considered to be the world's largest free trade area. The main aim of the AfCFTA is to boosting intra-African trade as a means of promoting socio-economic growth development. The AfCTA holds a lot of promise provided that Governments and people across countries can support its actual implementation beyond offices. Africa urgently needs it!.[29]

[28] UN DESA (2024) "The Sustainable Development Goals Report 2024 – June 2024", New York, USA, https://unstats.un.org/sdgs/report/2024/. United Nations (2024) "World Social Report 2024", New York, USA. UN DESA (2024) "Annual Highlights report 2023–2024", New York, USA

[29] The first author of this book (i.e. Karamo) has played roles in the transition from the OAU to the AU by drafting the Framework Paper for the African Economic Community (AEC), which became the AU, and training OAU staff in economic cooperation and integration. For more information on these pan-African organization, the interested reader may refer to the AU website, in particular to "60 years OAU to AU 1963–2000"; "2023 AU Handbook"; "The African Continental Free Trade Area"; and "Agenda 2063"; https://oau60.au.int/; https://au.int/en/handbook; https://oau60.au.int/; https://au.int/en/african-continental-free-trade-area; https://au.int/agenda2063, retrieved April 7, 2025; and https://www.brookings.edu/articles/the-future-of-african-trade-in-the-afcftaera/#:~:text=The%20region%20now%20accounts%20for,Africa%27s%20trade%20and%20economic%20landscape.

1.19 Conflicts in General

Despite the African Union's (AU) efforts in peacekeeping and conflict resolution, pockets of conflicts on the continent have persisted for extended periods. Those in Somalia, South Sudan, Libya and the Democratic Republic of Congo, among others, have been extremely difficult to resolve, exposing the limitations of the AU's peacekeeping initiatives. These initiatives have been criticized for their limited resources and impacts, undermining the AU's ability to effectively respond to complex and large-scale conflicts. Consequently, the missions have often been affected by delayed deployments and challenges in adequately protecting civilians, raising serious human rights concerns.

The AU's overdependence on external funding has limited the organization's autonomy and ability to implement programmes aligned with the continent's specific needs and priorities. There are also implementation gaps. While the AU has developed several ambitious frameworks and agendas, the gap between policy formulation and effective implementation remains large. Therefore, some of the Union's initiatives, such as Agenda 2063, have faced difficulties in translating visions into concrete actions on the ground.

Furthermore, the AU's ability to enforce its decisions and resolutions in member states is limited. Unlike other regional unions such as the European Union, the AU lacks supranational authority, which hampers its ability to ensure compliance with agreed-upon measures. This is further exacerbated by bureaucratic inefficiencies and slow decision-making processes, which hinder its ability to respond promptly to emerging crises and issues.

1.20 Looking Ahead

To fully realize "African solutions to African problems", African countries need to address their challenges and shortcomings through sustained efforts, pooling national resources, knowledge and expertise together, and investing in preventive diplomacy to address potential internal conflicts before they erupt or escalate. Other possible solutions involve building institutional capacity, including administrative structures and resources, addressing implementation gaps and increasing cooperation among member states. Another key area to focus on is technology and innovation. These issues and recommendations have been addressed throughout this book, particularly in Chaps. 2 (through a very broad perspective of education) and Chap. 4 (with a focus on tribalism, Africa's biggest social cause of conflict).

African states, led by the AU, should invest in research and development and Science, Technology, Engineering and Mathematics (STEM) to drive innovation in various sectors and in continental and regional organizations. This goes together with promoting digital literacy and access to technology for all populations to enable technological inclusion in this digital age. They should be able to harness technology for improving healthcare, agriculture and education. Addressing these problems also requires political will, unity and improved coordination. It is also worth noting that international partnerships and collaborations still play a role in supporting African countries' efforts; however, Africa must be able to stand up tall in these partnerships on behalf of its people.

1.21 Addressing Africa's Challenges: A Summary

We have attempted to cover many of Africa's main challenges in the economic, social and political spheres. Thus, in addition to the discussion in this introductory chapter, Chap. 2 discusses the state of existing African educational systems and how to transform them into purposeful education. Chapter 3 looks at development strategies for Africa in the twenty-first century beyond the commonly cited East Asian Model. The chapter shows how to integrate markets and the Enabling Developmental State. Chapter 4 exposes what may be Africa's most serious social challenge—tribalism, its causes, consequences, and how to deal with it, using primary data from a path-breaking Gambian field survey. Chapter 5 explores the relatively new area of Islamic finance as a means of resource mobilization and inclusion for Africa in an era of very serious financial constraints. Chapter 6 relates to the essential health sector, proposing how to build resilience in the post-COVID-19 African economy, based on a South African case study. Chapter 7 highlights two fundamental requirements of modern economic development: innovation and technological learning. It discusses the importance of these in Africa, drawing on lessons from East Africa. Chapter 8 draws attention to another critical sector, agriculture, using empirical evidence and policy analysis. Chapter 9 concludes.

The book uncovers many unpleasant realities of the African existence, honestly. Among others, these are colonialism, conflict, underdevelopment and poverty, hunger, climate crisis and the position of the underdog at the bottom of the international pecking order. Yet, Africa's immense potential for positive change or progress has also not been ignored but instead unravelled in the book. We call for aligned social contracts at national, regional and continental levels,[30] one integrating all African stakeholders, one capable of embedding the interests of our people and our continent at heart in dealing with each other within and across Africa and in dealing with the rest of the world. To be aligned, these contracts should take place under the auspices of an African Union that does not only bark but can do so with teeth.

We must stop appearing to each other and the world as beggars sitting on golden thrones and starving people with bowls of rice in their laps! These are bad positions for us, they are also unsustainable and the world will not let us go on like these forever, unless it is in their interest to do so forever. Regarding interest, we have emphasized the prevalence of self-interest in today's world, undesirable as it is! To prove the validity of our arguments and the timeliness of this book, we should look at Trump's decisions to freeze US foreign aid, followed by cuts, in January 2025, and his "Liberation Day" universal tariff declaration and impositions in April 2025. These vividly show that Africa should heed our clarion calls in this book for more and effective actions in the pursuit of unity and human-centred development. When Africans "fight" (symbolically) or fight (literally) each other, everyone must be seen as a loser! No one must celebrate and encourage them, directly or indirectly! As the common sense phrase goes, "United we stand, divided we fall"!

Our history has repeatedly proven us to be intelligent, resourceful and resilient, and these have enabled us to survive the worst traumas of history. However, major impediments seem to pull us back even when progress seems to be reassuring. Let us think about these impediments deeper, work harder on them to clear and put the interests of our continent and people at heart better at all times, with greater sincerity and selflessness. This book is but a modest contribution in this direction and discourse.

[30] A social contract is an implicit agreement among stakeholders to cooperate for the common good. In it the stakeholders in/members of the society agree on the need for compromise and cooperation for mutual benefits. There is an extensive literature on this which is complex and diverse, but we use the concept here in the simple sense of Africans (governments, civil societies, private/business sectors, etc.) implicitly and explicitly or formally agreeing to work working together as one in the interests of their countries and continent. For more discussions on the theories of social contracts, dating back to the sixteenth century, the interested reader may refer to the writings, or discussions of the works, of Thomas Hobbes, John Locke, Jean-Jacques Rousseau and others.

CHAPTER 2

Purposeful Education for Development: An Alternative Concept and Approach to Education in Africa

2.1 Introduction

The colonial administrations set up educational systems in Africa that were elitist, exclusive, even divisive and very narrow in their objectives. The beneficiaries were the children (mainly the sons) of African traditional rulers and other supporters or henchmen. Western education became both a means of rewarding loyalty and producing literate cadres who were essential for local governments. Consequently, at the dawn of independence in African countries, there were very much fewer educated Africans than one would have normally expected, taking into account the national populations and, in particular, the massive challenges and demands of nationhood and development. In this chapter, we look at how colonial educational systems have shaped the character of post-colonial educational setups and how this has impeded progress. We assess also recent reforms or developments and their impact and recommend what type of education Africans need in the twenty-first century to address both internal and external challenges. Figures 2.1 to 2.5 reveal the current sorry state of Africa's educational systems and provide the backdrop for the critical measures recommended in this chapter.

K. N. M. Sonko et al., *21st Century African Development Strategies*,
https://doi.org/10.1007/978-3-031-93079-9_2

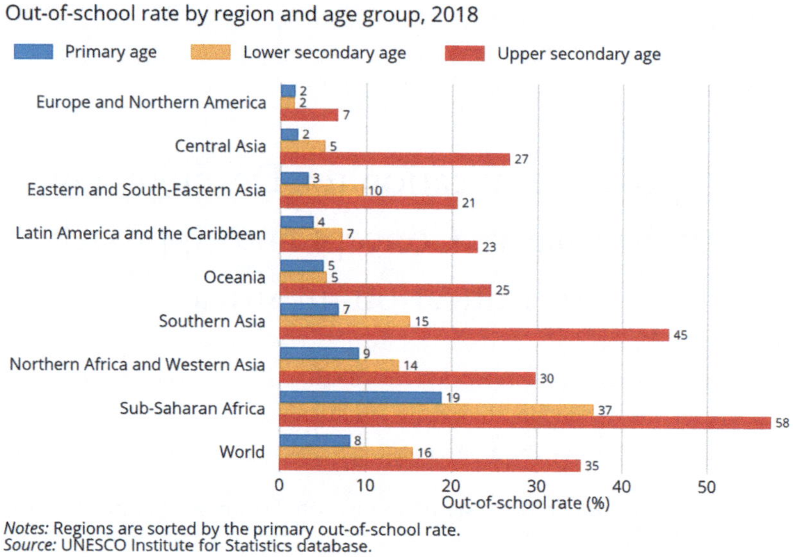

Fig. 2.1 Out-of-school rates

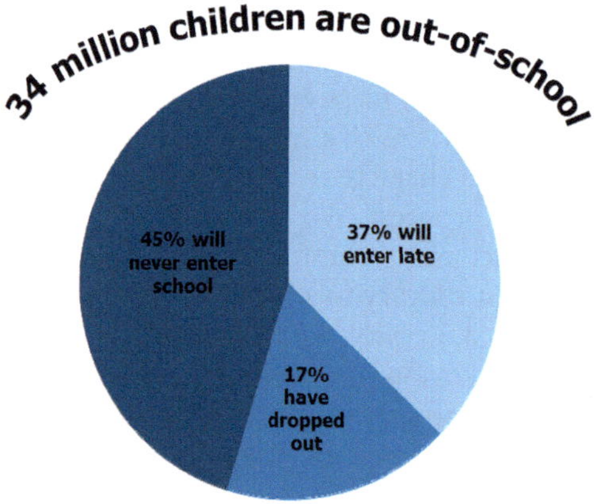

Fig. 2.2 Children out of school. (Source: UNESCO Institute of Statistics database 2025)

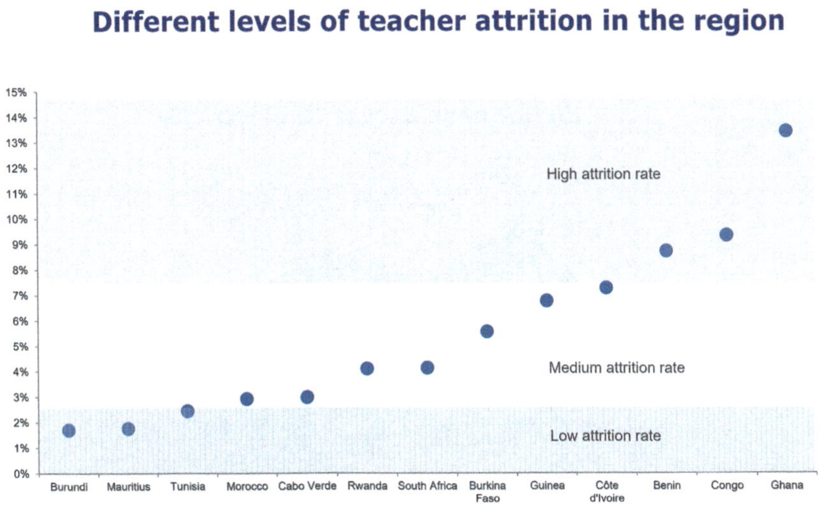

Fig. 2.3 Teacher attrition in schools. (Source: UNESCO Institute of Statistics database 2025)

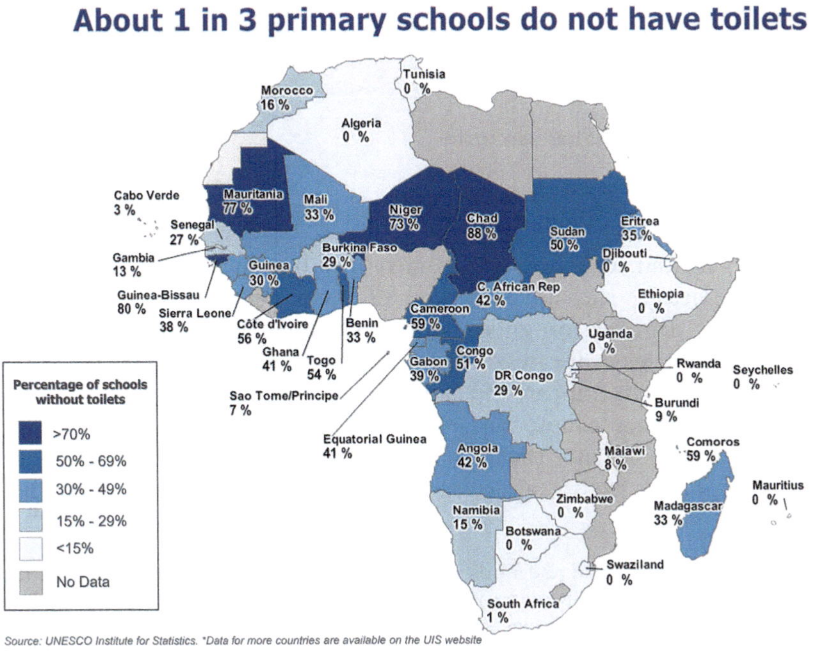

Fig. 2.4 Schools without toilets

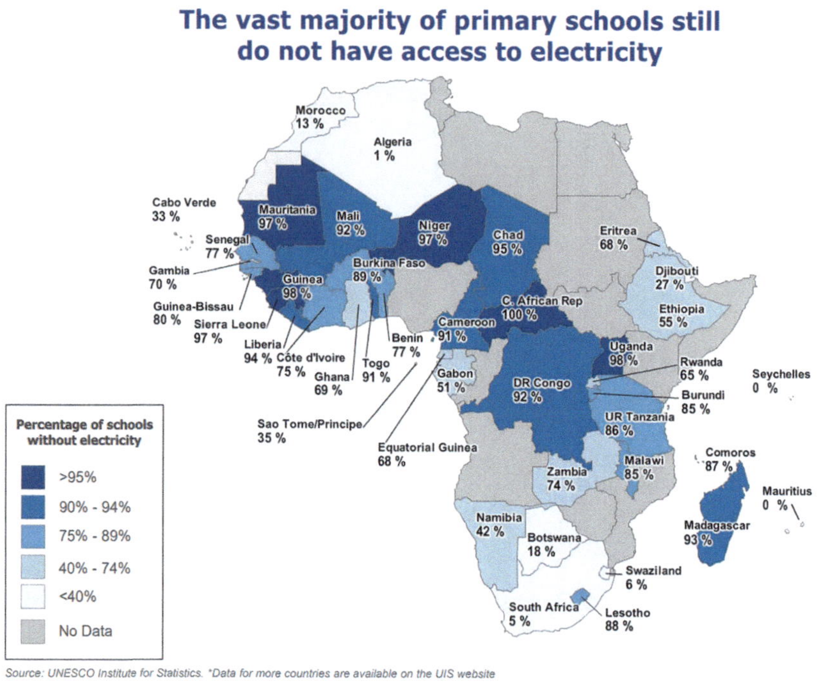

Fig. 2.5 Schools without electricity

2.2 Africa in the Twenty-First Century

Today's African economies are characterized by a mixture of positive and negative factors,[1] such as vast natural resources, fast-growing populations, increasing demand for goods and services, inflation, unemployment, indebtedness, new diseases/viruses, migration (legal and illegal), faster economic growth compared to earlier decades, etc. On the political front, there are military coups, warfare, influxes of refugees, and attempts at democratic governance (failures and successes), among others. The four most important sectors (agriculture, education, health and industry) that

[1] For these the interested reader may wish to refer, among numerous other studies, to the World Bank, "Leveraging Resource Wealth During the Low Carbon Transition," *Africa's Pulse*, No. 27 (April) 2023,. Washington, DC: World Bank. doi:10.1596/978-1-4648-1985-8. License: Creative Commons Attribution CC BY 3.0 IGO.

are critical for self-reliance and economic growth and social welfare are all very far from their full potential being tapped. On the social front, tribalism (the topic of Chap. 4), crime and gender inequity are common, generally. For these reasons, African educational systems have very many challenges to face. Their responsibilities are unlike those of their colonial antecedents, which were responsible mainly for the interest of the metropolis and an elitist minority of the local population, as pointed out above.

Internal factors are not all that the post-colonial African educational systems have to take into account or deal with, and external ones add to their immense responsibilities and hurdles. Therefore, external factors will also be discussed in this chapter. Thus, the discussions in the chapter are influenced by internal and external challenges which are outlined here and the abilities of the educational systems to address them. In fact, the realities of these challenges define the meaning of education in this chapter.

2.3 Features of African Economies Generally

2.3.1 Vast Natural Resources

Africa is known as a continent with vast natural resources: fisheries, animals, minerals, metals, etc. In 2018, Africa's combined GDP was about $2.5 trillion, which is 2.5 times lower than the estimated value of the continent's natural capital, valued at $6.2 trillion in the same year.[2] A very extensive diversity of natural habitats, such as highlands, forests, oceans, coasts, deserts and others, are spread throughout the continent. The continent is a leading producer of essential and luxury metals and minerals. Africa's two most profitable mineral resources are gold and diamonds. In 2021, for instance, Africa's officially recorded production of gold was 680.3 metric tons. The supply of diamonds globally is dominated by African countries. Africa is also becoming an increasingly important player in the world market for oil and gas. The amount of natural gas produced in the continent has doubled since 2000 and continues to increase

[2] Lennox Yieke, *"Green Wealth: African Development Bank Unites African Leaders at COP29 to Boost Carbon Markets for Sustainable Growth", African Business, November 22nd, 2024,* https://african.business/2024/11/economy/green-wealth-african-development-bank-unites-african-leaders-at-cop29-to-boost-carbon-markets-for-sustainable-growth?utm_source=MailerLite&utm_medium=email&utm_term=2025-05-13&utm_campaign=African%20Development%20Bank%20champions%20Africa%20at%20COP29%20Africa%20s%20Green%20Wealth%20opportunity%20and%20more.

annually, because of new discoveries. Algeria, Egypt and Nigeria are the major producers of natural gas. About 21% of Africa's land area is covered by forests, making Africa the third most forested continent.

Older oil-producing countries include Algeria, Angola, Egypt, Equatorial Guinea, Republic of Congo, Libya and Nigeria. Nigeria continues to be the largest producer of crude oil in Africa, with proven reserves of 37.50 billion barrels and production capacity of about 2.19 million barrels of oil per day (mbpd). Ghana, Ivory Coast, Mauritania, Senegal and several other countries have also made discoveries of oil and/or natural gas more recently.

Another very important industry in Africa is fishing. It has been valued at about $24 billion every year, accounting for about 1.3% of the combined GDP of African countries. The fisheries spread all over the marine coasts, in addition to inland waterways. The Great Lakes and Nile River, for instance, provide huge freshwater fisheries, such as the delicious Nile perch. With better management of marine fisheries, the industry can be much more lucrative.

2.3.2 *Increasing Demand for Goods and Services*

Population growth, larger access to education and better healthcare than in the past, and rising incomes have increased the demand for goods and services in Africa. As a result, there is an increase in the middle class across the continent. The class comprises Africans who can afford to spend from $2 to $20 a day.[3] Their share of the continental population has risen from 27% or 111 million persons in 1980, to 34.3% in 2010 and an estimated 42% or 1.1 billion persons in 2060.[4] This is the fastest growth rate of the middle class in the world. These growth trends have set Africa on the path of a middle-class boom that would outpace the numbers in the two conti-

[3] AfDB, "The Middle of the Pyramid: Dynamics of the Middle Class in Africa," *Market Brief*, April 20, 2011, https://www.afdb.org/fileadmin/uploads/afdb/Documents/Publications/The%20Middle%20of%20the%20Pyramid_The%20Middle%20of%20the%20Pyramid.pdf; Deloitte & Touche, "The Rise and Rise of the African Middle Class," 2013, https://sabc.ch/wp-content/uploads/2017/12/Deloitte-study-May20131.pdf, retrieved September 10, 2024. Also see UN, Growing Middle Class and Import Substitution Connecting the Dots to Unlock Made in Africa, *Policy Brief Africa Dialogue Series*, 10 May 2023, Retrieved September 11, 2023.

[4] AfDB, ibid.

nents with the biggest middle-class populations in the world—China and India. The class is the engine of growth in consumer spending or the demand for goods and services in Africa.

2.3.3 *Inflation and Unemployment*

Most African economies have become victims of inflation and unemployment at the same time. In many countries both inflation and unemployment have become chronic. Although the inflation is caused by both domestic (such as labour costs and government expenditures) and external factors, the latter seem to be more important, generally. These external causes include sharp rises in global commodity prices (in particular those which Africa imports), spikes in exchange rates, international supply chain disturbances, and natural and man-made disasters.[5]

2.3.4 *Indebtedness*

The 1980s are referred to as Africa's "lost decade", because of economic and political crises. One of the biggest indicators of the crisis at the time was its extremely heavy debt burden, which led to very stringent International Monetary Fund (IMF)-led structural adjustment programmes (SAPs). The debt burden led to a plethora of relief measures, which were actually successful enough (temporarily, with the benefit of hindsight) to enable Africa to redirect its meagre resources to developmental needs which enabled it to embark on the growth trajectory emanating from the end of the 1990s.[6] Today, however, Africa is facing the risk of another debt crisis. This is most concerning because of all that has been said and done about African debt in the 1980s and 1990s. According

[5] https://www.imf.org/en/Blogs/Articles/2022/10/20/africas-inflation-among-regions-most-urgent-challenges#:~:text=Instead%2C%20external%20developments%20have%20shaped,chain%20disruptions%2C%20and%20natural%20disasters; https://www.researchgate.net/publication/329971169_The_Main_Determinants_of_Inflation_in_South_Africa_an_Empirical_Investigation/fulltext/5c2662cda6fdccfc706e48a6/The-Main-Determinants-of-Inflation-in-South-Africa-an-Empirical-Investigation.pdf, last visited August 11, 2024.

[6] Mckinsey Global Institute, Reimagining economic growth in Africa: Turning diversity into opportunity, June 5, 2023, https://www.mckinsey.com/mgi/our-research/reimagining-economic-growth-in-africa-turning-diversity-into-opportunity, retrieved, 8th December 2024.

to the World Bank, the continent's total external debt has soared from $1.12 trillion in 2022, to about $1.152 trillion in 2023.[7] The threat of another major debt crisis is greater than ever before because global interest rates are at an all-time high in 40 years. The increasing indebtedness emanated from Africa's post-1990s' economic performance and the relatively more diverse and flexible international capital markets, which have made it possible for Africa to amass debt beyond what it was able to do in the conventional markets of the pre-2000 era. For example, bilateral debt dropped sharply to about 27% of total external debt in 2023/2024 compared to 52% in 2000, mainly due to the relative ease and attraction of commercial debt. On the other hand, commercial debt rose sharply to 43% of the total external debt in 2023/2024, compared to only 20% in 2000. Another example is the multiple bond debt securities issued by African countries. As these reach maturity in the early 2020s they face a $163 billion debt servicing responsibility by 2024, compared to $61 billion in 2010.[8] An unreasonable level of indebtedness, in relation to its usage and the capacity of an economy, has many negative consequences. These include the impossibility to attain economic and financial sustainability, enhance productivity and finance the most important or vulnerable sectors such as agriculture, education and health. Ultimately, employment, social welfare and economic growth become impossible to achieve desirously. The resurgence of heavy indebtedness by African governments in the 2020s points to very serious internal (within Africa) and external (outside Africa) factors many of which are outlined in this book. Africa needs more and better educated citizens in governments (particularly) and outside governments, at home and abroad, who care about their continent and people and are well trained to deal with these factors competently.

[7] World Bank, "Unlocking the Development Potential of Public Debt in Sub-Saharan Africa," Results Brief, December 2022, https://www.imf.org/external/pubs/ft/fandd/2001/06/loungani.htm

[8] The interested reader may refer to Hausmann, Ricardo, and Eduardo Fernández-Arias (2000), "Foreign Direct Investment: Good Cholesterol?" *IADB, Research Department Working Paper*, No. 417, 11 December 2000; and AfDB, "Annual Meetings 2024: old debt resolution for African countries – the cornerstone of reforming the global financial architecture," News and Events, 15 May, 2024, retrieved September 11, 2024.

2.3.5 *Migration (Legal and Illegal)*

Since1990, the number of African migrants living outside of the continent has more than doubled, with the rate of growth of the migrants in Europe the highest. Therefore, in 2020, most African-born migrants living outside Africa were found in Europe as residents (11 million). Europe is followed by Asia (about five million) and North America (approximately three million).

As in previous years, most of the internal displacements in 2022 happened in Sub-Saharan Africa, caused by internal conflicts and violence. Such conflicts and violence triggered massive displacements in the Democratic Republic of the Congo (surpassing more than four million), Ethiopia (in excess of two million) and Somalia (about 621,000). Natural disasters also took their toll, causing the largest displacements in Nigeria (about 2.4 million), Somalia (about 1.2 million), Ethiopia (around 873,000) and South Sudan (around 596,000).[9]

In recent years, a deadly form of migration has emerged in Africa, which has never been experienced before. Thousands of young people (men and women) risk their lives crossing or attempting to cross the Mediterranean and enter into Europe illegally. Most of them originate from West Africa, but more recently others from as far as the Sudan have joined them. According to the latest statistics, more than 157,651 illegal migrants crossed into Italy through the Central Mediterranean in very unsafe boats from Tunisia (62%), Algeria, Egypt and Libya.[10] The migrants (or would-be migrations) who choose this route do not include well-educated or skilled persons, which indicate that the educational systems with appropriate skilling can help in stemming this disturbing tide of voluntary immigration to Europe. Properly skilled persons are more likely to find opportunities and stay at home or seek migration legally than persons who are not properly trained.

[9] International Organization for Migration (IOM), "Migration and Migrants: Regional Dimensions and Developments," *World Migration Report*, 2024, http://worldmigrationreport.iom.int/what-we-do/world-migration-report-2024-chapter-3/africa, retrieved September 11, 2024.

[10] Roald Høvring, "10 things you should know about the Central Mediterranean migration route," Norwegian Refugee Council, 20. Mar 2024, https://www.nrc.no/feature/2024/10-things-you-should-know-about-the-Central-Mediterranean-migration-route/#:~:text=The%20Central%20Mediterranean%20route%20(the,cross%20the%20stretch%20in%202023.

2.3.6 *Faster Growth*

In spite of the many challenges, Africa's economic turnaround has been spotted and highlighted since the late 1990s, in marked contrast to the continent's performance in earlier years. During the period prior to the COVID-19 pandemic, seven out of the ten fastest growing economies in the world were in Africa. In 2019, the continent's average growth rate was about 3.4%, after consistent growth of more than a decade. With the improved economic performance of the continent, the middle class has also been rising in Africa as noted earlier. Although COVID-19 and political instability in several states have slowed down the continent's growth, and disease and political instability continue to seriously threaten a significant number of countries, the positive economic trends are expected to continue.[11] Africa's educational systems can and should be shaped to enhance the continuity or sustainability of the growth as well as its inclusiveness and greenness in the twenty-first century. Table 2.1 presents the latest growth statistics.

2.4 The Educational Systems in Particular

2.4.1 *Exclusion*

The United Nations Educational, Scientific and Cultural Organization (UNESCO) has observed that of all regions, globally, Sub-Saharan Africa has the highest rates of exclusion in education. More than one-fifth of children between the ages of about 6 and 11 are out of school, followed by a third of young persons between the ages of about 12 and 14. According to the UNESCO Institute of Statistics (UIS), nearly 60% of young Africans between the ages of about 15 and 17 are out of school, whilst, on the other hand, the school-age population is increasing.

2.4.2 *Low Quality of Education*

Whilst the increase in access to education in Africa has boosted literacy and increased the number of educated persons, evidence shows that quality has been sacrificed for quantity in some or many cases. The biggest negative

[11] International Monetary Fund (IMF), *World Economic Outlook*, January 2023. This point was also made in Sonko and Sonko (2023), p. 74.

impacts can be seen in the technical and medical fields in particular, where large outlays are always required for equipment, materials, the right environment and infrastructure for experiments and practical experience. Furthermore, grossly inadequate infrastructure has negatively impacted learning and the quality of the schools at all levels, generally. Therefore, cash-strapped public and private educational institutions cannot live up to expectations and the required standards.

2.4.3 *Overcrowded Classes*

Overcrowded classrooms hinder learning. In Africa classes are not only large but sometimes one room may seat more than one grade. For this reason, the average class size exceeds 70 in the Central African Republic, Malawi and Tanzania, for example. In a survey, UIS found that there are more than 50 students per class in primary schools in a third of the African countries studied, and 40 pupils or more per class in the overwhelming majority of the single-grade classes. The early grades, which are considered to be the most critical, are the most overcrowded too, with Grade 1 classes surpassing 50 pupils in about 50% of the countries; more than 80 pupils per class was found in the first three grades of primary schools in the Central African Republic (CAR) and about 50 pupils in the first two grades in Guinea, Togo and Uganda.[12]

2.4.4 *Shortage of Teachers and Stationery*

Teachers are the cornerstones of any educational system. Good teachers facilitate learning, whist the opposite hinder it. Shortage of teachers impedes the motivation of those on the job by overworking them. The inadequacy of the number of teachers in relation to the number of pupils or students hinders learning as well as the ability to fully tap the potential of the educational systems to satisfy the needs of the nation. This situation is aggravated by poor salaries and grossly insufficient opportunities for training and advancement in the educational systems. Unmotivated teachers lead to unmotivated students.

At the lower levels of the educational systems the increase in the school-age population is increasing the demand for schools and teachers, whilst

[12] https://uis.unesco.org/sites/default/files/school-resources-and-learning-environment-in-africa-2016-en/school-resources-and-learning-environment-in-africa-2016-en.pdf.

greater access to formal education as a whole does so too at higher levels of the system. At the same time, attrition from changes of jobs, retirement, mortality, migration, etc., makes teacher turnovers high in African countries.

Apart from the issues related to teaching staffs in African countries, students face shortages of textbooks. UNESCO found that, on average, 14 students share the same mathematics textbook in Cameroon, 5 in Chad and South Sudan and 4 in Equatorial Guinea. On average, two students or more in Sub-Saharan Africa as a whole share one reading book and about three students share one mathematics textbook.[13]

It is absolutely difficult to learn in an environment in which essential services, such are fresh water and adequate sanitation facilities, are in short supply. In most countries toilets are either unavailable altogether for girls in most schools, especially in the rural areas, or they have to share with boys. One in three primary schools in Africa does not provide toilets at all for the pupils. For example, 70% or more schools in Chad, the Comoros and Mauritania do not have toilets at all, and about 50% of the toilets are mixed toilets in the schools in Mali, Madagascar and Burundi. About 50% of primary schools do not have drinking water, and most schools have no access to electricity.[14] These conditions have been found to be one of the reasons why pupils are discouraged about schooling in most African countries. Girls are the most affected in many countries, and in some cases they have been found to refuse going to schools at all or regularly missing classes, so as to protect their dignity, health and security. This hidden cause of disadvantages to girls shows up later in their adulthood and creates barriers to their economic and professional progress.

2.4.5 *Surge in Domestic Educational Institutions*

There has been a surge across Africa in the number of domestic educational institutions, physical/in-person as well as those which provide online education. In particular, the proliferation of online courses has universalized access to education, opening doors for anyone who can afford to pay for it, in less time and with less resources than formally structured

[13] https://uis.unesco.org/sites/default/files/school-resources-and-learning-environment-in-africa-2016-en/school-resources-and-learning-environment-in-africa-2016-en.pdf.

[14] https://uis.unesco.org/sites/default/files/school-resources-and-learning-environment-in-africa-2016-en/school-resources-and-learning-environment-in-africa-2016-en.pdf.

schools requiring physical presence in classrooms. These have increased the rates of literacy and some levels of basic skill formation or proficiency. However, it has also culminated in mass education in which quantity and paper qualifications are pursued rather than quality and much-needed capacity building.

2.5 The World in the Twenty-First Century

Before the twenty-first century, revolutions were generally seen only as violent movements that overturned the status quo, especially in brutal ways. The twenty-first century world presents revolutions of a different form—non-violent overturn of the economic and social status quos through technology and radically new ideas. This is now commonly referred to as disruption. The pursuit of money is at the root and centre of these disruptive processes, as shown in the flourishing of financial institutions and other businesses. The essential and indispensable conduits of these new forms of revolutions are very dynamic and innovative educational systems which train individuals and groups to acquire and utilize ideas, values and skills for money-making in numerous ways, especially through new technologies and services. African educational systems are faced with additional challenges in this new world with new challenges, which are not bloodily violent but technologically and service-wise disruptive and eruptive.

2.5.1 Self-Interest

As advocates of a better world for all, we prefer a world where governments and people work together for mutual benefit across borders. However, we live in a world where the self-interest of nations determines international actions and relations. This is not a baseless belief or imagination but a practical reality which is no longer a hidden secret. President Trump's recent universal tariff declaration shows it in its clearest form (see Chap. 1), but it is not the only example. In this context, Africa has to know also its interests and protect them, better, in order to stop what African themselves always complain about and blame outsiders for—meddling in their affairs and shackling their progress. Without these, Africa will continue to be subjected to exploitation, disrespect and disregard.

2.5.2 Competition

Within the context described in the preceding paragraph, competition has become an inherent feature of contemporary economies, more intensely now than before. The feature is exhibited at international, national, organizational and individual levels. As nations struggle to dominate each other globally, within each nation itself organizations, regions, groups struggle for dominance over each other or winning in one form or the other. Some aspects of this competition are outrightly negative, but some are positive. The clearest negative aspect at the international level is the desire of nations to be dominant in their relations with others which often leads to the ignoring of the interests and needs of others and even to wars between nations. Examples of positive aspects of the competition exist in business when companies try to do better than each other in product innovation and customer service. Neoliberalism has justified, praised and defended competition particularly in the market and a reduction of the state in the economy to promote competition.[15]

Lagging behind or being uncompetitive has several consequences for a country. First, it impedes investment, limits markets and creates unemployment. Secondly, out of these, trade deficits, economic decline and poverty can emerge. Nevertheless, when competition becomes cut-throat among nations (and even individuals), it can create marginalization and alienation, unless effective institutions can be created that can contain the process (managing fears and balancing interests).[16]

2.5.3 Information and Communication Technology

Today's Information and Communication Technology (ICT) has revolutionized the level of technology and how information and communication are processed, packaged and transmitted in the modern era. Covering all technical means of handling information and communication, ICT comprises computer and network hardware and software, which deal with digitalization, connectivity and automation in various sectors, especially in industry. Industry 4.0 or the Fourth Industrial Revolution (4IR) has

[15] See, for instance, Ostry, Jonathan D., Prakash Loungani, and Davide Furceri, "Neoliberalism: Oversold?" *Finance & Development*, Vol. 53, No. 2, June 2016; also in the same issue of *Finance and Development*, "Evolution Not Revolution: Rethinking Policy at the IMF, an Interview with Chief Economist Maurice Obstfeld".

[16] Recommendations for such can institution have been detailed in Sonko and Sonko (2023).

brought the evolution of ICT to unprecedented heights through technologies such as robotics, automation, blockchain, artificial intelligence (AI), Internet of Things (IoT), cloud computing and analytics, machine learning, and robotics. The integrating of these technologies into production plants and operations has resulted in facilitating real-time decision making, productivity and how and what companies manufacture and distribute.[17]

It has been estimated that by 2025 (this year), Industry 4.0 technologies would create additional value, through new products and services, which would equal$3.7 trillion.[18] This potential is expected to be unlocked mainly by manufacturers who can change their conventional methods and adopt adaptive manufacturing that is capable of integrating production facilities using advanced data-generation and processing software. Advanced technologies such as AI and distributed computing can help in harnessing and increasing value-added, outcome-based services, productivity and profitability. According to the McKinsey Global Institute (2018), Industry 4.0 leaders can expect a 122% increase in their cashflows. Runners up can expect to receive 10%, whilst those who are unable to adapt will suffer from a 23% drop in their profits.[19]

African industries should be ready because the effects of Industry 4.0 will be sweeping sooner than expected by most. McKinsey & Company has further found that:

> Every single industry will be transformed during the Fourth Industrial Revolution, but some to a greater degree than others. The nature of the

[17] https://www.ibm.com/topics/industry-4-0#:~:text=IBM,What%20is%20Industry%20 4.0%3F,improve%20and%20distribute%20their%20products; https://www.mckinsey.com/featured-insights/mckinsey-explainers/what-are-industry-4-0-the-fourth-industrial-revolution-and-4ir;https://ec.europa.eu/eurostat/statistics-explained/index.php?title=Glossary:Information_and_communication_technology_(ICT)#:~:text=Information%20and%20communication%20technology%2C%20abbreviated,as%20well%20as%20their%20software.

[18] https://www.mckinsey.com/featured-insights/mckinsey-explainers/what-are-industry-4-0-the-fourth-industrial-revolution-and-4ir.

[19] https://www.studysmarter.co.uk/explanations/macroeconomics/economics-of-money/international-capital-market/#:~:text=The%20International%20Capital%20Market%20primarily,instruments%20like%20bonds%20and%20shares McKinsey & company, "What are Industry 4.0, the Fourth Industrial Revolution, and 4IR?" August 17, 2022, https://www.mckinsey.com/featured-insights/mckinsey-explainers/what-are-industry-4-0-the-fourth-industrial-revolution-and-4ir.

> Industry 4.0 transition will differ by the specific types of technology being adopted, as well as the existing infrastructure and skills of organizations.[20]

They projected that Industry 4.0 will also drastically transform the skill sets of workforces in the coming decades by shifting the standards of sought-after talents. These changes would emanate from companies embracing robotics. Hence the demand for skills will be affected as follows:

(1) Physical and manual labour in repeatable tasks, like those in assembly lines, will decline by about 30%;
(2) Basic literacy and numeracy skills will fall by nearly 20%;
(3) Technological skills such as coding will increase by more than 50%;
(4) The demand for complex cognitive skills will rise by almost 33% and
(5) High-level social and emotional skills will increase by more than 30%.

The predicted developments, some of which have already started, as AI (in particular) spreads like wild fire in countries that can afford, are threats to Africa because of the continent's low levels of industrial and technological advancements. The biggest responsibilities for preparing Africans for the new challenges lie in the educational systems. They should make it possible for Africans to learn and develop vertical or hard as well as horizontal, and transversal or soft digital skills. [21]As the global economy is transformed, Africa must catch up or be ahead through purposeful education, including skilling, reskilling and upskilling to avoid skills obsolescence in an era of rapid digital transformation.

2.5.4 *International Capital*

An international capital market is a system for trading securities (stocks and bonds) in more than one country and currency. Grasping its structure and operations is essential for Africans to be able to tap into its potential fully. It is where countries borrow and invest across borders, through companies, governments, governmental institutions and other investors.

[20] McKinsey & company, "What are Industry 4.0, the Fourth Industrial Revolution, and 4IR?" August 17, 2022, https://www.mckinsey.com/featured-insights/mckinsey-explainers/what-are-industry-4-0-the-fourth-industrial-revolution-and-4ir.

[21] Geeks Academy, "Hard vs Soft Skills: A Guide to Digital Skills," https://www.geeksacademy.it/en-en/article-268/hard-vs-soft-skills-a-guide-to-digital-skills, retrieved December 12, 2024.

By facilitating the global flow of capital, the international capital market enables traders to tap into larger pools of cash and financial assets than are available nationally in their countries.

Globalization has created the international capital market in the international financial sector, which transcends geographical frontiers. The market has three components. There is the foreign exchange market, which enables traders to buy and sell currencies, thereby setting exchange rates. There is the stock market, which enables businesses and individuals to raise capital through the shares of listed companies on stock exchanges. A third component is the bond market, where governments, municipalities and large corporations raise funds through bonds which are sold to interested investors.

As development is about both economics and its related subject of finance, Africa needs both good economists and financial analysts. The educational systems should be able to produce both and enable them to understand sound development policies and advise their colleagues and African leaders what are the good and bad choices when it comes to running economies. In particular, they should be able to advise them in their relations with the major development and financial institutions, especially those that are non-African and capital coming from outside Africa. For example, they should be able to advise them on the advantages and/or disadvantages of each type of capital. They should be informed that short-term lending is driven by speculative considerations, it is quick to fly and can cause serious economic instability through boom-bust cycles.[22] They should know the true costs of foreign debt and the benefits of creating win-win partnerships through private investments and trade.

2.5.5 *Sustainability*

Sustainability has become the catchword of the early twenty-first century encapsulating durability in business and economic development. However, it is not a new concept. In 1991 Khan and Sonko co-authored a ground-breaking work that compellingly advocates for the integration of sustainability and technology in economic development. They provide robust technical evidence supporting the benefits of this approach. Sustainability,

[22] https://www.studysmarter.co.uk/explanations/macroeconomics/economics-of-money/international-capital-market/#:~:text=The%20International%20Capital%20Market%20primarily,instruments%20like%20bonds%20and%20shares.

in essence, is about maintaining and supporting processes over the long term. In the realms of business and economic policy, it emphasizes conserving natural and physical resources to ensure their availability for the future.

Their "eco-economic" approach, introduced 23 years ago, underscores the importance of balancing the needs of current and future generations. This forward-thinking perspective not only is crucial for environmental stewardship but also presents significant opportunities for businesses to innovate and thrive sustainably. By adopting these principles, companies can secure a competitive edge and contribute to a sustainable future, ensuring long-term value for stakeholders and the planet. The process of accomplishing this noble but somewhat onerous duty is now embodied in what Sonko and Sonko (2023)[23] refer to as formal comprehensive or holistic Environmental, Social and Governance (ESG). These three groups of factors are considered in the primary challenges confronting both corporations and society at large, now including climate change, human rights and legal compliance, among others.

Africa is not spared from these challenges of the world but has been lagging behind in terms of both the awareness and implementation of ESG measures; in other words, the laggards in the classification of ESG implementers, as they have been referred to in the literature elsewhere.[24] Most businesses in Africa have to date not truly embraced ESG as a part of their daily operations. The big corporations tend to be more advanced and expected to be so, but many also tend to be merely focused on compliance and/or greenwashing at present. However, pressure has been mounting on businesses, in particular, to go beyond just tick-box compliance and care more substantially for the environment in which they operate. Many African governments also still have a very long way to go.

[23] Sonko, Karamo NM, and Mariama Sonko, *Demystifying ESG: Charting the ESG Course in Africa*, Palgrave Macmillan, London & New York, 2023.

[24] Helena Naffa, and Máté Fain, "A factor approach to the performance of ESG leaders and laggards," Finance Research Letters, Volume 44, January 2022, https://www.sciencedirect.com/science/article/pii/S1544612321001549, retrieved October 4, 2024; Roulland, Thomas, and Alex Bibani, "Achieving Sustainability. Leaders and laggards: how ESG data defines both, " Allianz Global Investors, 16/09/2024, https://www.allianzgi.com/en/insights/outlook-and-commentary/esg-data-defines-leaders-and-laggards, retrieved October 4, 2024; and Lewellyn, Krista, "ESG Leaders or Laggards? A Configurational Analysis of ESG Performance," *Business & Society,* Volume 63 Issue 5, May 2024, https://orcid.org/0000-0003-4924-6362, retrieved October 4, 2024.

2.6 Recommendations for Transforming African Educational Systems

Dual-Level Approaches: How Can the Educational Systems Address Internal and External Challenges?

There are two critical recommendations which we believe are particularly relevant for addressing the biggest challenges Africa faces at both the internal and external levels, simultaneously. To put it differently but with the same meaning, we are referring to the fundamental ways in which Africa can deal with the critical challenges that are manifested with momentous significance and have bearings on African development at both the internal (domestic) and external (foreign) levels. These ways are 1) purposeful education and 2) strategic thinking through strategic management.

2.6.1 Purposeful Education[25]

By purposeful education we mean educating and empowering people for very clear objectives or goals. This calls for well-thought-out reasons and policies for national educational systems, enabling them to align aims, objectives, skills and opportunities. The process should begin at the highest levels of governance where laws and policies are formulated, encompassing the legislature, executive and judiciary. The wider objectives of education in any African country should be set at these highest levels of decision making in the three organs and communicated down to policy makers who can translate the policies and stated objectives or goals into actionable programmes and projects with clearer definitions and targets. Further down the hierarchy, responsibilities, outputs and deadlines should be clearly laid out in each institution or department. This can be done in simple formats or through the more sophisticated Strategic Management Sustainability Framework (SMSF) or Tool (SMST),[26] which will be discussed below.

Before then, it is paramount for us to emphasize that purposeful education requires that parents understand the national purposes of education

[25] This may also be referred to as Purpose-led education.

[26] The Framework is utilized more like a spreadsheet, whilst the Tool is operated as an enlarged computer application requiring more knowledge about information technology than is required by the Framework.

and play a very active part in the education of their children. It also means that another cardinal part of making such a system more effective is for the government to be able to detect and nurture talent at a young age. This is due to the fact that, typically, many brilliant kids drop out of school or repeat classes, because they cannot afford the school fees, accommodation and/or transportation costs. The most desirable situation is one in which there is harmony between the aspirations of families and the goals of the governments and nation; in short, aligning national educational systems with national needs . Competitive educational systems emerge when governments can cater for the dreams of parents and their kids through education, and parents and children recognize and seize the opportunities the educational systems provide for them. For families to be able to take advantage of the potential opportunities presented by the educational systems (especially public, but private too), they must have the means to do so. The most important factors in determining this are their abilities to pay for their education or get it free and the availability of the necessary infrastructure and services pointed out earlier. However, it should be pointed out that, as illustrated in Fig. 2.6, even individuals have a role in purposeful education in the sense that the aspirations of the population/citizens should be aligned with those of the government and families. This implies the social contract mentioned in chap. 1. This can be extended to regional and continental levels in Africa with the frameworks of the regional economic communities (RECs) and the African Union (AU).

A purposeful educational system must be able to provide its "products" (students/graduands) to acquire employable or entrepreneurial skills. This requires informal (at home) or formal counselling that helps children to aspire for the right subjects at appropriate ages. It also requires developing inter-industry and multi-institutional linkages between the educational system and the private sector as well as others to enable students to go on internships whilst still going to school.

It is equally important that the national educational goals should be in line with a well-laid-out and implementable National Development Plan, harmonizing the purposes of national education with the development aspirations of the nation. Purposeful education is summarized and portrayed in Fig. 2.6. The capacity of the educational systems should match the demands of each African country. The attainment of sufficient levels of productivity by the people coming out of the educational systems directly contributes to higher levels of economic output and social welfare or living standards. When education is purposeful, it enables policy makers and

Fig. 2.6 Purposeful education

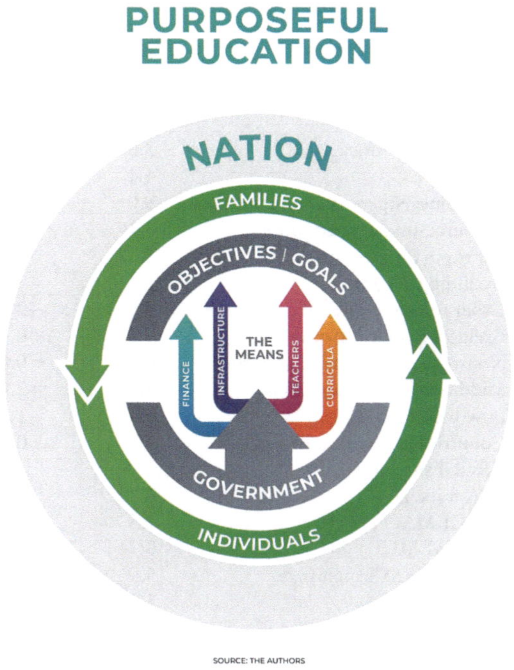

beneficiaries to also become aware of the importance of the identified purposes and how to attain them. That is the opposite of purposeless or meaninglessly purposeful education when schools are built and kids go there without any clear beneficial mission or vision for the nation. In such a situation, people (both kids and adults) may be picking up pieces of paper from educational institutions (credible or not) for no reason or for the wrong reasons. Honorary qualifications may also flourish only for the sake of having titles. On the other hand, purposeful education can enable nations and nationals to align their aspirations, education, plans and achievements for national and individual benefits. When these are aligned, unemployment and the waste of resources and time are managed better (Table 2.1). When a nation is able to meet its own skills demand, it can serve the rest of the world without the brain drain. Thus, with the growing population African countries, with purposeful educational systems may also be able to turn the continent into the world's "skills basket"!

Table 2.1 Real GDP growth - Sub-Saharan Africa (SSA)

Country/group	*Real GDP (annual percent change)*						
	2011–2019	*2020*	*2021*	*2022*	*2023*	*2024*	*2025*
Sub-Saharan Africa	3.8	−1.6	4.8	4.1	3.6	3.6	4.2
Median	4.4	−1.2	5.0	4.3	4.5	4.0	4.6
Excluding Nigeria and South Africa	5.0	−0.1	5.2	5.1	4.6	4.5	5.3
Resource-intensive countries	3.1	−2.4	4.2	3.6	2.7	2.8	3.5
Oil-exporting countries	2.8	−2.1	3.1	3.4	2.5	2.8	3.2
Excluding Nigeria	2.3	−2.9	2.0	3.6	1.6	2.6	3.4
Other resource-intensive countries	3.5	−2.7	5.3	3.8	3.0	2.8	3.7
Excluding South Africa	5.6	0.4	5.6	5.3	4.8	4.1	5.4
Non-resource-intensive countries	6.0	0.8	6.5	5.6	5.8	5.6	6.1
Middle-income countries	3.1	−2.8	4.6	3.5	2.7	3.0	3.5
Low-income countries	6.1	1.7	5.4	5.6	5.7	5.0	6.0
Countries in fragile and conflict-affected situations	4.2	−0.3	4.2	4.3	4.1	3.7	4.3
CFA franc zone	4.4	0.3	4.4	4.7	4.0	5.3	5.3
CEMAC	2.5	−1.5	1.7	3.3	2.3	3.7	3.0
WAEMU	5.7	1.3	6.0	5.5	5.1	6.2	6.6
COMESA (SSA members)	5.9	0.3	6.6	6.0	6.1	5.0	5.8
EAC-5	5.5	0.9	6.4	5.2	5.3	5.4	5.9
ECOWAS	4.0	−0.7	4.5	4.0	3.5	3.8	4.3
SACU	1.7	−6.3	5.3	2.2	1.0	1.2	1.8
SADC	2.8	−4.0	4.8	3.7	2.7	2.5	3.3

Source: IMF, World Economic Outlook, October 2024

In a purposeful educational system, institutions must be able to encourage and cater for research and innovation, the importance of which has already been highlighted. This is impossible without data generation and storage. For researchers, data is like the engine of a car, without which there can be no movement no matter how skilful the driver is. Data availability enhances research, helps to answer questions and enables researchers to turn imaginations into reality. In a purposeful system education, research and data should all be oriented to the needs of the nation.

Perhaps the biggest challenges of African educational systems are how to be inclusive and create sustainable opportunities for the fast-growing number of youth in particular. Purposeful education can address these by starting with the poorest and most vulnerable. These are those who can be found at the bottom of the national income ladder (when income criterion is used), at the bottom of the privilege spectrum (in terms of the distribution of public infrastructure and services) and those with physical or mental disabilities (variously referred to as the handicapped, persons of special needs, etc.). We refer to them as "the marginals". In a purposeful educational system, these marginalized populations should be an integral part of educational policies, planning and actions. The ability to integrate them into the mainstream from the margins is what can turn challenges into opportunities, potential beggars into productive professionals, potential criminals into law-abiding citizens and, in short, bane into boon.

2.6.2 *Strategic Thinking Through Strategic Management*

Strategic thinking through formal strategic management is a key to success in running companies and organizations, public and private. It is another dual-level approach to address Africa's educational challenges with a doubled-edged sword. When strategic management is combined with the systematic pursuits of external and internal goals, the goals become attainable. This can be demonstrated through our Strategic Management Sustainability Framework (SMSF) and Tool (SMST), also referred to as the African PESTLE Analysis (APA). The attainability arises from systematic and very clear approaches. As shown in the case of ESG, it comprehensively reveals and addresses challenges, organizing them consistently, defining and quantifying targets, assigning responsibilities and setting deadlines.

Additionally, the SMSF/SMST/APA, which has been presented to numerous audiences around the world, offers the following much-needed qualities in African institutions:

1. The Framework and Tool offer reporting and visualization features to present findings clearly in six fundamental categories that persons, organizations and the world at large need.
2. Either the Framework or Tool enables institutions or individuals to deliver actionable recommendations, based on the findings from their analysis. Thus, either can help them to identify and capitalize on challenges and opportunities and mitigate risks effectively.
3. This Framework and Tool are powerful yet simple and user-friendly with the capabilities of producing good employee/human insights when formulating strategies for the future.

4. The Framework and Tool encourage (in fact require) team building! The concept of "Teamability" is developed by Sonko (2024)[27] as part of the SMSF/SMST/APA process, and it is a unique concept/illustration of the importance of teamwork, which is now an almost universal desire.[28]
5. They are a Framework and Tool that encourage companies/organizations and any other user to draw on their internal resources first; i.e. to engage their employees first in addressing their challenges/problems and finding their answers.
6. They provide the unique concept of "the quartile approach" to challenge/problem identification and solutions.
7. They also provide the unique feature of "Performance Square" to measure, target, assign responsibilities and set deadlines for major tasks.
8. Through the Strategy Report, which they end up with, they provide formats to summarize the main challenges and their solutions.
9. They provide a window and a gate, a microscope and telescope, for companies/organizations and individuals, meaning that in their vast and comprehensive scopes they also enable focus, depending on the user's interest. Example: those who are interested in mainly the environment can focus mainly on the environment whist taking into account other relevant factors and those who are interested mainly in technology, governance or social challenges can do so the same way.
10. Finally, they provide a list of positive consequences for the concerned, highlighting how they can improve their performances or other activities by reducing something negative, stabilizing some-

[27] Sonko and Sonko (2023); and for "Teamability" refer to https://apatool.com/ and Karamo NM Sonko and Mariama Sonko, "Urban Challenges and Planning: Applications and Relevance of the Strategic Management Sustainability Framework (SMSF) and Tool (SMST)," Paper presented at "The 3rd International Conference on Sustainability: Development and Innovation," Jeddah, Saudi Arabia, February 8–12, 2026.

[28] Teamability—what does it mean?

(1) Doing what requires more than one person to be done by more than one person;
(2) The ability to develop the attitudes to work with others;
(3) The willingness to work with more than yourself;
(4) The belief that someone is almost as good, as good or even better than you in dealing with a challenge;
(5) To acknowledge and appreciate the contributions of others;
(6) To motivate teams and make every member of a team feel needed and useful; and
(7) To reward teams where teams have succeeded.

thing constant and increasing something positive which might be related to their performances.

Reducing Negativity

The SMSF/SMST/APA concept is inspired by the nine core values/principles of the African village woman:

1. Adaptability;
2. Coordination;
3. Confidence;
4. Discipline;
5. Energy;
6. Focus;
7. Patience;
8. Perseverance; and
9. Positivity.

All of the above enhance performance. They help to eliminate or reduce the negative attitudes which build emotional/psychological barriers to performance at work. Besides, they help to reduce or eliminate self-pity or sense of deprivation which undermines motivation.

Constantly Stabilizing What Is Desirous

The SMSF and SMST help to stabilize what is desirous:

1. In companies or organizations with team spirits, the SMSF and SMST provide justification to continue maintaining it through dynamic physical visualization of teamwork and the transformation of historic traditional cultural values into modern strategic management concepts;
2. The concept of "teamability" is developed as part of the SMSF and SMST process. It is a concept concept/illustration of the importance of teamwork, which is now an almost universal desire. "Teamability" means:

   (1) Doing what requires more than one person to be done by more than one person;
   (2) The ability to develop the attitudes to work with others;
   (3) The willingness to work with more than yourself;

(4) The belief that someone is almost as good as, as good as or even better than, you in dealing with challenges or the challenge you are facing;
(5) To acknowledge and appreciate the contributions of others;
(6) To motivate teams and make every member of a team feel needed and useful and (7) To reward teams where teams have succeeded.

Increasing What Is Positive

Whilst discouraging what is negative, the SMSF and SMST encourage what is positive:

> In life, as a whole, everywhere including school and the workplace, the right attitudes are essential.[29] In the workplace, they are of utmost importance because attitudes directly affect productivity. Even if you are the best engineer in the world, the wrong attitudes can prevent you from building the right bridges or innovating the kind of technology that can make you a Bill Gates. At the personal level, the wrong/bad attitudes can even lead you to suicide! The SMSF/SMST/APA is helpful in building positive attitudes. In fact, this is one of its best features. It does this in four ways, in addition to the principles/values of the African woman already listed—a. by giving you a comprehensive tool to identify and deal with your challenges/problems; b. enabling you to recognize and appreciate your relative privileges; c. by giving you hope; and d. enabling you to recognize your own ability to address your challenges/problems! Thus, the SMFT and SMST encourage companies/organizations or users generally to be the masters of their own destinies on their work floors or wherever else they may be. Thus, we provide the means with the inspiration and confidence in your ability to use the Framework and/or Tool in order to address your challenges by yourself as the person who knows them best and can solve them the best way!

2.6.3 *Private Education*

One of the features of colonially inherited educational systems in Africa is the over-reliance on public/governmental educational institutions. The expansion of public education after colonialism has enabled governments

[29] This why the right attitudes and values, such as discipline and others brought to attention in the SMSF/SMST/APA process, can be used to be used to shape or adjust Africa's development in the twenty-first century.

to serve their people and enabled ordinary citizens to have access to education. However, budgetary constraints make it impossible to cater for the needs of entire and growing populations in Africa. Therefore, in recent years, private schools have emerged and some of them have excelled, even in scientific/technical education. The motivation to invest in private education by local and international investors comes from incentives which make such investments attractive. Private education brings competition in the educational systems, increases access to education, provides skilled personnel for employers and enhances production and productivity. On the downside, the proliferation of private institutions, unchecked, can compromise standards in private schools, and result in inappropriate curricula and unjustifiably exorbitant fees. Therefore, to fully reap its potential, private education should be part of purposeful education discussed in this chapter, bearing in mind that private investors need to be encouraged to make reasonable returns on their investments in the educational sector.

2.7 Single-Level Approaches: How Can African Educational Systems Address Internal Challenges?

In order to make appropriate recommendations on how African educational systems can be more effective, one needs to understand what are or should be their appropriate objectives, where the challenges and shortcomings are and how to deal with them. The overriding objective of any educational system is to teach and train people to acquire the right ideas and skills to make them more productive in their careers and in the national economy. The differences in the systems lie in some of their contents, their rigour, priorities, resources, support to national capacity building, and abilities to seize national and international opportunities. Therefore, we have identified challenges that the African educational systems face both nationally and internationally. Addressing these at both levels again, but separately, with the objectives of making African educational systems serve Africa and the world better is done next. We start by relating education to some of the most important sectors in Africa's economic and social fabric, before proceeding to raise key, but not often discussed, issues that the educational systems must address to become more effective.

2.7.1 Health

As clearly shown in Chap. 4, Africa lags behind other regions of the world in almost all healthcare indicators. Not only is Africa behind, but the gap between its health indicators and those of the rest of the world continues to widen. On many of these indicators, Africa has been overtaken even by some countries of Southeast and South Asia, which ranked lower than some African countries a few decades ago. While progress is being made, it is not enough, which is the reason why we should expect that developments in the health sectors of African countries will continue to lag behind those in the rest of the world for some time. Except for COVID-19, pandemics seem to affect Africa more than other regions. The HIV/AIDS epidemic has hit Sub-Saharan Africa harder than any other region in the world, and is one of the reasons why the gap between Africa and the rest of the world has widened in health indicators since the 1980s. In addition, policy-related factors have played a major role, by rendering the responses of governments to epidemics less effective than they have been elsewhere. Political factors are among the most important causes: wars in many countries across the continent for much of the second half of the last century had terrible effects on local populations, directly pushing up death rates and indirectly increasing them by interrupting food production and distribution chains, and by impeding relief efforts and the provision of emergency medical assistance. Poverty, finally, is making Africa very unhealthy. Large percentages of the African population are too poor to afford transportation to treatment facilities, let alone to pay for medical treatment.

Therefore, health sector in African countries can be considered sources of major growth opportunities for two main reasons: because of the tremendous health challenges that the continent faces and because of the very serious deficiencies that still exist in Africa's healthcare. On the bright side, because of the many easily treatable conditions that still affect many Africans, current improvements in life expectancy can be expected to continue as African governments, with the help of foreign partners and the private sector, address the deficiencies in primary care, and large-scale communicable diseases. The non-communicable but life-threatening so-called lifestyle diseases are more complicated and require more attention and resources.

2.7.2 *Agriculture*

Through the health sector, Africa can create healthy Africans. For healthy people to remain healthy, proper nutrition is obligatory. That makes agriculture as important as the health sector. Apart from nourishing Africans, the agriculture is also a major source of employment and income for the vast majority of the Africans who live in rural areas. Thus, African education must incorporate agricultural knowledge and skills that can help to tap the huge potential of agriculture. There is a need to cut down on current account deficits partly caused by food imports, advance agriculture and diversify and industrialize economies from agricultural bases, and eradicate persistent food insecurity.[30] Specialized agricultural institutes can be very useful for the type of education and skills needed for success in these.

2.7.3 *Infrastructure*

The importance of infrastructure has been touched upon in different parts of this chapter, for example, when we highlighted its impact on the quality of education and the abilities of parents to afford to pay for infrastructure and services. Its gross inadequacy has been stated too. In addition to providing more financial resources for the needed infrastructure for African educational systems, these systems must be able to produce the skills for successful development. Effecting financing means spending money on what is useful and would yield positive returns on education.

2.7.4 *Policies and Budgets*

Development policies have been the subjects of extensive debates since the founding of modern economics. A survey of the literature and practice would reveal the following related questions:

1. What is the relative effectiveness of macroeconomic policies in economic development and how do you instrumentalize them?

[30] The urgency for dealing with this situation is shown by the projected increase in the number of undernourished Africans from about 240 million in 2015 to about 320 million by 2025 and increase in the net food imports from US$35 billion in 2015 to more than US$ 110 billion by 2025 https://assets.kpmg.com/content/dam/kpmg/za/pdf/Healthcare-in-Africa.pdf.

2. What is the relative effectiveness of microeconomic policies in economic development and how do you instrumentalize them?
3. How do you calibrate the relative effects of macroeconomic and microeconomic policies on income, employment and growth?
4. How do you deal with structural constraints in economic development?
5. What is the relative importance in development of the different economic sectors?
6. What are the roles of the state in economic development?

At first, these questions appear impossible to answer! Although not impossible, they are definitely not easy to answer. Before attempting to do so, at least in part, we would first like to draw attention to three broad categories of economic policy advocacy: (1) monetarists; (2) Keynesians/fiscalists and (3) socialists. The dominant one among these three tends to be "monetarism" as it is subscribed to by the most powerful institutions of this world and their backers, namely the International Monetary Fund (IMF) and the World Bank Group. Their conviction is best projected in the economic medicine they doze out to countries in trouble, particularly the developing countries, through structural adjustment programmes (SAPs), which combines IMF and World Bank approaches. In the 1980s and 1990s the IMF's was based on financial programming, an integration of monetary and credit elements in the balance of payments analysis, which derives a linkage between the domestic part of the money stock (credit) and international reserve changes. Khan and Sonko (1995) observed that unlike the Fund's concern with temporary balance of payments imbalances, the Bank focused on the real economy and growth in the medium term. Africa has had more than its fair share of the experience since the 1980s with the Bank and Fund, and this has been studied in detail in our earlier works.[31]

On the other hand, fiscalists believe that it is government spending and taxation (fiscal policy) that is of paramount importance in economic regulation and development. Thus, fiscalism is an economic ideology which

[31] See, for instance, Khan, Haider A., and Karamo NM Sonko, *"Adjustment, Ecology and Distribution," African Economic and Social Review, Vol. I, Nos. 1–2* (December) 1995; and Sonko, Karamo NM., Debt in the Eye of a Storm: the African Crisis in a Global Context," *Africa Today*, 4th Qtr., Vol. 37, No. 4. (4th Qtr., 1990), pp. 15–28.

emphasizes the use of government spending and taxation as means of influencing aggregate demand, employment and growth.

At the other end of the spectrum are the socialists and even much further the communists, whose main differences are that the former believe in limited markets and the latter does not tend to believe at all in any roles for, or importance of, free markets in economic development. Both also believe in the distribution of wealth among the population, through state intervention, with the latter going to a much greater, and even revolutionary, extent to do so.

Today on the socialist side, the Chinese model of market socialism tends to be the most successful model. The Chinese call their model socialism but with Chinese characteristics. Vietnam is following largely an open economy model similar to China. Strategic openness of this kind deserves to be taken seriously rather than the earlier dogmatic types. The Chinese experience, in particular, indicates the need to be innovative and take local conditions into account in shaping economic and political systems, a case for deeper reflections about the viability or otherwise of "Africracy" (Chap. 1).

2.7.5 Content, "Selfism" (Self-Esteem, Self-Confidence and Self-Reliance)

As indicated earlier, African educational systems during the colonial period were designed to serve the needs of the colonial administrations and a minority of the population. Furthermore, the nature of the quintessential colonial educational system was one that emulates the European educational systems in its contents. Therefore, the flaws of the African colonial educational systems can be traced to their origins and purposes which had determined their contents. Post-colonialism, these systems were adopted without any changes by the new governments. Although over the years some changes have been made in many countries in areas such as the introduction of local content (e.g. writing or integrating local languages, history and social studies), the colonial influence is still evident in the curricula of post-colonial systems across the continent.[32] The influence on the

[32] Also refer to Thompson, O.O. et al., "Destroy their Tongue and Identity so that they will Never build the House: Language, Identity and (Under)development of Africa," *Journal of Policy and Development Studies,* Vol. 15. Issue 2 (2024), pp. 16–30, htttps://www.ajol.info/index.php/jpds, retrieved April 4, 2024. This paper assesses the colonial impact on

post-colonial systems can be detected from the following features, among others:

1. Textbooks and supplementary books are significantly based on the curricula in the colonizing countries;
2. Focus on the arts rather than science and technology;
3. Ignoring or propagation of African history and culture from colonial perspectives and
4. Undermining African self-esteem, self-confidence and self-reliance.[33]

Although over the years reforms, which cannot be totally dismissed as insignificant, have been carried out in many countries, there is still work to be done, particularly in repurposing the educational systems through its overall direction and content. These outstanding tasks are complicated by realities such as:

1. The multiplicity of African languages in Sub-Saharan (unlike the Arabic in the North), makes it difficult, if not impossible, to have one-language curricula in which a single local language is chosen as the national language in each country, written (where not yet written) and promoted in the educational system;
2. Modern science and technical are taught and developed in former colonial languages, which makes interpretation and translation into local languages, at the same standards, very difficult and resource-intensive and
3. The shortage of financial and human resources to reform the inherited post-colonial systems and build world-class educational systems.

African education and identity and recommends, among other things, "reinvention" of "what works for us, recalibration of our identity, cultural values … through conscientious education".

[33] For some related discussions, see Ghajiga, Gideon Simon, and Dikeledi Jackie Warlimont, "The Challenge of Language and Cultural Identity in Post-Colonial Africa's National Economic Development," https://www.academia.edu/85678594/THE_CHALLENGE_OF_LANGUAGE_AND_CULTURAL_IDENTITY_IN_POST_COLONIAL_AFRICAS_NATIONAL_ECONOMIC_DEVELOPMENT?email_work_card=title, retrieved May 22, 2025; and Simpson, Andrew (ed.), *Language & National Identity in Africa*, Wiley-Blackwell, 2000.

It should be pointed out that having African languages as the basis of African educational systems, especially in purposeful educational systems, is ideal. However, the first constraint, in particular, is formidable.[34]

2.7.6 *Science, Technology and Innovation (STI)*

Science and technology enable students to acquire more practical skills that can address the most urgent needs of individuals, society and the economy in the modern world. They also facilitate self-employment, which is desirable in any country because governments, on their own and even with private companies, cannot employ everyone. Therefore, the self-employment of citizens can be encouraged by enabling individuals to acquire skills through science and technology, for example, through technical and medical schools.

Innovation leads to invention. It can precede or be the result of science and technology. Science and technology can be one or two, the same or different. Together, they lubricate the economy, make it shine and become a winner. They are at the core of modern economic progress and are its

[34] For further discussions on language the interested reader may refer to Richard Fardon and Graham Furniss, *African Languages, Development and the State*, y Routledge, London and New York, 1994; Roy-Campbell, Zaline, "Revitalizing African Languages for Transformation", Contemporary Journal of African Studies, 6 (1): 27–45, 2019, https://doi.org/10.4314/contjas.v6i1.2; Henriksen, Sarita M, "Identity and Plurilingualism in Africa - the case of Mozambique," *African Literacies: Ideologies, Scripts, Education*, 2014, https://doi.org/10.2307/3217827; Fridah Kanana Erastus, "Examining African Languages as Tools for National Development: The Case of Kiswahili, *The Journal of Pan African Studies*, vol.6, no.6, November 2013; Motsaathebe, Gilbert, "Language, Afrikology and the Tremor of the Political Moment: English as a Main Language of Discourse in Africa," *INDILINGA – African Journal of Indigenous Knowledge Systems* Vol 9 (1) 2010; Ugwu, Eucharia Okwudilichukwu, "Africa on the Verge of a Linguistic Genocide: The Need for Action," *European Scientific Journal, A*ugust 2019 edition Vol.15, No.23, pp. 57–75; Phillipson, Robert, "Linguistic imperialism: African perspectives," *ELT Journal*, Volume 50/2 April 1996, pp. 160–167; Maneechay, Jaruwan, "Linguistic imperialism: African perspectives," *ELT Journal*, January 1, 1996, https://www.academia.edu/1919961/Linguistic_imperialism_African_perspectives?email_work_card=thumbnail, retrieved May 22, 2025; Brock-Utne, Brigit, "Language and Democracy in Africa," *Inequality in Education* https://doi.org/10.1007/978-90-481-2652-1_7; and Barbouchi, Limame, "Power of Language, Language of Power: An Analysis of the Im/possibilities of African Unity through An African Standardized Regional Language," *Horizons in Humanities and Social Sciences*, 1 (1), pp. 88–101, 2015, retrieved May 28, 2025.

most distinct and distinguishing feature.[35] Evidence shows their primary role in the developed industrialized nations and the industrializing ones, particularly during the present Fourth Industrial Revolution. On the other hand, evidence shows that since the colonial period and until very recently, there has been a dire need for innovation, especially in the science and technology fields in Africa.

A study by Mugabe (2011)[36] shows that most African national systems of innovation are relatively weak.[37] While commendable efforts are being made now, much more needs to be done to enable countries, in general, to seize the many opportunities that exist or are emerging now in the continent and the world. Although there are many African and international[38] institutions with programmes of assistance for African countries in science and technology, he pointed out that they are not well coordinated to add value for more successful national and regional systems of innovation.

These institutions include the African Union (AU),[39] the New Partnership for Africa's Development (NEPAD), the African Development Bank (AfDB), the World Bank, United Nations Economic Commission for Africa (UNECA), United Nations Development Programme (UNDP)

[35] See Sonko and Sonko (2023).

[36] John O. Mugabe, "Science, technology and innovation in Africa's regional integration," ACODE Policy Research Series No.44, 2011, https://www.acode-u.org/uploadedFiles/PRS44.pdf, retrieved September 25, 2024.

[37] See Chap. 9 for what Khan refers to as "egalitarian innovation systems".

[38] UNESCO, "Humanitarian aid for education: why it matters and why more is needed," ED/EFA/MRT/2015/PP/21 REV.2, 2015, https://unesdoc.unesco.org/ark:/48223/pf0000233557, retrieved October 6, 2024.

[39] For more on the efforts of this most important continental union, see, for example: African Union (AU), *Plan of Action for the African Decade for Technical, Professional, Entrepreneurial Training and Youth Employment (2019–2028)*, https://au.int/sites/default/files/documents/43477-doc-TVET_Decade_Plan_of_Action._E.pdf, retrieved October 6, 2024; AU, Continental Strategy for Technical and Vocational Education and Training (TVET) to Foster Youth Employment, https://au.int/sites/default/files/documents/43476-doc-TVET_Continental_Strategy_E.pdf, retrieved October 6, 2024; AU, Science, Technology and Innovation Strategy for Africa 2024 (STISA-2024), https://au.int/sites/default/files/documents/38756-doc-stisa_science_tech_innovation_strategy.pdf, retrieved October 6, 2024; and AU, "Concept Note on Education as the AU Theme of the Year for 2024," Executive Council, Forty-fourth Ordinary Session, 15 January–15 February 2024, Addis Ababa, Ethiopia, https://au.int/sites/default/files/documents/43425-doc-EX_CL_1476_XLIV_Rev._1_-_CONCEPT_NOTE_with_Roadmap_AU_Theme_E.pdf.

and the United Nations Educational, Scientific and Cultural Organization (UNESCO). Mugabe further observed that most of the national and regional initiatives are largely focused on research and development with very little emphasis on technological innovation. Technological innovation is considered to be critical in converting scientific and technological knowledge into goods and services for boosting economic development. Therefore, he recommends that African countries develop explicit national innovation policies with clear benchmarks and implementation strategies to address the weaknesses in their science, technology and innovation (STI) systems. He recommends that they must increase their spending on STI to at least 3% of their national budgets.[40]

A more formal way of putting science and technology into a broader but more practical form has emerged in recent years as STEM (Science, Technology, Engineering and Mathematics).[41] STEM is related to our concept of purposeful education, because it is meant to not only provide education in these four areas but also to enable students to graduate and apply their knowledge in real-world settings. Thus, it does, or can, help them to develop realistic aspirations, when properly counselled and prepared for future careers, based on their potential in the four areas. STEM has emerged out of market trends which reflect present opportunities, changing trends and future career opportunities and demands. Integrating STEM into a national purposeful educational framework, strategically managed, can help African countries to systematically plan, implement and monitor education for present and future needs.

[40] IMF has also made a general call for more spending too, from both national and internal sources by stressing that "Making progress towards universal enrolment by 2030 may require doubling education expenditures as a share of GDP. Governments should act to safeguard and expand education budgets, while also ensuring that each dollar is well spent. The international community should also ensure that education remains at the forefront of their support" *Regional Economic Outlook Analytical Note Sub-Saharan Africa*, April 2024. https://www.imf.org/en/Publications/REO/SSA/Issues/2024/04/19/regional-economic-outlook-for-sub-saharan-africa-april-2024.

[41] Krystal DeVille, "What is STEM? What You Need to Know," Science, March 21, 2024, https://stemeducationguide.com/what-is-stem/, retrieved October 1, 2024; Hussim, Hairunnisa, Roslinda Rosli, Nurul Aisya Zahira Mohd Nor, Siti Mistima Maat, Muhammad Sofwan Mahmud, Zanaton Iksan, Azmin Sham Rambely, Siti Nurdiyana Mahmud, Lilia Halim, Kamisah Osman, Ah Nam Lay, "A Systematic Literature Review of Informal STEM Learning," *European Journal of STEM Education*, Volume 9, Issue 1, Article No: 07, 2024, retrieved October 1,2024; and Rifandi, R., "STEM education to fulfil the 21st century demand," *Journal of Physics: Conference series,* Vol. 1317, October 2018.

2.7.7 The Power of Educating the Youth

The total African population has now reached about 1.3 billion and growing faster than that of any other continent. It has been projected to double by 2050. The median age in 2020 was 19.7, and most of the population are under the age of 35—in other words, the youth. In 2020, this age cohort amounted to almost a billion people in all of Africa and about 22.7% of the world's youth population. The population of the youth has been projected to reach 47.7% of the global youth population in 2100, overtaking Asia's share of 37.8% (the second highest). By 2100, Africa's youth population will be equivalent to twice the entire population of Europe. In Sub-Saharan Africa, children and young persons between the ages of 0 and 34 years account for almost 80% of the poor. As this population increases and the numbers of women increase too, the pressure on the existing educational infrastructure and services and the search for livelihoods rise simultaneously. Thus, Africa's youthful population can be boon or bane; boon if African countries are able to cater for the youth in the educational systems and job markets, bane if they cannot and the youth turn their energy into violence, crime and other consequences of illiteracy, poor education and unemployment. In any case, there is the urgent need for inclusive educational systems (already discussed under purposeful education).

2.7.8 Education for Higher Levels of "Selfism" (Self-Esteem, Self-Confidence and Self-Reliance)

African education systems need to have enough content which de-emphasizes the negative elements of modernization or what some refer to as Westernization such as unfettered materialism, devaluation of indigenous/African culture, idealizing the cultural values of former colonial masters, self-centredness, etc. Instead, they should emphasize the positive ones such as Africanness and African history,[42] self-reliance, greater self-esteem and self-confidence which we refer to as "selfism", caring for the

[42] For a concise discussion of such aspects refer to Ebou Taal Ndongo Daara Afdaay, "Democracy, governance and peoples' and human rights in the pre-colonial states of the greater Senegambia basin: institutional framework, traditional and practices from the 13th to the 19th century," *The Point*, Friday, January 14, 2011, https://www.gambia.dk/forums/topic.asp?ARCHIVE=true&TOPIC_ID=10242, retrieved April 3, 2025. For more extensive scholarly debates on these, the interested reader may refer to any of the works of Ali

aged, family, community, poor and needy, respect for elders, etc. Purposeful education can promote economic progress and, thus, help Africans to rise out of poverty and perceived backwardness. As pride without progress is meaningless, purposeful education may also be referred to as meaningful education that generates pride through achievement.

2.7.9 Educating Communities and Nations for Resilient Development

One of the biggest negative consequences of colonialism and modernization is the breakdown of traditional/indigenous knowledge and values, a recurrent theme in this chapter and book. Sustainability can be enhanced if we can instil values, aspirations and behaviour that are economically and socially communal, national and resilient, and which may be appreciated even beyond national boundaries. These include Africanness, caring for the aged, family, community, poor and needy, respect for elders, etc. For the youth, we have presented elsewhere what we refer to as "The Heeno Principles", which we have already disseminated widely in the Gambia:

<u>The Heeno Principles</u>

1. Have Faith;
2. Love your Parents;
3. Seek Knowledge;
4. Love your Country;
5. Love your Community;
6. Respect your Elders;
7. Respect the Women;
8. Be Grateful;
9. Recognise your Relatives, especially your Uncles, Aunts and Cousins;
10. Respond to the Genuine Needs of others, if you can;
11. Avoid Greed;
12. Be Honest and Truthful;
13. Conserve the Environment and Avoid Waste;

Mazrui, Basil Davidson, Cheikh Anta Diop, and D.T. Niane, in particular, accessible through various links through Google Search.

14. Be Hardworking and Disciplined. [43]

The youth, Africa's future, are becoming the greatest victims of wholesale modernization/Westernization, as they get increasingly exposed to glamourous values through irresistible global media which glorifies the self, youthfulness, aggrandizement, limitless abilities and aggressive marketing. This is why in a purposeful educational system cooperation between the state and communities or citizens, families in particular, is essential to support, guide and protect children from negative external influences which can lead to instability of various forms in African nations and undermine their real long-term economic and social progress.

2.7.10 *Comprehensive or Holistic Environmental, Social and Governance (ESG)*

The best form of educating Africans about sustainability is through what we refer to as formal comprehensive or holistic ESG. We have written a book on the why and how of these three categories of sustainability in Africa.[44] In our research for the publication we found that there is very little knowledge of ESG in the continent but that the little that exists is gradually increasing. This trend (the increase) can be continued informally, and in fact the media is already playing a role in this, but the best way is to inculcate knowledge about and skills in sustainability through formal education. The global climate challenge has already become a very serious crisis and Africa is bearing the brunt of it. The continent's educational systems can demonstrate one of their greatest relevance through environmental engineering and other relevant studies that can equip Africans with the knowledge and skills to deal with the climate crisis which is increasingly being seen as a direct threat to human survival in and outside Africa.

[43] These principles were presented on December 6, 2025, by the Chairman of Heeno International (HI) (https://heenointernational.com/), our family foundation, to a group of Gambian youth, sponsored by HI, after a leadership training course conducted by Global Skills (UK).

[44] Sonko and Sonko, ibid. (2023).

2.8 Single-Level Approaches: How Can African Educational Systems Address External Challenges?

Here we seek to generate ideas which can be directed at challenges which exist mainly at the external level, that is, challenges that emanate from outside the continent but have significant bearings on African countries. In economic and political terms, we are referring to challenges which originate from the existence of more than one country in the globe and the competition among them for economic, political and social gains. These exist in two arenas—the world market and the global political system.

External challenges may be considered more elusive because Africa has no direct control over them. However, they would be secondary in importance if Africa is able to put its house in order. If Africans can attempt and succeed in doing this, they would be able to influence external relations in some very significant areas. Well-educated pan-African leadership with the interest of the continent and fellow African at heart would be the best way of exerting influence on the world, through concerted actions in regional cooperation and integration.

2.8.1 Competitiveness

Together or individually, African countries can be more competitive by being able to understand and competently defend their own in a brutally competitive and self-centred world. Economically, they can do so through boosting productivity, which, according to Krugman, "in the long run it is almost everything. A country's ability to improve its standard of living over time depends almost entirely on its ability to raise its output per worker."[45] Bhatt (2024) adds that: "Productivity is the foundation of prosperity. The only way a country can raise its standard of living sustainably is to produce more with existing or fewer resources. You cannot do that without improving productivity."

Krugman maintains that the important things that really matter in the economy, because of their impact on the standard of living, are productivity, income distribution and unemployment. According to him if these are

[45] Krugman, Paul, *The Age of Diminished Expectations, third edition,* MIT Press, Cambridge, 1997, p.11; Gita Bhatt, " Productivity and Prosperity," F&D. Finan*ce & Development,* Sept 2024, https://books.google.ae/books?id=awA0yp1V8c8C&printsec=frontcover&redir_esc=y#v=snippet&q=a%20country's%20&f=false, retrieved 10 December 2024.

satisfactory, nothing else can go wrong, whereas if they go wrong nothing else can be right. He argues that other things such as inflation, international competitiveness, the state of financial markets and budget deficits are secondary and are worthy of consideration mainly because of their indirect influence on national well-being through productivity. Although one may indeed argue that the other issues are also important, Krugman directly stresses the importance of "the big three issues" in the case of the American economy, for example, and indirectly touches upon the role of education by pointing out that: "Yet very little of the business of economic policy is concerned with these big trends." The reason for this is that in spite of the overwhelming importance of productivity, not everyone understands it, or they do so wrongly, he points out. As a result, he concludes, the American economy has been poorly performing in the growth of productivity over the years.

Given that productivity is so important for reasons explained above, it should be a primary objective of the educational systems to teach and equips students with the abilities to achieve productivity gains. That means that the educational systems themselves should be models of productivity in their performances. African students graduating from them should understand the importance of productivity, how to achieve it, and demonstrate it in their job performances.

Being mostly fragile nations and relatively small economies, concerted actions, especially in the economic and political spheres, are preferable to individual lone songs by African countries. Therefore, the educational systems should train political leaders, policy makers, intellectuals and the general population about the virtues of regional economic cooperation and integration (a point also raised in Sect. 2.8). Over the years there have been numerous attempts at these and a number of noteworthy successes, such as the creation of the African Union, Regional Economic Communities (RECs) and, recently, the African Continental Free Trade Area (AfCFTA). Nevertheless, very much still needs to be done in the areas of practically implementing trade agreements and educating the population about the importance of African unity and intra-African trade. [46]The urgency of the

[46]We have had the fortunes of drafting the Framework Paper that led to the African Union, training the Organisation for African Unity (OAU) staff in regional economic integration and cooperation, witnessing the struggles of the Regional Economic Communities (RECs), inspired by real African giants. Today, as we watch, far in distance but close at heart, we are keenly interested in Africa's successes in ushering in durable achievements and assurances that our continent desperately needs, reflecting the aspirations of great African men and

situation can be seen from the small amount of intra-African trade over the ten years from 2013 to 2022, for instance, when it increased from only US$98 billion to US$102 billion. The share of intra-African trade in total African trade shows a bleak picture, with it being small and declining from 21% in 2015 to 15% in 2023.[47]

2.8.2 *Servicing the World*

Africa has a unique advantage—the fastest population growth rate in the world. This can be a disadvantage too. However, it must not be and the only way to avoid that is to use its increasing population productively, inside and outside the continent. If productivity growth is achieved in tandem with population growth, biology, economics and sociology would be harmonized. Thus, population growth should not be a problem. If the former (productivity) outpaces the latter (population growth), Africa can service the world without drops in domestic outputs across countries. The excess population can be used to service the world. The opportunities to service the world are there, especially for the youth, in areas such as subcontracting/outsourcing in ICT, nursing, textiles, other manufacturing, etc. Here again the educational systems of countries can play the unrivalled roles of training the youth to go out into the world not as illegal, untrained and unwanted aliens but as productive and highly demanded skilled workers. The trend is already set as can be seen by the amounts of remittances skilled Africans are sending home each year. Presently, the transfers are huge, even in absolute terms, but they would be minuscule if the full potential for youth employment can be boosted through formal positive and productive education and job opportunities are available for them.

Although not traditionally recognized, productivity is directly related to sustainability. For example, optimal efficiency is achieved by eliminating all waste in the production process. Inefficiency arises from using more

women of the past, and the needs of the present and the future. For work during this era at the two organizations at the pinnacle of African regional cooperation and integration visit the following links: https://repository.uneca.org/handle/10855/5670; https://archives.au.int/handle/123456789/10138; https://archives.au.int/handle/123456789/5341; and https://archives.au.int/handle/123456789/10115.

[47] Infographics, Intra-African Trade: Facts and Figures 2022, AGOA, 19 December 2023, https://www.tralac.org/resources/infographic/16253-intra-africa-trade-facts-and-figures-2022.html, retrieved September 23, 2024.

goods than required in the production processes. On the other hand, production efficiency and allocative efficiency do the opposite (prevent waste) in similar (by looking at the inputs and outputs) and different ways.[48] The difference lies in whether the production process meets the demand for goods at optimized cost (production efficiency) and whether the company has the right quantity of goods to meet demand (allocative efficiency). Both types of productivity (in other words productivity as a whole) are concerned with minimizing waste and optimizing resources and outputs. Achieving desirable productivity growth rates can catapult Africa into becoming a service provider worldwide, thereby challenging Asia as the leading global service provider. It can also enable the continent to land on the shores of sustainability. Again, as explained, purposeful education can enhance this process by enabling African nations and nationals to align their aspirations, educational plans and achievements, systematically and with more discipline. When these are aligned, unemployment and the waste of resources and time are contained and, hence, productivity can be seen as a reality. The right attitudes, which can also be influenced by formal education (in addition to the informal, foundational and cardinal education at home), can enhance the proper usages of resources and time for higher productivity.

2.8.3 Interest of the Underdog

It has been pointed out in this chapter that we live in a world of national interests. Countries think about themselves much more than others. Instead of win-win, in spite of the political rhetoric, they play, in reality, mainly zero-sum or win-lose games. Although the net gain of such games for the world we now live in is zero, these games have become inherent in the very nature of contemporary international relations. Therefore, Africans need to be aware of this reality, in which as underdogs their interests are rarely at the forefront of global economic and political architecture

[48] The difference may be summarized as follows: productive efficiency takes place when the minimum inputs are used to give the maximum outputs. Allocative efficiency takes place when inputs are allocated in a way that maximizes their utility for consumers and hence society.

and power plays. African educational systems should be capable of integrating in their curricula understanding of this reality. The only choices they have are a) accept the zero-sum games and defend your own; or b) reject the zero-sum games and influence others to do so in the mutual interest of the global community of ***really united nations.*** Both are not easy to do, because both are impossible unity again among African countries (Sect. 2.8.4).

2.8.4 Unity, Regional Economic Cooperation and Integration

Following from the above points on national interests and the status of underdogs of Africans in the world, political unity, economic cooperation and regional integration are essential for Africa to wield influence and defend its own in the global political economy. The potential is there and immense but exploiting it, as much as they must, to their advantage has always been evasive. Numerous attempts have been made with some success stories such as the African Union, the African Continental Free Trade Area (AfCFTA) and the Regional Economic Communities (RECs). However, very much is yet to be done and achieved.

2.9 Concluding Remarks

It is not all lost in African education, not all doom and gloom! There are some very positive trends that make it particularly so. One is the tendency nowadays for Africans who study abroad, unlike their predecessors some two decades ago, to want to return home after their studies.[49] Instead of staying abroad, they now tend to want to return home, unless the situation there makes it absolutely impossible to do so (security reasons, e.g.). The other is for these graduates to desire entrepreneurship instead of employment by others, especially governments, and sit in their bureaucratic offices. The third is that more and more Africans are now studying at home instead of going abroad, because of the surge in the number of local educational institutions, in-person/offline and online. Although studying in these institutions has some shortcomings, which have been discussed in this chapter, it makes it relatively easier for home-grown talent to adjust to domestic realities than for externally trained manpower to

[49] Also refer to Sonko, Karamo, "Africa from another angle," *New Africa*, September 19, 2013, https://newafricanmagazine.com/1599/, retrieved April 25, 2025.

acclimatize or readjust to challenges of the home environments. Finally, there tends to be increasing numbers of Africans studying STEM, due to growing interests and efforts in these areas now, unlike in the past. Although this trend is yet to be studied more and understood better, general and available evidence across the continent is suggesting that the growth has already started.[50]

[50]For evidence see, for instance African Institute of Mathematical Sciences (AIMS), "Promoting STEM Education in Africa," 10-05-2022, https://nexteinstein.org/promoting-stem-education-in-africa/#:~:text=According%20to%20the%20African%20Development,economic%20development%20of%20Africa%20quickly, retrieved October 6, 2024; UNESCO, "Unlocking Africa's potential by investing in STEM education," 7 May 2024, retrieved October 6, 2024; and Cristina Duarte, "Transforming Africa with STI-driven Solutions," United Nations General Assembly (UNGA), 79th Session, 2024, https://www.un.org/africarenewal/magazine/september-2024/transforming-africa-sti-driven-solutions#:~:text=Science%2C%20Technology%2C%20and%20Innovation%20(STI)%20are%20the%20cornerstones,of%20sustainable%20growth%20and%20innovation, retrieved October 6, 2024.

CHAPTER 3

Agriculture and Economic Development in Africa: An Empirical Investigation with Policy Implications

3.1 Introduction

Particularly in developing countries, agriculture serves as the backbone of the national economies. The agricultural sector feeds the population, enhances social security and welfare, and provides employment and income, in short promotes industrialization and economic development. Africa has tremendous potential in the agricultural sector because of the abundance of labour and fertile land as well as other natural resources. Africa has 2.6 billion hectares of arable land, about 65% of global total of arable land.[1] Yet, the continent is the "hungriest continent in the

Authors "Karamo NM Sonko and Mariama Sonko" are grateful for the invaluable research assistance in this Chapter of Dr Ebrima K. Ceesay, Senior Lecturer and Researcher in Economics and Finance, University of the Gambia and Mamadou Alieu Jallow, Adjunct Lecturer, Department of Mathematics, Economics & Finance, University of the Gambia.

[1] To put this into perspective in relation to China, for instance, Africa has a population of 1,540,539,941, whereas China with a population of only 1.416 billion has *only* (relatively) 127.6 million hectares of arable land. Visit the following links for more information: https://data.worldbank.org/indicator/AG.LND.ARBL.HA?locations=ZG; https://africacheck.org/infofinder/explore-facts/how-much-africas-land-could-be-considered-arable-land; and https://www.grida.no/resources/7868.

K. N. M. Sonko et al., *21st Century African Development Strategies*, https://doi.org/10.1007/978-3-031-93079-9_3

world"[2] because of the gross underutilization of labour, technology and natural resources. For this reason, a vicious cycle of dependence, underdevelopment and poverty has been created. In this chapter, we empirically examine the relationships between agriculture, on the one hand, and economic development, social welfare, political stability and sustainability, on the other hand, in order to explore what policy formulations these relationships, if any, engender for economic and public policy in Africa.

3.2 Theoretical Model

We start by adopting the theoretical concept of the production function, including the agricultural sector and other control variables. Hence, the growth accounting equation offers guidance for the decomposition of the agricultural sector's potential impact on social welfare, economic growth and development, political stability and sustainability as derived below:

$$Y_{it} = e^{\alpha T_{it}} A_{it} L_{it} K_{it} \tag{3.1}$$

$$\frac{\Delta A_{it}}{A_{it}} = g_i + \beta T_{it} \tag{3.2}$$

where *Y* is the agricultural sector, *L* is labour force/population, *A* is technology and can also be referred to as labour productivity, *K* is human capital, *T* are the impacts of the agricultural sector measures, g is the growth rate of capital, *t* is the time period and e is an intercept term. Equation (3.1) captures the direct effects of the agricultural sector measures on social welfare, etc., for example, the effects of the agricultural sector measures on the labour force, and the profit and capital of the firms. Equation (3.2) captures the indirect (dynamic) effects of agricultural sector measures, for example, the effects of the sector on other variables such as political stability, social welfare, sustainability, economic growth and development. The negative impacts on poverty alleviation, food security, climate change and businesses are becoming larger because of agricultural failure.

[2] See various sources, such as Adesina's different statements to this effect in https://www.afdb.org/en/news-and-events/time-running-out-help-africa-feed-itself-65923, last visited 16 March 2025.

3.3 Methodology

The research methodology used to conduct this study is described in the chapter. It includes the research design, study area, studied population, sampling strategies, sample size, types and sources of data. In addition, we present variable definitions and measurements, validity, and reliability of research instruments, as well as the data analysis technique.

3.3.1 Population of the Study

There are 32 African countries used in this study. The analysis uses World Bank data from these countries spanning 64 years, from 1960 to 2023.[3] Given the state of data on African countries, we could not get data on all the 55 African countries[4] as we would have liked. Therefore, given the exceedingly challenging nature of trying to obtain data on the various African countries, 64 years on, 32 out of 55 countries is actually a very significant coverage.

3.3.2 Method of Data Analysis

Data collection is followed by data analysis. This study utilizes descriptive and inferential analyses using STATA version 16, based on a panel data analysis from 1960 to 2023. Standard statistical software such as STATA and R are supposed to contain data in a quantitative format. With the use of these softwares, the data is analysed using the panel data model, and the results are presented graphically and with descriptive statistics. To illustrate the distribution and dispersion of the data, descriptive analysis is performed using the mean, range, minima, maxima and standard deviations of the data. Additionally, the study's independent factor's potential impact on the dependent variables is illustrated using the panel pooled data analysis methodology.

The purpose of this research is to investigate the connection between agriculture, economic development, economic growth, social welfare, political stability and sustainability in African countries. As stated above, the study employs the agricultural sector as the independent variable,

[3] World Development Indicators (WDI), 2024.

[4] Based on the membership of the African Union (AU) (https://au.int/en/member_states/countryprofiles2, retrieved February 15, 2025.

measured by agricultural value added, and economic development, economic growth, social welfare, political stability and sustainability as the dependent variables interchangeably. The variables are selected because they are commonly used indicators to understand the overall welfare of a country. This approach is a refreshing and most important addition to the literature on agriculture and development, with very serious policy relevance in Africa, a continent in dire need of transformation in the essential sector of agriculture.

The general form of the regression model found in most of the relevant literature is as follows:

$$Y_{it} = \propto + \beta X_{it} + \varepsilon_{it} \tag{3.3}$$

where Y_{it} is the dependent variable for country i in year t, β is the vector of coefficient of the independent variables of interest that the study wants to estimate, α is the constant term,

X_{it} is the vector of the independent variable for country i in year t, and ε is the normal error term.

3.3.3 The Empirical Model Specification

This study is based on the conceptual model adapted from Ceesay (2020). The estimated models to be used in this study are modified and presented as follows:

$$\text{LNED}_{\text{it}} = \beta_0 + \beta_1 \text{LNAS}_{\text{it}} + \varepsilon_{\text{it}} \tag{3.4}$$

$$\text{LNEG}_{\text{it}} = \beta_0 + \beta_1 \text{LNAS}_{\text{it}} + \varepsilon_{\text{it}} t \tag{3.5}$$

$$\text{LNSW}_{\text{it}} = \beta_0 + \beta_1 \text{LNAS}_{\text{it}} + \varepsilon_{\text{it}} t \tag{3.6}$$

$$\text{LNPS}_{\text{it}} = \beta_0 + \beta_1 \text{LNAS}_{\text{it}} + \varepsilon_{\text{it}} t \tag{3.7}$$

$$\text{LNS}_{\text{it}} = \beta_0 + \beta_1 \text{LNAS}_{\text{it}} + \varepsilon_{\text{it}} t \tag{3.8}$$

where:

LNAS_{it} = growth rate of agricultural sector for country i at time t.

LNED_{it} = growth rate of economic development for country i at time t.

LNEG_{it} = growth rate of the economy for country i at time t.

LNSW_{it} = growth rate of social welfare for country i at time t.

LNPS_{it} = growth rate of political stability for country i at time t.

LNS_{it} = growth rate of sustainability for country i at time t.
β_0 = is the intercept term of the models.
β_1 = The coefficient of the explanatory variable.
$\varepsilon_{i.t}$ = the error term.

3.4 Types and Sources of Data Collection

3.4.1 Data Sources and the Definition of Variables Used

Table 3.1 provides an overview of the data sources and variable definitions used in our study. It relates to the agricultural sector, economic growth and development, social welfare, political stability and sustainability.

Table 3.1 uses proxy variables due to data availability or measurement limitations. Hence, agricultural value added is a proxy for the agricultural sector, and economic development is proxied by Gross Domestic Product (GDP) per capita, GDP (constant prices) is a proxy for economic growth, life expectancy at birth is a proxy for social welfare, current health expenditure is a proxy for political stability and food production is a proxy for sustainability. The proxies of agriculture, economic development and GDP may be self-explanatory. However, those of social welfare, political stability and sustainability need some explanation, as done below.

3.4.2 Definition and Measurement of Variables Used in the Study

Agriculture Sector: Agricultural value added is a proxy for this variable. It likely measures the contribution of the agricultural sector to the overall

Table 3.1 Data sources and the definition of variables used

Variable names	*Sources*	*Descriptions*
Agriculture sector	WDI	Agricultural value added (LNAS)
Economic development	WDI	GDP over the population (i.e. GDP per capita) (LNED)
Economic growth	WDI	Annual growth of the economy over time (LNEG)
Social welfare	WDI	Life expectancy (LNSW)
Political stability	WDI	Current health expenditure (LNPS)
Sustainability	WDI	Food production index (LNS)

Source: Authors

economy. It could be measured in terms of agricultural output, agricultural employment or agricultural exports.

Economic Development: This variable is proxied by GDP per capita. It represents the average income per person in a country, reflecting the overall level of economic development. It is typically measured in terms of Gross Domestic Product (GDP) divided by the population.

Economic Growth: The variable is directly represented by the annual growth rate of GDP. The variable measures the growth rate of the economy over a specific period, typically annually. It indicates the pace of economic expansion. It is usual to measure it as the percentage change in GDP from one year to the next.

Social Welfare: The variable is proxied by life expectancy at birth. It reflects the general health and well-being of the population, indicating the level of social development. Life expectancy is typically measured in years. A longer life expectancy indicates better social welfare.

Political Stability: This variable is proxied by current health expenditure as a percentage of GDP. It suggests that higher health expenditure may correlate with better political stability. It is measured as the percentage of GDP allocated to health expenditure. A good health system, evidence of adequate public financing, is an essential component of economic development, without which political stability comes under threat.

Sustainability: This variable is proxied by the food production index. It may measure the ability of the country to produce food sustainably, considering factors like environmental impact and resource use. The food production index could be a composite index that includes various indicators such as agricultural productivity, land degradation and water use efficiency. Food production is an essential component of sustainability, as it may indicate a country's ability to feed its people, without which sustainability is unimaginable; therefore, a positive relationship is envisaged in our study.

3.4.3 Diagnostic Tests

Diagnostic tests are done to examine normality and multi-collinearity and ensure research quality. These are the main assumptions of linear regressions which must be met before the panel data analysis is done. Multicollinearity test is conducted on the regression model so that wrong conclusions about the relationship between dependent variables and independent variables are avoided.

3.5 Presentation of Research Findings

3.5.1 *Introduction*

The current chapter presents the research findings obtained, data analysis and interpretation in relation to the specific objectives of the study. Descriptive, correlation and inferential statistics, especially panel data estimation and hypothesis testing, are used to achieve the study's objectives. Each objective has different variables, depending on the objective and the research question asked.

3.5.2 *Descriptive Statistics*

The descriptive statistics below indicate the number of observations, the mean, the standard deviation, the minimum and the maximum.

Table 3.2 displays the descriptive statistics for our six variables: LNAS, LNED, LNEG, LNSW, LNPS and LNS. The Observations column indicates the number of observations for each variable, ranging from 694 to 2016. The Mean shows the average value for each variable, while the Standard Deviation measures the variability of the data around the mean. The Min. (minimum) and Max. (maximum) display the minimum and maximum values observed for each variable under investigation. The mean of the growth rate of the agricultural sector is 21.372 with a standard deviation of 1.429, suggesting a relatively low variability associated with this variable. The mean of the growth rate of economic development is 7.093 with a standard deviation of 0.973. The mean of the economic growth is 22.97 with a standard deviation of 1.579 while the mean of the

Table 3.2 Descriptive statistics

Variable	*Obs.*	*Mean*	*Std. Dev.*	*Min.*	*Max.*
LNAS	1378	21.372	1.429	17.796	25.536
LNED	1883	7.093	0.973	5.124	10.045
LNEG	1883	22.97	1.579	18.699	27.034
LNSW	2016	3.946	0.179	2.646	4.317
LNPS	694	1.463	0.406	0.102	2.831
LNS	1920	3.953	0.586	2.176	5.212

Source: Authors, based on data set from the World Bank, WDI, 2024, used in this study and in all figures and tables growth rate of social welfare is 3.946 with a standard deviation of 0.179. The mean of the growth rate of political stability is 1.463 with a standard deviation of 0.406. The values range from 0.102 to 2.831, indicating a moderate spread. On average the growth rate of sustainability is 3.953 with a standard deviation of 0.586. In conclusion, the descriptive statistics provide a picture of the central tendency and variability of each variable used in this study.

The first line graph depicts the trends in the growth rate of the agricultural sector in various African countries from 1960 to 2023 (Fig. 3.1). Each line represents a group of countries with similar growth patterns, with the growth rate plotted on the y-axis and the year on the x-axis. The graph shows very relevant and interesting findings of a diverse range of trends, with some countries experiencing consistent growth, others showing fluctuations, and some experiencing periods of decline. There is a general upward trend in the growth rate of the agricultural sector for most countries, with some periods of stagnation or decline. This suggests that overall, the agricultural sector tends to have been growing over the past six decades, an encouraging finding, which must not hide the fact that there is still very much more work needs to be done. In fact, while Angola, Guinea and Senegal have experienced relatively consistent growth, others, such as Chad and Libya, have shown more fluctuating patterns. Several

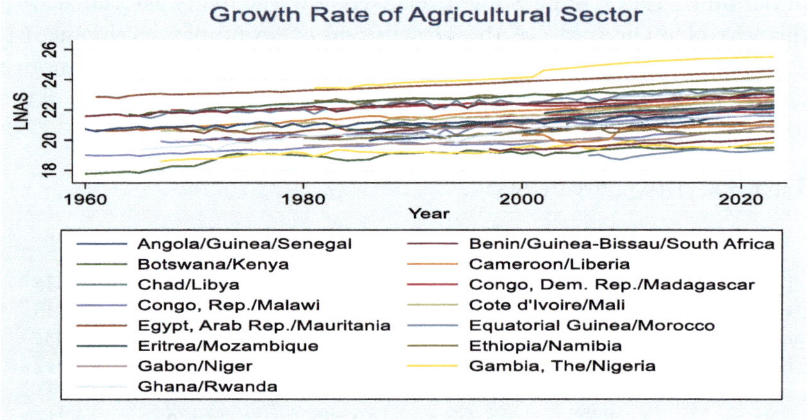

Fig. 3.1 Trends of growth rate of the agricultural sector in Africa. (Source: Authors using data set from the World Bank)

Table 3.3 Pairwise correlations

Variables	*(1)*	*(2)*	*(3)*	*(4)*	*(5)*	*(6)*
(1) LNAS	1.000					
(2) LNED	0.032	1.000				
(3) LNEG	0.845	0.511	1.000			
(4) LNSW	0.209	0.474	0.425	1.000		
(5) LNPS	0.020	−0.182	−0.070	0.043	1.000	
(6) LNS	0.130	0.243	0.234	0.680	0.183	1.000

Source: Authors using data set from the World Bank

factors could contribute to the variations, including climate conditions, government policies, access to technology, investment in agriculture and market demand.

The correlation matrix above (Table 3.3) shows the pairwise correlations between the different variables. The values in the table range from −1 to 1. A value close to 1 indicates a strong positive correlation, meaning that as one variable increases, the other tends to increase as well. A value close to −1 indicates a strong negative correlation, meaning that as one variable increases, the other tends to decrease. Looking at the table, we can see that several pairs of variables exhibit strong positive correlations. The table presents a correlation matrix, showing the pairwise correlations between the six variables: LNAS, LNED, LNEG, LNSW, LNPS and LNS. The values in the table represent the Pearson correlation coefficients. A value of 1 indicates a perfect positive correlation, −1 indicates a perfect negative correlation, and 0 indicates no linear relationship. The correlation between LNAS and LNEG is 0.845, indicating a strong positive relationship, while there is a moderate positive correlation between LNED and LNEG (0.511), LNSW and LNS (0.680) and LNSW and LNED (0.474). However, the correlations between LNAS and LNED (0.032), LNAS and LNPS (0.020), LNED and LNPS (−0.182), LNEG and LNPS (−0.070), LNSW and LNPS (0.043) and LNPS and LNS (0.183) are all relatively small, indicating weak or no linear relationship between these pairs of variables.

The second line graph depicting the trends in the growth rate of sustainability in various African countries from 1960 to 2020 (Fig. 3.2). As shown earlier, each line represents a group of countries, with the growth rate plotted on the y-axis and the year on the x-axis. The graph shows a diverse range of trends, with some countries experiencing consistent

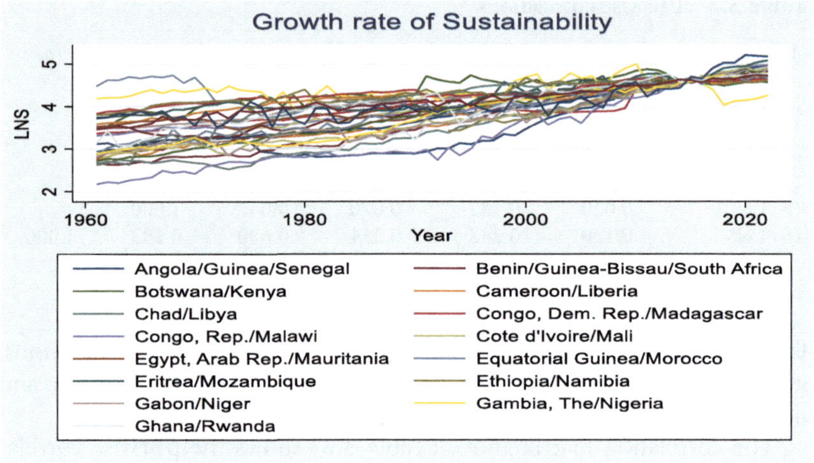

Fig. 3.2 Trends of growth rate of sustainability. (Source: Authors using data set from the World Bank)

growth, others showing fluctuations, and some experiencing periods of decline. There is a general upward trend in the growth rate of sustainability for most countries, but with some periods of stagnation or decline. This suggests that overall, sustainability tends to have been improving over the past six decades. The growth rates vary significantly across different countries. Some groups of countries, such as Angola, Guinea and Senegal, have experienced relatively consistent growth, while others, like Chad and Libya, have shown more fluctuating patterns. Several factors could contribute to these variations, including government policies, investment in sustainable practices, technological advancements and changing environmental and political conditions.

Table 3.4 presents the results of a pooled ordinary least squares (OLS) regression, where the dependent variable is the growth rate of economic development (LNED). The independent variable in the model is still LNAS. The regression results include the estimated coefficients, standard errors, *t*-values, *p*-values and 95% confidence intervals for each variable. Additionally, the table provides summary statistics such as the mean and standard deviation of the dependent variable, the overall *R*-squared, the number of observations and the results of the chi-square test. The coefficient for LNAS is estimated to be 0.417, with a statistically significant

t-value of 29.10 and a p-value of 0. This indicates a strong positive relationship between LNAS and the growth rate of economic development. In other words, a one-unit increase in LNAS is associated with a 0.417 unit increase in the growth rate of economic development, holding all other factors constant. The constant term is also statistically significant, with a negative coefficient of −1.792. This suggests that when LNAS is zero, the expected growth rate of economic development is negative. The overall R-squared of 0.001 indicates that the model explains little of the variation in the growth rate of economic development.

Table 3.5 presents the results of a pooled ordinary least squares (OLS) regression, where the dependent variable is the growth rate of the economy and the independent variable included in the model is LNAS. The regression results include the estimated coefficients, standard errors,

Table 3.4 Estimating pooled OLS results. The dependent variable is the growth rate of economic development

LNED	Coef.	St.Err.	t-Value	p-Value	[95% Conf	Interval]	Sig
LNAS	0.417	0.014	29.10	0	0.389	0.446	***
Constant	−1.792	0.354	−5.07	0	−2.485	−1.099	***
Mean dependent var	7.099			**SD dependent var**		0.926	
Overall R-squared	0.001			**Number of obs**		1377	
Chi-square	846.970			**Prob > chi^2**		0.000	
R-squared within	0.392			**R-squared between**		0.009	

***$p < 0.01$, **$p < 0.05$, *$p < 0.1$

Source: Authors' own evaluation using the data set from the World Bank used in this chapter

Table 3.5 Estimating pooled OLS results, with the dependent variable economic growth rate

LNEG	Coef.	St.Err.	t-Value	p-Value	[95% Conf	Interval]	Sig
LNAS	1.178	0.017	70.47	0	1.145	1.21	***
Constant	−1.987	0.389	−5.10	0	−2.75	−1.224	***
Mean dependent var	23.163			**SD dependent var**		1.569	
Overall R-squared	0.713			**Number of obs**		1377	
Chi-square	4965.909			**Prob > chi^2**		0.000	
R-squared within	0.786			**R-squared between**		0.656	

*** $p < 0.01$, **$p < 0.05$, *$p < 0.1$

Source: Authors' own evaluation using the same data set from the World Bank *t*-values, *p*-values, and 95% confidence intervals for each variable. Additionally, the table provides summary statistics such as the mean and standard deviation of the dependent variable, the overall *R*-squared, the number of observations and the results of the chi-square test. The coefficient for LNAS is estimated to be 1.178, with a statistically significant *t*-value of 70.47 and a *p*-value of 0. This indicates a strong positive relationship between LNAS and the growth rate of the economy. In other words, a one-unit increase in LNAS is associated with a 1.178 unit increase in the growth rate of the economy, holding all other factors constant. The constant term is also statistically significant, with a negative coefficient of −1.987. This suggests that when LNAS is zero, the expected growth rate of the economy is negative. The overall *R*-squared of 0.713 indicates that the model explains 71.3% of the variation in the growth rate of economic development. This suggests that the model has a relatively good fit to the data. In conclusion, the results suggest a strong positive relationship between LNAS and economic growth, which makes a lot of sense in Africa.

Table 3.6 presents the results of a pooled ordinary least squares (OLS) regression, where the dependent variable is the growth rate of social welfare (LNSW). The independent variable in the model is still LNAS. The regression results include the estimated coefficients, standard errors, *t*-values, *p*-values, and 95% confidence intervals for each variable. Additionally, the table provides summary statistics such as the mean and standard deviation of the dependent variable, the overall *R*-squared, the number of observations and the results of the chi-square test.

Table 3.6 Estimating pooled OLS results, with the dependent variable growth rate of social welfare

LNSW	**Coef.**	**St.Err.**	***t*-Value**	***p*-Value**	**[95% Conf**	**Interval]**	**Sig**
LNAS	0.176	0.005	37.83	0	0.167	0.185	***
Constant	0.257	0.101	2.54	0.011	0.058	0.455	**
Mean dependent var	4.006			**SD dependent var**		0.149	
Overall *R*-squared	0.044			**Number of obs**		1347	
Chi-square	1430.741			**Prob > chi^2**		0.000	
***R*-squared within**	0.588			***R*-squared between**		0.001	

***$p < 0.01$, **$p < 0.05$, *$p < 0.1$

Source: Authors' own evaluation using data set from the World Bank

The coefficient for LNAS is estimated to be 0.176, with a statistically significant *t*-value of 37.83 and a *p*-value of 0. This indicates a strong positive relationship between LNAS and the growth rate of social welfare. In other words, a one-unit increase in LNAS is associated with a 0.176 unit increase in the growth rate of social welfare, holding all other factors constant. The constant term is also statistically significant, with a positive coefficient of 0.257. This suggests that when LNAS is zero, the expected growth rate of social welfare is positive. The overall *R*-squared of 0.044 indicates that the model explains only 4.4% of the variation in the growth rate of social welfare. In conclusion, the results suggest a positive relationship between LNAS and the growth rate of social welfare, but the model's overall explanatory power is limited.

Table 3.7 presents the results of a pooled ordinary least squares (OLS) regression, where the dependent variable is the growth rate of political stability (LNPS). The independent variable included in the model is LNAS. The regression results include the estimated coefficients, standard errors, *t*-values, *p*-values and 95% confidence intervals for each variable. Additionally, the table provides summary statistics such as the mean and standard deviation of the dependent variable, the overall *R*-squared, the number of observations and the results of the chi-square test. The coefficient for LNAS is estimated to be 0.137, with a statistically significant *t*-value of 5.14 and a *p*-value of 0. This indicates a positive relationship between LNAS and the growth rate of political stability. In other words, a one-unit increase in LNAS is associated with a 0.137 unit increase in the growth rate of political stability, holding all other factors

Table 3.7 Estimating pooled OLS results, with the dependent variable growth rate of political stability

LNPS	Coef.	St.Err.	*t*-Value	*p*-Value	[95% Conf	Interval]	Sig
LNAS	0.137	0.027	5.14	0	0.085	0.189	***
Constant	−1.513	0.58	−2.61	0.009	−2.651	−0.375	***
Mean dependent var	1.469			**SD dependent var**		0.400	
Overall *R*-squared	0.000			**Number of obs**		640	
Chi-square	26.375			**Prob > chi²**		0.000	
***R*-squared within**	0.060			***R*-squared between**		0.001	

***$p < 0.01$, **$p < 0.05$, *$p < 0.1$

Source: Authors' own evaluation using data set from the World Bank

constant. The constant term is also statistically significant, with a negative coefficient of −1.513. This suggests that when LNAS is zero, the expected growth rate of political stability is negative. In conclusion, while the results suggest a positive relationship between LNAS and the growth rate of political stability, the model's overall explanatory power is limited.

Table 3.8 presents the results of a pooled ordinary least squares (OLS) regression, where the dependent variable is the growth rate of sustainability (LNS). The independent variable in the model is LNAS. The regression results include the estimated coefficients, standard errors, *t*-values, *p*-values and 95% confidence intervals for each variable. Additionally, the table provides summary statistics such as the mean and standard deviation of the dependent variable, the overall *R*-squared, the number of observations and the results of the chi-square test. The coefficient for LNAS is estimated to be 0.831, with a statistically significant *t*-value of 71.35 and a *p*-value of 0. This indicates a strong positive relationship between LNAS and the growth rate of sustainability. In other words, a one-unit increase in LNAS is associated with a 0.831 unit increase in the growth rate of sustainability, holding all other factors constant. The constant term is also statistically significant, with a negative coefficient of −13.599. This suggests that when LNAS is zero, the expected growth rate of sustainability is negative. In conclusion, while the results suggest a positive relationship between LNAS and the growth rate of sustainability, the model's overall explanatory power is limited.

Table 3.8 Estimating pooled OLS results, with the dependent variable growth rate of sustainability

LNS	Coef.	St.Err.	*t*-Value	*p*-Value	[95% Conf	Interval]	Sig
LNAS	0.831	0.012	71.35	0	0.808	0.854	***
Constant	−13.599	0.257	−52.88	0	−14.103	−13.095	***

Mean dependent var	4.101	**SD dependent var**	0.529
Overall *R*-squared	0.017	**Number of obs**	1331
Chi-square	5090.860	**Prob > chi²**	0.000
***R*-squared within**	0.853	***R*-squared between**	0.031

***$p < 0.01$, **$p < 0.05$, *$p < 0.1$

Source: Authors' own evaluation using data set from the World Bank

3.6 Post Estimation Tests

3.6.1 Autocorrelation Test in Panel

The Wooldridge test for autocorrelation in panel data is used to detect the presence of first-order autocorrelation in the residuals of a panel data model. The results indicate that the F-statistic and *P*-value are 10.095 and 0.0088 respectively.

The *p*-value (0.0088) is less than the conventional significance level of 0.05. Therefore, we reject the null hypothesis of no first-order autocorrelation. This suggests that there is evidence of first-order autocorrelation in the residuals of the panel data model.

The presence of autocorrelation indicates that the residuals are not independent across time, which can violate the assumptions of classical regression models and lead to inefficient and biased estimates. Autocorrelation can inflate the test statistics, leading to incorrect inferences.

3.6.2 Breusch and Pagan LM Test for Panel

The Breusch and Pagan Lagrangian Multiplier (LM) test for random effects evaluates whether a random effects model is more appropriate than a simple OLS regression. The *p*-value (0.0167) is less than the conventional significance level of 0.05. Therefore, we reject the null hypothesis that the variance of the random effects is zero.

3.7 Further Discussion of the Results

The results of the study offer an extensive analysis of the relationship between key variables, including the growth rate of the agricultural sector, economic development, sustainability, social welfare and political stability. These relationships were investigated through the use of descriptive statistics, correlation analysis and pooled ordinary least squares (OLS) regressions.

The correlation matrix illustrates the pairwise relationships between the variables. Strong positive correlations between the agricultural sector and economic growth signify that growth in the agricultural sector is closely associated with economic growth, a very sensible finding. Janvry and Sadoulet (2010) also discover in their study that agricultural growth exhibits a strong correlation with overall economic growth in developing economies, reinforcing the idea that agricultural development serves as a driving force for broader economic development. Similar findings are also highlighted by Barrett (2011). He observes a significant relationship between agricultural productivity and GDP growth. Agricultural development facilitates historically unprecedented increases in incomes, enhances life expectancy, mitigates the risk of chronic or acute malnutrition and allows for heightened investment in education and non-agricultural pursuits in today's advanced economies. When the agriculture sector (LNAS) is considered as an independent variable, its correlations with other variables illustrate its multifaceted impact on development. Its weak correlation with economic development may indicate that although extremely important agriculture alone is inadequate for broader economic progress, likely necessitating industrialization and services to further enhance growth. Nevertheless, the importance of agriculture must not be underestimated as it is historically shown that agricultural advancement is critical for industrial development. A strong correlation with economic growth highlights agriculture's pivotal role in GDP contributions, particularly within primary-sector-dominated economies. Its moderate correlation with social welfare signifies its contribution to improving livelihoods through employment and food security, although its effect may depend on policy and resource allocation. Weak correlations with political stability and sustainability imply indirect or mediated influences, as these factors frequently require systemic interventions that extend beyond agricultural activities.

The pooled ordinary least squares (OLS) results indicate that the growth rate of agriculture has positive significant impact on the growth rate of economic development. About 1% increase in agricultural growth translates to 0.417% increase in economic development.

This result was in line with the study done by Christiaensen et al. (2011), which demonstrates that in low-income nations, agricultural growth is very crucial at lowering poverty and promoting economic development. In addition, Thirtle et al. (2003) found that investments in agricultural research and development considerably raise value-added agricultural productivity, thereby reducing poverty and increasing overall economic growth. Thus, Diao et al. (2007) argue that the development of agriculture boosts food security, thereby generating jobs and raising rural incomes, all of which contribute to the country's economic development. This study highlights the necessity of focused policies to optimize the developmental impact of agriculture. Furthermore, Irz et al. (2001), who employ cross-country estimation models, discover a strong positive correlation between economic growth and agricultural productivity, illustrating the ripple effects on poverty alleviation and human development in general. The relationship between productivity and social welfare has been stressed by Krugman (1997) and Bhatt (2024) and is discussed in Chap. 2 of this book.[5]

The diverse economic paths of African nations between 1960 and 2020 are highlighted by the visual trends shown in Figs. 3.3 and 3.4 and are discussed. Some nations exhibit volatility. These variations can be

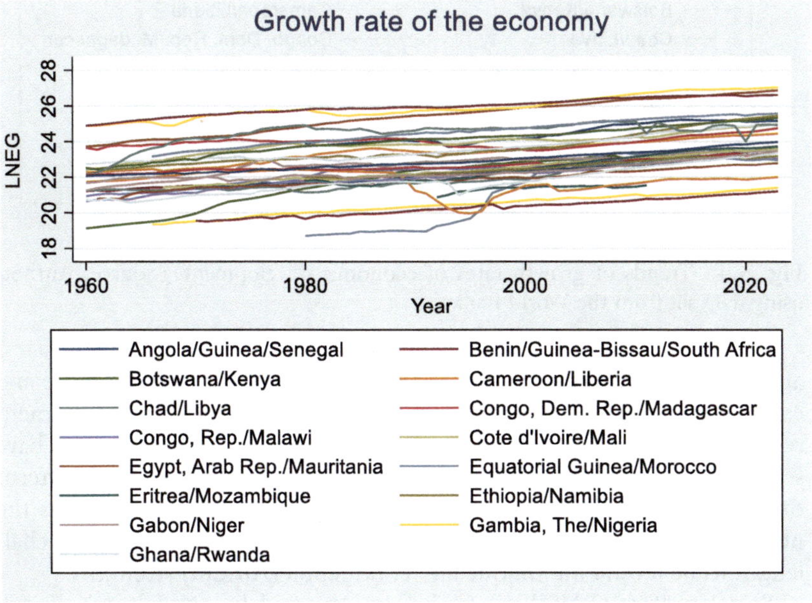

Fig. 3.3 Trends of growth rates of the economy. (Source: Authors using data set from the World Bank)

[5] Krugman, Paul, The Age of Diminished Expectations, third edition, MIT Press, Cambridge, 1997, p.11; Gita Bhatt, " Productivity and Prosperity," F&D. Finance & Development, Sept 2024, https://books.google.ae/books?id=awA0yp1V8c8C&printsec=frontcover&redir_esc=y#v=snippet&q=a%20country's%20&f=false, retrieved 10 December 2024.

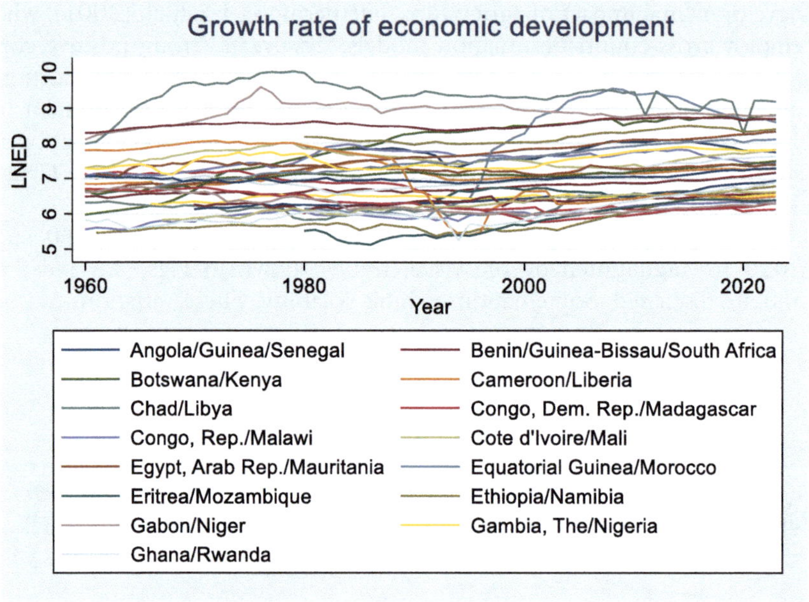

Fig. 3.4 Trends of growth rates of economic development. (Source: Authors using data set from the World Bank)

attributed mainly to differences in resource management, governance and external economic shocks. The upward trend in economic development reflects broader regional progress, albeit unevenly distributed. Some have seen periods of rapid growth while other countries exhibit cyclical patterns of growth and decline. The diversity in these trajectories highlights the need for tailored policy interventions that address specific national challenges while leveraging unique and continental (African) strengths.

Social welfare (LNSW) is positively impacted by agricultural growth (LNAS). This suggests that although to a lesser extent than its direct economic benefits, agricultural growth raises living standards and promotes social well-being. According to Shikur (2020), Ethiopian agricultural policies show that improved agricultural productivity, fuelled by initiatives like irrigation and market liberalization, has a significant positive impact on the social welfare of rural households. Particularly in areas that rely significantly on agriculture, these policies have enabled increased incomes, better resource use and enhanced social welfare.

Our study indicates a positive statistically significant influence of the growth rate of agriculture on political stability (LNPS). Kimenyi et al. (2014) also investigate the relationship between agricultural investments and political instability especially in countries that are prone to conflicts, such as Nigeria and Mali. Although their study implies that instability reduces agricultural productivity, it also points out that investments in agriculture can help to reduce conflict and promote stability when backed by initiatives to increase resilience. Carlson (2022) examines how Egypt's political stability is affected by environmental factors and discovers that agricultural production and arable land have influences. The research findings indicate that the decline in agricultural productivity and arable land in the case study increased the strain on social and economic structures ultimately leading to political instability or revolutions in Egypt.

The coefficient indicates a significant positive relationship between agricultural growth (LNAS) and sustainability (LNS). This emphasizes the critical role that agriculture plays in advancing sustainable practices especially when connected to economic and environmental regulations. These findings imply that agriculture plays a role in enhancing sustainability, although attaining sustainable growth requires other systemic elements too. Agro-ecological intensification and climate-smart techniques in general are examples of sustainable agricultural practices that have been shown to greatly enhance resource optimization and environmental resilience (Adamsone and Grivins 2024). These methods support sustainability objectives and increase productivity over the long run. By guaranteeing food security and bolstering rural livelihoods, better agricultural practices, such as precision agriculture and some indigenous methods, are shown to increase resource efficiency and biodiversity, lessen environmental degradation and improve sustainability.

Agriculture plays a crucial role in boosting GDP and promoting socioeconomic advancement as evidenced by the high coefficients and strong correlations across several variables. The correlations varied in degrees of strength (e.g. weak with political stability, moderate with social welfare), suggesting that contextual factors like policies, institutional quality and external economic activities mediate the impact of agriculture. As economies mature, the "negative" effects of economic development on agriculture point to a shift towards the industrial and service sectors highlighting the intricate relationship between agriculture and development paths.

Results of the regression analysis of the growth of the agricultural sector (LNAS) against other variables including social welfare (LNSW), economic development (LNED) and economic growth (LNEG) are not uniform. Overall, the study emphasizes how agricultural growth affects social, economic and environmental outcomes. Even though agriculture plays a major role in social welfare, sustainability and economic growth, some models' explanatory powers may still be limited indicating the need to include more variables and broader contextual factors. Nevertheless, these findings offer insightful information to policy makers who aim to acknowledge the complexity of socio-political dynamics while utilizing agricultural development as a catalyst for sustainability and economic advancement.

3.8 Limitations of the Study

Although this study's methodology and conclusions have certain limitations, it offers insightful information about agricultural growth and economic development in Africa. One major drawback is the use of static panel data techniques like pooled OLS, which might not adequately capture the dynamic relationships over time. The study also focuses on associations rather than causation, as it does not employ techniques like instrumental variables or difference-in-differences that could establish causal links between independent variables and outcomes. Therefore, there is the need for more research. Future research could build on the current findings and offer a more thorough understanding of agricultural growth, economic development, political stability, social welfare, sustainability growth dynamics by utilizing dynamic panel models, incorporating additional variables, applying robust error corrections, expanding geographic scope and exploring causal relationships.

3.9 Conclusions and Policy Recommendations

3.9.1 Concluding Remarks

This research offers significant understanding of the intricate relationships between the agricultural sector, social welfare political stability, economic development and sustainability in African economies. Descriptive statistics, correlation analysis and pooled OLS are used to show how important agriculture is for boosting economic growth, sustainability, political stability and social welfare. Key findings show that, while agricultural growth remains moderately to strongly related to social welfare, and political stability, it significantly supports economic development and sustainability, indicating the influence of larger socio-economic and institutional factors. Along with highlighting the structural shift towards industry and services in more developed stages of economic development elsewhere, the study also highlights the importance of agriculture as a pillar of GDP growth in African primary-sector economies. Though unevenly distributed, the upward trend in economic development is indicative of broader regional/continental progress. The variety of these paths emphasizes the necessity of specialized policy interventions that take advantage of distinctive national strengths and address particular national challenges, whilst drawing on regional economic cooperation and development.

3.9.2 Key Policy Implications

Key policy recommendations include the following: promoting agricultural productivity and diversification ought to be a top priority in Africa.[6] Policy makers need to invest in irrigation systems, research and contemporary agricultural technologies to boost yields and improve climate change resilience. Moreover, encouraging diversification into value-added processing, agro-industrial activities and high-value crops can lessen dependency on traditional agriculture while generating more jobs, particularly in rural areas.

Strengthening sustainability practices is another crucial policy area. Policies that support agroforestry, conservation agriculture and sustainable land management are examples of sustainable agricultural practices that governments ought to develop and implement. These measures are vital for reducing environmental degradation and ensuring long-term agricultural productivity. Furthermore, to incentivize farmers to embrace eco-friendly practices, access should be introduced to carbon credits, subsidies, green finance and technology.

Increasing the connection between agriculture and other sectors can significantly amplify agriculture's contributions to economic development. Strengthening connections between agriculture, manufacturing

[6] For a detailed and comprehensive discussion of the agricultural sector and agricultural policies in Africa, refer to David Luke (ed.), How Africa Eats Trades, LSE Press, 2023, and David Luke (ed.), How Africa Eats. Trade, Food Security and Climate Risks, LSE Press, 2025. and https://www.google.com/search?q=David+Fashole+Luke+How+Africa+trades&sca_esv=602bc0460517bd79&source=hp&ei=-W_yaJ7JHJiTkdUP2Jm4sAQ&iflsig=AOw8s4IAAAAAaPJCREi3Hog6QjPDy1Q7IF7qHn5Tstd& ved=0ahUKEwjeqeHo1KuQAxWYSaQEHdgMDkYQ4dUDCBs&oq=David+Fashole+Luke+How+Africa+trades&gs_lp=Egdnd3Mtd2l6IiREYXZpZCBGYXNob2xlIEx1a2UgSG93IEFmcmljYSB0cmFkZXNIk5oBUABYuowBcAB4AJABAJgBlAWgAblUqgELMi0yMi4xMC4xLjO4AQzIAQD4AQGfpstate=ive&vld=cid:a5ea24ed,vid:T2O2zuG7Q_E,st:0

and services is crucial for developing a value chain that increases the sector's potential. Enhancing storage facilities, digital trading platforms and transportation infrastructure should be the main priorities of policy makers to help farmers access markets and reduce losses after harvest.

Promoting social welfare through agricultural policies is critical for equitable development. Governments with an emphasis on rural communities should implement social protection programmes like conditional cash transfers, subsidized agricultural inputs and capacity-building initiatives. Besides, since women farmers make up a large portion of the agricultural workforce, gender-sensitive policies are important for fostering equity and inclusivity.

Sustainable agricultural development is largely dependent on institutional capacity, technology and political stability. Political stability, technology and institutional capacity are fundamental for sustainable agricultural development as they create the conditions for continuity, productivity and the ability to convert Africa's huge but unutilized and poorly utilized arable resources. Africa has the potential to become the world's food basket; the question is "Can Africa?"

In order to boost agricultural production, fair resource allocation, conflict resolution and a stable environment for agricultural growth, transparent and inclusive governance structures must be established. A balanced blend of smallholder, medium-scale and large-scale farmers can fully tap the full potential of African agriculture, given the right means, attitudes and conditions.

To promote growth and resilience in the industry, it is equally important to strengthen institutional frameworks to enhance policy implementation, uphold property rights and draw in both domestic and foreign investment. Global, but more importantly, regional collaboration can successfully handle common issues and opportunities in Africa. To address issues like food insecurity, trade barriers and climate change, African countries should strengthen their cooperation through institutions like the African Union and Regional Economic Communities (RECs). Collaborating with international organizations that can genuinely enhance African efforts can also help support agricultural development projects by facilitating access to capital, technology transfer and technical knowledge.

Additionally, better monitoring systems and data quality are critical to successful policy making. Governments ought to spend money on reliable systems for gathering, organizing and evaluating economic and agricultural data. This involves updating and relevant metrics regularly to account for multifaceted elements, such as environmental resilience and social inclusion, guaranteeing that policies continue to be applicable and efficient.

In short, African economies can fully utilize agriculture's potential as a catalyst for social welfare, sustainability, political stability, economic development and economic growth by implementing dynamic and effective policies. Along with promoting inclusive growth, these recommendations lay the groundwork for reducing the vulnerabilities of the sector and those who depend on the sector and help them in building and maintaining resilience. In all of these and more, two factors need critical attention and their importance cannot be overemphasized. One is that African educational systems must be able to cater for Africa's agricultural systems (Chap. 2). The other is that the continent with all the resources to feed itself and the world cannot continue to be the one that is constantly begging the rest of the world for food and draining its very scarce foreign exchange resources on food! Africa cannot live and achieve sustainable progress on producing what it does not eat and eating what it does not produce.

References

Adamsone-Fiskovica, A., & Grivins, M. (2024). Understanding the potential of sustainability turn in farming: review of sociotechnical adoption factors of agri-environmental cropping practices. *Renewable Agriculture and Food Systems*, *39*, e16.

Barrett, C. B. (ed.) (2011). "The economics of agricultural development: An overview," chapt.1, *Agricultural Development*, Routledge; and Barrett, C. B. (2011). "The economics of agricultural development: An overview. *Original Essay*, *1*(63), 1–25.

Carlson, A. (2022). Political Stability and Agriculture: A Case Study of Egypt. *Minnesota Undergraduate Research & Academic Journal*, *5*(4) pp. 1–30.

Ceesay, E. K. (2020). The impact of migration and remittances on employment in agriculture in the Gambia. *Journal of Agronomy and Research*, *3*(2), 1–16.

Christiaensen, L., Demery, L., & Kuhl, J. (2011). The (evolving) role of agriculture in poverty reduction—An empirical perspective. *Journal of development economics*, *96*(2), 239–254.

De Janvry, A., & Sadoulet, E. (2010). Agricultural growth and poverty reduction: Additional evidence. *The World bank research observer*, *25*(1), 1–20.

Diao, X., Hazell, P. B., Resnick, D., & Thurlow, J. (2007). *The role of agriculture in development: Implications for Sub-Saharan Africa* (Vol. 153). Intl Food Policy Res Inst.

Irz, X., Lin, L., Thirtle, C., & Wiggins, S. (2001). Agricultural productivity growth and poverty alleviation. *Development policy review*, *19*(4), 449–466.
Kimenyi, M., Adibe, J., Djiré, M., Jirgi, A. J., Kergna, A., Deressa, T. T., ... & Westbury, A. (2014). The impact of conflict and political instability on agricultural investments in Mali and Nigeria. *Brook. Afr. Growth Initiat. Work. Pap, 17.*
Shikur, Z. H. (2020). Agricultural policies, agricultural production and rural households' welfare in Ethiopia. *Journal of Economic Structures*, *9*(1), 50.
Thirtle, C., Lin, L., & Piesse, J. (2003). The impact of research-led agricultural productivity growth on poverty reduction in Africa, Asia and Latin America. *World Development*, *31*(12), 1959–1975.

CHAPTER 4

Reviving Africa's Health Sector: Examining the Roles of Public and Private Healthcare Services

4.1 Introduction: Africa's Health Challenges

Africa needs a well-educated, well-fed, well-protected and healthy population. These are the fundamental requirements of economic progress and happiness in any nation. All of these topics have been discussed at different extents in this book, but a closer look at the health sector is essential and is what we do in this chapter, somewhat briefly, as well as in Chap. 5. It may be remiss to discuss Africa's healthcare challenges without recalling the biggest pandemic in modern medical history (COVID-19), how it was dealt with and the lessons we can draw from it in dealing with future widespread diseases. Therefore, our discussions in this chapter cover not only the need for better attention to regular diseases, but also preparedness for epidemics, pandemics and other widespread diseases, using the COVID-19 pandemic an experience to learn from.

4.2 Africa: A Health Portrait

As shown in Figs. 4.1–4.20, our analysis of health statistics on Africa reveals the following very disturbing picture, in absolute and relative terms:

(1) Africa has the lowest life expectancy at birth, compared to all other regions;

K. N. M. Sonko et al., *21st Century African Development Strategies*,
https://doi.org/10.1007/978-3-031-93079-9_4

(2) On the other hand, the maternity mortality ratio is higher than that of all other regions of the world;
(3) The under-five mortality rate is higher than that of any other region;
(4) The neonatal mortality rate is higher than that of any other region;
(5) New HIV infections are more than in any other region;
(6) The incidence of tuberculosis is the second highest in the world;
(7) The incidence of malaria is the highest in the world;
(8) Hepatitis B surface antigen prevalence among children is the highest in the world;
(9) The reported number of people requiring interventions against Neglected Tropical Diseases (NTDs) is the second highest in the world;
(10) Adolescent birth rates for all ages are the highest in the world;
(11) Density of medical doctors is the lowest in the world;
(12) Density of nursing and midwifery personnel is the lowest in the world;
(13) Density of dentists is the lowest in the world;
(14) Density of pharmacists is lower than that of any other region;
(15) The average of 15 international health regulations core capacity scores is the lowest in the world;
(16) Prevalence of stunting in children is the highest in the world;
(17) Proportions of the population using safely managed drinking water services and those using safely treated domestic water waste flows are the lowest in the world;
(18) Proportion of the population using safely managed sanitation services is the lowest in the world;
(19) The proportion of births attended by skilled health personnel is lower than that of any other region; and
(20) The age-standardized prevalence of hypertension among adults aged 30–79 years is the third highest in the world and equivalent to that of the Americas.

The above picture is bleak, very bleak, showing an Africa with anything but a smiling face in spite of the rapid economic growth we have cited in this book. An unhealthy population has far-reaching consequences for development across all sectors, and it is difficult to argue that there is an "Africa rising!" when healthcare for our people is stagnant or falling at the bottom of the same indicators for the rest of the world. This is not an acceptable situation at all.

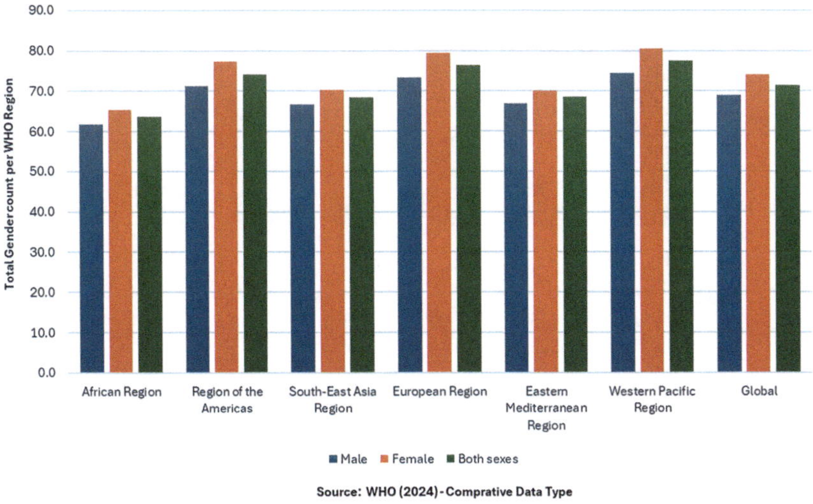

Fig. 4.1 Life expectancy at birth (years) – 2021

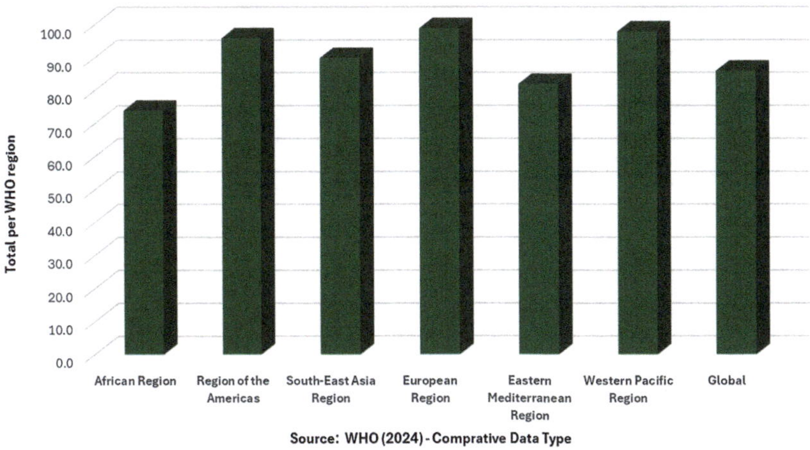

Fig. 4.2 Maternal mortality ratio (per 100 000 live births) – 2023

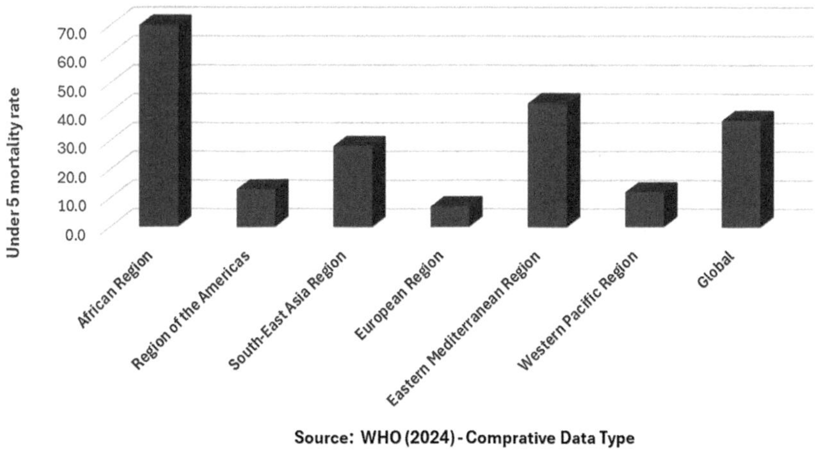

Fig. 4.3 Under-five mortality rate (per 1000 live births)

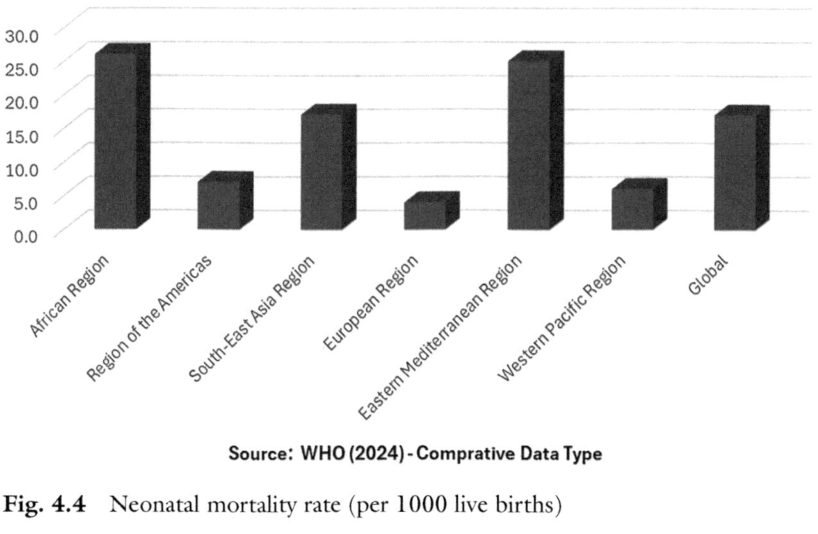

Fig. 4.4 Neonatal mortality rate (per 1000 live births)

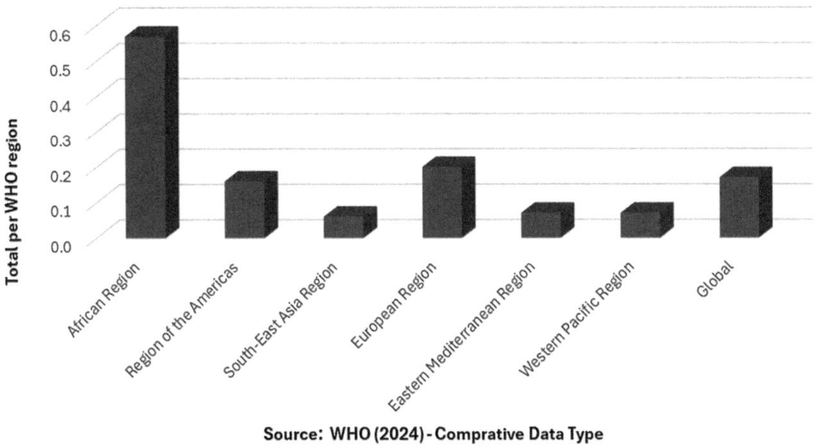

Fig. 4.5 New HIV infections (per 1000 uninfected population) – 2022

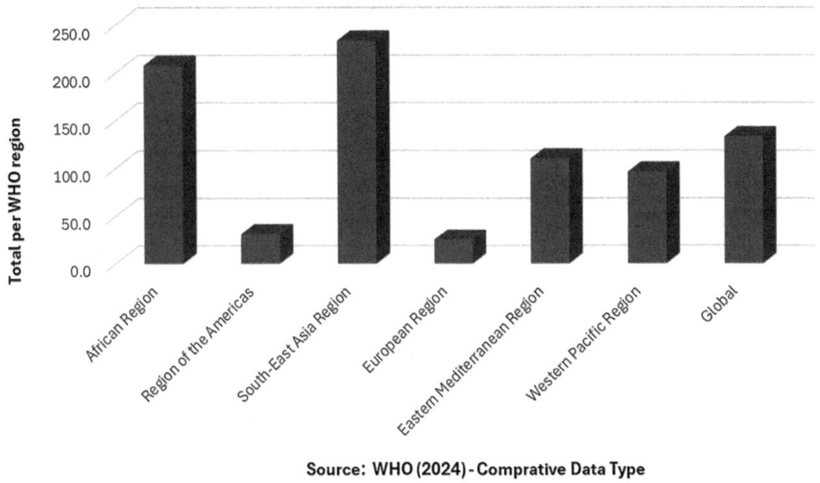

Fig. 4.6 Tuberculosis incidence (per 100 000 population) – 2022

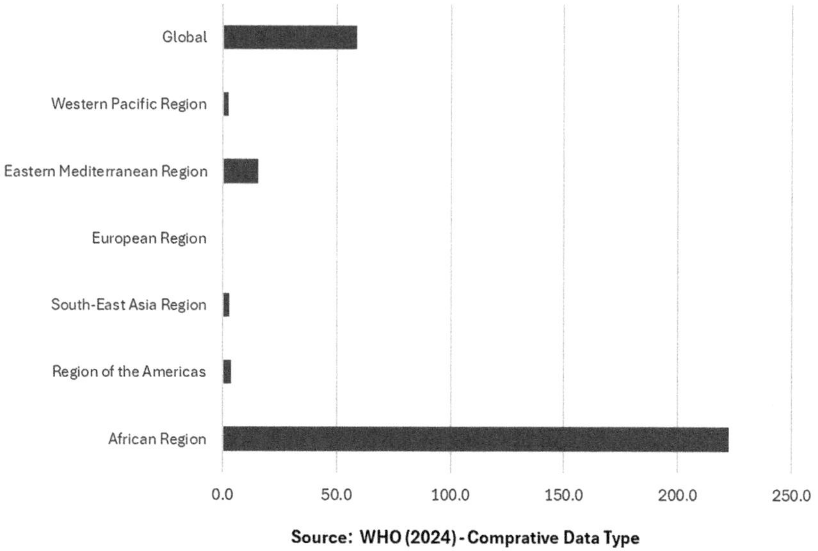

Fig. 4.7 Malaria incidence (per 1000 population at risk) – 2022

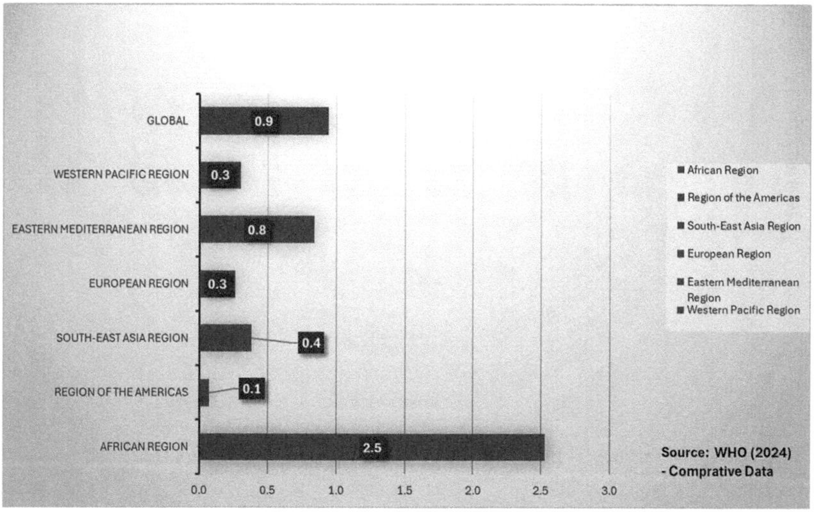

Fig. 4.8 Hepatitis B surface antigen (HBsAg) prevalence among children under 5 years (%) – 2020

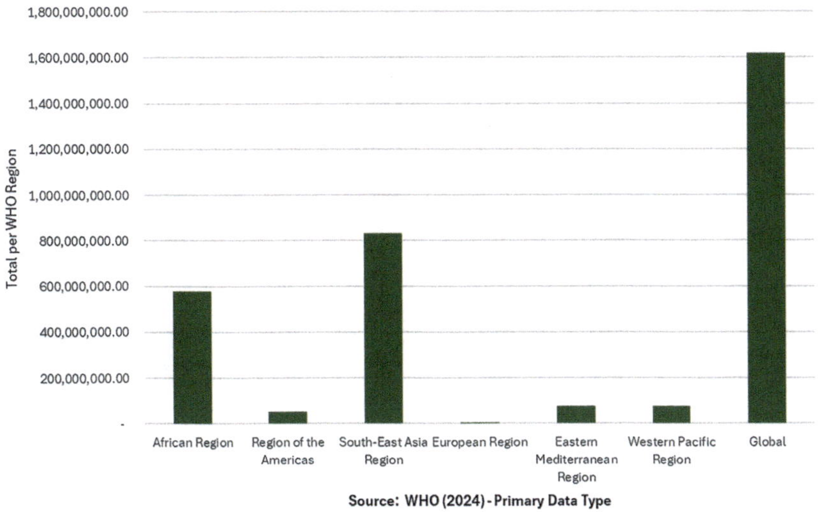

Fig. 4.9 Reported number of people requiring interventions against NTDs – 2022

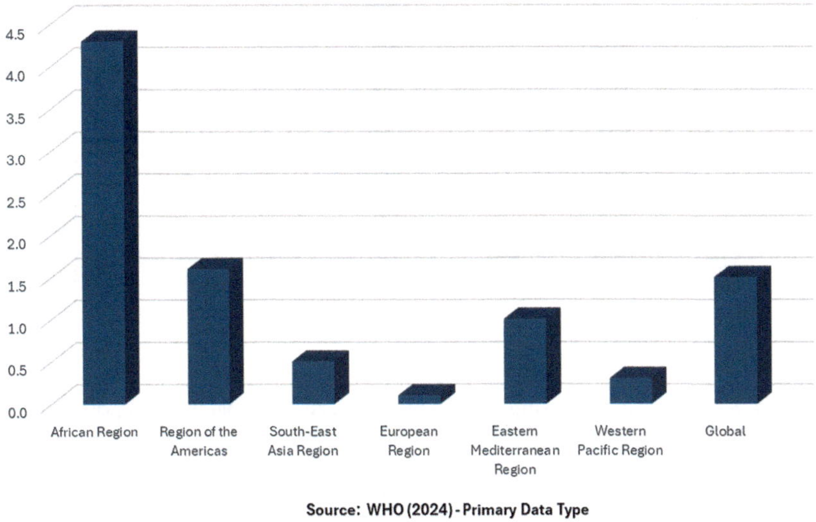

Fig. 4.10 Adolescent birth rate (per 1000 women aged 10–14 years)

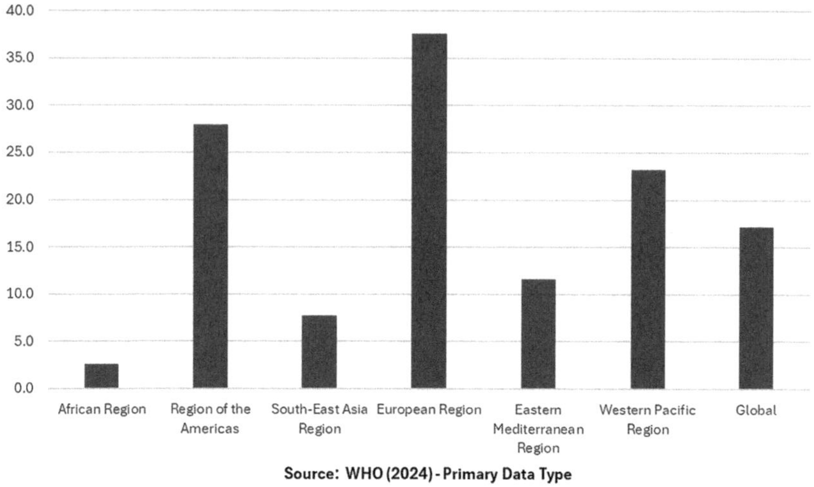

Fig. 4.11 Density of medical doctors (per 10 000 population) / 2014–2022

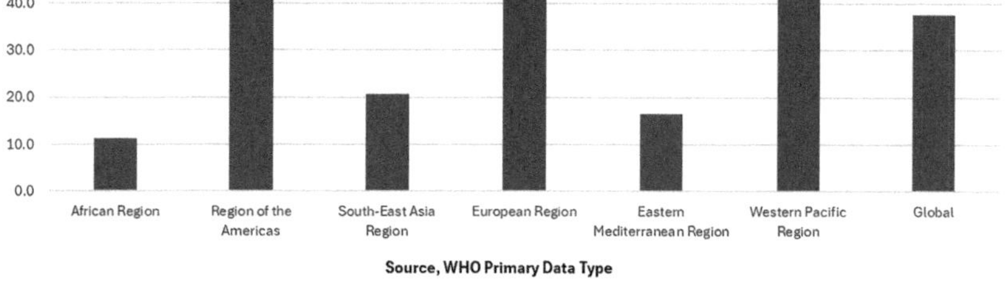

Fig. 4.12 Density of nursing and midwifery personnel (per 10 000 population) 2014–2023

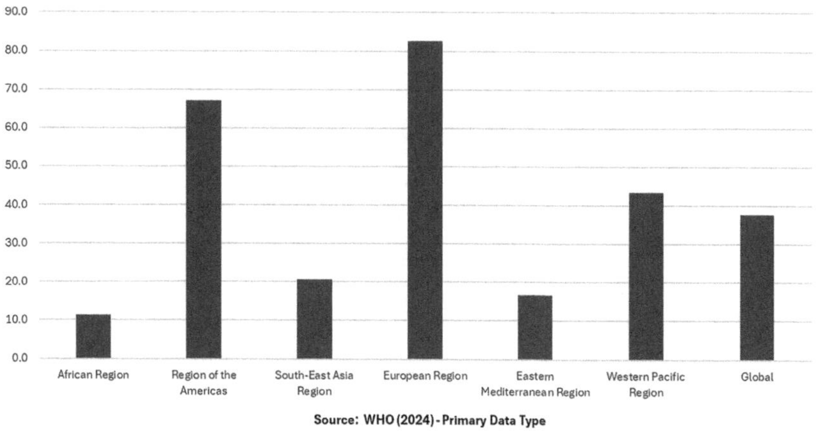

Fig. 4.13 Density of dentists (per 10 000 population) 2014–2024

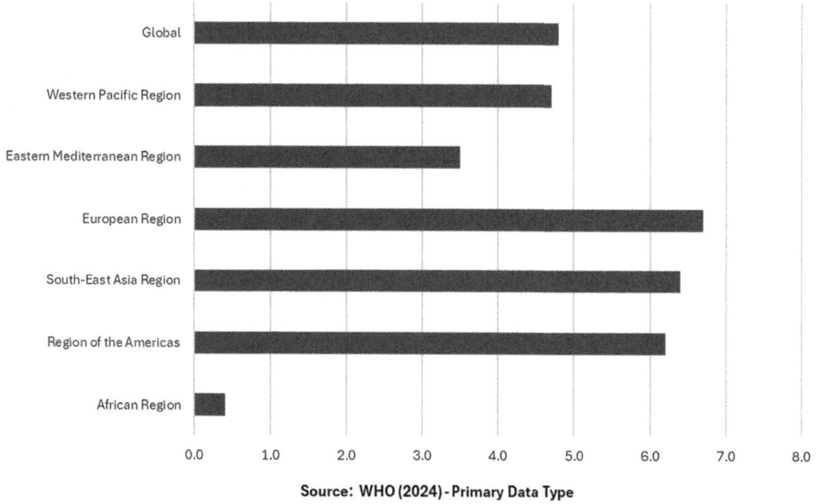

Fig. 4.14 Density of pharmacists (per 10 000 population) 2014–2025

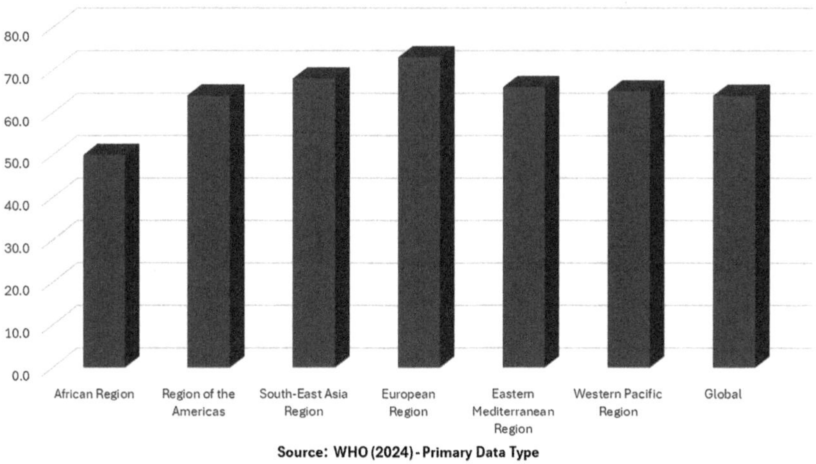

Fig. 4.15 Average of 15 International Health Regulations core capacity scores 2023

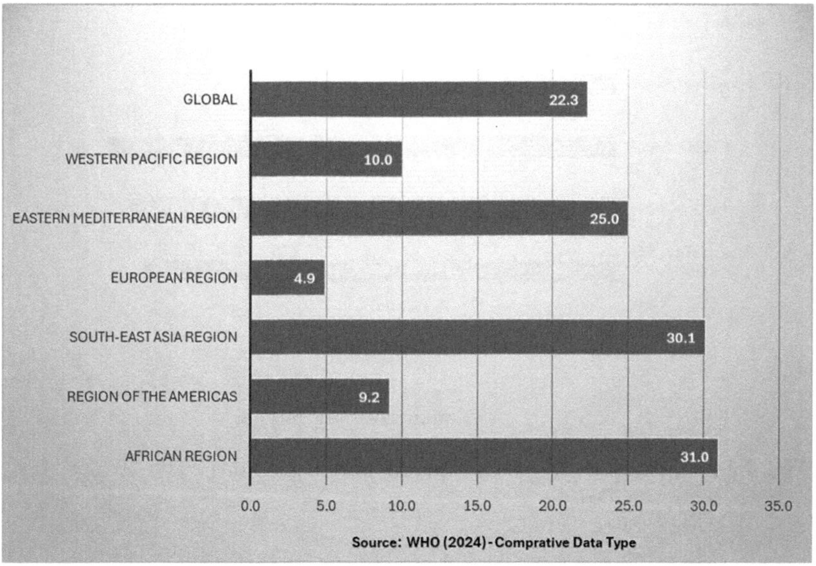

Fig. 4.16 Prevalence of stunting in children under 5 (%) 2022

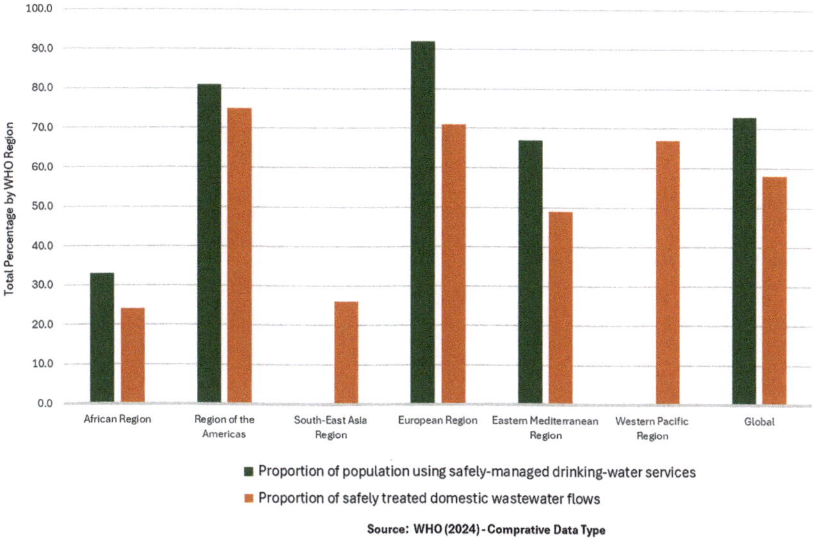

Fig. 4.17 Proportion of population using safely-managed drinking water services and those using safely treated domestic wastewater flows (%) 2022

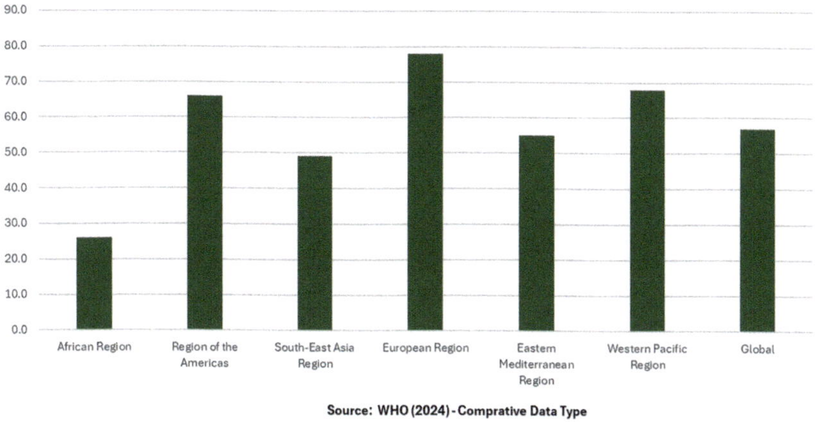

Fig. 4.18 Proportion of population using safely-managed sanitation services (%) 2022

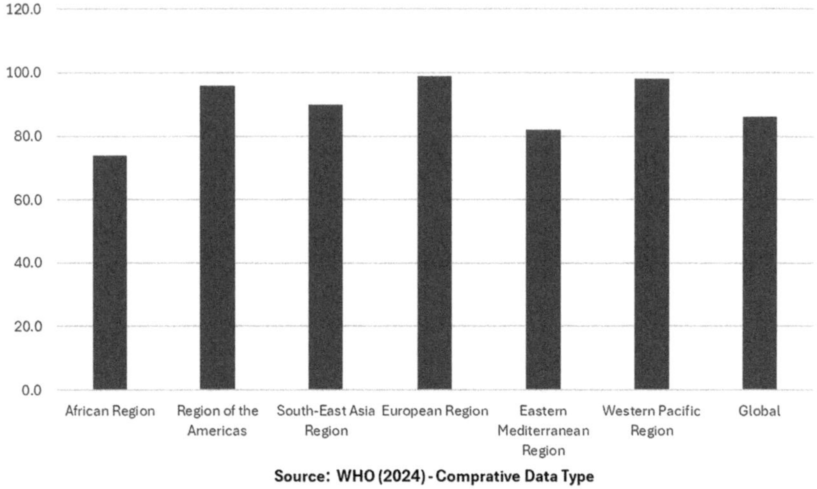

Fig. 4.19 Proportion of births attended by skilled health personnel (%) 2023

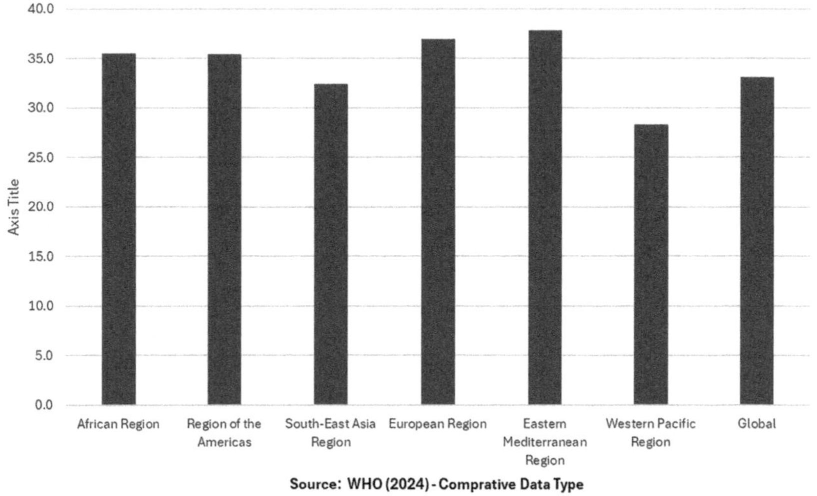

Fig. 4.20 Age-standardized prevalence of hypertension among adults aged 30-79 years (%) 2019

Our discussions in this chapter cover the needs for addressing not only regular diseases but also epidemics, pandemics and other widespread diseases, particularly in Africa. For this reason, it may be remiss to discuss Africa's healthcare challenges without recalling the biggest pandemic in modern medical history (COVID-19), how it was dealt with and the lessons we can draw from it in dealing with future widespread diseases.[1]

4.3 COVID-19 in Africa: The Benefits of Hindsight

In late 2019, a novel coronavirus, identified as SARS-CoV-2, was found to cause a pandemic of respiratory illness called COVID-19. Africa was not spared from the global economic meltdown that followed. The pandemic resulted in a global recession reflected in a historic economic slump in output of 3.1% in 2020, followed by a steep rise of 6.0% in 2021. In Sub-Saharan Africa, the combined GDP fell by −1.7% in 2020 and then rose by 4.7% in 2022. Although IMF data puts the Middle East and North Africa (MENA) together, the negative effects of the pandemic in 2019 were universal in all the subregions of Africa, including the African countries in MENA. A study by the Fund found that the pandemic created the risks of wiping out some of the progress made in MENA over the past decades in poverty reduction, literacy rates, increasing lifespans and reducing inequality.[2]

According to widely available data from sources, such as the INFORM Severity Index[3] and World Health Organization (WHO), Africa had the

[1] Some of the points on COVID-19 can be found in our earlier work, Sonko, Karamo NM Sonko, and Mariama Sonko, Demystifying Environmental, Social and Governance (ESG) in Africa: Charting the ESG Course in Africa, Palgrave Macmillan, London and New York, 2023.

[2] Roberto Cardarelli, Mercedes Vera-Martín and Mr. Subir Lall (eds.), *Promoting Inclusive Growth in the Middle East and North Africa Challenges and Opportunities in a Post-Pandemic World*, IMF, October 2022.

[3] The INFORM Severity Index is a composite index, which puts together 31 core indicators, in three groups: impact, conditions of affected people, and complexity. The indicators are calculated on a scale of 1 to 5. The scores are then aggregated into the three groups or components to determine the overall severity, with scores ranging from very low to high. The three dimensions are weighted according to their contribution to severity through the impact of the crisis, conditions of affected people and complexity. More information on the Index can be found in https://www.acaps.org/methodology/severity#:~:text=The%20INFORM%20Severity%20Index%20is%20a%20composite%20index%2C%20which%20brings,scale%20of%201%20to%205, last visited January 16, 2023.

lowest cumulative number of cases and deaths, compared to all other regions. The number of cases (9,390,554) and deaths (174, 993) were lower than even the United Kingdom's alone (24,000,101 and 196,821, respectively).[4]

According to the INFORM Severity Index,[5] only 18 African countries were classified as having very high levels of severity of the COVID-19 pandemic. However, data for the calculation of this composite Index was not available for about half of the total number of African countries.[6] Elsewhere we have pointed out the shortcomings of data and computational methods which left us with an unclear picture of the full extent of COVID-19 in Africa.[7]

4.4 Preventative Measures

COVID-19 caught the world off guard and there was panic across the world largely because the world was put in a shock as no one was prepared for anything like it.[8] There was a dramatic rise in the number of cases at the beginning of what first looked like an occasional outbreak of a flu-like new or old sickness, then a global warning from the medical profession that there was an emergent epidemic caused by a new disease called COVID-19. Finally, as the reality sank in, the international medical

https://data.humdata.org/visualization/covid19-humanitarian-operations/?layer=inform_severity_index, last visited January 16, 2023.

[4] https://covid19.who.int/table/, last visited on November 26, 2022.

[5] The INFORM Severity Index is a composite index, which puts together 31 core indicators, in three groups: impact, conditions of affected people, and complexity. The indicators are calculated on a scale of 1 to 5. The scores are then aggregated into the three groups or components to determine the overall severity, with scores ranging from very low to high. The three dimensions are weighted according to their contribution to severity through the impact of the crisis, conditions of affected people and complexity. More information on the Index can be found in https://www.acaps.org/methodology/severity#:~:text=The%20INFORM%20Severity%20Index%20is%20a%20composite%20index%2C%20which%20brings,scale%20of%201%20to%205, last visited January 16, 2023.

[6] https://data.humdata.org/visualization/covid19-humanitarian-operations/?layer=inform_severity_index, last visited January 16, 2023.

[7] Sonko, Karamo NM Sonko, and Mariama Sonko, Demystifying ESG in Africa: Charting the ESG Course in Africa, Palgrave Macmillan, London and New York, 2023.

[8] For the economic impacts of COVID-19 on the world and the responses, the reader also refer to the World Bank, "The Economic Impacts of the COVID-19 crisis," chapter 1, *World Development Report 2022*, last accessed on April 12, 2023, at https://www.worldbank.org/en/publication/wdr2022/brief/chapter-1-introduction-the-economic-impacts-of-the-covid-19-crisis.

community declared the COVID-19 pandemic. In the panic mode, the responses to the pandemic by authorities around the world, including African governments, took the following forms:

(1) *Detection*. Increases in screening and treatment;
(2) *Food*. Hoarding food and feeding underprivileged communities;
(3) *Aid*. International development finance institutions, such as the International Monetary Fund (IMF) and World Bank, dished out grants to the underdeveloped countries to help them to undertake emergency measures;
(4) *Information*. Public awareness campaigns;
(5) *Domestic Movements*. Restrictions on domestic movement and public transport. Stay-at-homes and curfews;
(6) *Masks*. Facial coverings and/or wearing masks;
(7) *Schools*. Adaptation or closure of schools;
(8) *Businesses*. Adaptation, closure of businesses and massive layoffs;
(9) *Gatherings*. Limits on or restrictions on public and private gatherings;
(10) *International Travel*. International travel restrictions or lockdowns (entry restrictions, quarantining and testing).[9]

At the height of the pandemic the above containment measures cost Africa an estimated US$ 13.8 billion in lost GDP each month and 40 million people were thrown into extreme poverty.[10] The continent and most of the underdeveloped countries started to drum for funds right from the beginning of the pandemic. In Africa, the then Chairperson of the African Union, President Cyril Ramaphosa of South Africa; the former President of the African Development Bank (AfDB), Donald Kaberuka; the former Nigerian Minister of Finance and now Director General of the World Trade Organization, Ngozi Okonjo-Iweala; the former South African Finance Minister, Trevor Manuel; and the former CEO of Credit Suisse, Tidjane Thiam, were appointed Special Envoys to mobilize international

[9] https://covid19.who.int/region/amro/country/ca/measures, last visited November 11, 2022.

[10] World Bank, The World Bank in Africa. COVID-19 (Coronavirus) Response", October 1, 2021, https://www.worldbank.org/en/region/afr/coronavirus, last visited December 10, 2022. The number of those thrown into extreme poverty has been estimated at 53 million in 2020 by Etayibtalnam Koudjom, Sévérin Tamwo and Koffi D. Kpognon, "Does poverty increase COVID-19 in Africa? A cross-country analysis," *Health Economics Review*, volume 12, Article number: 51, 2022.

support for the fight against Africa's COVID-19-induced economic woes. This was not the first time for such action in Africa—the African Development Bank (AfDB), African Union (AU), UN Economic Commission for Africa (ECA) and the New Partnership for Africa's Development (NEPAD) are all well known for their frequent calls for financial resources for their programmes and directly for Africa.

Some of the preventative measures, such as disease detection, information, social distancing, masks and hygiene-related measures, are still relevant, even after the COVID-19 pandemic, especially during the initial stages of the outbreaks of any widespread diseases. Some are relevant even before outbreaks if the threats are felt.

Apart from direct medical measures and medically related measures, adequate financing for medical sectors are essential. As government budgets are never enough for this, external aid is often needed. However, past experience strongly shows the failure of aid at national and even regional levels (organizations) because of the lack of accountability and other reasons that have been widely studied. The best way to make sure that funds mobilized for containment measures against diseases are used exactly for the purposes that they are raised for is to ensure that there is accountability for every cent raised. The scandals in a number of African countries in their use of COVID-related aid should serve as lessons for the administration of future financing for Africa's medical sectors, from both internal and external sources.[11]

4.5 Curative Rather than Preventative Measures

Apart from the above preventive measures, the curative measures against COVID-19 consisted of in- and outpatient treatments in medical facilities. Although in many African countries there was widespread disbelief in the existence of COVID-19, thus limiting screenings and treatments, the number of actual tests and admissions still imposed a huge burden on already overstretched medical facilities even with the creation of new ones. There were general shortages of medical and support staff, equipment, medication and infrastructure across the continent. No disease had ever

[11] See, for example, APA News, "Gambian minister makes sensational Covid-19 corruption claims", May 17, 2020; BBC News, "Coronavirus in South Africa: Misuse of Covid-19 funds 'frightening'", September 2, 2020; and Africanews, "Africa's Covid-19 corruption that outweighs pandemic", May 25, 2021; last visited December 10, 2022.

before exposed the inadequacies of African healthcare services than COVID-19 did. COVID-19 did proof right the old adage that "prevention is better than cure".

4.6 The Pandemic Has Ended, but the Threats of Widespread Diseases Have Not

The COVID-19 pandemic has officially ended, but the threats of widespread diseases continue around the world. In a world that has now become "a global village", Africa has to look at threats of diseases within and outside the continent. As far as any part of the world is threatened by a deadly virus, Africa is threated too and measures to prevent and cure the disease and deal with its inevitable consequences have to be taken very seriously by Africans. Thus, our healthy strategies have to have several components to be able to address the different layers of internal and external medical threats.

4.7 Global Measures for Dealing with Widespread Diseases

It follows from the above that to contain the direct and indirect effects of any widespread disease in Africa, now or in the future, COVID-19 or any other, African political leaders and policy makers must behave like and prepare for the long haul, act with speed, coordination and for the common good. However, although actions at the national levels are great and are what we are calling for here first, we cannot prevent the spread of diseases which originate from outside the continent unless the global aspects of health threats become equally important in a "global village" strategy. A successful Africa-wide programme can be harmonized with such a global approach and, in fact, be more beneficial. It can protect the African countries and continent whilst insulating them from externally generated viruses. The world would also be safer from a healthier Africa.

4.8 COVID-19, ESG and Africa: What Can Be Done by Companies for the Health Sectors?

Environmental, Social and Governance (ESG) is very important in making governments more socially responsive and companies more socially responsible. As better and inclusive healthcare services call for effective roles of both the public and private sectors, what we refer to as formal comprehensive or holistic ESG[12] comes into play, with the public and private sectors teaming up. It is for this reason that we now discuss the question of what governments and private companies in Africa can do to address the challenges of their health sectors. To encourage others in applying the new concepts and to seize the new opportunities presented through ESG, African governments not only must be advocates of ESG, but should themselves be more interested in the implementation of Environmental, Social and Governance measures in the health sectors of African countries. Practical interests in ESG can make governments role models for the private sectors. As holistic ESG is about caring for people and the planet, the health sectors are natural homes for it. The sectors offer perfect playing fields for governments, businesses and others to score goals for the benefit of lives and even the natural environment. Private companies can help in developing Africa's health sectors, with the support of governments, as discussed next.

4.8.1 *Existing Medical Facilities*

One of the reasons for the poor state of healthcare in Africa is that operating medical facilities, especially outside the urban areas, generally exist in dismal states. Even in the urban areas of Africa generally, a very few of these facilities (serving very small percentages of the populations who can afford them) meet international standards. The unappealing facilities dent the abilities and morale of smart and dedicated personnel working there, resulting in substandard patient care. Therefore, companies can provide equipment to the hospitals, clinics and other medical facilities and help renovate them as part of their ESG programmes.

4.8.2 *Working Medical Personnel*

Medical personnel in Africa can be grouped into three categories: (1) those trained in recognized schools in developed countries at international standards; (2) those trained at institutions at home or in other African

[12] Formal comprehensive or holistic ESG is defined as deliberate, structured, coordinated and monitorable programme of pursuing clearly defined environmental, social and corporate governance objectives in companies. When applicable outside companies, corporate governance becomes organizational governance than can be tailored to the structure and functioning of the organization concerned.

countries; and (3) those who studied in other developing countries outside Africa. Many (but not all) of the latter institutions lack the resources to train at international standards. Companies can help, through their ESG programmes, by inviting medical experts from different parts of the world for short-term refresher or upgrading courses for African doctors, nurses and other health workers, especially those without the required international-level professional exposure.

4.8.3 New Medical Facilities

Existing medical facilities in Africa are not only generally substandard, but their numbers are also grossly insufficient for the growing populations of African countries. Furthermore, they are very much unevenly distributed in favour of the urban areas, especially in and near the capital cities. Therefore, new, better and more evenly distributed facilities are needed to expand the access of the populations to medical services. Companies can allocate part of their CSR budgets, under ESG, for achieving this objective.

4.8.4 Additional Medical Personnel Through Academic Institutions

Related to the need for new medical facilities, there is also the need to train more medical personnel in order to help attain international standards of competence. This calls for better equipment, more and better qualified teaching staffs and more appropriate curricula in academic institutions. Companies can allocate part of their CSR budgets, under ESG, for this purpose. Private companies can help attract the best brains to poorly funded academic institutions in Africa by providing endowment chairs and research grants for faculty and scholarships for the best students in these African institutions. This is a very common practice for supporting academic institutions in some of the developed countries, especially the United States.

4.9 Profit-Making Private Healthcare in Africa

Around the world, private healthcare services have proven to be useful in increasing the quality and quantity of available healthcare to populations. Like private education, this is a new area for private investors in Africa, in fact more recent than private education which is now gaining ground in many African countries (Chap. 2). The poor medical infrastructure and services in Africa's health sector, generally, deprive most of the people of proper healthcare and it is common knowledge that those who can afford it (an affluent minority of public officials and business persons) go abroad to seek the medical attention they need for themselves and their families. Thus, the urgency for improving domestic healthcare may not be felt by precisely those who can something about it. Therefore, enabling private investment in the health sector, through the necessary incentives from governments, can attract and encourage local and foreign investors to put money in Africa's health sectors, improving the infrastructure and services in the sectors.

4.10 Requirements for a Successful Pan-African Health Strategy

As we have maintained in this chapter, the COVID-19 pandemic is officially over, but the threats of large-scale diseases in the world, including Africa, remain. The pandemic has left the world and Africa with lessons that must not be forgotten. Elsewhere, we have called global "community" efforts to deal with present and future threats, on the basis of mutual interests and interdependence. African countries need each other even more in such a context where they can potentially do better working together than working in isolation as individual countries. A successful pan-African health strategy means the abilities of African countries to protect themselves against internal within the continent and external outbreaks, such as COVID-19, from outside the continent. What are the requirements for such a strategy? These are discussed next and they have national relevance too.

4.10.1 Planning

African Ministries of Health must have well thought out medical plans, which include very clear aims and objectives, milestones and measurable performance indicators. For this to happen strategic thinking should serve as the basis of policy conceptualization and formation or development.

4.10.2 *Financial Resources*

Plans without financing do that make any, or much, sense, so medical plans must be aligned with resources. Measures of resources not only should be based on what is already and easily available, but must also take into account the capacity of a government to mobilize more resources. This capacity can be boosted through innovative ideas, some of which have been brought up in this book.

4.10.3 *Implementation*

The planning process moves into a more advanced dimension, closer to reality, only when the implementation starts. The implementation stage should consist of milestones and measurable performance indicators, deadlines, accompanied by the ability to monitor progress with deadlines.

4.10.4 *Clarity of Roles*

Additional to clarity of aims and objectives identified above, under "Planning", there must also be clarity of who are those responsible for the implementation of plans and what their individual and joint roles are.

4.10.5 *Coordination*

Coordination is essential, especially for big projects with multiple players. It helps to align efforts, combine strengths, address weakness and enhance achievements.

4.10.6 *Strategic Management and Sustainability*

All the above points and more under this last section (4.10) may be achievable through the applications of our Strategic Management Sustainability Framework (SMSF) and Tool (SMST), also referred to as the African PESTLE Analysis (APA). Chapter 2 discusses how this can be done by examining the detailed features, approaches and methodologies of the SMSF/SMST/APA.

4.10.7 Conclusion: A Pan-African Health Strategy

From our arguments in this chapter, a coordinated and effective pan-African health strategy is a requirement for enabling African countries to protect themselves, individually and collectively in a "global village". It would enable them to mobilize and combine resources, skills and measures that may be difficult to do individually. African continental and sub-regional organizations can and should facilitate the process. As these are mostly governmental organizations, they can initiate and succeed in developing a continental health strategy (elements of which already exist in the organizations), only with the full support of African governments.

CHAPTER 5

Building Resilience in the Post-COVID African Economy: An Intersectional Perspective Based on Socio-Economic Modelling and the Indigenous Knowledge Base

5.1 Introduction

Our world, including Africa, is prone to epidemics and pandemics, which (COVID-19 clearly demonstrated) can cause devastating harm on economies and societies, as outlined in Chap. 4 and by Sonko and Sonko (2023) in their path-breaking study on Environmental, Social and Governance (ESG).[1] Therefore, by now it is a well-established empirical proposition that a global pandemic, particularly one of the scale and reach of COVID-19, places insurmountable policy challenges upon most governing bodies. These challenges are further exacerbated when the nation being governed is a country like South Africa with deep racial-ethnic and

[1] My co-authors in this book are at the forefront of promotion and research in ESG in Africa. See, for example, Karamo NM Sonko, *Demystifying Environmental, Social and Governance (ESG): Charting the ESG Course in Africa*, London and New York: Palgrave Macmillan, 2023; Mariama Sonko, "ESG: Relevant and Applicabilty in Africa", presentation at the First High-level Webinar on ESG and Stakeholder Capitalism in Africa, January 28, 2022; and Mariama Sonko, "ESG: Meaning, Materiality and Mode", presentation to the Etisalat Academy, Dubai, UAE, June 30, 2022; and Mariama Sonko, "ESG in Africa", presentation to the senior staff of the Arab Bank for Economic Development in Africa (BADEA), Khartoum, Sudan, September 24, 2021.

K. N. M. Sonko et al., *21st Century African Development Strategies*,
https://doi.org/10.1007/978-3-031-93079-9_5

class inequalities even in the post-Apartheid period. The disadvantaged groups face in their communities the constraints of limited resources, inadequate infrastructure and oftentimes multiple other obstacles that prevent them from receiving the full benefits even if the government is relatively successful in designing appropriate pandemic relief packages for their populations. Therefore, it is imperative that the economic and policy concerns of South Africa be examined through a different lens—one that prioritizes immediate issues like hunger and disease prevention, but also emphasizes short-, medium- and long-term recovery. In keeping with the goals of post-Apartheid South Africa, the recovery and growth strategies should be pro-poor among other things.

The goal is to present a plan that ultimately respects the poor and also meshes with their own vision of development from a socially embedded intersectional perspective. For this to work, a socially embedded intersectional capabilities approach (SEICA) is necessary (Khan 1998, 2004a, b, 2006, 2010, 2011, 2013, 2020a, b, 2021a, b).[2] One important debate in many parts of the world including South Africa has been centred around the role of indigenous knowledge in general and in healthcare and medicine in particular, which can also be part of our conversation. While there is criticism to be noted of all knowledge systems, including indigenous ones (Green 2012), there has been recent studies identifying the merits of incorporating indigenous knowledge systems (IKS) in improving health and public health education outcomes (Cocks et al. 2012; Dahlberg and Trygger 2009; Botha 2010).

I make a preliminary attempt in this chapter to include indigenous knowledge both as a complement to the standard public health model and as an integral part of any formal multisectoral model. In the latter area, our work points to important gaps in data gathering and focuses our attention on the kind and quality of data needed. This looms as an urgent socially

[2] For further information of Socially Embedded Intersectional Capabilities Approach, see also Khan, Haider A. and Joshua Villanueva (2020). Women's Socially Embedded Intersectional Capabilities and Development: A Theory of Inclusive Development Applied to the Philippines, Working paper, JKSIS, University of Denver.

Khan, Haider A and Shamayeta Rahman (2020a). Women's Socially Embedded Intersectional Capabilities and Development: A Theory-based Empirical Investigation in the ASEAN economies, Working Paper, JKSIS, University of Denver.

———. (2020b). Covid-19 and Development: An Economy Wide Model and Data-based Approach to Impact and Resolutions, Working Paper, JKSIS, University of Denver.

———., M. Mahapatro and K.Morshed (2020). COVID-19 and Gender Justice: How are women faring? Evidence from a statistical analysis of the BRAC Rapid Perception Survey for Bangladesh, Working Paper, JKSIS, University of Denver.

relevant research task. Khan (1998, 2004a, and 2012) raised the prospects of including indigenous knowledge-based innovations in national and regional (augmented) innovation systems and offered some formal guidelines. It will be possible to do this within the South Africa SAM by breaking down knowledge production activities along the lines of characteristics of non-indigenous (NIK) and indigenous knowledge (IK), their production functions and economy-wide consequences and complementarities between NIK and IK.

This chapter utilizes South Africa as a case study and examines the strengths and weaknesses of their current and past COVID-19, fiscal, monetary and sectoral policies. This case study also helps to present a fairly comprehensive framework regarding the allocation of limited resources to the most vulnerable groups in a country. It addresses both immediate impact and the medium to long-run effects of economic stimuluses via multiplier analysis by examining both supply-side and demand-side elements of the economy.

The section goes onto elaborate on South Africa and optimal decision-making strategies and then outlines the government's COVID-19 fiscal package. Following that, there is an extensive methodology section that elaborates on Social Accounting Matrix (SAM) and Susceptibility Exposure-Infection-Recovery (SEIR) calculations and the possible integrations of indigenous knowledge in both. The chapter then focuses on its findings about the economy of South Africa and highlights areas that would require the highest priority and would ultimately help the most people, particularly the impoverished groups. The final section demonstrates this by presenting and examining the government's COVID-19 plan and highlighting its strengths and limitations.

5.2 Case Study: South Africa

As reported by Sonko and Sonko (2023), South Africa was the most affected country in Africa during the COVID-19 pandemic.[3] Therefore, the government of South Africa took some bold and timely steps for countering the negative impact of the global pandemic on the South African economy. Like many other countries, South Africa recognized the need to

[3] Karamo NM Sonko, and Sonko, Mariama, *Demystifying Environmental, Social and Governance (ESG): Charting the ESG Course in Africa,* London and New York: Palgrave Macmillan 2023.

effectively address the severe consequences of COVID-19, the resulting economic lockdowns with curtailed economic activities manifested in factory closures, sudden loss of employment and income with significant reduction in national output. Cancellation of export orders and depressed demand for domestically produced goods and services had an adverse impact. The services sector which includes trade, tourism, transport, communication, hotels, restaurants, banking, finance, education, etc. as in other countries, had predictably shrunk in capacity utilization. The 2020 IMF projections (World Economic Outlook 2020) depicted overall economic decline in 2020 at −5.8% but painted a picture of optimistic economic recovery in 2021 with GDP growth at 4.0%. In a more pessimistic scenario assuming a slower recovery, the UNDP estimated the GDP to have fallen by 7.9%, estimating nearly five years before the economy returns to its pre-pandemic state (IMF 2020, UNDP 2020).

Though a R500 billion (amounting to approximately 10% of the 2019 GDP) stimulus package was introduced, only R130 billion was repurposed from the current budget and tax programmes and utilized. The rest of the R330 billion (approximately 65% of the stimulus) was expected to be financed through international loans, with approximately US$4 billion expected from the IMF and 40–60 million coming from the World Bank (UNDP 2020). A stimulus package of this size was very necessary to combat both the immediate and long-run impact of this crisis, however it was also vital that it be distributed in a timely manner for maximal effectiveness. It was also important to optimize allocation by identifying the most affected sectors and their relative importance in terms of value added, employment and income generation, and their effects on other aspects of inclusivity within marginalized and disadvantaged populations (particularly in factors of gender, race, ethnicity and location amongst other things).

The fiscal package (better called a “relief package” rather than “stimulus package”) included a fairly generous quantum of financial support to various groups of the vulnerable population. One of the purposes of this chapter is to help direct the strategic allocation of this support to the affected population on the basis of some preliminary data analysis and economic modelling using both sectoral data and the economy-wide consistent multisectoral data captured by the detailed 2015 SAM of South Africa. The chapter also hopes to identify integration of the economic and socially embedded capabilities approach with the inclusion of indigenous knowledge production sectors within its methodology for future policy analyses.

For optimal decision making it is necessary to think in terms of distinct but overlapping decision and implementation phases during large-scale economic crises. In order to keep the different time frames of analysis distinct, I propose to deal with three different time scales: addressing (with South Africa as an example) the immediate crisis at the time during the first 3–6 months of the financial year (FY21 (March–June)), the restorative phase during the 6–12 months for FY21 (June–December/June) and FY22, and a plan beyond that designed to be consistent with South Africa's long-run economic goals.

The first two time periods are of utmost priority, where the main problem during the first phase would be containing the infection, preventing widespread hunger and shortages and being able to create incentives for the private sector to follow an optimal restorative path. It is imperative to pay attention to the Susceptibility-Infections-Recovery (SIR) or Susceptibility Exposure-Infection-Recovery (SEIR) model to derive optimal lockdown periods from and implement it strictly. The March 15 lockdown period prevented 50,000 additional deaths (Garba et al. 2020). It is also important in the near future to guide more resources to public health bodies like the National Institute for Communicable Disease (NICD) to be able to undertake more of these important analyses in a timely manner (Atkeson 2020a, b). It also appears that in South Africa and other African countries a two-tiered strategic budgetary approach is appropriate in terms of directing aid towards testing and buying medical equipment, but this should still be utilized strategically based on areas that are likely to see most of the outbreak initially during epidemics and pandemics. It is thus imperative that significant investments are made into the public health research infrastructure for proper utilization of the limited healthcare resources in African countries.

Second, it is highly important to prevent starvation and hunger, a frequent threat in Africa. Both cash transfers and aid-in-kind to affected groups have been and will be necessary in South Africa and other African countries. Some of these were done in South Africa through the delivery of food parcels to affected populations, creating unemployment insurance, and via the creation of loan programmes to keep small- and medium-run businesses running. Quick identification of poor families and effective delivery of food aid in particular are key required actions during such a crisis. Though, undoubtedly, there will be some leakage, working with reliable government officials, volunteers and local people who have a reputation for being reliable is crucial.

The package that the South African government came up with was not adequate enough to support the workers and families who needed at least R500 per month for the next 6 to 12 months. The Quarterly Labor Force Survey for 2019 and SAM-2015 indicate that less than 20% of workers are in the informal sector (which appears to be an underestimation). The official unemployment rate for South Africa is at 30%, which implies that there are significant barriers to employment even in the informal sectors (also refer to Department of Statistics 2020). However, if the economic stagnation continues, it is likely that unemployment will continue to rise and even more people, particularly low-skilled workers, will be pushed into lower wage jobs in the informal sector even in this post-pandemic era. This will have further adverse implications for gender and racial inequality, as more women and black workers are currently employed in lower-skilled positions (UNDP 2020).

The fiscal stimulus package was designed to provide the necessary budget needed for medical equipment and healthcare services, prevent starvation, and provide the financial support needed by small and medium companies to keep their businesses running until the eventual phasing out of the lockdown (UNDP 2020).

Additionally, the government had taken the following steps:

(a) Food distribution and basic services for the poor;
(b) Building a programme for cash transfer to the targeted vulnerable population through social relief grants, wage protection programmes and a broader unemployment insurance;
(c) Developing a state infrastructure fund; investing in remote education and renewable energy for job creation;
(d) Promoting industrialization through easier licensing opportunities and encouraging local production;
(e) Delayed tax programmes and credit guarantee programmes for small and medium-sized enterprises (including informal business) to benefit from and promote employment.

All of this including additional support for health services accounted for almost 90% of the stimulus package. More specifically, 10% was allocated for cash transfers, social grants, COVID-19 relief and unemployment support grants (Bhorat and Köhler 2020). From the SAM-based multipliers derived, it is possible to confirm that all of these measures will have immediate and longer-term impacts if implemented immediately with some degree of effectiveness. The objective should be to minimize leakage and deliver aid to the targeted groups immediately. This chapter evaluates the impact of the current plan and makes recommendations based on quantitative estimates in order to target the most vulnerable populations in South Africa.

5.3 Methodology

5.3.1 COVID-19: An Economy-Wide Multisectoral SAM-Based Model—Distributional, Employment and Growth Impacts of the Countervailing Public Policies to Overcome the Adverse Impacts of COVID-19

South Africa's SAM-2015: A Brief Description

The SAM utilized for this chapter was constructed for South Africa for the year 2015, which is recent enough for our purposes. It is a square table consisting of equal numbers of rows and columns. There are 197 rows and columns within the purposes of this table. The expenditures of each variable are noted by convention as flows from a column to the various rows intersecting that particular column, whereas the receipts of each variable are noted in the respective rows. By definition, the sum of expenditures for the variables must equal the sum of the receipts of the same variables, thus leading the total expenditures to match the total receipts (appearing in the bottom corner of the table). The SAM South Africa table contains four sets of endogenous accounts for our modelling approach, that is, (1) 62 activities numbered from 2 to 63; (2) 104 commodities numbered from 64 to 167; (3) factors which are broken down between labour with primary education, middle school education, secondary education, tertiary education and capital in the rows 169–173; and (4) households which have been subdivided by income deciles in the rows 175–188 (per decile until the top 10% which is divided per 2%). There are also margins on 168 and enterprises on 174. The table also includes exogenous accounts including activity government (189), direct tax (190), import tax (191), direct tax (192), sales tax (193), savings-investment (194), change in stocks (195) and rest of the world (196).

Though not currently available, a possible improvement to the current SAM would be the integration of gender data and indigenous sectors (including indigenous knowledge-based sectors). This indigenous knowledge-inclusive SAM or IKI-SAM would allow for endogenous modelling of the indigenous sectors and allow the government to identify resource flows for this very essential sector.

Fixed Price Modelling in a SAM-Based Framework
In this section the social accounting matrix and an IKI-inclusive framework is presented as a data-gathering framework, as well as an analytical tool, for studying the effects of the COVID-19 on growth. The origins of social accounting can be traced as far back as Gregory King's efforts in 1681, but more recent work stems from the attempts by Richard Stone, Graham Pyatt, Erik Thorbecke and others.[4]

In the methodological framework of this study, the IKI-SAM is used for mapping production and distribution at the economy-wide level. In this section, first a general SAM is described. Then it is shown how the method for studying the effect of growth within this framework follows logically from its structure. The model used in this chapter is a simple version of a class of SAM-based general equilibrium models.[5] However, presented below is an improvement based on the incorporation of indigenous knowledge-based activities. It summarizes succinctly the interdependence between productive activities (including indigenous knowledge-based activities), factor shares, household income distribution, balance of payments, capital accounts and so on, for the economy as a whole at a point in time. Given the technical conditions of production, the value added is distributed to the factors in a determinate fashion. The value added accrued by the factors is further received by households according to their ownership of assets and the prevailing wage structure. In the matrix form the SAM consists of rows and columns representing receipts and expenditures, respectively. As an accounting constraint receipts must equal expenditures. As mentioned before, the existing SAM for South Africa does not separate out indigenous knowledge sectors; this is a shortcoming that I hope to come back to later.

As is elaborated further in Khan and Thorbecke (1988, Khan 1999, 2006, 2010), the SAM framework can be used to depict a set of linear

[4] For a description of SAM as a data-gathering device, see Pyatt and Thorbecke (1976). Khan (1997) also has a chapter on this alone.

[5] In Walrasian general equilibrium models the flexible price vector determines the equilibrium. In a Keynesian (dis)equilibrium model in the short-run the quantities vary while the price vector remains fixed.

Table 5.1 Simplified schematic of indigenous knowledge-inclusive Social Accounting Matrix

		Expenditures				
		Endogenous accounts			*Exogenous*	*Total*
Receipts		1	2	3	4	5
	Endogenous accounts					
Factors	1	0	0	$T_{1.3}$	x_1	y_1
Households	2	$T_{2.1}$	$T_{2.2}$	0	x_2	y_2
Production activities, including indigenous knowledge (IK) activities	3	0	$T_{3.2}$	$T_{3.3}$	x_3	y_3
	Exogenous accounts					
Sum. of other accounts	4	l_1'	l_2'	l_3'	t	y_x
Total	5	y_1'	y_2'	y_3'	y_x'	

Source: Author's schematization

relationships in a fixed coefficient model. For deciding the question of determination, the accounts need to be divided into exogenous and endogenous ones. For instance, in the South Africa SAM, there are three endogenous accounts. These are factors, households and production activities, leaving the government, capital and the rest of the world accounts as exogenous (Tables 5.1 and 5.2).[6]

Looking at the table above which represents a SAM, we can see immediately that

$$y = n + x \tag{5.1}$$

$$y = 1 + t \tag{5.2}$$

Now if we divide the entries in the matrix T_{nn} by the corresponding total income (that is, y_n), we can define a corresponding matrix of average expenditure propensities. Let us call this matrix A. We now have:

$$y = n + x = Ay + x \tag{5.3}$$

$$y = (1 - A)^{-1} x = Mx \tag{5.4}$$

[6] See Khan and Thorbecke (1988: Ch. 2) for more theoretical details and empirical examples. The presentations here follow the cited work closely.

Table 5.2 Schematic representation of endogenous and exogenous accounts in a SAM

		Expenditures				
		Endogenous	*Sum*	*Exogenous*	*Sum*	*Totals*
Receipts	**Endogenous**	T_{nn}	N	Injections T_{nx}	X	y_n
	Exogenous	Leakages T_{xn}	1	Residual balances T_{xx}	T	y_x
	Totals	y_n'		y_x'		

Source: Author's schematization

M has been called the matrix of accounting multipliers by Thorbecke, for these multipliers, when computed, can account for the results (e.g., income and consumption) obtained in the SAM without explaining the process that led to them. Let us now partition the matrix *A* in the following way (Khan and Thorbecke 1988).

$$A = \begin{bmatrix} 0 & 0 & A_{13} \\ A_{21} & A_{22} & 0 \\ 0 & A_{32} & A_{33} \end{bmatrix} \tag{5.5}$$

Given the accounts factors, household and the production activities, now we see that the income levels of these accounts (call them y_1, y_2, y_3, respectively) are determined as functions of the exogenous demand of all other accounts. In this respect, what we have is a reduced-form model which can be consistent with a number of structural forms. This is quite satisfactory as far as tracing the effects of a certain injection in the economy is concerned or for prediction purposes when the structural coefficients are more or less unchanged.

One limitation of the accounting multiplier matrix *M* as derived in Eq. (5.4) is that it implies unitary expenditure elasticities (the prevailing average expenditure propensities in *A* are assumed to apply to any incremental injection). A more realistic alternative is to specify a matrix of marginal expenditure propensities (C_n below) corresponding to the observed income and expenditure elasticities of the different agents, under the assumption that prices remain fixed. The C_n matrix can be partitioned in the same way as the A matrix above. The most important difference between the two partitioned matrices is that $C_{32} \neq A_{32}$. Expressing the changes in income (dy) resulting from changes in injections (dx), one obtains

$$\mathrm{d}y_n = C_n \mathrm{d}y_n + \mathrm{d}x \tag{5.6}$$

$$= \left(I - C_n\right)^{-1} \mathrm{d}x = M_c \mathrm{d}x \tag{5.7}$$

M_c has been called a fixed price multiplier matrix and its advantage is that it allows any nonnegative income and expenditure elasticities to be reflected in M_c. In particular, in exploring the macroeconomic effects of exogenous changes in the output of different product-cum-technologies on other macroeconomic variables, it would be very unrealistic to assume that consumers react to any given proportional change in their incomes by increasing expenditures on the different commodities by exactly that same proportion (i.e., assuming that the income elasticities of demand of the various socio-economic household groups for the various commodities were all unity). Since the expenditure (income) elasticity is equal to the ratio of the marginal expenditure propensity (MEP_i) to the average expenditure propensity (AEP_i) for any given good i, it follows that the marginal expenditure propensity can be readily obtained once the expenditure elasticity and the average expenditure propensities are known, that is,

$$\varepsilon_j = MEP_i \,/\, AEP_i \tag{5.8}$$

$$MEP_i = \varepsilon_i AEP_i \tag{5.9}$$

and

$$\sum_i MEP_i = 1 \tag{5.10}$$

Thus, given the matrix A_{32} of average expenditure propensities, and the corresponding expenditure elasticities of demand, ε_i the corresponding marginal expenditure propensities matrix C_{32} could easily be derived.[7]

[7] See Khan and Thorbecke (1988, Khan 1999, 2004a, b, 2006, 2010) for some examples. See also Pyatt and Round (1979: 861).

These multipliers can be further decomposed for more refined causal analysis of direct, indirect and feedback loop causal influence paths and graphs.

5.3.2 *Targeting for Optimality, Taking into Account the Presence of IK Within the SIR and SEIR—Models of Epidemic/Pandemic Assessment and Policy Strategy*

The term targeting denotes in this chapter some modifications of the classical SIR model in the manner described below in order to optimize the effects of countervailing policies. The simplest version of the SIR model consists of three differential equations and provides a good first approximation to the dynamics of a range of infections. Several recent papers cited in the references have started incorporating economic trade-offs and conducting optimal policy analysis within this framework for a country like South Africa targeting in formulating proper public policy response needs to take into account the following:

First, demographically, different groups typically have different risks of infection and mortality implying specific health risks and aggregate costs of treatment differentiated for each group.

Furthermore, each group might interact with other groups at rates that are variable. This fits the description of what Easley and Kleinberg (2010) call a "network version"—in this case, a "network version" of the basic SIR model. Such network differentiation among subgroups of South African population will necessitate treating different demographic subgroups appropriately giving appropriate consideration to relevant differentiating factors at play within each subgroup.

Secondly, the interactive term in SIR model which renders the relevant differential equation (see below) nonlinear may vary among subgroups. Finally, the parameters of contact and infection may not necessarily be constants. They may vary because of endogenous behavioural changes of individuals or because community norms vary from one subgroup to another.

The third point may be too difficult to assess in a country like South Africa, but the first two points may be addressed in a multi-risk version of the basic SIR model proposed by Acemoglu et al. (2020).

As a starting point for South Africa, we could focus following Acemoglu et al. (2020) on the special case of the MR-SIR model consisting of three groups: young (20–44), middle-aged (45–65) and old (65+). Like them we could also consider initially the lockdown policies that took place during the pandemic, that is, consider the special case where the only differences in interactions between the three groups come from differential parameters faced by them. To simplify a bit more initially, the simple epidemiological model can be used to analyse what might be called "zone-based social distancing" (ZSD). Here too we have to be sensitive to indigenous knowledge base and emphasize culturally sensitive social distancing that can enhance social learning. Therefore, we expand the notion of ZSD to socially learned ZSD or SLZSD. The SLZSD can offer a framework for estimating the efficacy of alternative social distancing measures. For this purpose, we can develop a simple SIR epidemic model on a structured network, for which it is possible to compute the inter-zonal reproduction number that can be used to guide further empirical analysis and decision making.

By doing the above exercise on the basis of rather incomplete and imprecise data for South Africa in this area, we can nevertheless derive results that are highly suggestive. Our model suggests that there are advantages of organizing people into zones (i.e., a particular structure of groups) according to demographic characteristics and geographic locations. Therefore, it is possible to arrive at zonal demographic lockdown policies.

The Multi-Risk SIR model can be set in both discrete and continuous time. The latter permits the standard differential equation approach. For the most general scenario, individuals can be partitioned into risk groups j = 1, … , J with Nj initial members. The total population is normalized to unity so that sum over all groups equals 1.

At any point in time t, individuals in group j can be subdivided into those susceptible (S), those infected (I), those recovered (R) and those deceased (D), so that:

$$Sj(t)+Ij(t)+Rj(t)+Dj(t)=Nj$$

Agents move from susceptible to infected, then either recover or die. The states—in temporal order—are

St = Susceptible
It = Infectious
Rt = Resolving
Dt = Dead
Ct = Recovered based on a number of factors including IK-based SLZSD

Any susceptible person might fall prey to the disease by coming into contact with an infectious person. Therefore, the model needs a time-varying contact rate parameter. It varies over time to capture behavioural changes such as social distancing. In the SEIR model four differential equations can be solved with specified initial conditions and parameter values. However, to get the correct statistically defensible estimates of key numbers such as the number infected and the number recovered, we need large-scale randomized testing and detection. That does not seem to have been the case in South Africa. Thus, there is a "calibration gap" in the model for such countries. In South Africa we need the best estimates we can get and then solve the differential equations to estimate the optimal lockdown, social distancing and zonal compartmentalization along with demographic partitioning. Although some attempts have already been made to build these models, better testing will facilitate accurate results.

While this important work is undertaken, we need nevertheless to find approximately optimal fiscal and monetary targeting in a multisectoral setting with differentially located labour and household groups. This is what I do in the main body of this chapter.

5.4 Results and Interpretations

For the purposes of this chapter, the multipliers for South Africa are taken at 1.5 and 2, the first being close to the figure determined through the inclusion of direct, indirect effect, induced household consumption effects while the second is closer to the estimate including the induced investment effects (Burrows and Botha 2013; Picek and Schröder 2018; Sibeko and Isaacs 2020). This suggests that a stimulus of R500 billion will lead to R750 billion in growth (assuming a multiplier of 1.5), and R1 trillion in growth (assuming a multiplier of 2). Being a more conservative estimate, the former is more likely and is poised to get back economic growth to 3.8% if enacted properly. Similarly, if the country-wide employment effects are to be held at 6.1, this package could lead to the creation of over 3 million jobs (Sibeko and Isaacs 2020). So while another stimulus package was not necessary immediate, it may be necessary to augment the current one to alleviate the increased levels of poverty resulting from the long-term effects of this crisis. This is the ongoing challenge in the broader context of South African development in the 2025–2040 period.

Table 5.3 presents the SAM-based calculations of direct and indirect effects of injection of funds into the top 10 value-added sectors in the

South African economy on the 14 different household groups classified according fourteen different income groups. Due to the unavailability of data, gender, race and location data could not be added to this, but could have presented vital insights on the disparities present.

Scrutinizing Table 5.3, we can see that in addition to the public sector which is the most prominent, there are other sectors that also contribute significantly in terms of total value added going to the various households including the poor households. If we follow the first row of the table which gives the sectoral value added for the top 10 sectors as a percentage of GDP, we can see that other sectors such as the informal sector (specifically in household sector), land transport, real estate, wholesale trade and construction are also large sectors and some are quite important in generating employment and incomes, especially for impoverished households in the lower-income deciles.

Industrial energy consumption data suggest that COVID-19 particularly hit industries like mining, manufacturing and construction very hard, with energy consumption falling by over 50% in these sectors (Norland 2020). These are also sectors primarily employing low-skilled workers, earning low wages in the lower- and medium-income deciles. Overall, earnings for lower educated workers did fall by 40% (compared to 30% for skilled labour) which made the former groups more vulnerable and susceptible to food insecurity (Arndt et al. 2020a, b; Karl Pauw 2020). For future policies for development, when contextualized against the fact that more women and black Africans are likely to be employed in lower-skilled jobs, it is not surprising that more female-headed and black households are likely to fall below the poverty line than their male and white counterparts. This also has additional implications for increased gender and race-based inequality on top of the rise in expected income inequality as measured by the Gini coefficient.

However, it is also important to note that in the post-COVID period now, those in the middle-income deciles are less likely to receive government transfers while also being vulnerable to income loss. Unlike wealthier households, those in the middle-income deciles are more likely to be employed in lower educated jobs, but less cushioned during a crisis than lower-income deciles due to not having access to government transfers at the same rate. It is important for cash transfer programmes to acknowledge recent loss of income in these income groups or in the long run far more families may be pushed down to poverty.

Table 5.3 Multipliers for 14 different household groups for the top 10 value-added sectors (in million rands)

	Government	*Informal sector, households*	*Land transport*	*Real estate*	*Wholesale trade*	*Financial intermediation*	*Retail trade*	*Mining*	*Business activities*	*Construction*
Sectoral VA	619,302	301,764	203,225	179,497	174,356	161,420	141,811	127,527	124,240	122,310
Rank	1	2	3	4	5	6	7	8	9	10
GTVA %	17.43%	8.49%	5.72%	5.05%	4.91%	4.54%	3.99%	3.59%	3.50%	3.44%
hhd-0	0.005	0.012	0.004	0.002	0.004	0.003	0.006	0.006	0.004	0.005
hhd-1	0.008	0.018	0.007	0.005	0.007	0.005	0.010	0.009	0.007	0.008
hhd-2	0.011	0.020	0.010	0.007	0.010	0.008	0.013	0.011	0.009	0.009
hhd-3	0.016	0.025	0.013	0.009	0.013	0.011	0.017	0.015	0.013	0.012
hhd-4	0.022	0.030	0.018	0.013	0.018	0.017	0.022	0.019	0.018	0.016
hhd-5	0.037	0.043	0.028	0.021	0.028	0.029	0.035	0.030	0.029	0.025
hhd-6	0.055	0.050	0.038	0.030	0.040	0.045	0.047	0.041	0.042	0.034
hhd-7	0.095	0.072	0.059	0.048	0.065	0.078	0.074	0.064	0.070	0.053
hhd-8	0.203	0.111	0.105	0.091	0.127	0.170	0.135	0.119	0.142	0.096
hhd-91	0.055	0.030	0.030	0.027	0.035	0.048	0.037	0.033	0.039	0.026
hhd-92	0.060	0.030	0.031	0.027	0.037	0.051	0.039	0.034	0.042	0.028
hhd-93	0.087	0.043	0.043	0.040	0.054	0.075	0.054	0.049	0.060	0.039
hhd-94	0.106	0.043	0.046	0.043	0.061	0.089	0.060	0.054	0.071	0.043
hhd-95	0.172	0.073	0.081	0.078	0.104	0.151	0.101	0.092	0.118	0.073

Source: Author's calculation based on 2015 South Africa SAM

There are other steps the government has taken all of which need to be channelled efficiently. There are issues regarding financing efficiently these and other expenditures that do not necessarily require austerity. The approach to public finance in difficult times discussed in the context of Global Financial Crises (Khan 2004b, 2011, White&Case 2020) prefigures what Krugman (2013) and others have suggested more recently. In times of crisis such as the present one, out-of-the-box anti-austerity financing is the needed strategy for the next decade.

Here are tables representing the impact on employment that would result from a 10 million rand injection in the top 10 value-added sectors. The results have been differentiated by education level closer analysis and using standard wages for the industry. It appears that the informal sector (specifically in household sector), land transport and real estate sectors will see the most job growth upon this injection. A lot of the jobs created will be in sectors that employ lower educated workers; targeted aid could not only sustain these industries but also low-skilled worker who are most at risk.

5.5 Further Observations and Evaluation of the Programmes: Implications for a Strategy of Pro-poor Development in Africa

There are non-export sectors such as construction and transportation sectors shown in Table 5.4 and others in the subsequent tables in the text that make a large contribution to GDP and employment. In fact, through the input-output table and SAM, we can identify and derive a larger list of sectors which should receive government support. If gender, race and location-specific data were available, adjustments could be made to improve disparities in those areas as well.

We now separate out the different worker situations for the top 10 sectors in our attempt to look closely at the component of household income coming from labour (Table 5.5). Here we can see that food manufacturing is the sector that comes out on top from this angle. However, machinery, chemical products, fabricated metals and production of motor vehicle parts are also significant. Thus, the package for increasing aggregate demand through aid to various sectors will need to include these sectors as strategic also.

Table 5.4 Employment outcomes in skilled and unskilled sector for 10 million rand injection (using standard industry wages)

	Government	*Informal sector, households*	*Land transport*	*Real estate*	*Wholesale trade*	*Financial intermediation*	*Retail trade*	*Mining*	*Business activities*	*Construction*
Rank %	**1**	**2**	**3**	**4**	**5**	**6**	7	**8**	**9**	**10**
% GTVA	**17.43%**	**8.49%**	**5.72%**	**5.05%**	**4.91%**	**4.54%**	**3.99%**	**3.59%**	**3.50%**	**3.44%**
No. of extra Labour w/ primary	5.97	55.68	39.58	37.79	1.78	22.70	1.69	2.30	23.56	16.08
No. of extra labour w/ middle	6.52	55.40	35.34	40.35	1.77	23.94	1.71	2.23	23.96	15.78
No. of extra labour w/ secondary	6.96	52.91	25.38	41.31	1.66	24.58	1.64	2.05	23.71	14.17
No. of extra labour w/ tertiary	6.95	48.13	13.97	39.96	1.48	23.86	1.51	1.78	22.64	11.73

Source: Author's calculation based on 2015 South Africa SAM

Table 5.5 Multipliers for top 10 VA in manufacturing sector for different labour levels

Commodity	*Sectoral value added*	*Rank of % of GTVA*	*% of GTVA*	*Multiplier for labour w/ primary ed.*	*Multiplier for labour w/ middle ed.*	*Multiplier for labour w/ secondary ed.*	*Multiplier for labour w/ tertiary*
Food	88,002	1	2.48%	0.015	0.035	0.090	0.286
Machinery	31,420	2	0.88%	0.017	0.043	0.104	0.284
Other chemical products	27,789	3	0.78%	0.015	0.038	0.104	0.284
Fabricated metals	26,551	4	0.75%	0.030	0.079	0.156	0.243
Motor vehicle parts	25,367	5	0.71%	0.013	0.032	0.078	0.209
Basic chemicals, nuclear	21,963	6	0.62%	0.030	0.079	0.156	0.243
Misc. manufacturing	20,228	7	0.57%	0.014	0.031	0.079	0.148
Paper	18,843	8	0.53%	0.021	0.039	0.084	0.219
Plastic	12,626	9	0.36%	0.017	0.085	0.195	0.272
Computer-related activities	7739	10	0.22%	0.013	0.026	0.081	0.360

Source: Author's calculation based on 2015 South Africa SAM

We now turn to Table 5.6 which gives a picture of employment in the top 10 manufacturing sectors by looking at unskilled and skilled labour situation separately. It is important to highlight that these sectors create not only high-skilled jobs, but also a significant amount of medium- and low-skilled jobs as well which would not only create employment opportunities, but specifically create jobs with better wages.

Below are some of the tables for the multipliers in the health sector and the construction sectors, both of which have received significant investments in this stimulus in order to improve public health infrastructure, overall infrastructure and jobs in the economy. This was a particularly needed investment and will have long-run effects in creating high-paying jobs and improving human capabilities overall. This is also one of the scenarios where the integration of indigenous productive activities could have

Table 5.6 Employment in top 10 VA in manufacturing sector for different labour sectors

Commodity	*Sectoral value added*	*Rank of % of GTVA*	*% of GTVA*	*Lab. prim./ GTVA per cent*	*Lab. mid. / GTVA per cent*	*Lab. sec./ GTVA per cent*	*Lab. tert. /GTVA per cent*	*Lab. prim./ VA per cent*	*Lab. mid. / VA per cent*	*Lab. sec./ VA per cent*	*Lab. tert. /VA per cent*
Food	88,002	1	2.48%	0.06%	0.16%	0.37%	0.69%	2.45%	6.36%	14.99%	27.97%
machinery	31,420	2	0.88%	0.01%	0.05%	0.14%	0.44%	1.68%	5.59%	15.89%	49.82%
Other chemical products	27,789	3	0.78%	0.00%	0.05%	0.17%	0.20%	0.16%	7.40%	26.82%	32.71%
Fabricated metals	26,551	4	0.75%	0.04%	0.13%	0.25%	0.27%	5.67%	17.35%	33.07%	36.73%
Motor vehicle parts	25,367	5	0.71%	0.01%	0.05%	0.15%	0.50%	1.84%	6.78%	20.44%	69.55%
Basic chemicals, nuclear	21,963	6	0.62%	0.00%	0.05%	0.17%	0.20%	0.16%	7.40%	26.82%	32.71%
Misc. manufacturing	20,228	7	0.57%	0.01%	0.02%	0.05%	0.07%	1.06%	3.16%	8.92%	12.29%
Paper	18,843	8	0.53%	0.01%	0.03%	0.07%	0.20%	1.07%	5.27%	12.32%	37.56%
Plastic	12,626	9	0.36%	0.01%	0.06%	0.13%	0.14%	1.82%	17.14%	37.86%	39.93%
Computer-related activities	7739	10	0.22%	0.00%	0.00%	0.02%	0.18%	0.44%	1.22%	9.39%	84.68%

Source: Author's calculation based on 2015 South Africa SAM

Table 5.7 Multipliers for workers in health and related service sectors

	Health and social work	*Insurance and pension*	*Medical appliances*
Labour w/ primary	0.015	0.016	0.002
Labour w/ middle	0.031	0.024	0.005
Labour w/ secondary	0.087	0.120	0.015
Labour w/ tertiary	0.327	0.398	0.043

Source: Author's calculation based on 2015 South Africa SAM

Table 5.8 Multipliers for workers in construction and related sectors from SAM-based calculations

	Construction	*Construction, Related Services*
Labour w/ primary	0.026	0.046
Labour w/ middle	0.047	0.068
Labour w/ secondary	0.095	0.096
Labour w/ tertiary	0.188	0.167

Source: Author's calculation based on 2015 South Africa SAM

allowed the integration of indigenous healing, medicinal and educational practices, much of which has a lot of value in public health beyond preserving cultural practices. These investments could have not only wide-reaching effects on the indigenous populations but disparity-reducing effects on the greater population at hand. Tables 5.7 and 5.8 show multipliers for workers in health and related sectors and multipliers for workers in construction and related sectors, respectively.

The multipliers for the sectors broadly related to the agriculture sector are presented below (Table 5.9). It is important to continue investment into these sectors due to the large amount of job opportunities it creates for lower-skilled and lower-income populations. Though the data is not present, it is important to highlight that a lot of the agricultural.

Work and production is undertaken by black and indigenous workers. It is important for the government to not only pay attention to other productive activities undertaken by indigenous groups but also ensure that certain indigenous practices are sustained through this support. These actions are necessary to alleviate marginalized groups from poverty and reduce inequality, particularly in these times when they are more susceptible to vulnerabilities and insecurities.

Finally, a more expansive look at the top 20 value-added sectors is presented next in order to highlight some more sectors which could benefit from the economic stimulus (Table 5.10). This table also allows us to recognize the sectors that would in particular benefit the poorest and the most vulnerable of the population, especially those who might have the least amount of transferable skills. This could allow policy makers to focus on sectors like agriculture and mining which see some of the poorest populations in them while also recognizing sectors which might bring in more jobs for lower-skilled people like the informal sector (specifically in household sector), agriculture and retail trade.

We acknowledge that the government of South Africa credibly announced a plan with strategic programmes to be implemented in immediate, short-term and long-term span, during and after the pandemic. In the post-pandemic period from 2025 to 2040, the positive aspects of these plans need to be followed up consistently. The four major strategies the government adopted in this regard during and after the pandemic are as follows (KPMG 2020):

I. Focusing on keeping small and medium-run enterprises running through debt relief programmes, especially providing finances and capital to local producers of essential goods. This has also been supplemented with delayed tax programmes to aid such businesses. From the analysis of SAM 2015, we can see that retail, wholesale trade and business activities account for a large proportion of the value added to the economy. It is thus useful to prioritize the resources needed to sustain these sectors during this crisis.
II. The government also began programmes to reduce youth unemployment numbers by providing cash transfers to employers financially affected by COVID-19, who continue to employ a certain number of employees at certain wage levels. In addition to encouraging employment, the government has also expanded its unemployment insurance programmes in light of this pandemic, and the resulting rise in job loss.
III. Creating and investing in the National Empowerment Fund to specifically make loans available to black entrepreneurs and manufacturers to help grant access to resources to the most vulnerable populations and help reduce racial inequality exacerbated by the pandemic.

Table 5.9 Multipliers for related agricultural sectors for labour at different education levels and lower income household groups

	Agriculture	*Forestry*	*Fishing*	*Meat*	*Fish*	*Vegetable*	*Fruit and nuts*	*Dairy products*	*Grain mill products*	*Starches products*	*Animal feeding products*
Labour w/ primary	0.037	0.071	0.046	0.020	0.019	0.018	0.021	0.015	0.015	0.019	0.012
Labour w/ middle	0.043	0.051	0.048	0.034	0.032	0.029	0.036	0.027	0.027	0.034	0.022
Labour w/ secondary	0.069	0.074	0.136	0.068	0.062	0.055	0.074	0.058	0.058	0.075	0.047
labour w/ tertiary	0.157	0.159	0.170	0.136	0.124	0.109	0.152	0.120	0.122	0.156	0.099
hhd-0	0.006	0.009	0.007	0.004	0.003	0.003	0.004	0.003	0.003	0.004	0.002
hhd-1	0.009	0.013	0.011	0.006	0.005	0.005	0.006	0.004	0.004	0.006	0.004
hhd-2	0.010	0.014	0.014	0.007	0.007	0.006	0.007	0.006	0.006	0.007	0.005
hhd-3	0.013	0.017	0.018	0.009	0.009	0.008	0.010	0.007	0.008	0.010	0.006

Source: Author's calculation based on 2015 South Africa SAM

Table 5.10 SAM-based multipliers for top 20 VA sectors for output, labour and 14 HH groups

	Government	*Informal sector, households*	*Land transport*	*Real estate*	*Wholesale trade*	*Financial intermediation*	*Retail trade*	*Mining*	*Business activities*	*Construction*
Sectoral VA	619,302	301,764	203,225	179,497	174,356	161,420	141,811	127,527	124,240	122,310
Rank %	**1**	**2**	**3**	**4**	**5**	**6**	7	**8**	**9**	**10**
%GTVA	17.43%	8.49%	5.72%	5.05%	4.91%	4.54%	3.99%	3.59%	3.50%	3.44%
Labour w/ primary	0.024	0.081	0.021	0.011	0.021	0.012	0.030	0.033	0.019	0.026
Labour w/ middle	0.047	0.102	0.046	0.018	0.044	0.017	0.064	0.049	0.041	0.047
Labour w/ secondary	0.201	0.099	0.095	0.055	0.113	0.130	0.143	0.115	0.133	0.096
Labour w/ tertiary	0.570	0.133	0.177	0.160	0.288	0.456	0.258	0.236	0.355	0.189
hhd-0	0.005	0.012	0.004	0.002	0.004	0.003	0.006	0.006	0.004	0.005
hhd-1	0.008	0.018	0.007	0.005	0.007	0.005	0.010	0.009	0.007	0.008
hhd-2	0.011	0.020	0.010	0.007	0.010	0.008	0.013	0.011	0.009	0.009
hhd-3	0.016	0.025	0.013	0.009	0.013	0.011	0.017	0.015	0.013	0.012
hhd-4	0.022	0.030	0.018	0.013	0.018	0.017	0.022	0.019	0.018	0.016
hhd-5	0.037	0.043	0.028	0.021	0.028	0.029	0.035	0.030	0.029	0.025
hhd-6	0.055	0.050	0.038	0.030	0.040	0.045	0.047	0.041	0.042	0.034
hhd-7	0.095	0.072	0.059	0.048	0.065	0.078	0.074	0.064	0.070	0.053
hhd-8	0.203	0.111	0.105	0.091	0.127	0.170	0.135	0.119	0.142	0.096
hhd-91	0.055	0.030	0.030	0.027	0.035	0.048	0.037	0.033	0.039	0.026

hhd-92	0.060	0.030	0.031	0.027	0.037	0.051	0.039	0.034	0.042	0.028
hhd-93	0.087	0.043	0.043	0.040	0.054	0.075	0.054	0.049	0.060	0.039
hhd-94	0.106	0.043	0.046	0.043	0.061	0.089	0.060	0.054	0.071	0.043
hhd-95	0.172	0.073	0.081	0.078	0.104	0.151	0.101	0.092	0.118	0.073

	Electricity, gas, power	*Activities to financial intermediation*	*Food*	*Insurance and pension funding*	*Sale of motor vehicles*	*Agriculture*	*Health and social work*	*Post and telecom*	*Coal mining*	*Other mining*
Sectoral VA	107,583	98,016	95,649	88,002	80,489	76,754	71,773	69,424	67,562	66,042
Rank %	**11**	**12**	**13**	**14**	**15**	**16**	**17**	**18**	**19**	**20**
%GTVA	3.03%	2.76%	2.69%	2.48%	2.27%	2.16%	2.02%	1.95%	1.90%	1.86%
Labour w/ primary	0.012	0.008	0.025	0.016	0.025	0.037	0.015	0.011	0.021	0.015
Labour w/ middle	0.019	0.014	0.045	0.024	0.059	0.043	0.031	0.026	0.034	0.035
Labour w/ secondary	0.058	0.256	0.098	0.120	0.158	0.069	0.087	0.074	0.093	0.090
Labour w/ tertiary	0.254	0.445	0.205	0.398	0.280	0.157	0.327	0.251	0.226	0.286
hhd-0	0.003	0.002	0.005	0.003	0.005	0.006	0.003	0.003	0.004	0.003
hhd-1	0.005	0.006	0.007	0.006	0.009	0.009	0.006	0.005	0.007	0.006
hhd-2	0.007	0.010	0.009	0.009	0.012	0.010	0.008	0.006	0.009	0.008
hhd-3	0.010	0.015	0.013	0.012	0.017	0.013	0.010	0.009	0.013	0.012
hhd-4	0.014	0.021	0.017	0.017	0.022	0.017	0.014	0.012	0.017	0.016
hhd-5	0.022	0.037	0.026	0.029	0.035	0.025	0.024	0.020	0.027	0.026

(*continued*)

Table 5.10 (continued)

	Electricity, gas, power	*Activities to financial intermediation*	*Food*	*Insurance and pension funding*	*Sale of motor vehicles*	*Agriculture*	*Health and social work*	*Post and telecom*	*Coal mining*	*Other mining*
hhd-6	0.033	0.059	0.035	0.044	0.049	0.033	0.034	0.030	0.039	0.037
hhd-7	0.056	0.095	0.056	0.075	0.077	0.050	0.059	0.050	0.062	0.062
hhd-8	0.114	0.195	0.103	0.158	0.142	0.089	0.125	0.103	0.117	0.123
hhd-91	0.034	0.053	0.028	0.045	0.039	0.025	0.035	0.029	0.033	0.035
hhd-92	0.034	0.057	0.030	0.047	0.041	0.026	0.037	0.031	0.034	0.037
hhd-93	0.051	0.081	0.042	0.069	0.057	0.037	0.055	0.045	0.050	0.053
hhd-94	0.057	0.094	0.047	0.081	0.064	0.040	0.065	0.052	0.055	0.061
hhd-95	0.102	0.155	0.080	0.138	0.108	0.069	0.109	0.089	0.095	0.105

Source: Author's calculation based on 2015 South Africa SAM

IV. Dedicate funds towards infrastructure development, particularly for renewable energy and remote learning needs to meet the immediate and long-run demands of South African development while also creating employment opportunities.

While specificity is required within each of the categories, the government's declared policy support measures in dealing with the economic fallout of COVID-19 certainly deserve appreciation. The support analysed above includes working capital loan fund for manufacturing and service industries, renewable energy fund, infrastructure growth fund, working capital support for cottage, micro, small and medium enterprises and safety net expansion. However, the upshot of our quantitative estimates based on the SAM-2015, and labour force survey, indicates that while this package is sufficient in the short run (based on strategic allocation of the aid for maximum countervailing impact), there needs to be a second stimulus package once the impact of the crisis and the first stimulus is assessed. It is highly likely that the poverty and inequality exacerbated by the crisis is unlikely to be fully addressed by the amount within this stimulus, as many within the middle-income deciles are susceptible to becoming poorer in the long-run. Thus, an additional quantum of aid package will be needed for both social safety net protection and achieving a reasonable rate of economic growth after the first two quarters of the COVID-19 external shock. Based on earlier work done by Khan (1999) and other literature on IK, we can reasonably conclude that including trading based on IK in addition to the standard public health procedures will improve the effectiveness of the aid package by 10–20%.

5.6 Summary, Policy Recommendations and Conclusions

The analysis done in this chapter demonstrates the crucial salience of thinking about pandemics, similar challenges and development, intersectionally from a SEICA perspective, in a world that has now become rather vulnerable to such shocks. The following conclusions and recommendations for South Africa also hold lessons for other African and developing nations, not only during but after the COVID-19 pandemic. Thus follow-up development strategy will continue to protect the vulnerable groups in particular.

- Aid going towards buying PPE and other medical equipment, and for adequate testing, during health crisis such as COVID-19 should be given to the affected areas first while a reserve fund should be maintained for future affected areas or for those areas where there will be an intensification of the infection, sickness and mortalities and future emergencies from 2025 to 2040 at least. The amount and proportions should be up to the discretion of expert advisor groups of public health professionals and including social scientists who have studied public health issues.
- Certain areas may be more prone to experiencing the most acute food shortages especially during an epidemic, pandemic or widespread crisis than others. Quick identification of the poor families in these areas and effective delivery of cash transfers and food aid will be the key required actions. While there will inevitably be some leakage, its scope should be minimized by working with reliable government officials, volunteers and local people who have a reputation for being reliable. Headcount indexes and other methods may be implemented to identify key areas to prioritize for aid in countries for strategic utilization of limited resources.
- There are advantages in combining industrial location data with data for hotspots of economic and social vulnerabilities. Aid needs to be rushed and kept flowing in an appropriate amount with constant feedback through monitoring. It is important to be attentive to such trends and contexts in data to better administer stimuluses to areas that will not only help the most amount of people during the crisis but will also yield the most short- and long-run growth for the most labour-intensive sectors.
- The relief packages (such as food aid, cash transfers, building houses for homeless) may be reasonable steps if the amount allocated is adequate. The SAM-based multipliers derived through this exercise confirm that all of these measures can have immediate and long-term impacts if implemented immediately with some degree of effectiveness. The objective should be to minimize leakage and deliver aid to the targeted groups immediately in the country concerned. An emphasis should be given to cash transfer programmes implemented while upholding the social distancing rules, with the beneficiaries receiving their allowances in either mobile financial system accounts or locations where social distance guidelines can be maintained. If such cash transfer systems are not present, then

resources should be directed towards the creation of such programmes. It is imperative for African and other developing countries to evaluate the effectiveness of relief packages, even if it is a modelled quantitative estimate, to properly examine what sectors need attention and to what degree it will need to generate positive demand-side effects.

The SAM-based calculations identify the direct and indirect effects of injection of funds into the top 10 value-added sectors in the case of the South African economy on 14 different household groups. These groups include households at various levels of income. The results indicate that the government and informal, household sectors are certainly important, but in addition to these sectors on which most commentators have focused on so far, there are other sectors that are important as well. Other service sectors such as retail and wholesale trade, land transport, housing and infrastructure construction and mining are also large sectors. These are quite important in generating employment and incomes, especially for impoverished households such as small farmers and day labourers. These sectors deserve support as well. As mentioned earlier, the strategy is to ultimately lead into long-run development plans and thus the focus should remain on revitalizing the largest sectors of the economy to restart growth with equity.

The SAM-based calculations also identified the direct and indirect effects of injection of funds into the top 10 value added sectors in the South African economy on overall employment, and on employment of skilled and unskilled workers differentiated by education level. Additional information from Labour Force Survey is used to supplement the SAM-based data. Here are a few interesting insights based on analysing that combined data set:

- The public sector continues to be the largest in terms of sectoral value added, followed by the informal sector (specifically in household sector), land transport, real estate, wholesale and retail trade. However, when the multipliers are examined in terms of household income, it can specifically be seen that the households with lower incomes are most likely to benefit from money going into the informal sector (specifically in household sector), retail trade, mining and construction. It is also important to note that more people are likely to be pushed into the informal sector as a result of this pandemic. In order to counter this, a strategy of formalizing the rights for well-being, that is, capabilities enhancement, is an urgent necessity that must go on over the next decade and longer if need be.

- In terms of job growth, upon an injection of funds, the most growth in opportunities can be seen in the informal sector (specifically in household sector), land transport and business activities sector when wages are taken into account. It should also be noted that job growth is relatively similar for people of all education levels except tertiary level education, where less opportunities are created as expected due to the higher need for qualifications. For the informal sector in particular, the previous point regarding capabilities enhancement must be implemented over the next decade or even longer.
- The largest value-added sectors in the manufacturing industries are food, machinery, chemical product and fabricated metals production. Labour with tertiary and secondary education is more likely to see higher yield when these sectors are invested in comparison to labour with lower academic qualifications.

In this chapter, I have emphasized the importance of integrating indigenous knowledge during crises like the COVID-19 debacle or other large-scale global crisis with similar impacts to build inclusive, sustainable and socially aware development plans for the future. For too long, vital traditional knowledge has been ignored, especially when it comes to finding and employing solutions for indigenous lands. The merits of modern science and technology cannot be denied, but at the same time, it is important to acknowledge that it is only through the unity and integration of both types of knowledge that we can form sustainable solutions in all spheres of policy making, be it health, education or economic growth.[8] In the methodology section, I specifically highlighted how current models in multisectoral analysis and public health evaluations could benefit from the integration of indigenous sectors, notably with concepts like the IKI-SAM and the SLZSD. It is through such integrations that little by little, indigenous knowledge can become commonplace in academia and policy-making forums.

[8] In reference to personal communication to author by Dr Mammo Muchie. December 7, 2020.

This chapter with a detailed empirical study highlights the *Socially Embedded Capabilities* perspective for addressing economic and social crisis in Africa with wide-ranging impact. It also emphasizes that while short-term small fiscal stimuli are necessary, middle-income and lower-income African countries in particular need to approach future crisis-fighting policies by both offsetting immediate instabilities and stimulating long-run equitable growth with justice for all. Such an intertemporally consistent approach will ensure that the limited resources are being strategically used to fulfil overall development goals. Our chapter also underlines how important it is to gear resources towards building healthcare infrastructure and investing in public health resources—not just in a temporary manner during the crisis period, but also as a part of a long-term investment programme towards the country's human capital formation. Such a strategy will create a reliable healthcare system for everyone, capable of tackling future crises in Africa. Thus, a case for equitable African development strategies can be made.

References

Acemoglu, D., Chernozhukov, V., Werning, I & Whinston. M. D. (2020). A Multi-risk SIR Model with Optimally Targeted Lockdown. *NBER*, Working Paper 27102. http://www.nber.org/papers/w27102

Annika C. Dahlberg, & Sophie B. Trygger. (2009). Indigenous Medicine and Primary Health Care: The Importance of Lay Knowledge and Use of Medicinal Plants in Rural South Africa. Human Ecology: An Interdisciplinary Journal, 37(1), 79–94.

Arndt, C., R. Davies, S. Gabriel, L. Harris, K. Makrelov, S. Robinson, S. Levy, W. Simbanegavi, D. van Saventer, L. Anderson. (2020a). Covid-19 Lockdowns, income distribution, and food security: An Analysis for South Africa. *Global Food Security*, 26. https://reader.elsevier.com/reader/sd/pii/S221191242030064X?token=31258257B00AAD77624CD73B4F2A95D0E4F06BA053D7ED137188E7B62F94AFC2420E71D5A915FD27EB5075D7CBBC7494

Arndt, C., R. Davies, S. Gabriel, L. Harris, K. Makrelov, B. Modise, S. Robinson, W. Simbanegavi, D. van Saventer, L. Anderson. (2020b). Impact of Covid-19 on the South African Economy. *SA-TIED* Working Paper, UNU-WIDER. https://sa-tied.wider.unu.edu/sites/default/files/pdf/SA-TIED-WP-111.pdf

Atkeson, A. (2020a). How Deadly Is COVID-19? Understanding The Difficulties With Estimation Of Its Fatality Rate. *National Bureau of Economic Research*, Working Paper 26965.

———. (2020b). What Will Be the Economic Impact of COVID-19 in the US? Rough Estimates of Disease Scenarios", *National Bureau of Economic Research*, Working Paper 26867

Botha, L. R. (2010). Indigenous knowledge as culturally-centred education in South Africa. Africa Education Review, 7(1), 34–50.

Bhorat, H. and Tim Köhler. (2020). Lockdown Economics in South Africa: Social Assistance and the Ramaphosa Stimulus Package. Africa in Focus. *Brookings Institute.* https://www.brookings.edu/blog/africa-in-focus/2020/11/20/lockdown-economics-in-south-africa-social-assistance-and-the-ramaphosa-stimulus-package/

Burrows, L.R. & Botha, A.P. (2013). Explaining the changing input-output multipliers in South African: 1980–2010. http://www.essa2013.org.za/fullpaper/essa2013_2636.pdf

Department of Statistics. (2020). Quarterly Employment Statistics. Economic Data, Department of Statistics, South Africa.http://www.statssa.gov.za/?page_id=1854&PPN=P0277&SCH=7898

Cocks, Michelle L, Alexander, Jamie, & Dold, Tony. (2012). Inkcubeko Nendalo: A Bio-cultural Diversity Schools Education Project in South Africa and its Implications for Inclusive Indigenous Knowledge Systems (IKS) Sustainability. Journal of Education for Sustainable Development, 6(2), 241–252.

Easley, D. and Kleinberg, J. (2010). *Networks, Crowds and Markets: Reasoning About a Highly Connected World.* (Cambridge: Cambridge University Press)

Garba, S. M., Lubuma, J. M. S., Tsanou, B. (2020). Modelling the transmission dynamics of the Covid-19 Pandemic on South Africa. Elsevier Public Health Emergency List. https://www.ncbi.nlm.nih.gov/pmc/articles/PMC7402282/

Green, L. J. (2012). Beyond South Africa's 'Indigenous Knowledge – Science' Wars. South African Journal of Science, 108(7/8), 1.

International Monetary Fund. (2020). The Great Lockdown. *World Economic Outlook 2020.* April, 2020. https://www.imf.org/en/Publications/WEO/Issues/2020/04/14/weo-april-2020

Khan, H.A. (2021a). Human Capabilities in Complex Global System and Financial Governance: A Theory with Application to the BRICS. in P. Anand et al. eds. *BRICS Handbook* (Oxford University Press: Oxford)

———. (2021b). A Sustainable Development Strategy for Bangladesh in the Post-COVID 19 Era: A Socially Embedded Intersectional Capabilities Perspective. *Journal of Bangladesh Studies.* January/February. Vol.22, No. 2:1–14.

———. (2020a). "On Socially Embedded Intersectional Capabilities Theory (SEICT)—An Example from the Philippines" In H. A. Khan, *Women's Socially Embedded Capabilities and Development: A Theory-based Empirical Investigation of Some ASEAN Countries*, Background paper for the Cambridge University Project on Human Development in ASEAN, 2020.

———. (2020b). Economic Impact of COVID-19 On Bangladesh: Agenda for Immediate Action and Planning for the Future, EconPapers, https://econpapers.repec.org/paper/pramprapa/100380.htm (last visited on Dec.6, 2020)

Khan, H.A. and Joshua Villanueva (2020). Women's Socially Embedded Intersectional Capabilities and Development: A Theory of Inclusive Development Applied to the Philippines, Working paper, JKSIS, University of Denver

Khan, H.A. and Shamayeta Rahman (2020a). Women's Socially Embedded Intersectional Capabilities and Development: A Theory-based Empirical Investigation in the ASEAN economies, Working Paper, JKSIS, University of Denver.

Khan, H.A. and Shamayeta Rahman (2020b). Covid-19 and Development: An Economy Wide Model and Data-based Approach to Impact and Resolutions, Working Paper, JKSIS, University of Denver.

Khan, H.A., M. Mahapatro and K.Morshed (2020). COVID-19 and Gender Justice: How are women faring? Evidence from a statistical analysis of the BRAC Rapid Perception Survey for Bangladesh, Working Paper, JKSIS, University of Denver

Khan, H. A. (2014) Development and Women's Rights as Human Rights: A Political and Social Economy Approach within a Deep Democratic Framework, *Denver Journal of International Law and Policy* Vol. 42, No. 3(Aug. 2014).

——— (2013). Development Strategies: Lessons from the Experiences of South Korea, Malaysia, Thailand and Vietnam. in Augustin K. Fosu ed. *Achieving Development Success* (Oxford University Press: Oxford): 119–132.

———. (2012). Enhancing Economic Integration in the Asia-Pacific through the Strengthening of National Innovation Systems - Challenges and Strategies. *Asia-Pacific Technology Monitor*, March–April

———. (2011). Analyzing the impact on financial crisis on developing countries. Report submitted to the UNDP, NYC.

———. (2010). China's Development Strategy and Energy Security. in Amelia Santos-Paulino and Guanghua Wan ed. *The Rise of China and India: Development Strategies and Lessons*, (Palgrave/Macmillan: New York)

———. (2006).Trade Liberalization and Poverty Reduction in CGE Models: The Dual-Dual Approach in H. Khan and J. Weiss, eds. *Poverty Strategies in Asia*, (E. Elgar: Cheltenham)

———. (2004a). *Innovation and Growth in East Asia: The Future of Miracles.* (Houndsmills and Macmillan/Palgrave: New York)

———. (2004b). *Global Markets and Financial Crisis in Asia: Towards a Theory for the Twenty First Century* (Houndsmills and Macmillan/Palgrave: New York)

———. (1999). Sectoral Growth and Poverty Alleviation: A Multiplier Decomposition Technique Applied to South Africa. *World Development.*

———. (1998) Technology, Development and Democracy, Cheltenham, UK: Edward Elgar.

———. (1997) Technology, Energy and Development: The South Korean Transition Cheltenham, UK: Edward Elgar.

———. and Thorbecke E. (1988) *Macroeconomic Effects and Diffusion of Alternative Technologies Within a Social Accounting Matrix Framework: the Case of Indonesia.* (Gower Publication: CO. Aldershot, U.K.)

Krugman, P. (2013). *End this Depression Now.* (W.W. Norton: New York)

KPMG (2020). *South Africa: Government and Institution Measures in Response to Covid-19.* Insights. https://home.kpmg/xx/en/home/insights/2020/04/south-africa-government-and-institution-measures-in-response-to-covid.html

Mammo, M. (2020). Personal Communication with author. Email. December 7, 2020.

Norland, E. (2020). South Africa: Stimulus, Low Rates Face Challenges. *CME Group.* https://www.cmegroup.com/education/featured-reports/south-africa-stimulus-low-rates-face-challenges.html?source=rss&utm_source=benzinga&utm_medium=feedburner&utm_campaign=distribution&utm_content=BenzingaEconomicResearch

Pauw, K. (2020). Personal Communication with authors. Email. January 4, 2020.

Picek, O. & E. Schröder. (2018). Spillover effects of Germany's final demand on Southern Europe. World Economy. 41, 2216–2242.

Pyatt, G. and E. Thorbecke (1976). *Planning Techniques for a Better Future.* ILO, Geneva.

Pyatt, G., and J.I. Round (1979). Accounting and Fixed-price Multipliers in a Social Accounting Matrix Framework. *The Economic Journal 89:850–73.*

Sibeko, B. and G. Isaacs. (2020). A Fiscal Stimulus for South Africa. Working Paper, *Institute for Economic Justice: Research, Policy and Advocacy.* June, 2020. https://iej.org.za/wp-content/uploads/2020/08/A-fiscal-stimulus-for-South-Africa-Final-IEJ.pdf

UNDP (2020). Socio-Economic Impact of COVID-19 on South Africa. *UNDP Report.* https://www.za.undp.org/content/south_africa/en/home/library/socio-economic-impact-of-covid-19-on-south-africa/

White&Case. (2020). COVID-19: South African Government Financial Assistance Measures: Rescue Measures for South African Businesses to Stay Afloat in Turbulent Waters. *Government Assistance Measures, Coronavirus, EMEA.* https://www.whitecase.com/publications/alert/COVID-19-south-african-government-financial-assistance-measures#:~:text=donations%20made%20to%20a%20COVID,2020%20to%2031%20July%202020.&text=taxpayers%20who%20donate%20to%20the,deduction%20from%20their%20taxable%20income.

CHAPTER 6

Africa as Part of the Global South: A Framework for Building Innovation Systems and Technological Learning in an Unevenly Developing Africa

6.1 Introduction

As noted in the chapter on development strategies for Africa, innovation and technological learning are crucial for future development trajectories. Particularly for capabilities enhancing trajectories, innovation and learning are of crucial strategic salience (Gurib-Fakim and Signe 2022; African Union Commission STISA 2024).[1] Here we look at both techno-institutional aspects and African roots of technological learning. We also emphasize the geoeconomic aspects of African development.

Geoeconomics requires us to think in terms of new and old transportation corridors, international trade and finance, economic development or maldevelopment in a complex unevenly developed world of political economy and great power rivalry. In our complex, uneven world of international competition, technological innovation needs to be reconceptualized as a complex dynamic system with national systems facing imperatives of both competition and cooperation. In this context, regional technical cooperation in Africa becomes a key ingredient of African institution building for innovation systems. From this perspective, Africa presents important case study material for the rest of the twenty-first century as the

[1] For some specific application aspects of digital technologies in particular, see also Adeniran et al. (2023)

K. N. M. Sonko et al., *21st Century African Development Strategies*,
https://doi.org/10.1007/978-3-031-93079-9_6

Fourth Industrial Revolution unfolds. Our approach applied below offers new insights into the geoeconomics of Africa's prospects for building a dynamic innovation system. In addition to presenting an analytical framework for developing strategic policy perspectives for African economies at different stages of development, we conclude with an emphasis on regional collaboration in Africa and global cooperation that will be essential for constructing a coherent people-centred and ecologically sustainable African innovation system.

We should note that earlier the African Union Commission (AUC) had established a Conference of Ministers in charge of Science and Technology (AMCOST). AMCOST was formed in order to enable the Union to periodically deliberate and articulate a collective position on science and technology issues. The first Summit was held in Maputo, Mozambique, in July 2003. Importantly, the Consolidated Plan of Action (CPA) was presented in 2005 as an instrument for the implementation of the decisions of the African Union Assembly of Heads of State and Government on STI and endorsed for immediate implementation in 2006 at the Khartoum Summit of the African Heads of State. However, Africa has fallen short in both specificities of coordination mechanisms and rigorous analysis without which the implementation of a strategic vision is not possible (AUC STISA 2024).

We need to point out that the analysis here does not include the North African Arabic-speaking countries that are included under the UN MENA category. Although these countries and the rest of Africa have many aspects that are similar, the UN MENA category economies have their own histories and diversities which would require an entire book-length treatment. This is beyond the scope of our current endeavour.

In the next section, we deal conceptually with challenges of building an African Innovation System in a complex and uneven world. In Sect. 6.3, we use crucial empirical aspects of African underdevelopment to broadly look at three types of African countries and their specific innovation challenges in the face of the unfolding Fourth Industrial Revolution in other parts of the world. We argue that Africans can learn a lot technologically if some conditions are met through strategic steps as the case of the People's Republic of China (PRC) demonstrates. To emphasize the relevance of the Chinese example, we have added an appendix dealing with China's journey from a low level earlier to be well on its way to participating fully in the Fourth Industrial Revolution in the twenty-first century. The crucial task for Africa is to think creatively and strategically and build appropriate institutions of innovation and technological learning. Here we introduce the key concept of an Augmented National Innovation System (ANIS) for Africa that will take unevenness and inequalities within and among African countries seriously and pose the question of creating an African Innovation System for enhancing African people's capabilities (in the sense that Amartya Sen and others have elaborated on this term) within an ecologically sustainable overall development strategy. Within the concrete empirical context of Africa, we illustrate the key aspects of ANIS building for Africa.

The penultimate Sect. 6.5 presents some ideas for consistent systemic data base creation across Africa. This section argues for starting the work on this level for building a Unified Information and Modelling System for Innovation in Africa. Concretely, ideas for constructing a Social Accounting Matrix (SAM) System-based modelling methodology for constructing an Augmented African Innovation System presented here briefly references to work that have been done already. Section 6.6 summarizes and emphasizes the need for Africa-wide coordinated cooperative efforts along with help from other partners in both the Global North and the Global South. The appendix that follows gives a detailed picture of how China created an NIS starting with a very low base and great unevenness. Therefore, without imitating China mechanically Africa can also learn to do the same by imaginative long-term perspective and collaborative efforts for appropriate institution building.

6.2 Towards Building an African Innovation System: Complex Innovation Systems in an Uneven World

We begin with the observation that even the non-MENA part of the African continent represents close to 20% of the earth's surface and is home to more than one billion people. This part of the world will likely have more than 2 billion people by 2050. It will have a large cadre of young workers. It already has more than 50% of the world's arable lands, large forests, 30% of the world's reserve of minerals. Combined with human resources, Africa is potentially very wealthy. But currently, it produces only 3% of global GDP with less than 3% of international trade (mainly exporting primary commodities and natural resources) and has very low level of human development.[2] One important explanatory factor is the weakness of Africa in research and innovation: Africa accounts for only 1.3% of research spending, and produces 0.1% of all patents. As we elaborate further below, both the financial and real institutional support for innovation remains weak and unevenly developed across Africa.

We recognize that a lack of investment in science and technology has held back Africa's economic transformation at both the structural level (the shift of workers and resources from low- to higher-productivity sectors) and the sectoral level (the growth of productivity within sectors) with far-reaching consequences. For instance, lacking the economic and scientific infrastructure necessary for innovation, Africa has continued to rely on the colonial exploitative model of resource extraction and export. This model is unsustainable and harmful for Africa. This becomes particularly evident when we look at the low and uneven levels of development, particularly human development. The colonial model is contrary to a strategy for enhancing human capabilities in the sense of Sen.[3] Furthermore, this colonial model which benefits a small dependent elite group is largely responsible for Africa's debilitating poverty and aid dependency. These challenges have been compounded by economic fragmentation, as smaller markets constrain the long-term investments and formation of human capital that would foster innovation and drive technology transfer as has happened in East Asia—particularly China (Khan and Thorbecke 1988, 89; Khan 1997, 2023a, b, c).

In contrast to Afro-pessimists, we argue that there is potential here for innovation. But this will require growing recognition by policy makers of the role that science and technology can play in achieving national development goals and transforming Africa by 2050.

Related to this scenario is the larger framework of building Africa as a geoeconomic region to be taken seriously. The accelerated march towards building a geoeconomic region in Africa will require linked innovation systems, transportation corridors, resource exchange and geopolitical

[2] On innovation and human development in Africa, see Azuh et al. (2020). See also Kahn (2022) and Kasongo et al. (2023).

[3] This model has also held back public R&D for crucial capabilities-enhancing technologies such as developing biotechnology for food security. See Altshul et al. (2019)

understanding of Africa's place in the World Economic System. Therefore, intra-African and trans-African partnerships may be pivotal in constructing a successful African Innovation System.

These partnerships towards enhancing African innovation capacities will be crucial. In particular Africa's rapid catch up and technological learning through a strategic mix of both collaboration and self-reliance will be critical. Africa must catch up quickly in high productivity and equitable innovation that can improve the standard of living of all people. Furthermore, it must plan to participate in the ongoing Fourth Industrial Revolution.

It should also be noted that the Fourth Industrial-Technological Revolution will fundamentally alter the scale, scope and complexity of human societies. To reap the benefits and avoid possible catastrophe, the global response including Africa must be integrated and comprehensive. To briefly recapitulate the historical trajectory of these revolutions so far, we can begin with the First Industrial Revolution which used water and steam power to mechanize production. The Second used chemical industries, hydrocarbons and electric power to create mass production and distribution as well as a huge military-industrial complex in the bigger economies. Following on its heels, the Third Industrial Revolution used mainly electronics and information technology to automate production. It also promoted biotechnology and began the path to nanotechnology (Khan, 2005). More recently, a Fourth Industrial Revolution is building on the Third along the lines predicted early in this century (Khan 2004a, b, 2005). This is integrating the digital revolution with other technology systems to create a grand synthesis or super convergence of advanced technology systems through AI, robotics, biotechnology and nanotechnology. We present a section on China which started in a very impoverished low productivity state in the 1980s catching up and reaching the frontiers of the Fourth Industrial Revolution. Starting with advanced parts such as South Africa, through effective regional cooperation centred around going through different stages, Africa as a whole can achieve successes similar to China and other smaller East Asian economies such as Korea and Taiwan.

Three features of these transformations are particularly to be noted: velocity, scope and systems impact. The Fourth Industrial Revolution is evolving at an exponential rate, and this evolution is disrupting almost every industry and institution in every major country in our planet. In fact, beyond the advanced countries, billions of people connected by mobile devices, storage capacity, and access to knowledge guided by AI will present challenges for new forms of innovation systems. If the challenge is taken up by Africa as it must, possibilities for human and planetary well-being will be multiplied by emerging technology breakthroughs in fields such as artificial intelligence, robotics, the Internet of Things, autonomous vehicles, 3-D printing, nanotechnology, biotechnology, materials science, energy storage and quantum computing. This will indeed present a new prospect for global prosperity. PRC can play a leading role in this endeavour.[4] But we need a new integrated political economy model to analyse the prospects and ensure that optimal good can be extracted from the latest scientific-technological revolution. But it should be also emphasized that productivity increases through innovation in food, housing, healthcare, education and other basic capabilities enhancing activities must receive the highest priority in Africa, particularly for the poor.

How can Africa overcome its handicaps and great unevenness to start a catch up process to build an efficient and equitable innovation system? It has to be emphasized that even the most advanced economies in Africa such as South Africa and Nigeria have limited innovation capacities at present. In the next two sections we first present some analytical categories and do a quick survey of the current state of African innovation capabilities underlining both current limitations and the need for an even accelerated development of innovation systems and technological learning. Sections 6.3 and 6.4 advance these ideas by considering ANIS, Sectoral Innovation Subsystems and Cross-border African Innovation Systems in the face of unevenness. One key human development strategic point is emphasized throughout: innovation for food security, better housing, healthcare and innovation must receive strategic priority. With enough human development as a base, African countries even currently at a low level of development can embark on the Fourth Industrial Revolution meaningfully. For this to happen strategically, African countries must build cooperative structures of innovation and South-South skill and technology transfer mechanisms.

[4] See also Jin (2023) and Miller (2022).

6.3 Constructing a New African Innovation System: Going from a Low-Level Equilibrium Trap Towards THE Fourth Industrial Revolution and an Augmented National Innovation System (ANIS)

In a national context, treating innovations in specific sectors—e.g., the ICT sectors—as part of the techno-economic paradigm embedded in the nation state requires viewing the innovation process as a complex network within a National Innovation System (NIS)—also abbreviated as NSI or National System of Innovation—and Sectoral Innovation Sub-systems (SISS). The key to understanding the systemic economics of innovation, particularly in the dynamic semiconductor, AI, biotechnology, nanotechnology and other knowledge-intensive sectors is to realize that a policy-driven disequilibrium process has set in within the world economy of which the NISs and SSISs are parts. The COVID-19 crisis has put in bold relief the contrast between Africa and other parts of the world with the possible exception of South Africa on which this book has a chapter already. During this process, unfortunately but consistent with the complex systems uneven development approach followed here, the gap between the advanced countries of the world and most of the rest is widening while visionary African leaders are focusing on reducing the gap in high technology. Unfortunately, for countries trapped by neoliberalism under US hegemony, this disequilibrium process is leading to rapid economic changes in the direction of even a greater unevenness in the Global Political Economy (GPE). These changes include intersectoral shifts towards the ICT, other high technology and knowledge sectors including the AI subsectors, changing skill requirements, high volatility of wages, profits and financial variables and consequent increase in uncertainty about the future states of the national economies in Africa and GPE as a system. The dynamics of this disequilibrium process must be studied through methods of understanding complexity. Clearly, our knowledge of such dynamic systems is still in its infancy, but much can be learned by studying some known features. In the last few decades, the frontiers of economics have moved far beyond the standard models of decreasing or constant returns where costs cannot be decreased beyond a certain point, unless factor markets behave in a peculiarly decreasing marginal cost fashion. Leaving the perfectly competitive world behind, economists at the frontiers have been focusing on increasing returns to scale, economies of scope and network externalities. The world of high technology in general and the ICT and knowledge sectors are characterized much better through these approaches than the old perfectly competitive models. Many models of imperfect competition have also been developed to study interesting and relevant phenomena such as R&D rivalry and R&D expenditures. The upshot of these developments is that economists at the frontiers of their discipline are much closer to understanding many aspects of the digital economy than they were ten years ago. In this chapter I want to illustrate this point by discussing a recently developed theoretical approach within the context of NIS and SISS in an uneven world economy. The policy implications for the development of new technologies, particularly semiconductors, AI, biotechnology, nanotechnology and robotics, are quite striking.

6.4 Constructing the New Africa: National Innovation Systems (NIS), SECENIS, Social Learning and Complexity[5]

The National Innovation System—also abbreviated as NSI or National System of Innovation—can be broadly defined as the intersectoral flow of technology and information in the economy including households and individuals, productive enterprises and various institutions including both public and private educational and R&D institutions. All these can form a network which under appropriate circumstances can generate a self-sustaining innovative process on the national level (Nelson, 1990, 1993a, b; Kim and Nelson, 2015; Lee, 2006; Khan, 1983, 1997, 1998, 2002, 2004a, b, 2005; Khan and Thorbecke, 1988, 1989). According to this

[5] We build our analytical framework here from concrete problems and possibilities for innovation in Africa. For existing information on the African countries in this area, the reader is referred to: African Development Bank, Various Years. African Development Outlook, African Union Commission. STISA (Science Technology and Innovation Strategy for Africa) (2024), Boakye (2024), Chukwuma et al. (2012), Fry (2023), Gaillard and Mouton (2022), Gutowsk et al. (2020), Juma, and Serageldin (2007), Juma and Yee-Cheong (2005), Kahn (2022), Kasongo et al. (2023), Mouton (2008), Mugabe (2006, 2008), Naidoo (2015), NEPAD (2006), Nyugha, P. G. (2024), OECD Reviews of Innovation Policy: Africa (Various Years), Olyanga et al.(2022), SARUA (2008), Schmoch, U (2005), UK National Commission for UNESCO (2005), UNCTAD (2003, 2007, 2008);UNIDO (2008), WIPO. Various Years. World Bank (2006, 2009), World Economic Forum (Various Years).

approach, which we generally follow with some modifications described later, technological development requires a system of well-functioning institutional networks and such development when it occurs results from this complex system of relationships among different groups of actors who respond to appropriate policies in the socio-economic system. Most advanced countries are already societies with highly evolved NIS. Some economies in the Asia Pacific region like Japan, China, India, Korea and Taiwan have developed such NIS with various degrees of success. Many poor countries are far behind. This is an example of what I mean by the unevenness of the global economy and globalization. My previous work on NIS (Khan 1998, 2002, 2004a, b) of the requirements of technical progress shows that we need both a deeper understanding of the disequilibrium processes at work leading towards multiple equilibria and complex dynamics and the economic implications of the complexities of the production and distribution aspects of new technologies. It is with a view towards capturing these complexities leading towards multiple equilibria that an alternative conceptualization of technology systems transition in terms of an Augmented NIS (ANIS) has been formulated by some economists (Khan, 1983, 1985, 1998, 2002, 2003a, b, 2004a, b; Gabriele and Khan, 2010). In addition to capturing both equilibrium and disequilibrium features of technological transitions, this broad approach can illuminate *distributional* issues as well. Since poverty reduction remains on the agenda of the national governments of many African developing countries and the international development agencies, it can be argued that from this perspective at least the new approach has relevance for the African developing countries. But such distributional considerations are of importance in all advanced countries as well. From here on, we wish to highlight the fact that our framework can be viewed as simply a variety of Augmented NIS (ANIS) and its various subsystems, and therefore, we will be using the more general term from now on which also has the virtue of maintaining intellectual continuity with NIS and at the same time augmenting the range of the concept. One important extension captured in this formulation is the explicit consideration of both factorial and household income distributions which interact in a causally reciprocal way with the technology systems (Khan and Thorbecke 1988, 89). We point out the importance of these two types of income distributions for Africa in the section on building unified economy-wide data base for creating efficient and equitable ANIS for Africa.

We note that the main institutional actors in the complete augmented national innovation system include universities, public R&D institutes, private enterprises, financial institutions such as commercial banks, technology support agencies, policy-making bodies and the government in general. Understanding the linkages among the institutional actors involved in innovation activities or processes is crucial to improving a country's technological and economic performance. Linkages in a national system of innovation usually take different forms. These will include in Africa joint research projects among public R&D institutions, joint technology development and transfer activities between public and private sector institutions, mobility and exchange of scientists and engineers, technology licensing agreements, and the sharing of information and technology infrastructure. Assessing the performance of a national system of innovation entails tracing the various institutional links and measuring the intensity of the interactions among various knowledge producers and economic actors. The interactions are supposed to be continuous and characterized by positive feedback (Khan and Thorbecke, 1988, 89; Khan 1998, 2004a, b: African Union Commission 2024). The linkages and interactions among the various institutions in a national system of innovation are purposefully stimulated and nurtured by public policies and various incentives that the government puts in place. Public policies pertaining to intellectual property protection, competition, FDI, taxes, mobility of scientists and engineers, and technology regulation and licensing influence the evolution and growth of a national system of innovation. The performance of a national system of innovation is also influenced by political, economic and social conditions. Open and democratic political systems are likely to encourage the search for new information and introduction of new knowledge and promote learning capabilities. Institutional linkages and interactions, including strategic complementarity, positive feedback and general exchange of information, tend to flourish in countries where policies and political practices encourage open dialogue and debate. National systems of innovation are open systems. They are characterized by inflow and outflow of information, skills and technology. The main activity in the national systems of innovation is learning. This involves interactions between people and between institutions. The learning is interactive, characterized by positive feedback. The feedback takes place between economic firms and consumers; between R&D institutions and industry; between R&D institutions and financial bodies; between policy-making bodies and R&D institutions; between policy-making institutions and private firms; and between education and training institutions and industrial firms. Later in our discussion of technical modelling of an ANIS, we emphasize these points formally.

The capacity of countries or economies to innovate is also dependent on existing physical infrastructure and how that infrastructure is utilized. Infrastructure such as laboratories for scientific research, electricity, telecommunications and internet connectivity is critical for firms to be able to design and develop new products and processes and to create new applicable knowledge. Indisputably, the state of infrastructure critically shapes the institutions' ability to produce and apply knowledge. Therefore, in assessing ANIS, the state of infrastructure should play a crucial role.

In addition, other important aspects/determinants of innovation systems include: research and innovation priorities; policies for R&D and innovation; quality of scientific research institutions; public and private sector investment in R&D; protection of intellectual property rights; institutional linkages particularly university-industry collaborations; availability and utilization of skills in science, engineering and entrepreneurship fields; existence and use of technology standards and regulatory agencies; and the participation of countries in regional and international programmes.

Unfortunately for Africa, many low-income countries have no innovation systems at present. These countries require basic needs-related innovation in agriculture and related activities. Most of them spend very little in public sector R&D and on public private innovation partnerships. Here, there is a lot to learn from China's policies under opening and reform policy regime.

Even countries like South Africa the overall R&D is barely 1% of GDP. More starkly, oil rich Nigeria invests lower than 0.5% on R&D on the average. Thus together with upgrading of labour-intensive technologies, a more comprehensive approach for catching up with East Asian economies will be essential.

What strategic policy areas and modes of financing are of crucial importance for African countries? Throughout this discussion, we consider both new opportunities and challenges.

As observed, ANIS for innovation in Africa varies from country to country. Each national system has its peculiarities that are largely based on national macroeconomic conditions, political histories and culture, resource endowments, stage of economic and technological development, and social systems and capabilities. Generally, African countries can be grouped into three categories based on the content, dynamism and capacities of their national systems of innovation. The first group is that of leading countries with well-established and relatively high-quality research institutions, high level of technological readiness, explicit innovation policies and agencies for funding innovation. The private sector is involved in funding R&D, and collaborations between universities and industry are nurtured. South Africa is the only country in this group. Other countries like Kenya, Uganda, Nigeria and Ghana have a good chance of joining this category if policies can mobilize resources in the right direction.

Consistent with the above we can identify a second group of potential leaders in the next few decades. In this category are countries with currently low levels of technological readiness, research institutions that are weak. On the positive side the institutions are being strengthened, science and technology policy regimes exist, and there are ongoing processes to formulate explicit innovation policies. There are also agencies for funding R&D which have been or are being established. But the private sector is weak and does not fund R&D. Also links between universities and industry are non-existent or weak at best. We can present a larger list here: Botswana, Ghana, Kenya, Malawi, Mauritius, Madagascar, Rwanda, Seychelles, Uganda, Tanzania and Zambia. The level of technological readiness and innovation capacities of these countries are below that of middle-income economies. Therefore, policies must be formulated rigorously and implemented carefully.

The final group is in need of more regional and international cooperation. These are African countries with very poor research institutions. They have no Science and Technology (S&T) policy regimes. S&T institutions are few and weak, university-industry collaborations are non-existent, and funding for R&D is meagre. Also both the public and the private sectors are small. Consequently, participation in R&D is very weak. Angola, Namibia, Lesotho, Niger, Mali, Gambia, Gabon, Senegal, Ivory Coast, Niger and Swaziland are examples. Concerted regional and international efforts need to focus on this group as soon as possible.

The above is a realistic starting point. However, we argue that Africa today has relatively more opportunities than before for economic transformation and development.

We must recognize first that macroeconomic and political conditions in many African countries are becoming more favourable to economic change and growth for increasing wealth and people's capabilities. In spite of many crises, many African countries have experienced impressive economic growth in the twenty-first century. Foreign Direct Investment

(FDI) inflows to the continent have increased. Trade opportunities are becoming relatively more diversified although there is a long way to go. Trade in particular between Africa and Asia is growing in many different sectors. Further diversification is necessary and possible. Furthermore, conditions for private capital investment are more favourable today compared to 20 years ago, as most economies have opened up and the investment climate has improved. Although here selective strategic sectors need to be studied carefully—as we emphasize in our strategy chapter—a policy of developmentalist strategic openness needs to be pursued. Finally, on the harmful conflict side, today there are fewer political and civil conflicts in Africa compared to the situation in the 1970s, 1980s and 1990s.

Next, we consider new technological opportunities for Africa. We note that there is a wide range of new technologies available for increasing the productivity and diversity of African economies. An important factor in realistic appraisal of twenty-first-century technological systems for a knowledge economy is now emerging in Africa. We are referring here to the stock of knowledge and related innovations available to Africa over the next few decades. More of these are now available to African countries than before at an accelerated pace, and more will be available under a concerted cooperative African ANIS building project. Technological diversity and convergence will make it relatively easy and economical to access and apply knowledge. Inter alia, such applications not only will add value to the proper use of Africa's natural resources but will also enable Africa to use the natural resources as inputs to produce more valuable finished items. This is an important point to remember when we discuss African innovation in productive activities within the proposed future methodology of social accounting matrix-based economy-wide modelling of innovation prospects in Africa in a realistic manner. For example, in accordance with Khan's (2005) predictions about technological convergence, Information and Communication Technologies (ICTs) have converged with biotechnology to create bioinformatics that make it possible to improve biodiversity and mineral prospecting in Africa. The application of biosystematics and bacterial leaching will enable oil-producing African countries to export high-value oil products. Consistent with our analysis, technology is breaking barriers to capital access and movement as well. Technological developments associated with mobile telephony make it possible to move or transfer capital to rural areas and across most of Africa rapidly. As we will emphasize in strategy recommendation, such new developments in technology are the foundations on which a sound capabilities enhancing technology system for Africa can be constructed in the next few decades by 2050 and beyond.

Next we consider the important issue of institutional diversity. It must be admitted that in spite of many false starts and haphazard policies, Africa has more institutional diversity today compared to a few decades ago. There is a growing industrial sector with a diverse range of industrial firms—small and large—engaged in various economic activities in many countries. African economies have private enterprises co-evolving with public ones. Though not an unmixed blessing, many transnational corporations have increased their presence and activities in the continent over the past decade. There is also growth in numbers and diversity of knowledge, financial and technical institutions and overall skill mix. There is a growing political will in many African countries to improve and/or develop their institutions for scientific research and promote technological innovation. This is manifested in the ongoing efforts by countries to review their R&D organizations, formulate new science and technology policies and, in many cases, develop science and technology strategies. Some of these efforts are receiving international support in the form of funding and technical assistance. These trends can be harnessed systematically to build what we have called an Augmented NIS or ANIS that will systemically deliver both efficiency and equity.

Next, we are also observing as a fourth important development a renewed focus on accelerating regional economic and political integration. If Africa can continue and deepen this trend, building an ANIS can become feasible. Some important examples are: African countries are integrating their economies through institutional arrangements such as the Common Market for Eastern and Southern Africa (COMESA), EAC, Economic Community of West African States (ECOWAS) and SADC. Regional economic integration makes it possible for African countries to pool their economic diversity and assets together and build bigger markets as well as trading blocs. It is also an important mechanism for assembling resources for the production of regional public goods. The EAC created the East African Science and Technology Council in 2007. SADC established a desk dedicated to science and technology and is finalizing a protocol to promote cooperation in science and technology. In 2005, ECOWAS designed a framework for common science and technology programmes. COMESA has been implementing programmes to harmonize regulatory measures for biotechnology and ICT development. These are indicative of what countries can do through regional economic integration to foster technological innovation. From our strategic perspective, we endorse and suggest regional efforts to combine technical and normative analysis for building multi-country African ANIS at an accelerated pace.

As a fifth factor for being optimistic in a realistic manner, we observe that many African leaders and the international community are increasingly recognizing that science, technology and innovation are critical for the transformation of economies, reduction of poverty, attainment of the Sustainable Development Goals (SDGs) and integration of the continent into the global knowledge economy on the basis of equal sovereignty. For example, in January 2007, African leaders dedicated their African Union (AU) Summit to discussing ways to promote the development and application of science and technology for development. Through the AU and NEPAD, a high-level council of ministers of science and technology was already established in 2003, and since then a number of framework programmes have been developed. Development agencies such as the AfDB and international institutions such as the World Bank and UNESCO have designed frameworks to guide their support to Africa's scientific and technological development. These efforts might have increased financial resources for research and innovation activities in Africa. However, so far the quantity has been much smaller than necessary. As a result, leaders are now putting new partnerships and self-reliance as the key strategic aspects to pursue. This is fully in accord with our strategic focus on building a cooperative African ANIS with interrelated national systems as key components. We now turn to the important task regarding national priorities and capacities.

6.5 National Research and Development Priorities and Capacities

We have cited many studies that form the empirical foundation for our analytical advice. We recognize that there are a number of studies that have reviewed the national R&D systems of the 19 Sub-Saharan countries and other African countries. There are also new initiatives to conduct national R&D surveys. For example, NEPAD is supporting most of the Sub-Saharan countries to conduct surveys. Individual countries have also initiated activities to set their R&D priorities and formulate related science and technology policies. These efforts vary from one country to another. Some countries (e.g., Botswana, Mozambique, Mauritius and South

Africa) have already outlined R&D priorities in their science and technology strategies or plans. Others, such as Ghana and Kenya, have R&D priorities in draft science and technology policy documents. Yet some other countries, such as Swaziland, have recently launched national R&D priority setting and policy formulation exercises. Some systematic unified framework such as the one we offer here will be helpful since different approaches are used by individual African countries to set their R&D priorities. In many cases, there are no organized national R&D priority setting processes. Priorities of R&D seem to emerge from political statements, sometimes as wish lists that are at best aspirational. For most countries, R&D priorities are often set by or at the level of individual research institutions based on the institutions' anticipation of funding from national governments or international donors. R&D priorities are also set within sectors such as agriculture and health, and at the level of individual departments or ministries. There have been efforts to set R&D priorities in specific technology fields such as biotechnology, nanotechnology and nuclear sciences. In the area of biotechnology, for example, most of the countries have identified needs and set R&D priorities. National biotechnology R&D priority setting exercises have been undertaken in Ghana, Kenya, Namibia, South Africa, Uganda, Tanzania and Zimbabwe in the past decade. The extent to which these exercises have influenced the direction of research and funding decisions remains unclear. Clarity in these regards is essential for strategic building of ANIS with sectoral systems of innovation.

Consistent with our observations above, the degree of sophistication of R&D priority setting varies from country to country. In some countries, priority setting is done through stakeholders' meetings or consultations. This largely involves getting scientists, NGOs, business representatives and government officials into workshops to identify national R&D priorities. In some cases, background studies may be prepared for the workshops. Stakeholders' meetings or workshops are the most common approach for R&D priority setting in most African countries. Despite the differences in approach to R&D priority setting, countries have identified a number of common areas for R&D focus. This is encouraging but needs further systematization and focus for the project of building the African ANIS.

We can find some basis for hope in at least some important sectors. For example, especially from the perspective of building resilience in food security in the area of agriculture, all African countries have for a long time identified crop breeding (with an emphasis on cereals) and livestock disease research. Ghana has placed emphasis on research to improve varieties of cassava in order to increase its capacity for industrial starch production. Ghana, Kenya, Mauritius, Mozambique, Seychelles, South Africa and Tanzania have over many years prioritized research on the conservation and use of marine resources. A growing number of African countries are starting to identify agricultural biotechnology as a priority. Among these African countries are Botswana, Ghana, Kenya, Uganda, Tanzania, Namibia, Malawi, Mozambique, Mauritius, Rwanda, South Africa and Zimbabwe. Some of these countries have even identified specific crops and/or traits upon which biotechnology R&D should focus. For example, Mauritius has identified sugarcane, while Zimbabwe has identified tobacco and cereals. This trend needs to be accelerated. Clearly there is much scope here for competent cooperation.

We now turn to another strategically important area covering public expenditure on research and development statistics.

6.6 Public Expenditure on Research and Development Statistics

We recognize that data on public expenditure on R&D in most African countries are scarce. Here collaboration with advanced countries for building specific focused institutions will be essential because the great majority of these countries do not have institutions and/or programmes that undertake regular R&D surveys and collect systematic data on R&D expenditure. National statistics offices do not seem to have a focus on surveying or collecting statistics on expenditure on R&D. Of all African countries, South Africa has the most advanced institutional and programmatic activities on R&D surveys. Its Centre for Science, Technology and Innovation Indicators of the Human Sciences Research Council (HSRC) is specifically funded by the Department of Science and Technology (DST) to undertake R&D and innovation surveys on a regular basis. There are various attempts at collecting statistics on R&D expenditure in the other countries. The UNESCO Institute for Statistics conducts R&D surveys in some of the countries which this study focuses on. NEPAD is supporting Angola, Ghana, Kenya, Lesotho, Malawi, Mozambique, Uganda, Tanzania and Zambia to undertake R&D surveys, with an emphasis on collecting data on expenditure on R&D. Studies such as SARUA (2008) have generated estimates of public expenditure on R&D for some of the SADC countries. These estimates show that none of the countries under study expends 1% its GDP on R&D.

Most African countries have created institutions for R&D. Universities and other institutions of higher learning also conduct R&D in addition to their core business of education and training. A baseline study of science and technology conducted for SARUA in 2008 provides a good profile of R&D institutions in 14 SADC countries. UNESCO has also commissioned and undertaken surveys that provide profiles of R&D or related institutions in Africa. These studies or profiles are mainly regional in coverage and do not discuss specific institutions in the different countries. There have been a number of more detailed specific reviews of some countries' STI systems. These reviews show that African countries have various institutional arrangements for STI in general and R&D in particular. Our proposal strategically is to integrate systems through building economy wide consistent data sets.

Some countries have concentrated their R&D activities in universities. Examples of such countries are Angola, Botswana, Lesotho, Mauritius, Mozambique, Namibia and Swaziland. Some countries have sectoral R&D activities concentrated in public research institutes. For example, in Kenya, R&D in the area of health is largely concentrated in the Kenya Medical Research Institute (KEMRI). Other countries (e.g., South Africa) have R&D efforts spread across universities, public R&D institutions and the private sector. In Ghana, most of the R&D activities are concentrated in the Council for Scientific and Industrial Research (CSIR) and a few other research institutes.

Ghana, Kenya and South Africa have the highest concentration of relatively large public R&D institutions and universities. Ghana has seven public universities three of which specifically focus on scientific R&D. In addition, Ghana has more than 15 research institutes. Kenya has seven public universities (most of them with faculties of science and some related R&D activities) and at least seven public R&D institutes. It hosts headquarters and laboratories of the International Centre for Agroforestry (ICRAF), the International Livestock Research Institute (ILRI) and the International Centre for Insect Physiology and Ecology (ICIPE) as well as several regional research programmes.

South Africa has the highest concentration of R&D institutions and R&D-performing universities in Sub-Saharan Africa. It has 7 large science councils with numerous research institutes and 18 public universities of which 5 are dedicated to scientific research and technology. The country also has specialized national laboratories or facilities that are managed by the National Research Foundation (NRF). It hosts the African-component of the International Centre for Genetic Engineering and Biotechnology (ICEGB), the African Institute for Mathematical Sciences (AIMS) and the Southern Africa Biosciences (SANBio) Hub of NEPAD.

Only a few universities in Africa are in a position to boast of quality scientific journals in their libraries; few university staff have access to computers in their offices (even in computer science departments); many of the libraries in African universities do not have computers and are not computerized; and in old universities the age of equipment is about a quarter of a century old. The report establishes that engineering schools or university institutes are the ones most lacking in equipment compared to those for basic sciences. Its overall conclusion "the average age of laboratory equipment is too high (11.6 years for basic sciences and 15.8 years for that of the engineering sciences). Significant changes in laboratory technology have occurred in the last 10 years in Asian developing countries and other Latin American countries such as Brazil. Hence, by comparison, African institutions are clearly much behind their counterparts in other continents in the areas of experimental science. This gap needs to be closed through increasing expenditures, building infrastructure and new laboratories through international collaboration and systematic skill transfer.

What are the right policy instruments for promoting scientific research in Africa for building ANIS?

6.7 Promoting Scientific Research: African Countries' Policy Instruments

The number of African countries that are identifying specific policy instruments for STI is growing. We can observe now that a number of countries now use explicit policies written in science and technology-specific policy and legal documents or frameworks to govern R&D activities. These tend to be articulated through formal legislation. Thus Kenya, an early example, started with a Science and Technology Act of 1977, amended in 1980, and is further updating it for the emerging Fourth Industrial Revolution. Furthermore, plans and strategies, such as Botswana's National Research, Science and Technology Plan of 2005 and Mozambique's 2005 Science,

Technology and Innovation Strategy, and in white papers, such as South Africa's Science and Technology White Paper of 1996 and further steps in the twenty-first century, are notable advances.

In Africa, some countries have multiple policy framework documents. To take the Botswana case again, for example, we can find that in addition to the 2005 National Research, Science and Technology Plan, Botswana has the Science and Technology Policy documents for more recent years as well. Uganda has recently adopted a new National Science, Technology and Innovation policy in addition to other sectoral specific policies. South Africa has the National Research and Development Strategy of 2002, and the Ten-Year Innovation Plan of 2007 in addition to the white paper. It updates these plans frequently. We have several such updates almost every other year. Although Angola, Democratic Republic of the Congo, Madagascar, Mauritius, Seychelles and Swaziland do not have science and technology-specific policy frameworks, even these lagging countries also have explicit policies scattered in sectoral policy documents such as national plans for agriculture, national health policy, energy plans and strategies, and ICT plans. Trade and industrial policy documents, annual national budget statements, investment policies and legislation, and intellectual property protection legislation also tend to contain explicit policies for R&D for STI in most of the countries. All African countries' agricultural plans include policies for promoting R&D. Countries such as Botswana, Ghana, Kenya, Mozambique, Namibia, Mauritius, Seychelles and South Africa have measures for promoting R&D, particularly in their ICT plans.

There are some common threads among the science and technology-specific policy frameworks of the different African countries. All of them put emphasis on strengthening national public R&D institutions by improving infrastructure, improving coordination of institutions, building and/or strengthening collaborations between public R&D institutions with private companies, increasing investments in R&D, promoting science and technology education and raising public awareness, and increasing and retaining numbers of scientists and engineers. Some of the policy and legal frameworks (such as Kenya's Science and Technology Act as amended recently and Tanzania's Science and Technology Act) create institutions for coordinating science and technology and committees to provide leadership in specific fields of R&D. These efforts can be strengthened further through regional cooperation and institution building.

If regional cooperation and institution building can be started in earnest, African countries will also be able to rely on a wide range of implicit policies coordinated to promote R&D and science and technology in general. These include tax regulations, customs and excise duties, immigration laws, fiscal policies, foreign affairs policies, industrial policies, health regulations, environmental impact regulations and import and export regulations. There is no systematic review or assessment of how well African countries use implicit policies to promote R&D. A case-based review of the use of implicit policies may be useful to inform efforts aimed at integrating science and technology considerations into national economic policy frameworks. It may also be helpful in informing the reform or development of science and technology policies and legal frameworks. Here cooperation between advanced countries like South Africa and other African countries is essential.

Further cause for optimism comes from some initiatives already taken in Africa. Some of the African countries have begun national processes to develop explicit science, technology and innovation policy frameworks. Angola's government has been working with UNCTAD to review its implicit policies and institutional landscape in order to identify gaps. Swaziland is being supported by UNESCO to hold national stakeholders' consultations to identify R&D priorities and establish a science and technology policy-making process. Ghana (since 2004) and Kenya (since 1998) have been investing in various studies and events to review and reform their STI policies. These trends can be further generalized and deepened.

6.8 Measuring Technological Readiness and Innovation Capacity

There is a saying among the policy makers that what is not measured is ignored. Therefore, it is critical for African countries to work collaboratively to organize efforts towards creating a unified set of indicators for measuring technological innovation capabilities to identify areas for creating basic capacities as well as further advanced capabilities for joining ultimately the march towards the Fourth Industrial Revolution. On the positive side, we note that several indices have already been developed to measure and provide some assessment of countries' technological status and performance. These include the Technology Achievement Index (TAI) used in the United Nations Development Programme's (UNDP) Human Development Reports, the Industrial-Cum-Technological

Advance Index (ITA) used by UNIDO's Industrial Development Reports and Technological Readiness (TR) measures used by the World Economic Forum in the Global Competitiveness reports. TAI focuses on a country's innovative capacity. It is used to measure a country's ability to create new products and processes through R&D and to use new and old technologies to increase economic productivity. According to the Human Development Report's TAI ranking, the Organisation for Economic Co-operation and Development (OECD) countries and a few developing countries are the main source identifying a range of new technologies. OECD countries still account for more than 80% of patent applications in the 2020s a similar percentage of scientific and technical journal articles published worldwide. So far, African countries are not significant sources of technological innovations. They are not really engaged in the creation of technology. South Africa is the innovation hub in Africa. The UNDP Human Development Report ranks South Africa in the middle ranks of innovating countries. But in Africa, it is certainly the most dynamic adopters of technology. Other African countries are technologically marginalized at present but can learn from the South African example.

Thus most African countries are also lagging in innovation capacity. They are also lagging behind in technological readiness (TR) as well. TR "measures the ability with which an economy adopts existing technologies to enhance the productivity of its industries." It is an assessment of a country's preparedness to procure, absorb and use technology. Technological readiness is determined by considering factors such as firm-level technology absorption, laws relating to information and communication technologies, FDI and technology transfer, personal computers per 100 inhabitants, and internet users and mobile phone subscribers. It is separate from innovation capacity, which is about the ability of a country to expand the frontiers of knowledge and create new technology. Technological innovation is important for countries with diminishing possibilities of adopting and using existing technologies. In these circumstances, firms cannot increase their productivity by relying on or using existing technologies or by merely undertaking incremental innovations. They must push the frontiers of knowledge and create cutting-edge products and processes in order to be competitive. The Global Competitiveness Report ranks the countries' competitiveness based on TR and innovative capacities. Most Sub-Saharan African countries are ranked very low. They have low levels of TR and innovative capacities. South Africa and Kenya are ranked relatively higher. Much can be done here through regional cooperation in specific areas of innovation.

There is no room for pessimism. We note that African countries are exposed to a wide range of technologies. Many such technologies are embedded in foreign products. The share of imported high technology products in Sub-Saharan Africa has risen in the past decade or so. Between 2000 and 2004, high technology imports accounted for 4.5% of Sub-Saharan Africa's GDP having risen from 3.2% for the period 1994–1996. Now these are in the 8–10% range. Mauritius and South Africa import the most high-tech goods relative to the size of their economies, between 10% and 15% of GDP in any given year, while Somalia imports the least, i.e., less than 1% of GDP. However, most of the countries are not technologically ready to adopt, adapt and successfully apply the technologies in their economies. This situation can be changed through active support by the advanced countries and international organizations. We discuss this further in the next segment on funding. Complementary policies for technological learning through efforts to improve and upgrade levels of education provide continuous technical training and adopting policies that deliberately promote technology diffusion and adaptation. Improving physical infrastructure will be a necessary part of such a comprehensive effort as well.

We now turn to the important subject of financing innovation in Africa.

6.9 Financing Technological Innovation in Africa: Possible Institutional Arrangements

It is of utmost importance for Africa to be supported by the international community for this project of building a cooperative Africa-wide ANIS with individual country components. It is well known that financial capital is critical for starting and staying on the path towards the promotion of technological innovation, catching up and ultimately being ready for participation in the Fourth Industrial Revolution. Cooperative cross-African countries finance over the next few decades will be crucial for the development of firms, particularly start-ups now, which are the central locus of innovation for practical applications. Evidently, African research and training institutions over the next few decades will require financial resources to be able to test their ideas. These research centres must work with specific firms to commercialize research results, and generally turn their ideas into new goods and services. We have argued that lack of financial support is one of the main barriers to technological innovation in Africa. At present, African countries rely on a narrow range of institutional arrangements to finance innovation activities. This is far from being an optimal strategy. Africans do not have institutions dedicated to funding commercialization of research findings, technology prospecting and diffusion, or even funding activities aimed at testing technologies. Common funding instruments in advanced countries such as venture capital are either underdeveloped or non-existent in many of the African countries. In most of the African countries, venture capital, tax relief and other instruments are not available to universities at present. The same can be said with respect to conditions in small and medium enterprises (SMEs) and, in many cases, even R&D institutions.

Clearly, private equity industry, commercial and development banks, microfinance institutions, private foundations, and even many bilateral and multilateral donors have not given attention to providing financial resources for technological innovation in Africa. Africa has few start-up firms in fields such as biotechnology and energy technology development. Early stage investment in such areas is often unattractive to private banks, microfinance institutions and private foundations because it frequently involves higher risks with little or no returns in the short run. In Africa, new firms in such areas often start with business models that have not been proven in Africa and possess few tangible assets as collateral. The long gestation period will require alternative modes of financing with bilateral and multilateral longer-term arrangements, especially in such fields as biotechnology and life sciences. However, many African governments are increasingly recognizing that without the development of firms or companies that engage in innovation and without financial resources for commercializing new ideas from R&D institutions, their current paltry investments in R&D will not contribute to technological development and economic growth. This recognition gives some hope but needs concrete funding commitments. Thus the recognition of the gaps in funding articulated in some of the recent science and technology policies of countries such as Botswana, Ghana, Rwanda, Kenya, Mozambique and South Africa need concrete cross-country plan of action. There is an urgent need to develop a diverse range of financial instruments and funding institutions for innovation in Africa. African countries can strengthen the trend in some of the countries that have established new public institutions for funding technological innovation and mobilize resources for others to catch up, and coordinate these new financing arrangements. As positive examples, we can mention Botswana which established the Botswana Research, Science and Technology Investment Agency, South Africa which established the Innovation Fund, Uganda which established the National Innovation Fund and Zimbabwe which established the Innovation Commercialization Fund. These trends need to be accelerated and supported through regional cooperative institution building for innovation.

Some countries have proposed or are creating such institutions within and across countries. South Africa has created another agency—the Technology Innovation Agency—which will have sole responsibility for funding and promoting technological innovation. This needs to be followed up by coordinating with other African countries. Ghana and Kenya have launched efforts to establish new institutions for funding innovation. Both countries are establishing endowment funds for scientific research and technological innovation. But they need cross-country support even as they help other countries in group one in their catching up efforts. Thus the challenge for these countries is both to build their own ANIS and to help other African countries. Therefore, in addition to ensuring that adequate financial resources are available from national budgets or treasuries to build and sustain the endowment funds or agencies and to make sure that resources are allocated to innovation activities rather than locking or devoting most resources to abstract scientific research, they must also take steps towards regional cooperation in building African ANIS. Given the scarcity of funding African countries will need to make difficult choices in order to balance funding allocations for scientific research versus investing in technological innovation activities such as promoting the creation of innovative firms or companies. Not all countries can attempt to reach the frontiers of research in one leap. A pragmatic step-by-step strategy that builds on country-specific features pragmatically is the optimal strategy.

There are trends at the micro level that can be accelerated strategically as well. At the micro level, in addition to the current efforts of many African governments, some development banks are starting to focus more on supporting innovation creation and diffusion through enterprises. For example in Ghana, the Presidential Special Initiatives (PSI) was established five years ago to enable the Ministry of Trade, Industry, Private Sector Development and Presidential Special Initiatives to promote the emergence and growth of companies that work to add value to the country's cassava, cocoa and other natural resources. Specifically, the government is funding a number of companies to produce and export industrial starch from cassava. In South Africa, the Industrial Development Corporation (IDC) is engaged in funding start-up companies, some of them linked to universities and the research councils. Other African countries can learn from such experiences—and through cross-border collaboration with actors in Ghana, South Africa and similar African countries.

6.10 Towards a Unified Information and Modelling System for Innovation in Africa: A Social Accounting Matrix (SAM) System-Based Modelling Methodology for a Diversified African Innovation System

Although the innovation systems in Africa can proceed in a piecemeal manner extracting valuable policy-relevant information from the existing disparate data sources, a more systematic approach will aid in identifying key issues for regions at different stages of development—for example, the three groupings we have identified—and help recommend systematically a coherent set of policies. So far only South Africa has engaged in the task of building system wide data sets in the form of Social Accounting Matrices over time. We recommend that resources be mobilized to do this for Africa as a whole. This can be a major area of collaborative research that will yield valuable databases for building African ANIS. As the debate on the "East Asian miracle" underlines, the key strategic question for a geo-economic area such as Africa that has made a technological transition at least partially from a traditional to a modern system concerns the prospects for long-term economic growth and distribution through innovation. Ultimately, it is the sustainable long-term rate of growth that will determine the wealth that can be distributed among personal consumption, investment, government spending on infrastructure and public services, etc.

Therefore, it is the creation of an innovation system that will determine the viability of a technology-based growth process. This process of building an innovation system is very much an evolutionary and path-dependent process (Nelson, 1993a, b). The central idea is that the provision of appropriate types of capital, labour and forms of organization for high value-added industries will lead to rapid productivity increases. However, to sustain such an increase, a domestic innovation system must be set up. There is a further requirement that this innovation system must fulfil. This is the requirement of a positive feedback loop or a virtuous cycle of innovations.

This problem is intimately connected with the existence of multiple equilibria in complex economies. A positive feedback loop leading to a virtuous cycle of growth and technology development is one particular sequence of equilibria in this context. In general, such a sequence also involves increasing returns. In order to capture this complexity and include output, employment, factorial and household incomes in a detailed disaggregated manner the disaggregated SAM framework is an ideal consistent conceptual and data system for ANIS analysis. South Africa has produced a series of SAMs since 1978. Using such SAMs for South Africa Khan derived important results on impact of technology on output, employment and incomes as well as poverty reduction. For technical details of such modelling the reader is referred to Khan (1998, 2004a, b, 2021a).

Here we can mention the main modules of the SAM as they relate to innovation. These are: productive activities, factors, households, government and rest of the world. Innovation takes place in productive activities and affects the rest of the economy and society via multiple causal pathways. These can be captured via complex structural path analysis. We present below the key modules as the basis of a systemic modelling to measure the impact of various innovation policies on the economy and socio-economic system.

We note the structure of the economic flows in an African economy given by figure one below. This can be used in disaggregated form to model ANIS in detail and get relevant quantitative empirical results by using a corresponding series of SAMs over time (Khan 2004a, b). Such models fall in the general category of Structural Computable General Equilibrium (CGE) Models of Complex Systems. We emphasize that we must note both the domestic production structure and the open economy relations that are related to building ANIS for Africa. The initial step will be to integrate systematically the disparate data sources on production, employment, factorial and household incomes in a disaggregated form structurally with the open economy data set in a consistent manner in a series of SAMs. South Africa has already developed technical expertise and institutional arrangements that can inspire and assist other African economies. The scope for regional collaboration here is substantial.

The virtue of an economy-wide approach to technology systems is the embodiment of various inter-sectoral linkages. In a SAM, such linkages are mappings from one set of accounts to another. In terms of technology systems, the production activities can be broken down into a production (sub-)system and a set of innovative activities. In practice, this presents considerable difficulties of classification and empirical estimation.

One major component of the entire innovation system is, of course, the expenditures on R&D. In the SAM for Africa, this can appear either as an aggregate expenditure along the column labelled R&D or as a set of disaggregated expenditures. In the latter case these may be specified according to productive activities (e.g., construction and electrical equipment) or by institutions (e.g., private R&D expenditures and government R&D expenditures). It should be emphasized that the dynamic effects of R&D on the economy can be captured only in a series of such SAMs over time. One can contrast the possible policy experiments that can be undertaken within such a framework with the apparently ad hoc science and technology policies in many developing countries. In particular, the impact over time of a Social Capabilities Enhancing National Innovation System (SCENIS) can be traced by building and maintaining such SAMs.

Choice of new technology in Africa is affected by research and development in at least three different ways. Such a country can attempt to develop new technology through R&D, as mentioned previously. This ultimately requires a positive feedback loop innovation system in order to be self-sustaining. Another alternative is to adapt to existing technology. This too requires a production system geared towards innovation in a limited way. A third alternative is to import technology or to acquire it through attracting foreign direct investment. In practice, all these different forms may be combined. The abstract model embodies all these different possibilities. However, the first option requires, among other things, a presence of multiple equilibria. In a unique equilibrium world, the competitive equilibrium (under the assumption of complete markets) will always be the most efficient one. The presence of increasing returns usually destroys such competitive conditions.

In a market economy, "success" is often cumulative or self-reinforcing. Typically outcomes are not predictable in advance. However, once equilibrium gets selected out of a number of long-run equilibria, there is a tendency to be locked in. Technically, economic processes exhibit non-convexities—violating the generic assumption of competitive equilibrium economics. The presence of self-reinforcing mechanisms sharing common features found in fields as far apart as enzyme reactions and the economics of technical change underlines the importance of such mechanisms in governing the dynamics of self-reinforcing processes regardless of the field in which they occur. In a socialist economy, such an innovation process can be at least partially controlled. Furthermore, distributional and related political power concerns including moves towards deeper forms of democracy can also be better analysed in a model of a complex and adaptive social and political economy.

6.11 Taking into Account Complex Dynamics and Out-of-Equilibrium Behaviour for African Innovation Systems

Complex Adaptive Systems (CAS) for innovation are dynamic systems that can evolve with a changing environment. In CAS evolutionary trajectories there is no separation between a system and its environment in the sense that a system does not necessarily passively adapt to a changing environment. On the contrary, we have a system closely linked with all other related systems making up an ecosystem. In this larger ecosystem, change is necessarily that of co-evolution with all other related systems, rather than as adaptation to a separate and distinct environment.

As is well known, nonlinear dynamic systems can display a wide range of dynamic behaviours. Dissipative systems with a big enough perturbation can move to a new basin of attraction with much disorganization during transition. Also, even with bifurcations, we do not know for certain the expected path. Furthermore, catastrophic singularities are also possible.

Our systemic argument can be summarized in terms of dissipative systems dynamics in a world of multiple equilibria. Instead, a neoliberal global economy may simply go through cycles of instabilities. In Africa as a late starter it is within the realm of possible dynamic futures to set up a new capability enhancing system of production and distribution during the Fourth Industrial Revolution

6.12 Conclusions: Need for Coherent Developing Regional and International Collaboration in Africa—Learning from the East Asian Model

Throughout this chapter we have emphasized the systemic nature of innovation. In Africa in particular, recognition of this crucial point has led us to take institution building and regional cooperation in an interconnected way.

To summarize, the main institutional actors in the complete national innovation system include universities, public R&D institutes, private enterprises, financial institutions such as commercial banks, technology support agencies, policy-making bodies and the government in general. To build the linkages among the institutional actors involved in innovation activities or processes is crucial to improving a country's technological and economic performance. In Africa, although the most advanced, even South Africa has not developed these linkages sufficiently. Tier 2 and tier 3 countries will require substantive regional and global cooperative connections and investments in physical and intellectual capital to catch up and make further progress.

Linkages inter alia will include in Africa joint research projects among public R&D institutions, joint technology development and transfer activities between public and private sector institutions, mobility and exchange of scientists and engineers, technology licensing agreements and the sharing of information and technology infrastructure. The interactions among the various actors nationally and internationally will need to be multidimensional. As some researchers have pointed out (Khan and Thorbecke, 1988, 89; Khan 1998, 2004a, b), these multidimensional interactions in order to be effective will need to be continuous and characterized by positive feedback loops to grow over time

It needs to be emphasized that indigenous knowledge systems (IKS) will need to be taken seriously. These systems are to be integrated with the other components of an African capabilities-enhancing ANIS. So far South Africa has shown some interest in doing this. South Africa and other African countries will need to collaborate with one another so that the S are used in a holistic fashion to further the innovation capacities in every dimension.

Clearly, public policies and various incentives that the government puts in place will be important. But these must be coordinated and concerted among African countries. Cross-border institutions geared towards such coordination and implementation will need to be organized.

Institutional linkages and interactions, including strategic complementarity, positive feedback and general exchange of information, will thus be facilitated. As we have observed, ANIS is an open system with important feedback loops that are characterized by inflow and outflow of information, skills, integrated knowledge and technology. Technological learning cannot take place without these institutional linkages. The feedback will be particularly important between firms and consumers, between R&D

institutions and industry, between R&D institutions and financial bodies, between policy-making bodies and R&D institutions, between policy-making institutions and private firms, and between education and training institutions and industrial firms among others.

We have also emphasized that the capacity of countries or economies to innovate is also dependent on existing physical infrastructure and how that infrastructure is utilized across the African countries. Perhaps the need for cross-border collaboration with proper assistance from abroad is even more crucial strategically at this point in African history. In addition to traditional sources of funding, Africa needs to negotiate with all possible sources including Brazil, Russia, India, China and South Africa (BRICS) facilities, the New Development Bank and bilateral possibilities.

We have suggested that along with creation of food security, decent housing, healthcare and education systems, Africa should also build the foundations for ANIS in other sectors. This is most challenging, particularly for group 2 and group 3 African countries. The individual countries cannot overcome the resource constraints by themselves even under the best governance systems. Therefore, careful consideration and formulation of individual country policies need to be coordinated with regional bodies. This task should receive the highest priority in building the African ANIS. Our technical suggestions for building integrated data and modelling capacities can also be best pursued within such regional institutions.

Appendix

What can Africa learn from the development of innovation systems in a country that started out as very poor: PRC from poverty in the 1970s to wealth in the twenty-first century with an Augmented NIS and the linkages between industry and science?

As an example of Augmented NIS with some lessons for Africa, we can look at China. The claim is not that Africa can leap into the stage where China is today but rather that a step-by-step approach is needed. Africa through regional cooperation can have an area larger than PRC in total and through selective openness as in China—and earlier, Japan, Korea and Taiwan—move up the value added-chain, ultimately participating in the Fourth Industrial Revolution. The important step is to begin now without losing any time.

One important point we emphasize is the pitfalls of following the Chinese model mechanically is the adverse distributional outcome because of neglecting the distributional issues. In China there is finally some official recognition in China that issues related to distribution and the maintenance of reasonably harmonious social relations cannot be completely neglected in overall development strategy including the strategy for innovation. A second issue is the ecologically harmful consequences of indiscriminate industrialization. China has finally recognized this issue also and has become a global leader in green energy and technology development. Africa can have the advantage of paying attention to ecological and distributional issues right from the steps it takes at present.

As of now, China has achieved remarkable coherence in the Fourth Industrial Revolution and AI (Khan, 2021a, b; Lundvall and Rikap 2022), forming new types of platform business groups (Jia and Kenney 2021). China's Augmented NIS has witnessed remarkable advances because of a series of reforms aimed mainly at improving its effectiveness and closing the excessive gap which traditionally separated university-based research activities from the technology absorption and innovation needs of the enterprises system. The main thrust of reforms has been to diversify the country's Augmented NIS and to strengthen its market orientation and market compatibility, but the role of centrally managed large, long-term research programmes has also been enhanced. These reforms, along with the ever-expanding availability of financial resources made possible by economic growth and by the strong role of the state, have allowed China to achieve remarkable advances. This has also led to deeper integration with other economies through international trade, investment and joint technological and infrastructural projects. Several organizational and institutional structures which proved their validity in the context of developed market economies were studied, experimented with and in some cases adopted in China, but such a pragmatic approach does not amount to an attempt to ape Western examples. The most visible change in China's Augmented NIS is probably the progressive shift of the bulk of R&D activities away from universities and specialized research centres and towards industrial enterprises. However, universities participate in many of the most ambitious basic research endeavours and often play a crucial role in their implementation. For instance, universities carry out about 70% of the projects funded by National Natural Science Foundation (NNSF). The Chinese government is earmarking an increasing volume of funds to elite universities, mainly through the relevant ministries. Elite universities are expected to lead in national R&D programmes and projects, facilitate technology diffusion and pullovers, promote spin-off companies and incubation centres, and open laboratories for R&D sharing, to bridge in foreign technology and partners. This emphasis on the role of universities in engaging directly in the development, production and commercialization stages of their research results has been dubbed "forward engineering" by Lee. According to him, forward engineering is a peculiarly Chinese component of the "Beijing Consensus", a comprehensive and proactive catch-up strategy very different from the "Washington Consensus" and partly but not fully like that followed before by other successful Asian latecomers such as Korea and Taiwan. A pioneering one was project 211, aimed at funding the construction of campuses and developing new academic programmes in key scientific areas all over the country. Other programmes continue to promote university-industry links. The first one of this kind was launched jointly in 2001 by the State Economic and Trade Commission (SETC). The goal of this programme was to set up state technology transfer centres in six universities, to promote the commercialization of technological achievements. Research and technological innovations are now seen as crucial channels through which universities contribute to national and local economies. As mentioned above, however, the bulk of China's R&D is presently being carried out by enterprises, many of which are large state-owned enterprises (SOEs). SOE reforms were carried out in the framework of a complex, ever-changing institutional environment. The behaviour of Chinese SOEs is also becoming more modern and effective in several areas, including their ability to attract top executive talents. In China as elsewhere, R&D expenditure is positive and significantly correlated with firm productivity. The contribution of government R&D to firm productivity works mainly through an indirect channel, via the promotion of firms' own R&D, which appears to be a more effective policy tool than direct R&D grants. Other key sources of production improvement and innovation growth are each firm's absorptive capacity, the production network, openness and managers' education. Market-oriented, competition-enhancing innovation system reforms and corporate governance with clear performance indicators in reformed SOEs have been improving the effectiveness of the incentive structure and fostering S&T linkage activities. As a result, SOEs and private firms in high technology sectors including semiconductors and AI now perform as highly innovative firms. In many SOEs, managers apply the technical innovation audit tool for benchmarking, thereby improving their ability to choose among different types of innovation mechanisms. Due to the influence of the two main stakeholders (government and end-users), firms with a higher degree of government involvement and a correspondently lower degree of openness to the market exhibit a more widespread use of innovation mechanisms, thereby apparently contradicting the positive relationship between market focus and innovativeness traditionally posited by "Western" innovation management theories. This phenomenon is due largely to strong government intervention and strategic planning in SOEs' behaviour. The government puts paramount emphasis on long-term investments to promote technological innovations, targeting them as important indicators of SOE performance and awarding resources to SOEs accordingly. SOEs rely more on government-allocated resources and therefore tend to perform better in areas that are encouraged by the government, such as new product development. As new product output is an important indicator of SOE performance, SOEs are incentivized to operate at the frontier of new product development. There are dynamic advantages in terms of innovative capacity and technological progress, with major spillovers benefiting the national economy. One also needs to consider the existence of virtuous synergies with the non-state-owned sector (Lin 2012).

Notwithstanding China's Augmented NIS's remarkable strengths, remaining challenges are formidable. For instance, there is still a dualistic pattern in China's of technological development, with the export-oriented segments of the economy being relatively isolated from those producing mainly for the domestic market. There could be more synergy technological cooperation between universities and industry and the inadequate integration of the country's Augmented NIS into the global innovation networks. Without being exhaustive, one last feature of the still evolving Chinese Augmented NIS can be mentioned. Since the beginning of the new regime in the twenty-first century the increasing social and political tensions which inevitably accompany worsening income distribution have been noted carefully. The worsening distributional situation sets China apart from the other East Asian latecomer innovators. The Xi regime seems committed to changing the distributional picture and managing social and political tensions effectively. The overall macroeconomic and innovation policies are influenced by these goals. Apart from the already developed ANIS of Japan, the region's other players with strong capabilities for developing ANIS are India, Korea, Taiwan, Singapore, Malaysia, Thailand, the Philippines and Indonesia. Vietnam is at a lower stage of development but can potentially develop its ANIS integrated with the Asia Pacific. The present author has carried out studies on a number of these countries and several are ongoing. What can we conclude from the Chinese case study and these other Asian examples?

Since the late 1990s, the Chinese government has approved a number of crucial strategic decisions to build up a world-class National Innovation System. In 1998 the government instructed the Chinese Academy of Sciences (CAS)—a vast network of research institutes that are presently undergoing feverish expansion and reorganization—to initiate the Pilot Project of Knowledge Innovation Program (KIP). An action plan was carried out for rejuvenating education in the twenty-first century, in addition to a national meeting on technology innovation and a working conference on basic science research, to further enhance the reform of the scientific research system. Plans are also drawn to open a second-board stock exchange in the securities market, like the American Nasdaq. The KIP piloted at CAS has been a major component of the National Innovation System. In January 2006 China launched the "National Medium- and Long-Term Program for Scientific and Technological Development" (2006–2020), commonly known as the 15-year Plan for science and technology. The Plan's long-term goal is to allow China to become a pre-eminent global economic and technological power, relying on "independent, indigenous innovation": China planned to establish an improved scientific and technological innovation system by 2020. The Chinese planned to leapfrog the development of their country's information science and technology and to acquire core technologies with proprietary intellectual property rights in the IT sector (https://en.most.gov.cn/pressroom/201211/t20121119_98014.htm#:~:text=Main%20goals:By%202020%2C%20we%20will%20aim%20to,innovation%20system%20with%20Chinese%20characteristics%20that%20is). The list below gives the strategic sectors identified by China for gaining ascendancy in these areas by 2025.

Advanced Storage Technologies
Alternative and Renewable Energies
Biotechnology/Genetics
Electronic Components
Environmental Technologies
Integrated Circuits/Semiconductors
Manned Space Exploration
Materials Technology
Nanotechnology

Network and Communication Technologies
Optical and Biological Computing
Software and Related Services

China has a leadership mainly composed by engineers who are in a favourable position to understand the nature and the strategic centrality of research and technology. It is notable that by 2010, China had already built-up remarkable elements of strength in the S&T and R&D area. For instance, it had been pouring huge societal investments into higher education and research (state financing for higher education more than doubled in 1998–2003, reaching over US$10 billion by the end of that period; China's number of researchers increased by almost 80% in 1995–2004 and is now second only to the United States). Large SOEs are now investing heavily in technological upgrading and human capital formation, and there are several start-up innovative firms, some of them already established in international markets (such as Lenovo, Haier and Huawei), and others active in crucial areas such as the provision of Internet services for the domestic market.

It is important to locate China's 15-year S&T Plan in the framework of the worldwide scenario shaped by the converging trends of key frontier technologies. As the APEC (2005) workshop on this topic has made clear, the convergence of information technology, biotechnology and nanotechnology (called by Khan *super convergence*) might be the most significant technological event of the twenty-first century (Khan 2005). The process of convergence is already underway. All the major national and regional players including the United States, the EU and Japan have already taken significant steps to maintain and gain further advantage in these technologies. China was a latecomer, but in the last two decades catch up has accelerated. In 2022, it has formidable momentum.

What can China do to be in the same league as the three major players mentioned above? Considering the challenges posed by a very competitive international environment where the other major players still hold a significant advantage, China can achieve super convergence only through the creation of a self-sustaining innovation system that can move forward over time, this paramount strategic goal must be properly seen as the logical evolution of the present S&T strategy, basically centred around perfecting China's NSI, towards a qualitatively superior, self-propelling innovation system. The 15-year Plan, if successful, will complete the catch-up process by 2020. Between 2020 and 2050, the strategic goal should be to build up autonomously advanced technological capabilities in the three crucial areas, with a view towards moving towards super convergence. Regional cooperation with Japan, Korea and Taiwan can play an important role in this strategy. Ultimately, a pan-Asian regional innovation network including India and the ASEAN countries might also be established. China's National Development and Reform Commission (NDRC) can start the process of national capacity building and regional cooperation by supporting key strategic ventures. Increasing the number of competent staff in the areas of planning for high technology development is a cornerstone. In Khan (1998, 2002, 2004a, b, 2008a) the overall planning framework is presented as part of a system-wide effort to create positive feedback loop for innovation, which is at the same time ***progressive, equitable and ecologically sustainable.*** I show that of such a wholistic model is a nonlinear complex innovation system. The Socially Embedded Intersectional NIS (SECENIS) framework can be applied through quantitative economy-wide modelling techniques, to analyse the challenges for transition from now to 2020 and then from 2020 to 2050.

The SECENIS approach is based on a somewhat novel theory of innovation in the economy-wide setting. Its first and most important feature is that the analysis of a SECENIS can be thought of as part of the institutional turn in economic theory. However, in contrast with much institutional literature, its propositions can also be expressed in a formal language, through models that can be estimated quantitatively for both rigorous, empirical scientific testing and policy-making purposes. The starting point of the SECENIS theory is the creative destruction process at the firm and industry level. However, an extension to an economy-wide setting requires the explicit theorization of the role of the state as well as an interacting nonlinear market process. The direction in which the theory leads is a complex interaction between state policies and market processes that influence the decisions taken by specific firms' areas of innovative activities. The key concept that is developed in this context can be called a Managed Creative Destruction (MCD) process. In a national (or regional) MCD, the creative destruction process characterizing innovation is structured more consciously by the state (or the states in a particular region). It can be argued that China is now going through this process. Following Schumpeter, we assume that innovation in specific firms can have economy-wide effects. As models based on this approach have multiple equilibria, the concept of a complex sustainable capabilities-enhancing innovation system or SECENIS is formalized by picking an appropriate sequence of equilibria over time. It can be also shown that SECENIS has empirical relevance by applying the formal model to an actual economy. Ultimately, technological transformation—in particular the creation of a SECENIS—is what makes the difference between sustained growth and gradual or sudden decline.

In addition to the system-wide approach to innovation over time, the SECENIS theory offers two other distinct advantages. One is the linkage between micro and meso or macro levels. One can start with firm-level data on innovation activities and link these to sectoral and intersectoral information flows. In this way, what happens at the firm level can be seen from a larger, economy-wide perspective. At the same time, the impact of firm-level activities on overall level and pace of innovation can also be ascertained qualitatively and quantitatively.

The third aspect of SECENIS is distributional. The complex system dynamics of SECENIS integrates production with distribution. Thus, the distribution of value added in production at both the factorial and household levels can be formulated as part of a general equilibrium (or, under circumstances of internal or external shocks, disequilibrium) framework. Given the levels and distribution of income among households, the consumption patterns and effective demand feedback mechanisms complete the formulation of a system-wide model.

While acknowledging the impressive progress achieved so far, a comprehensive recent OECD study on China's innovation system concluded with a sobering warning: "China needs a better return on its fast-rising investments in research and development (R&D) and higher education if it is to meet its goal of becoming an 'innovation-oriented' economy by 2020...China still has a long way to go to build a modern, high-performance national innovation system" (https://sciencebusiness.net/news/71775/Should-do-better%3A-OECD-verdict-on-China). This statement is realistic, as it stresses the uncertainties of the future without underestimating Chinese government's firm strategic determination to achieve the 15-year Plan's goals. China's leadership seems to be fully aware of the centrality of science and technology, not only for economic growth, but also with respect to other crucial challenges, such as the ultimate environmental sustainability of its market socialist development model and for the sake of enhancing China's relative place among the world leading nations. Consistent with this goal, it has been earmarking towards research and the broader S&T sector an increasing share of China's fast-growing GDP. As a result, China has now achieved a substantial critical mass in the area of research and innovation, second only (according to some estimates) to that of the United States, and growing four times faster than that of any of the major world technological leaders, among which there are signs that the enthusiasm for ever-increasing investment in R&D might be someway declining, in both the public and the private sectors. There is by now plenty of evidence showing that over the last decade China has witnessed major efficiency-enhancing institutional and organizational changes, including in property rights, a massive accumulation of human capital, and a very sustained rate of scientific and technical progress. Labour productivity has been rising fast, and a major part of the improvement is likely to be due to the aforementioned factors, even considering China's extraordinary rate of non-human capital accumulation. R&D input indicators and output indicators such as patents and scientific papers have been rising fast. Yet, a closer look shows that China is doing an excellent job at absorbing, adapting and developing existing technologies, but is still lagging significantly behind world technological leaders in terms of capability to generate state-of-the-art, world-class innovation proper, as is shown, for instance, by data on basic research and inventions patents.

With respect to state industry, the assessment of available evidence on SOEs' performance is more complex. Most sources indicate that, until the end of the past century, SOEs had been absorbing a major share of investment funds while exhibiting efficiency and profitability levels lower than enterprises belonging to other forms of ownership. Yet, their propensity to innovate (not always in an effective way) was high, and their productivity climbed dramatically, especially during the late 1990s. Latest available evidence appears to show that, during the present decade, the policy of concentrating huge resources on a small number of large and advanced SOEs while letting smaller and less efficient state enterprises to fend for themselves (recurring increasingly to extreme measures such as closures or ownership changes) has begun to bring significant qualitative fruit, as testified by core SOEs' increasing profitability and international competitiveness and by the embryonic emergence of some world-class state-owned TNCs. Both SOEs and large industrial enterprises operating in China under different forms of ownership—such as joint ventures and private (national and foreign) firms—manifest a very strong willingness to innovate, at a time when their counterparts in the United States and—to a lesser extent—other OECD countries appear to show a sort of innovation fatigue. The economic sustainability of China's historically unprecedented

S&T effort does not presently appear an issue, at least in the short-to-medium term, taking into account the leadership's determination in prioritizing the S&T sector and the resilience of China's GDP growth rates, even in presence of diverse unfavourable exogenous phenomena such as the Sichuan earthquake and the overall slowdown in the international economy triggered by the US subprime crisis.

On the one hand, the relationship between most R&D activities and the market is becoming closer and closer. Most of the R&D is already being carried out inside the enterprise sector, while universities and research institutes are intensifying their contacts with firms and generating themselves start-up ventures to develop, produce and commercialize their innovations. The IPR protection system is evolving towards a higher level of protection, partly to respect China's WTO obligations, but mainly to suit the present development stage, characterized by an increasing degree of commercialization of the bulk of technological knowledge (essentially, the one stemming from applied research and development activities). On the other hand, in order to tackle the crucial weaknesses mentioned above, vast financial, human and institutional resources are being channelled towards long-term basic research endeavour, concentrating on a limited number of strategic high-tech sectors. This major effort is articulated institutionally in a decentralized fashion, yet operates in a broadly consistent organizational and financial framework set up as a key component of China's specific form of strategic development planning. The challenge, at the present stage, is to engineer in a relative short period (10–15 years) a decisive qualitative leap in China's NIS, developing a systemic ability to generate world-class indigenous innovations. In addition to generating technical progress, China's development strategy shall also consider the challenge of establishing a model of innovation compatible with an equitable pattern of income distribution and environmental sustainability, thereby paving the way to the eventual evolution towards a higher and more developed form of socialism. This is the expressed aim of the Chinese leadership and enjoys considerable popular support.

However, the conventional NSI approach does not include a set of social and other informational requirements which are crucial to policy makers to steer successfully such a complex transition. Therefore, there is a need for more advanced analytical and planning tools. In this respect, we briefly refer to one particular approach, exemplified by the models introduced by Khan (1998, 2002, 2004a, b, 2008a, b, 2012, 2015, 2021a, b) within the context of nonlinear positive feedback innovation systems or

SECENIS. SECENIS can be thought as a generalization of NIS that embodies distributional, ecological and other issues relating to socio-economic (and even political) development.

Therefore, SECENIS-type models are sensitive to many of the above-mentioned concerns relevant to the strategy of development in China. SECENIS-type models can be used to chart strategically the market socialist course, as their internal logic is also consistent with China's "walking-on-two-legs" catch up strategy.

This strategy aims at embodying world-class best practices from technological world leaders and successful late industrializers but is also uniquely Chinese in at least two crucial aspects. The first is China's sheer size, which allowed her to leapfrog to rank 2 worldwide in terms of the absolute quantitative magnitude of its NIS, at a stage when it still lagged far behind all technological leaders. The second aspect has to do with China's still unsettled internal politics of distribution. A move away from ignoring distributional and related well-being issues is being attempted. Within the CPC, there is a lively and serious debate about the distributional and well-being aspects for the Chinese people. This is the more positive part of the so-called China Dream. More broadly, this is part of the complex debates surrounding the Fourth Industrial Revolution.

Eurasia and China's Innovation Systems: Technological Great Leap Forward (TGLF)—China's NSI/NIS[6] *and the Linkages Between Industry and Science*

Evidence of China's innovative capabilities evolution towards the Fourth Industrial Revolution

Growing quantitative evidence is becoming available on various aspects of China's economy, institutions and innovative capabilities, and they broadly converge towards suggesting that China is in fact climbing fast the economic and technological development ladder. Figures on economy-wide and industrial GDP, export and labour productivity growths are too well known to be worth mentioning here. S&T, R&D and high-tech trade indicators are discussed in Section 3.2. Various other sources mention statistics bearing indirect evidence of China's growing technological power.

[6] We will be using NSI to keep continuity with the standard usage. But we will also be referring to NIS when we develop the concept of SCENIS which is an augmented (defined carefully later) type of NIS/NSI or ANIS.

Comparative evidence on companies' productivity growth and propensity to innovate appear to show that Chinese firms are doing reasonably well, European firms are maintaining their positions and (surprisingly) US firms are losing ground. Productivity growth in China is more than three times the rate of that in the United States and Europe. A survey carried out on more than 500 chiefs information officers (CIOs) in the United States, Europe and China provides even more striking results. Only 32% of US executives and 41% of Europeans said they wanted to be early adopters of new technologies, compared to 70% of Chinese CIOs. Consistently, 70% of companies in China are committing most of their business to web services, against 42% in Europe and 38% in the United States: "As companies use these new standards for communicating with other systems, people, and companies, they cut manual business process costs to one- tenth of current levels and can flexibly change features and services in less time for substantially less money.... Newer systems, during this second wave of web-based innovations, outperform older technology. These technologies have improved substantially in the past five years, making them easier to implement. As a result, more business processes will be online, driving higher levels of productivity". Moreover, many indicators on productivity, revenue and profit growth show that US companies are doing significantly worse than what conventional data on productivity growth might suggest. Among US S&P 500 large companies, employee growth was faster than both revenue and profit growth in 2001–2005. Thus, the growth of average revenue gains per employee was 58% lower than total average revenue growth, and profits per employee growth were only 75% of total profit growth. In contrast, among US S&P 350 companies recorded revenue and profit growth rates higher than employee growth rates.

Further indirect evidence of major advances in the areas of governance, management and technology in China's industry is provided by the very marked improvements in SOEs' economic and financial performance. In the aftermath of the 1997 Asian financial crisis, China's SOEs sector, long plagued by the deficiencies common to most publicly owned productive enterprises, saw its average profit margin fall close to zero, with many firms reporting big losses. After ten years of restructuring, which implied a dramatic decrease in employment and in enterprise numbers but also massive injections of capital and technology and a major leap in managers' and workers' education and skills, the SOEs sector was finally in good financial health.

In sum, by 2012, China has created a group of large leading SOEs in highly competitive sectors, where technology, design and marketing capabilities are key for ultimate survival, thereby overcoming a traditional weakness of public enterprises worldwide. The ultimate outcome of this major upgrading and restructuring exercise in China's public industry has played a crucial role in launching the Fourth Industrial Revolution in China.

R&D and S&T Indicators

Input indicators show that China not only earmarked huge and ever-increasing resources towards research, science and technology, but also intensified its efforts in relative terms, thereby exposing a strong and effective pro-R&D and S&T bias in both government and business sector policies. Gross Domestic Expenditure on R&D in nominal terms almost tripled (in nominal terms) in the early 2000s, reaching 300 billion Yuan by 2006. In a period of very fast economic growth, the GERD/GDP percentage ratio also increased markedly, from 0.95 in 2001 to 1.42 in 2006. Now it is close to 2. Government S&T appropriation also increased as a percentage of total government expenditure, with a high level of priority being accorded to special projects and operating funds.

Available, simple international comparative indicators of R&D inputs and outputs confirm the basic features of an overall scenario in which China has undoubtedly joined the worldwide League, pouring towards the research sectors enormous and ever-increasing human and financial resources. China's R&D effort far outpaces that of other large, semi-industrialized countries such as Brazil and India and is far ahead of many countries formerly seen as among the most industrialized ones, such as Italy. In terms of R&D intensity of the national economy, measured by the GERD/GDP percentage ratio, China has clearly left behind Italy, Russia, Brazil and India. We show in the next section that China is catching up rapidly in semiconductors with the leaders in the field and, most probably, will overtake them by 2030 at the latest. Basic comparative indicators of international R&D outputs show that China now figures among the global leaders, as it ranks fourth worldwide in terms of domestic invention patents granted, second in terms of indexed papers published and fifth in terms of SCI-indexed papers published. These data, however, are not adequate to provide firm evidence on a much-discussed issue, i.e., whether China's ability to translate R&D inputs into output is structurally lower than that of world technological leaders. The next section shows that in semiconductors and the most significant areas of artificial intelligence, China is already at par with the advanced countries or even ahead in many areas.

Semiconductor Industry, AI and Fourth Industrial Revolution in China Within a Geoeconomics Framework: Data and Analysis

We analyse the semiconductor industry as advanced material foundation for a significant part of the Fourth Industrial Revolution as well as a part of the material foundation for AI in the twenty-first century. I list in great detail the key AI technologies and their applications for China and the world. These are important parts of evolving twenty-first-century geoeconomics. Geoeconomics can be defined as the "geostrategic use of economic power" by states (Khan, 2021a, b; Lundvall and Rikap 2022). Geoeconomics proposes that an important part of economic and military power derives increasingly from control over markets and advanced technologies. Economic statecraft is analogous to geopolitics with "disposable capital in lieu of firepower, civilian innovation in lieu of military-technical advancement, and market penetration in lieu of garrisons and bases".[7] In the twenty-first century power therefore depends largely on "productive efficiency, market control, trade surplus, strong currency, foreign exchange reserves, ownership of foreign companies, factories and technology". Economic interdependence is also coterminous with competition among countries. According to realist geoeconomics, states intervene in the market to develop asymmetrical economic interdependence as the stronger and less dependent side in an economic partnership can extract political concessions from the weaker and more dependent side. Geoeconomics theory therefore expects that the international system gravitates towards a "balance of dependence", the equivalent of a balance of power, as governments seek to reduce excessive reliance on any one state or region (Diesen 2017). Furthermore, three categories of economic dependency can be defined: (1) strategic industries create dependency due to the human-made scarcity of high technology products or natural resources; (2) transportation corridors are important for economic competitiveness; and (3)

[7] Huntington (1993, p. 73).

financial instruments such as trade/reserve currencies and banks. All these propositions are understood by Chinese high technology policy makers.[8]

The history of the United States' rise to superpower status has relied on taking over the three geoeconomics pillars with strategic industries by building technological leadership, control over the world's maritime corridors, and financial instruments by establishing the US dollar as the reserve currency—first because of unique dominance of the United States after World War II (WWII) and then through US treasury bills purchases by the central banks of balance of payments surplus countries from 1973 onwards. This has allowed for the US leadership position in international banking and finance till now. Will this dominance end with the rise of China and dedollarization? Chinese dominance in the Fourth Industrial Revolution and AI together with international politics and geoeconomics will decide the answer to this crucial question.

Without doubt, the current disruption to the international economic system comes from the spectacular rise of China. Following Deng's wisdom ("hide your strength, bide your time"), Beijing followed initially a strategy of catching up without attracting unwanted attention from great powers. As China's economy in PPP terms surpassed the United States in 2014, the system inevitably entered the early stages of turbulent dynamics. Clearly, as this paper demonstrates, the PRC has succeeded with its own three-pillared geoeconomics strategy. As Khan (2010, 2018, 2021a, b) and Gabriele and Khan (2010) show, the PRC is asserting control over strategic industries by establishing technological leadership with the China 2025 industrial strategy and through the acquisition of natural resources around the world. Furthermore, since 2013, the PRC has developed the Belt and Road Initiative (BRI) for infrastructure and physical economic connectivity. Finally, though this is in its early stage, financial instruments of power are being established under Chinese control by gradually but strategically internationalizing its currency and building up gold reserves instead of dollar denominated T-bills and US financial assets. As Khan (2015) shows, establishing new development banks such as the Asia Infrastructure Investment Bank and the China International Payment System (CIPS) as an alternative transaction system to SWIFT are important steps in China's geoeconomic strategy. Perhaps in East Asia, the Chinese-led Regional Comprehensive Economic Partnership (RCEP) will lead soon to a geoeconomics region.

[8] For the Fourth Industrial Revolution in PRC and AI in particular see Zeng (2021).

Chinese Semiconductor Industry as a Key Twenty-First-Century Fourth Industrial Revolution and as Hardware Support for AI

The Chinese semiconductor industry has expanded dramatically from its small size in the early 2000's. It grew on average by 15.8% per annum from 56.2 billion yuan in 2000 to 281.4 billion yuan in 2011, while the global semiconductor output grew on average only by 8.8% per annum over the same period. Rapid growth has enabled the share of China's semiconductor output in world output to rise from 4.8% in 2002 to 14.5% in 2011. The manufacture of discrete semiconductor appliances grew on average by an impressive 22.1% per annum over the period 2002–2011. China had nearly 3000 semiconductor firms with over 600 of them producing integrated circuits by 2013. And yet, even with this strong growth, the Chinese semiconductor industry has faced many challenges over the last 10 years.

Semiconductors, otherwise known as "chips", are essential components at the heart of economic growth, security and technological innovation. Smaller than the size of a postage stamp, thinner than a human hair and made of nearly 40 billion components, the impact that semiconductors are having on world development exceeds that of the Industrial Revolution. From smartphones, PCs and pacemakers to the internet, electric vehicles, aircrafts and hypersonic weapons, semiconductors are ubiquitous in electrical devices and the digitization of goods and services such as global e-commerce. And demand is skyrocketing, with the industry facing numerous challenges and opportunities as emerging technologies such as artificial intelligence (AI), quantum computing, Internet of Things (IoT) and advanced wireless communications, notably 5G, all require cutting-edge semiconductor-enabled devices. But the COVID-19 pandemic and international trade disputes are straining the industry's supply and value chains while the battle between the United States and China over tech supremacy risks splintering the supply chain further, contributing to technological fragmentation and significant disruption in international commerce.

Government Promotion

Undoubtedly, Chinese semiconductor industrial development has benefited from strong institutional support. Two distinct stages could be identified, the first before 2000 characterized by specific national programmes, while the later stage by overall systemic support. A comprehensive policy framework was established to support development of the semiconductor and supporting industries. The period 2000–2014 witnessed the maturation of the supporting policy, which grew from an abstract national strategy to a concrete policy. Several policy pillars have been set up following issuance by the *State Council of the Software and Integrated Circuit Industries* in June 2000, the *Notification of the Long-Term Development Plan for Strategic Emerging Industries* over the 12th Five-Year Plan in July 7, 2012. The State Council strengthened policy direction further by encouraging the Development of the Software and Integrated Circuit Industries in January 28, 2011, which provided further support through financial incentive, preferential investment policies, R&D incentives, import and export subsidies, human resources initiatives and intellectual property rights protection. Human resources initiatives and IPRs protection are both the policy aspects in the document issues in January 2011. Human resources aspect includes detailed policies to support the IC-related talents attraction and cultivation through industry academia collaboration, establish the microelectronics institute and reform the educational methods and talents stimulations policies. The IPR aspect encourages software companies' copyright registration, strictly implementing the software and integrated circuit intellectual property protection system. With strong policy support through tax exemptions, subsidies and R&D grants, the government has managed to promote technological capabilities, including in indigenous IC design firms. Through reinforcement of the advantages of the IC sector and upgrading into backward packages, a complete industrial value chain is expected to emerge like a "necklace" of "pearls". The goal of such a scheme is to make China a major player in the global IC industry with domestic brands and national intellectual property rights. This, the government has done through a development roadmap with timeline, development goals, action initiatives and regulations. The sectoral development policy has stimulated industrial upgrading in the semiconductor industry through two ways. Firstly, the shifting of support from particular three segments to the entire value chain, with special emphasis on interaction between different industry players in the value chain, has benefited upgrading. One example of upgrading is indicated by the Value-Added Tax reform, which has since benefited all companies in the value chain, including design, manufacturing, assembly, testing and special purpose materials and equipment manufacturing. Secondly, the policy encourages cross-regional industrial integration, merger and acquisitions.

Industrial Expansion

The Chinese IC industry has been gradually moving up along the value chain of the global production network, witnessed by rapid growth of R&D input and output by domestic firms. The combination of inner strength and external forces significantly promoted the overall advancement of semiconductor industry, where reinforcement of inner strengths is featured by the growing number of firms and domestic research institutes, and external forces means the foreign firms with cutting-edge technology synchronize domestic firms to learn and upgrade. Meanwhile, strong domestic demand and national supporting policies provide local semiconductor firms a strong favourable external environment to thrive. The size of IC industry has been growing rapidly, with production volume increasing from 3500 million items in 1984 to 71.4 billion items in 2012 (the first three quarters). Table 6.1 profiles a growing IC industry of China with main economic indicator. The number of employees increases 14.7% every year, jumping from 74,004 people in 2000 to 293,023 people in 2010. The growing number of firms brought an increase in industrial gross output, which increased from 27.23 billion yuan in 2000 to 234.02 billion yuan in 2010 with an average annual growth rate of 24% throughout the period. A yearly increase of 22.32% in the profits lasted over the period, and exports grew 25.5% every year from 15.95 billion yuan in 2000 to 154.57 billion yuan in 2010. During the rapid growth, the Chinese semiconductor industry has become an important part in the global production network. Countries which have developed semiconductor industries have set up industry bases or some research and development centres in China, including the United States, the EU, Japan, South Korea and Taiwan region. So far in China, semiconductor industrial

Table 6.1 Operating models in the semiconductor industry and leading firms

Integrated device manufacturer (IDM) model	*Intel, Micron, Samsung, Texas Instruments*
Design (fabless)	AMD, Broadcom, MediaTek, HiSilicon, Qualcomm
Manufacturing (foundries)	GlobalFoundries, SMIC, TSMC, UMC
Assembly, test and packaging (ATP)	Amkor, ASE, ChipPAC, JCET, J-Devices, Power-tech, SPIL

Source: Adapted from SIA, "Beyond Borders", May 2016

clusters have formed in the Bohai Area, Yangtze River Delta and Pearl River Delta. The middle and west region has become the base for IC packaging and testing, for instance LED, packaging. Despite its status as a latecomer in the industry, China semiconductor sales grew 29.5% every year on average from 12 billion yuan in 2001 to 158 billion in 2011, with its market share in the world increasing from 1.9% in 2001 to 9.8% in 2011. While the sales shot up to 325 billion yuan in 2008 from 125 billion in 2007, sales fell back to 110 billion in 2009. The share in the world shows a stable rise, suggesting a sudden rise in demand from the international market in 2008. The development of China's IC industry was reflected not only by quantity, but also on its industrial structure to enjoy significant participation in global production activities. The sales of IC design grew 41.2% every year from 1.5 billion yuan in 2001 to 47.4 billion yuan in 2011. Throughout the period, the share of packing and testing significantly dropped from 79.3% to 38.9%, while the share of design increased from 7.3% to 30.1%. This dramatic structural change indicates the speeding up of industrialization of China's IC industry. The production activities are shifting away from low-value-added exercise and gradually upgrading technological capacity in high-value-added product design.

Current State of the Semiconductor Industry in China

Global chip sales from Chinese companies are on the rise, largely due to increasing US-China tensions and a whole-of-nation effort to advance China's chip sector, including government subsidies, procurement preferences and other preferential policies.

Just five years ago, China's semiconductor device sales were $13 billion, accounting for only 3.8% of global chip sales. In 2020, however, the Chinese semiconductor industry registered an unprecedented annual growth rate of 30.6% to reach $39.8 billion in total annual sales, according to an SIA analysis. The jump in growth helped China capture 9% of the global semiconductor market in 2020, surpassing Taiwan for two consecutive years and closely following Japan and the EU, which each took 10% of market share. Sales data for 2021 are not yet available. If China's semiconductor development continues its strong momentum—maintaining 30% CAGR over the next three years—and assuming growth rates of industries in other countries stay the same, the Chinese semiconductor industry could generate $116 billion in annual revenue by 2024, capturing upwards of 17.4% of global market share. This would place China behind only the United States and South Korea in global market share. Equally startling is the number of new firms in China rushing into the semiconductor industry. Nearly 15,000 Chinese firms registered as semiconductor enterprises in 2020. A large number of these new firms are fabless start-ups specializing in GPU, EDA, FPGA, AI computing and other higher-end chip design. Many of these firms are developing advanced chips, designing and taping out devices on bleeding-edge process nodes. Sales of Chinese high-end logic devices are also accelerating, with the combined revenue of China's CPU, GPU, and FPGA sectors growing at an annual rate of 128% to nearly $1 billion in revenue in 2020, up from a meagre $60 million in 2015. Across all four subsegments of the Chinese semiconductor supply chain—fabless, Integrated Device Manufacturer (IDM), foundry, and outsourced assembly, packaging, and testing (OSAT)—Chinese firms recorded rapid increases in revenue last year, representing annual growth rates of 36%, 23%, 32% and 23%, respectively, based on an SIA analysis. Leading Chinese semiconductor firms are on track to expand domestically, and even globally, in several submarkets. SIA analysis further shows that in 2020, China held an impressive 16% market share in the global fabless semiconductor segment, ranking third after the United States and Taiwan, and up from 10% in 2015. Benefiting from China's massive consumer and 5G market, Huawei's HiSilicon, China's largest chip designer, generated nearly $10 billion in revenue in 2020, despite tightened export control restrictions (largely due to significant stockpiling suggested by official Chinese trade data). Other Chinese fabless firms, such as communications chip supplier UNISOC, MCU and NOR flash designer GigaDevice, fingerprint chip firm Goodix and image sensor designers Galaxycore and OmniVision (a US-headquartered corporation acquired by China), have all reported a 20–40% annual growth rate to become China's top fabless firms. Moreover, in addition to supplying Chinese OMEs, GigaDevice, OmniVision and Goodix have entered the top three global smartphone vendors' supply chains.

Meanwhile, Chinese consumer electronics and home appliance OEMs and leading internet firms have also been ramping up efforts to expand into the semiconductor sector by designing chips in-house and making investments in established semiconductor firms, with notable progress made in designing advanced chips and building domestic supply chains over the past two years. China also maintains robust growth in building out its semiconductor manufacturing supply chain, with 28 additional fab construction projects totalling $26 billion in new planned funding announced in 2021; SMIC and other Chinese semiconductor leaders have further expanded their partnerships with local governments to construct additional joint venture fabs, with a focus on mature technology nodes. Wafer manufacturing start-ups are continuing to spring up in the trailing-edge fabrication field, backed by government incentives. On the chip manufacturing front, due to the inclusion of Huawei and SMIC on the US government's Entity List (China's most advanced chip designer and foundry, respectively), the Chinese semiconductor industry has largely suspended advanced logic node manufacturing development and redirected most capital to mature fabrication technology. As a result of this change, from September 2020 to November 2021, Chinese wafer manufacturers have added nearly 500K wafer per month (WPM) capacities in trailing nodes (>=14 nm) and only an additional 10K in capacity for advanced nodes. China's wafer capacity increase alone accounted for 26% of the worldwide total. In 2021, China also started commercial shipments of indigenously manufactured mobile 19 nm DDR4 DRAM devices and 64-layer 3D NAND Flash chips and started 128-layer products. While the Chinese memory industry is still at an early stage of development, Chinese memory firms are expected to achieve a compound annual growth rate of 40–50% in output and become highly competitive over the next five years. Regarding backend production, China is a global leader in outsourced assembly, packaging and testing (OSAT), with its top three OSAT players collectively holding more than 35% of the global market share.

All indications are that China's rapid growth in semiconductor chip sales is likely to continue due in large part to the unwavering commitment from the central government and robust policy support in the face of deteriorating US-China relations. While there remains a long way to go for China to catch up with existing industry leaders—especially in advanced node foundry production, equipment and materials—the gap is expected to narrow over the next decade as Beijing sharpens its focus on semiconductor self-reliance during the current 14th Five-Year Plan

Trump and Biden Administration Sanctions

In September of 2019, the Trump administration placed restrictions on exports to Semiconductor Manufacturing International Corporation, China's most advanced maker of computer chips. Dozens of Chinese companies, including SMIC and drone maker DJI, were added to the Commerce Department's so-called Entity List, which effectively cuts them off from US suppliers and technology. Some industry leaders were not worried about the ban initially as the ban only applies to those technologies that are "uniquely" capable of producing semiconductors at 10 nanometers in size or below. However, since the ban, China has faced immense pressure on the self-reliability of China's technology industry as a whole. Currently, experts predict that China is at least two generations (four years) behind the chip makers in the United States. These US companies include but are not constrained to Apple, Google, Nvidia, Intel and Qualcomm, to note a few.

The following tables and charts summarize the analysis of the evolution of this sector as part of a Chinese SECENIS.

Table 6.1 depicts the operating models in the semiconductor industry globally. One can also find the leading firms that utilize said operating models (Table 6.2).

Table 6.3 shows a worldwide ranking of the top 15 suppliers of semiconductors in 2018 globally.

Table 6.3 describes the notable semiconductor-related Chinese industrial plans from 1956 to 2016.

Table 6.4 lists the announced Chinese semiconductor-related investment into the United States by the year.

Figure 6.1 depicts the worldwide semiconductor consumption market by region from 2003 to 2016. The graph shows us that China has come out on top year after year with an all-time high in 2016.

Figure 6.2 goes further to show us the global market share of the semiconductor industry as of 2020. The United States has the largest global market share.

Figure 6.3 describes the semiconductor manufacturing capacity of 2021 with Taiwan coming out on top.

Figure 6.4 analyses where semiconductors are manufactured or assembled globally. The graph shows us that most semiconductors are manufactured or assembled in China.

Figure 6.5 analyses the global chip shortage starting in 2018 to present. It mentions various factory fires.

Figure 6.6 shows the global semiconductor market share by major country and/or region from 2003 to 2019. China remains stagnant throughout.

Figure 6.7 analyses China-based fabs that become more cost competitive due to government support for an estimated 10-year total cost of ownership (TCO) of reference facts by location (US indexed to 100).

Table 6.2 Worldwide ranking of the top-15 suppliers of semiconductors in 2018

Company	*Headquarters*	*Operating model*	*2018 forecasted sales (billion)*
Samsung	South Korea	IDM	$65.90
Intel	United States	IDM	$61.70
TSMC	Taiwan	Foundry	$32.20
SK Hynix	South Korea	IDM	$26.70
Micron	United States	IDM	$23.90
Broadcom	United States	Fabless	$17.80
Qualcomm	United States	Fabless	$17.00
Texas Instruments	United States	IDM	$13.90
Toshiba/Toshiba Memory	Japan	IDM	$13.30
Nvidia	United States	Fabless	$9.40
NXP	Europe	IDM	$9.30
STMicroelectronics	Europe	IDM	$8.30
Infineon	Europe	IDM	$8.10
Sony	Japan	IDM	$7.90
Western Digital/Sandisk	United States	IDM	$7.80

Source: IC Insights, "Nine Top-15 2018 Semi Suppliers Forecast to Post Double-Digit Gains", November 12, 2018

Table 6.3 Notable semiconductor-related Chinese industrial plans

Year	*Title*	*Semiconductor-related provisions*
1956	Outline for Science and Technology Development, 1956–1967	Identified semiconductor technology as a "key priority" for China's future
1983	"Build Two Bases (North and South) and One Point"	Designated a "South Base" (around Shanghai, Jiangsu and Zhejiang) and "North Base" (Beijing, Tianjin and Shenyang) where firms could share resources and develop semiconductor industry supply chains
1982	The Strategy for the Development of China's Electronics and Information Industries	6 strategies outlined focused on using foreign technology to advance China's technology via joint ventures, creation of a domestic electronics supply chain with an emphasis on quality mass production and large-scale ICs
1990	Project 908	Advocating Project 908, which sought to establish China's first world-class I.D.M. at Wuxi's #742 Factory
1991	8th Five-Year National Economic and Social Development Plan	Called the development of the domestic IC industry a "main task" of the state. Articulated "Project 908"

(*continued*)

Table 6.3 (continued)

Year	*Title*	*Semiconductor-related provisions*
1995	Project 908 Breaks ground	Goal was to establish a 150 mm (6-inch) wafer fab run as China Huajing Electronics Group (IDM)
1996	9th Five-Year National Economic and Social Development Plan and 2010 Long-Term Goals	Called for development of next-generation ICs
2001	10th Five-Year National Economic and Social Development Plan Outline	Called for the focused development of high-tech industries and to "vigorously develop the IC… industry"
2005	National Medium- and Long-Term Science and Technology Development Plan Outline (2006–2020)	Articulated China's long-term technology development strategy. Of 13 key projects identified, development of core electronics (including chips) and chip manufacturing are prioritized as numbers one and two
2006	11th Five-Year National Economic and Social Development Plan Outline	Called for the "vigorous" development of ICs and other industries at the core of the "digitization trend"
2011	12th Five-Year National Economic and Social Development Plan Outline	Inaugurated a "high performance ICs project"
2014	Guidelines for the Development and Promotion of the Integrated Circuit Industry	Called for establishing a National IC Industry Development Leading Small Group to coordinate design of the industry's development and starting a National Integrated Circuit Investment Fund
2015	Made in China 2025	Strategy calling for accelerated advances in key manufacturing technologies, including chips
2015	Made in China 2025: Major Technical Area Roadmap	Established specific sales values and market share targets for the IC industry to be met by domestic production
2016	13th Five-Year National Economic and Social Development Plan Outline	Called for the active promotion of advanced semiconductor technology

Source: USTR, Section 301, Report, March 2018, pp. 111–113; Lewis, "Learning from the Superior Techniques", 2019, pp. 32–35

Table 6.4 Announced Chinese semiconductor-related investment into the United States

Announced	*US target*	*Chinese investor*	*Value*
Jul-06	LSI Logic- ZSR(R) Digital Signal Unit	VeriSilicon Holdings	$13 million
Jan-08	Quorum Systems	Spreadtrum Communications	$77 million
Nov-10	Creation of US subsidiary	China WLCSP Co. Ltd.	$1 million
Jun-11	MobilePeak Systems stake	Spreadtrum Communications	$27.2 million
Aug-11	Telegent Systems	Spreadtrum Communications	$92 million
Sep-11	MobilePeak Systems stake	Spreadtrum Communications	$3.6 million
Mar-15	Integrated Silicon Solutions Inc.	Hua Capital Management, SummitView Capital, E-Town Memtek	$640 million
Apr-15	FlipChip International	Tianshui Huatian Technology	$41 million
May-15	WiSpry	AAC Technologies Holdings	$10 million
May-15	Static Control Components	Apex Microelectronics	$63 million
Jun-16	Marvell Technology*	Datang Telecom	$2 billion
Jul-15	Bridgelux	China Electronics Corporation, Chongqing Linkong Development Investment	$130 million
Jul-15	Micron Technology*	Tsinghua Holdings	$23 billion
Aug-15	Micrel Technology*	Unnamed Chinese buyer	$839 million
Sep-15	Atmel*	China Electronics Corporation	$3.4 billion
Sep-15	Western Digital*	Tsinghua Unisplendour	$3.8 billion
Sep-15	Pericom Semiconductor	Montage Technology Group (subsidiary of China Electronics Corp.)	$442 million

(*continued*)

Table 6.4 (continued)

Announced	*US target*	*Chinese investor*	*Value*
Dec-15	Xcerra- interface board business	Fastprint	$23 million
Dec-15	Mattson Technology	Beijing E-Town Dragon Semiconductor Industry Investment Center	$300 million
Dec-15	Fairchild Semiconductor*	China Resources, Hua Capital Management	$2.5 billion
Jan-16	OmniVision Technologies	CITIC Capital Holdings, Goldstone Investment, Hua Capital Management	$1.9 billion
Jan-16	Initio	Sage Microelectronics	$40 million
Jan-16	Vivante	VeriSilicon Holdings	Not known
Mar-16	Global Communications Semiconductors	Sanan Optoelectronics	$226 million
Mar-16	GigOptix	Shanghai Pudong Science and Technology	$5 million
Mar-16	Anadigics	Unnamed Chinese buyer	$78.2 million
Apr-16	Lattice Semiconductor	Tsinghua Holdings	$41.6 million
May-16	Marvell Technology Group	Tsinghua Holdings	$78.2 million
Jun-16	Multi-Fineline Electronix	Suzhou Dongshan Precision Manufacturing	$610 million
Jun-16	Integrated Memory Logic	Beijing E-Town Chipone Technology	$136 million
Aug-16	MEMSIC	HC Semitek; China Reform Holdings Corporation	
Sep-16	Analogix	Beijing Shanhai Capital Management & National IC Fund	$500 million
Nov-16	Lattice Semiconductor*	Canyon Bridge Capital Partners	$1.3 billion
Feb-18	Xcerra Corp*	Hubei Xinyan	$580 million

Source: Semiconductor Industry Association Factbook 2020

Note: * = Proposed Transaction Terminated. Source: Rhodium Group

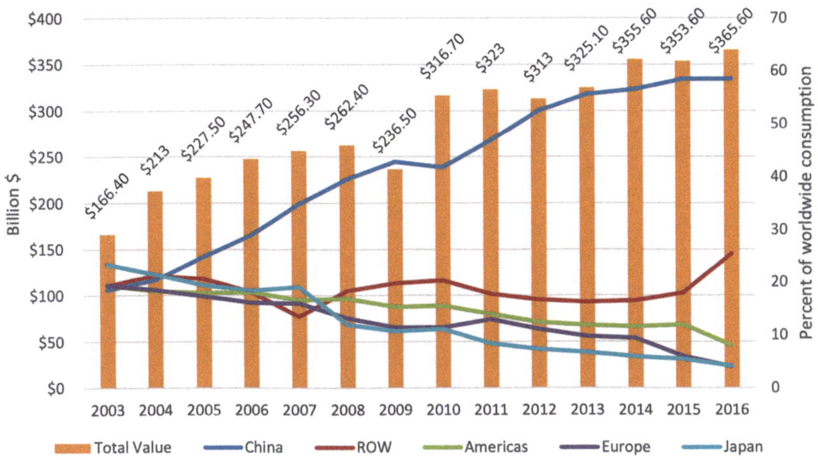

Fig. 6.1 Worldwide semiconductor consumption market by region, 2003–2016. (Source: PwC, "China's Semiconductor Market", 2017)

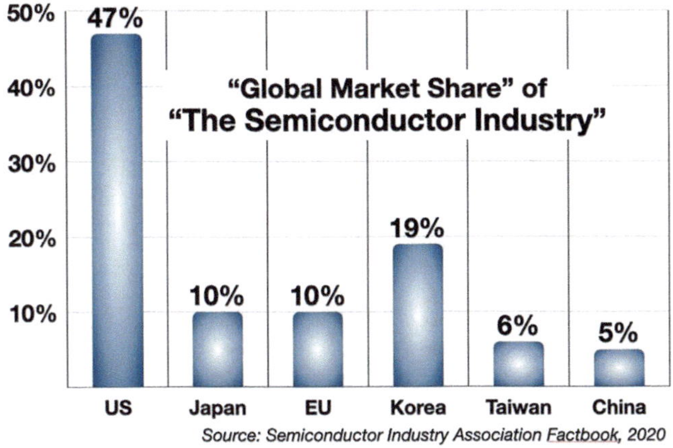

Fig. 6.2 The "global market share" of the semiconductor industry (2020)

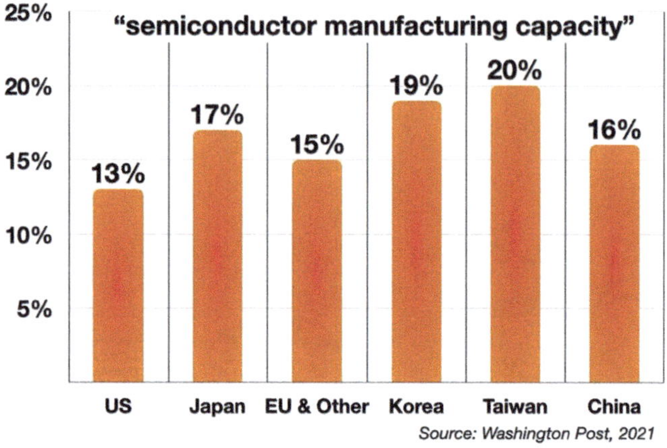

Fig. 6.3 Semiconductor manufacturing capacity (2021)

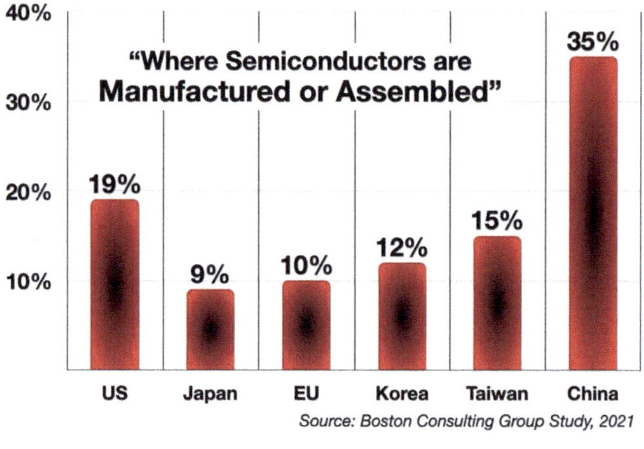

Fig. 6.4 Where semiconductors are manufactured or assembled (2021)

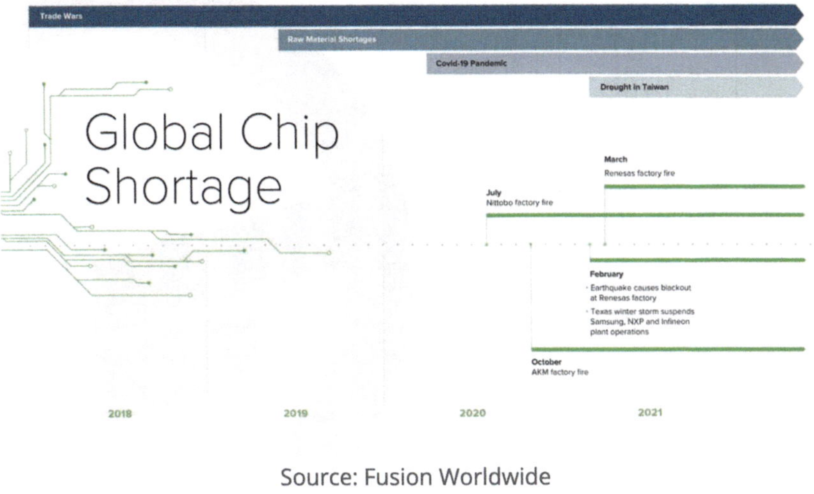

Fig. 6.5 Global chip shortage

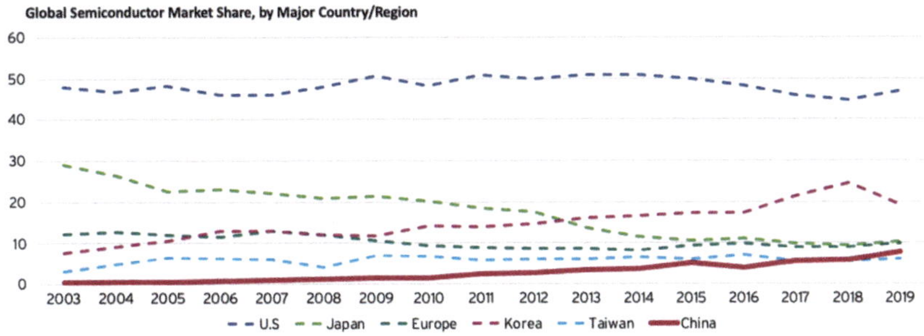

Fig. 6.6 Global semiconductor market share, by major country/region. (Source: Semiconductor Industry Association Factbook 2020)

Figure 6.8 further describes China's share of worldwide semiconductor fabrication capacities (Fig. 6.8).

A Detailed List of AI-related Technologies in China

China has made rapid progress in catching up and is either at the frontier or already dominant in the following AI areas:

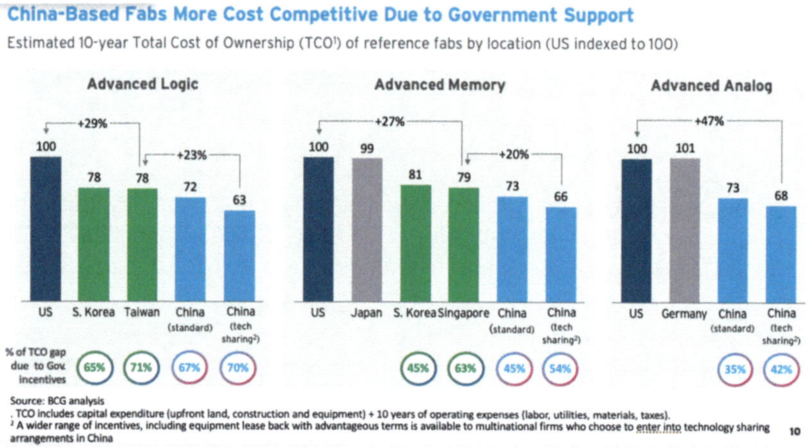

Fig. 6.7 China-based fabs more cost competitive due to government support. (Source: Semiconductor Industry Association Factbook 2020)

Fig. 6.8 China share of worldwide semiconductor fabrication capacities. (Source: Semiconductor Industry Association Factbook 2020)

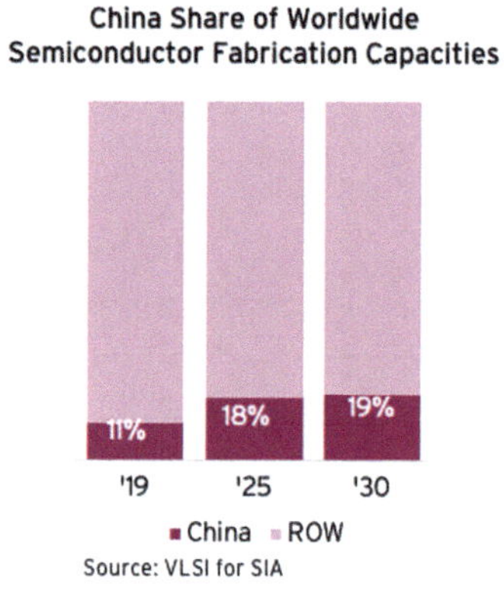

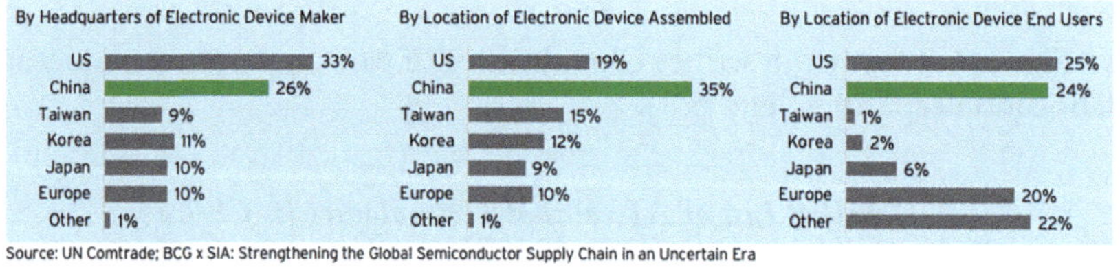

Fig. 6.9 Global elctronic device sales by geographic area, 2019 (%)

- Brain models, brain mapping, cognitive science
- Natural language processing
- Fuzzy logic and soft computing
- Expert systems
- Decision support systems
- Automated problem solving
- Knowledge discovery
- Knowledge representation
- Knowledge acquisition
- Knowledge-intensive problem-solving techniques
- Knowledge networks and management
- Intelligent information systems
- Intelligent web-based business
- Intelligent agents
- AI and evolutionary algorithms
- Distributed AI algorithms and techniques
- Neural networks and variations, including deep learning
- Heuristic searching methods
- Constraint-based reasoning and constraint programming
- Intelligent information fusion
- Learning and adaptive sensor fusion
- Search and meta-heuristics
- Integration of AI with other technologies
- Social intelligence (markets and computational societies)
- Social impact of AI
- Emerging technologies
- Applications (including computer vision, signal processing, military, surveillance, robotics, medicine, pattern recognition, face recognition, finger print recognition, finance and marketing, stock market, education, emerging applications, etc.)

Machine learning; models, technologies and applications:

- Statistical learning theory
- Unsupervised and supervised learning
- Multivariate analysis
- Hierarchical learning models
- Relational learning models
- Bayesian methods

- Meta learning
- Stochastic optimization
- Heuristic optimization techniques
- Neural networks and variations (e.g., Deep Learning)
- Reinforcement learning
- Multi-criteria reinforcement learning
- General learning models
- Multiple hypothesis testing
- Markov chain Monte Carlo (MCMC) methods
- Non-parametric methods
- Graphical models
- Bayesian networks
- Cross-Entropy method
- Time series prediction
- Fuzzy logic and learning
- Inductive learning and applications
- Graph kernel and graph distance methods
- Graph-based semi-supervised learning
- Graph clustering
- Graph learning-based methods
- Motif search
- Aspects of knowledge structures
- Computational intelligence
- General structure-based approaches in information retrieval,
- web authoring, information extraction and web content mining
- Latent semantic analysis
- Aspects of natural language processing
- Intelligent linguistics
- Computational neuroscience

- Algorithms for big data:

Data and information fusion
Algorithms (including scalable methods)
Signal processing
Data-intensive computing
High-dimensional big data
Multilinear subspace learning
Sampling methodologies

Streaming

– Big data fundamentals:

Novel computational methodologies
Algorithms for enhancing data quality
Models and frameworks for big data
Graph algorithms and big data

– Infrastructures for big data:

Cloud-based infrastructures (storage and resources)
Grid and stream computing for big data
Autonomic computing
Programming models and environments to support big data
Software and tools for big data
Emerging architectural frameworks for big data
Paradigms and models for big data

– Big data management and frameworks:

Database and web applications
Federated database systems
Distributed database systems
Knowledge management and engineering
Novel data models
Data preservation and provenance
Data protection methods
Data integrity and privacy standards and policies
Scientific data management

– Big data search:

Multimedia and big data
Social networks
Web search and information extraction
Scalable search architectures
Cleaning big data, acquisition and integration
Visualization methods for search
Graph-based search and similar technologies

– Privacy in the era of big data:

Cryptography
Threat detection using big data analytics
Privacy preserving big data collection
Intrusion detection

- Data mining/machine learning tasks:

Regression/classification
Segmentation/clustering/association
Deviation and outlier detection
Explorative and visual data mining
Mining text and semi-structured data
Temporal and spatial data mining

- Data mining algorithms:

Artificial neural networks/deep learning
Fuzzy logic and rough sets
Decision trees/rule learners
Evolutionary computation/meta-heuristics
Statistical methods
Collaborative filtering
Case based reasoning
Ensembles/committee approaches

- Data mining integration:

Mining large-scale data/big data
Data and knowledge representation
Data warehousing and OLAP integration
Integration of prior domain knowledge
Metadata and ontologies
Legal and social aspects of data mining

- Applications and further research areas:

Bioinformatics, medicine data mining, business/corporate
Industrial data mining, direct marketing, database marketing
Engineering mining, military data mining, security data mining, etc.

- Data to information to knowledge mapping
- Knowledge mining
- Business intelligence

- Information retrieval systems
- Knowledge management and cyber-learning
- Database engineering and systems
- Data and knowledge processing
- Data warehousing and data centres
- Data security and privacy issues
- Information reliability and security
- Information and knowledge structures
- Knowledge and information extraction and discovery techniques
- Knowledge and information management techniques
- Knowledge extraction from images
- Knowledge representation and acquisition
- Large-scale information processing methods
- Intelligent knowledge-based systems
- Decision support and expert systems
- e-Libraries (digital libraries) + e-publishing
- Ontology: Engineering, sharing and reuse, matching and alignment
- Agent-based techniques and systems
- Workflow management
- Content management
- Data and knowledge fusion
- Global contextual processing and management implementation
- Data/information/knowledge models
- Managing copyright laws
- Interoperability issues
- Transaction systems
- Ontologies and semantics
- Object-oriented modelling and systems
- Case-based reasoning
- Classical Aspects of Information Theory
- Applications (e-commerce, multimedia, business, banking, etc.)
- Natural language processing
- Information integration
- Multi-cultural information systems
- Domain analysis and modelling
- Metamodelling

Theoretical, mathematical, empirical and experimental aspects of cognitive computing, including:

- Bio-inspired cognitive algorithms
- Improving cognition in machine learning systems
- Modelling human brain processing systems
- Multimodal learning systems
- Reinforced learning
- Cognitive evolution
- Cognitive inferential systems
- Cognitive improvement in deep learning networks
- Advancements in neural networks
- Multiscale learning systems
- Fractal-based learning and decision support systems
- Application of chaos engineering in machine intelligence
- Dynamical learning systems
- Application of information theory in machine intelligence
- Application of linear and nonlinear optimization theory in ML
- Self-adaptive and self-Organizing systems
- Manifold and metric learning
- Cognitive modelling, visualization and analytics of big data
- Graph theoretic approaches in dimensionality reduction
- Information and knowledge retrieval and searching algorithms
- Big data knowledge mining
- Mathematical modelling of big data and artificial intelligence
- Cognitive signal processing
- Rough set theory
- Agent-based modelling in machine learning systems
- Information processing and decision-making systems
- Big data fusion and information retrieval
- Time and space analysis in machine learning
- New application of classical stochastic and statistical analysis for big data machine learning
- Nature-inspired cognitive computing algorithms
- Cognitive feature extraction
- Extraction of latent semantics from big data

SECENIS in China and Its Prospects During the Fourth Industrial Revolution

The main thesis of this chapter has been that construction of New East Eurasia as a geoeconomic region requires an innovating China which is increasingly being forced to delink from the US-led global order/disorder. It is clear from the above analysis that China is firmly on its way towards forming a SECENIS for the Fourth Industrial Revolution. Among other things, this has led to a new model for indigenous platform economy. A study of the Chinese platform firms such as Tencent and Alibaba demonstrate that in contrast to the US Silicon Valley model (internal development and introduction, acquisition and venture capital investment) PRC firms have developed two different strategies. The first is listing some of their existing operations separately on the stock market but still maintaining control. The second strategy is interfirm cross investments. They are not identical but have similarities with the Japanese *Keiretsus*. As the Fourth Industrial Revolution in China proceeds further the corporate forms for AI-related firms will evolve further and corporate governance in Chinese state-private sector mode will develop. Khan (2004a, b) indicated this line of development for corporate governance in technology sectors for Japan, Taiwan, Singapore and Korea in particular that prefigured the path for China today. Of course, since 2012 if not earlier, Chinese state has become even more involved in corporate governance of high technology sectors during the Fourth Industrial Revolution.

Consideration of the East Asian high technology development experience and the Chinese innovation system within the theoretical framework of critical trans-neoclassical realism (CTNR) leads to an important geoeconomic conclusion regarding China during the Fourth Industrial Revolution (https://mpra.ub.uni-muenchen.de/117362/1/2023%20May%20Geoeconomics%20Chinese%20Economy.pdf). China is an exceptional case that will be impossible to replicate under the current neoliberal geoeconomic rules of the game instituted by the United States and other advanced capitalist countries since the 1980s. Even if these rules change and some other countries can move forward on the path of industrialization, the older twentieth-century modes of industrialization based on fossil fuel-based technology will not be sustainable. I have sketched such an alternative strategy for China in Khan (2010) and Jiang and Khan (2017) that relies much less on fossil fuels and emphasizes regional cooperation. Here I have shown how the ANIS of China can begin to move towards an ecologically sustainable SECENIS. This SECENIS building and deepening strategy will lead to a sustainable economy based on growth with equity. If this trend can first be firmly established in PRC with follow-ups by Russia, Central Asia and Iran among others, a new development, trade, investment and monetary order can take root. This new order will have to offer both efficiency and equity for all partners under the guiding principle of sovereign equality.

However, time is of the essence. Given the path dependence of development unless strategic disengagement from the existing path followed by a strategic engagement with the alternative strategy is begun within the next five years, it may well be too late. The stakes are indeed very high. A more detailed strategy paper based on the key ideas from the alternative strategy outlined here with concrete quantitative scenarios and feasibility studies along the lines of models sketched in the Appendix (and other, more detailed models) will go some distance towards giving the appropriate analytical foundations for the policy makers. Methodologically, the nonlinear modelling approach might prove to be especially relevant for studying the properties of multiple equilibria and complex dynamics.

The crucial question is what kind of transformations in the global economic environment and development discourse will influence the policies in the right direction. A related question is: how can China play an enabling role in furthering sustainable industrialization and development for the developing countries? Most importantly, how the construction of a new East Eurasian order can help other developing countries?

Therefore, more broadly, we can conclude from the systemic analysis of Eurasian Geoeconomics that during the Fourth Industrial Revolution, the geoeconomics for region-building, much like the economics of nation-building earlier, will consist of developing connectivity and dependencies with strategic industries, transportation corridors and financial instruments. Our analysis predicts that these are indeed the areas that will receive increased attention from PRC strategists. The existing cooperative arrangements among Russia, China, Iran—more generally among expanded BRICS—already shows one possible positive path for future Eurasia and its partners.

References

Adeniran, A., Balogun, K., & Ihezie, E. (2023). Towards digital governance in Africa. In *Handbook of Public Management in Africa* (pp. 355–373). Edward Elgar Publishing.

African Development Bank, Various Years. African Development Outlook.

African Union Commission. STISA(Science Technology and Innovation Strategy for Africa) (2024). Addis Ababa.: 1–51.

Altshul, H. J., McMillan, L., & Hall, A. (2019). The role of public research agencies in building agri-food bioscience impact and innovation capacity in sub-Saharan Africa: The challenge beyond science capability. *International Journal of Technology Management & Sustainable Development, 18*(2), 105–125.

APEC (2005). "Biosecurity Planning and Surveillance Capacity for APEC…" Accessed February 26, 2022. https://www.apec.org/docs/default-source/publications/2005/8/apec-workshop-on-building-biosecurity-planning-for-apec-member-economies/05_atc_biosecurity.pdf.

Azuh, D. E., Ejemeyovwi, J. O., Adiat, Q., & Ayanda, B. A. (2020). Innovation and human development perspectives in West Africa. *Sage Open, 10*(4), 215–277.

Boakye, A. (2024). Estimating the impact of digital technologies on government operations, business operations and general welfare: The case of South Africa. *African Journal of Science, Technology, Innovation and Development, 16*(2), 274–282.

Chukwuma, S. Ezeonu., Richard, Tagbo., Ephraim, N. Anike., Obinna, A. Oje., and Ikechukwu, NE. Onwurah. 2012. Biotechnological Tools for Environmental Sustainability: Prospects and Challenges for Environments in Nigeria-A Standard Review. Biotechnology Research International 2012: 1–6.

Diesen, G. (2017). *Russia's Geoeconomic Strategy for a Greater Eurasia*. London: Taylor & Francis Ltd.

Fry, C. V. (2023). A lasting connection: colonial ties and scientific capabilities in sub-Saharan Africa. *Economics of Innovation and New Technology, 32*(4), 476–497.

Gabriele, A., & Khan, H. (2010). *Enhancing Technological Progress in a Market-Socialist Context: China's National Innovation System at the Crossroads.* Saarbrücken: Lap Lambert Academic Publishing.

Gaillard, J., & Mouton, J. (2022). The State of Science, Technology and Innovation in Africa: Trends, Progress and Limitations. *Science, Technology and Society, 27*(3), 318–326. https://doi.org/10.1177/09717218221078548

Gurib-Fakim, A. and L. Signe. 2022. Investment in Science and Technology Key to an African Economic Boom, Brookings Institution Commentary: 1–3.

Gutowski, A., Hassan, N. M., Knedlik, T., Tong, C. M. N., & Wholmuth, K. (Eds.). (2020). *Science, Technology and Innovation Policies for Inclusive Growth in Africa: Human Skills Development and Country Cases* (Vol. 21). Lit Verlag.

Huntington, S. P. (1993). "Why International Primacy Matters." *International Security* 17, no. 4: 68. https://doi.org/10.2307/2539022.

Jia, K., & Kenney, M. (2021). "The Chinese Platform Business Group: An Alternative to the Silicon Valley Model?" *Journal of Chinese Governance* 7, no. 1: 58–80. https://doi.org/10.1080/23812346.2021.1877446.

Jiang, X., & Khan, A. H. (2017). "Structural Change and Energy Use in China: A SAM-Based CGE Analysis." *The Chinese Economy* 50, no. 6: 405–24. https://doi.org/10.1080/10971475.2017.1380021.

Jin, Keyu (2023). *The New China Playbook.* New York: Penguin.

Juma, C., and Serageldin, I. (2007), Freedom to Innovate: Biotechnology in Africa's Development. A Report of the High-Level African Panel on Modern Biotechnology. African Union (AU) and the New Partnership for Africa's Development (NEPAD).

Juma, C., and Yee-Cheong, L., (2005), Innovation: Applying Knowledge in Development. Earthscan, UK.

Kahn, M. J. (2022). The Status of Science, Technology and Innovation in Africa. *Science, Technology and Society, 27*(3), 327–350. https://doi.org/10.1177/09717218221078540

Kasongo, A., Sithole, M., & Buchana, Y. (2023). Empirical analysis of innovation and productivity in services firms: The case of South Africa. *African Journal of Science, Technology, Innovation and Development, 15*(1), 1–13.

Khan, H. A. (1983). "Technology, Energy, Distribution and Balance of Payments: A Macroeconomic Framework." *Unpublished dissertation, Cornell University, Ithaca, New York.*

Khan, H. (1985). "Technology Choice in the Energy and Textile Sectors in the Republic of Korea." Essay. In Bhalla, A. S., ed. *Technology and Employment in Industry*, 3rd ed. Geneva: International Labour Office.

Khan, H. A. (1997). *Technology, Energy, and Development: the South Korean Transition.* Cheltenham, UK: Edward Elgar Pub.

Khan, H. A. (1998). *Technology, Development and Democracy: Limits of National Innovation Systems in the Age of Postmodernism.* Cheltenham, UK: Edward Elgar Pub.

Khan, H. A. (2002). "Innovation and Growth: A Schumpeterian Model of Innovation Applied to Taiwan." *Oxford development studies* 30, no. 3: 289–306. DOI: https://doi.org/10.1080/1360081022000012707.

Khan, H. A. (2003a). "Technology and Modernity: Creating Social Capabilities in a POLIS." *Modernity and Technology*, pp. 327–358.

Khan, H. A. (2003b). "What Can the African Countries Learn from the Macroeconomics of Foreign Aid in Southeast Asia." *Aryeetey, E., Court, J., Nissanke, M. and Weder, B.*

Khan, H. A. (2004a). *Interpreting East Asian Growth and Innovation: The Future of Miracles.* Basingstoke, Hampshire England: Palgrave Macmillan.

Khan, H. A. (2004b). *Global Markets and Financial Crises in Asia: Towards a Theory for the 21st Century.* London: Palgrave Macmillan Limited.

Khan, H. A. (2005). " A New Theory with Case Studies in Globalization, Convergence, and Superconvergence of Emerging Technologies" In the *International Workshop on Emerging Technologies: The Global Challenges of*

Convergence, Bangkok,14–15 Dec. http://www.apecforesight.org/emerging_tech/docs/HaiderPresentation_Dec05.ppt

Khan, H. A. (2008a). "Building an Innovative Economy through Managed Creative Destruction: A Theory with Applications to South Korea." *Econpapers.*

Khan, H. A. (2008b). "Democracy in Bangladesh: from Crisis to Sustainability." *Journal of Bangladesh Studies* 9: 13–25.

Khan, H. A. (2010). "China's Development Strategy and Energy Security." *The Rise of China and India*, 108–37. https://doi.org/10.1057/9780230282094_6.

Khan, H. A. (2012). "Enhancing Economic Integration in the Asia-Pacific through the Strengthening of National Innovation Systems - Challenges and Strategies." *Asia-Pacific Technology Monitor.*

Khan, H. A. (2015). "What Should the AIIB's Priorities Be?" *World Economic Forum*, April 27. https://www.weforum.org/agenda/2015/04/what-should-the-aiibs-priorities-be/.

Khan, H. A. (2018). "The Future of Bangladesh: ICT and Technological Superconvergence." *Journal of Bangladesh Studies* 18, no. 1–2, pp. 1–21.

Khan, H. A. (2021a). "AI, Deep Machine Learning via Neuro-Fuzzy Models: Complexities of International Financial Economics of Crises." *International Journal of Computational & Neural Engineering*, 122–34. https://doi.org/10.19070/2572-7389-2100016.

Khan, H. A. (2021b). "Governing a Complex Global Financial System in the Age of Global Instabilities and BRICS." *Handbook of BRICS and Emerging Economies*, 940–79. https://doi.org/https://doi.org/10.1093/oso/9780198827535.003.0037.

———. (2023a). Can BRI be the Road to Peace and Prosperity?. Econpapers https://econpapers.repec.org/paper/pramprapa/117081.htm

———. (2023b). Towards a General Complex Systems Model of Economic Sanctions with Some Results Outlining Consequences of Sanctions on the Russian Economy and the World. Econpapers https://econpapers.repec.org/paper/pramprapa/116806.htm

———. (2023c). The Economic and Geopolitical Consequences of Belt and Road Initiative (BRI) for China: A preliminary model-based analysis. Econpapers https://econpapers.repec.org/paper/pramprapa/117005.htm

Khan, H., & Thorbecke, E. (1988). *Macroeconomic Effects and Diffusion of Alternative Technologies Within a Social Accounting Matrix Framework: the Case of Indonesia.* Aldershot, Hants, England: Gower Pub. Co. Print.

Khan, H. A., & Thorbecke, E. (1989). "Macroeconomic Effects of Technology Choice: Multiplier and Structural Path Analysis Within a SAM Framework." *Journal of policy modeling* 11, no. 1: 131–156. DOI: https://doi.org/10.1016/0161-8938(89)90028-8.

Kim, L., & Nelson, R. R. (2015). *Technology, Learning, and Innovation: Experiences of Newly Industrializing Economies.* Cambridge: Cambridge University Press.

Lee, K. (2006). "China's Economic Catch-up: Washington Consensus or the Beijing Consensus, Selected Papers from the 2nd World Forum on China Studies (Abstracts)." In *Exploration into the Theory and Practice of the Mode of China's Development* Panel 2.

Lin, J. Y. (2012). *Demystifying the Chinese Economy.* Cambridge: Cambridge University Press.

Lundvall, B., & Rikap, C. (2022). "China's Catching-up in Artificial Intelligence Seen as a Co-Evolution of Corporate and National Innovation Systems." *Research Policy* 51, no. 1: 104395. https://doi.org/10.1016/j.respol.2021.104395.

Miller, C. (2022). *Chip War.* New York: Scribner. Smith Institute, UK.

Mouton, J (2008), Regional Report on Sub-Saharan Africa: A Study of National Research Systems. United Nations Educational, Scientific and Cultural Organization

Mugabe, J (2008), A Review of Ghana's Science, Technology and Innovation System, A Study for the United Nations Conference on Trade and Development

Mugabe, J. 'Regionalism and science and technology development in Africa' in Louk Box and Rutger Engelhard, eds., (2006), Science and Technology Policy for Development: Dialogues at the Interface. Anthem Press.

Naidoo, S. (2015). Linking the South African system of innovation with the rest of Africa: exploring challenges and opportunities.

Nelson, R. R. (1990). "U.S. Technological Leadership: Where Did It Come from and Where Did It Go?" *Research policy* 19, no. 2: 117–132. DOI: https://doi.org/10.1016/0048-7333(90)90042-5.

Nelson, R. R. (1993a). "Technical Change as Cultural Evolution." *Learning and TechnologicalChange*,9–23.https://doi.org/10.1007/978-1-349-22855-3_2.

Nelson, R. R. (1993b). *National Innovation Systems: a Comparative Analysis.* New York: Oxford University Press.

NEPAD (2006), Africa's Science and Technology Consolidated Plan of Action. New Partnership for Africa's Development, Pretoria.

Nyugha, P. G. (2024). The Importance of Artificial Intelligence to Africa's Development Process: Prospects and Challenges. *PriMera Scientific Engineering*, *4*, 20–30.

OECD ' Various Years. OECD Reviews of Innovation Policy: South Africa. Organisation for Economic Cooperation and Development, Paris.

Olyanga, A. M., Shinyekwa, I. M., Ngoma, M., Nkote, I. N., Esemu, T., & Kamya, M. (2022). Innovativeness and export competitiveness in the East African Community. *Modern Supply Chain Research and Applications*, *4*(3), 177–201.

SARUA (2008), Science and Technology: A Baseline Study on Science and Technology and Higher Education in the SADC Region. Southern Africa Regional Universities Association, Johannesburg South Africa.

Schmoch, U (2005), The Knowledge Basis of Africa—Status and Perspectives. Paper for Globelics.

UK National Commission for UNESCO (2005), Mapping of Science and Technology Activities in Sub-Saharan Africa.

UNCTAD (2003), Africa's Technology Gap. United Nations Conference on Trade and Development, Geneva

UNCTAD (2007), The Least Developed Countries Report 2007: Knowledge, Technological Learning and Innovation for Development, Geneva.

UNIDO (2008), Creating an enabling environment for private sector development in sub-Saharan Africa. United Nations Industrial Development Organization, Vienna.

UNCTAD (2008) Science, Technology and Innovation Policy Review of Angola. United Nations Conference on Trade and Development, Geneva

WIPO. Various Years. World Patent Report: A Statistical Review. World Intellectual Property Organization, Geneva.

World Bank (2006), Benchmarking FDI Competitiveness in Sub-Saharan African Countries. World Bank, Washington, DC.

World Bank (2009), Accelerating Catch-Up: Tertiary Education for Growth in Sub-Saharan Africa. World Bank, Washington DC.

World Economic Forum. Various Years, The Global Competitiveness Report. World Economic Forum, Geneva

Zeng, J. (2021). "China's Artificial Intelligence Innovation: A Top-down National Command Approach?" *Global Policy* 12, no. 3: 399–409. https://doi.org/10.1111/1758-5899.12914.

CHAPTER 7

Islamic Finance: An Exploratory Survey of an Emergent New Opportunity in Resource Mobilization and Inclusion for Africa

7.1 Introduction

The total value of global Islamic finance[1] assets in 2022 grew by 11% from 2021 to US$4.5 trillion and are projected to reach $6.7 trillion in 2027.[2] Islamic finance in Africa is of growing interest among scholars and practitioners (businesspersons and economic development officials). Yet succinct surveys of what is happening, together with the challenges and prospects of Islamic finance in resource mobilization in closing Africa's massive financing gap and fostering financial and religious inclusion, are hardly existent. Therefore, this exploratory chapter is intended to ask and answer the basic research questions of: "What is presently going on in the Islamic finance sector in Africa?" and "What is the potential of Islamic finance in as a means of resource mobilization and financial and religious inclusion in Africa?" Our concept of "religious inclusion" is new in the literature on Islamic finance. The chapter is intended to enable the multiple stakeholders and numerous researchers of Islamic finance to find the answers they need with regard to the contemporary status of Islamic finance and the opportunities the sector presents, particularly in Africa, in one comprehensive study such as this one.

[1] The simplest definition of Islamic finance is interest-free finance, based on the Islamic prohibition of usury, of which interest is considered to be the clearest manifestation.

[2] ICD-LSEG, *Islamic Finance Development Report 2023*, London: LSEG, 2023.

K. N. M. Sonko et al., *21st Century African Development Strategies*,
https://doi.org/10.1007/978-3-031-93079-9_7

After outlining in detail different aspects of the current situation of Islamic finance in both Sub-Saharan African and North Africa, the chapter concludes with recommendations on the way forward. The research finds that: (1) although major challenges remain, significant progress and growth of potential (which has been very slow until recently) has been made in spite of the COVID-19 pandemic which is now officially considered to be over; (2) the potential is vast and the market is growing; and (3) there are many reasons, including commonly unknown historical ones, that indicate the true but untapped potential of Islamic finance n Africa. Based on the findings, we argue that it is very important to also determine how the post-pandemic Islamic finance sector in Africa ought to be shaped strategically in order to develop the vast but largely unexploited potential for Muslims and non-Muslims, thus enhancing resource mobilization and inclusion (financial and religious) in the continent. Synergistically, the theme of the post-COVID-19 pandemic is also contained in other chapters in this book, especially Chap. 6 by Khan.

7.2 The Unexploited Potential

Despite the challenges of COVID-19 and its consequences since it has ended, Islamic finance's advances in Africa continue. A number of significant developments have taken place in the midst of the pandemic and there is no doubt that Africa is also witnessing progress in the development of this brand of finance since then. In fact, Islamic finance has experienced a faster growth during the pandemic than any other period in the continent's modern history. According to the *Islamic Finance Development Report 2021*, total global Islamic finance assets reached US$3.4 trillion in 2020. The biggest share of this was in the form of Islamic banking assets ($2.3 trillion) and the smallest ($62 billion) was takaful. See Tables 7.1 and 7.2.[3]

[3] Earlier research carried out by the authors of this chapter presents snapshots of the number of Islamic finance institutions in Africa. Sonko and Sonko (2020) found that there were 60 Islamic banks, 34 takaful companies, 8 private equity funds and 5 Islamic windows in the continent. See Karamo N.M. Sonko and Mariama Sonko, "Promoting Islamic finance in Africa: 'Top-bottom' or 'Bottom up'? A Case study of Banking in the Gambia", in Haider A. Khan and Karamo N.M. Sonko (eds.), *Islamic Finance as a Complex System*, Lanham, MD: Lexington Books, 2020, table 3.1, p.56.

Table 7.1 Islamic finance asset distribution by category (2020, US$ billion)

	Total assets (US$ Billion)	*Share (%)*	*Number of institutions/ instruments*
Islamic banking	2349	69.6	527
Sukuk	631	18.7	3805
Other IFIs	178	5.2	1698
Islamic funds	152	4.5	745
Takaful	62	1.8	323
Total	3372	100[a]	7098

[a]Rounded up

Data source: Islamic Finance Development Report 2021

Table 7.2 Islamic finance asset distribution by category (2021, US$ billion)

	Total assets (US$ Billion)	*Share (%)*	*Number of institutions/ instruments*
Islamic banking	2765	69.0	566
Sukuk	713	21.1 18.0	4426
Other IFIs	169	5.0	778
Islamic funds	238	7.0	1903
Takaful	73	2.2	323
Total	3958	100	7996

Data source: Islamic Finance Development Report 2022

However, Africa's share of Islamic finance assets in 2020 was equal to only $8 billion of the total (Table 7.3). The latest available data (2022) is provided in Table 7.4. As in the rest of the world, the Islamic finance landscape in Africa is dominated by banking, although takaful and sukuk issuances have picked up in recent years.

Africa is a late-starter to modern advanced Islamic finance and certain factors inhibit the *full* pace of progress. These include the fact that African Muslims are largely unbanked and the African Muslim-majority countries are themselves vastly Islamically unbanked. The World Bank confirmed the former; that is, the Muslims in Africa have a higher unbanked proportion than the non-Muslims and they are less likely to open bank accounts

Table 7.3 Islamic finance assets by region (2020, US$ billion)

Region	*Islamic finance assets (US$ Billion)*
GCC	1499
Other MENA	902
Southeast Asia	754
Europe	119
South Asia	87
Sub-Saharan Africa	8
Americas	3
Other Asia	1
Total	3373

Data source: Islamic Finance Development Report 2021

Table 7.4 Islamic finance assets by region (2021, US$ billion)

Region	*Islamic finance assets (US$ Billion)*
GCC	1617
Other MENA	1300
Southeast Asia	803
Europe	113
South Asia	107
Sub-Saharan Africa	10
Americas	8
Other Asia	1
Total	3958

Data source: Islamic Finance Development Report 2022

t save than their non-Muslim counterparts.[4] With regard to the latter (that the Muslim-majority countries are themselves highly unbanked Islamically), the evidence is provided in Fig. 7.1.

For instance, the Gambia with a population of about 2.4 million (more than 90% of whom are Muslims) offers the following statistics: Total number of banks is 12, and only 1 is Islamic. The total number of insurance companies is 11, and only 2 are takaful. The total number of microfinance institutions equals five, and only two are Islamic. The total number of

[4] Enrique Gelbard, Mumtaz Hussain, Rodolfo Maino, Yibin Mu and Etienne B. Yehoue. "Islamic Finance in SubSaharan Africa: Status and Prospects". IMF Working Paper, 14/149 (2014).

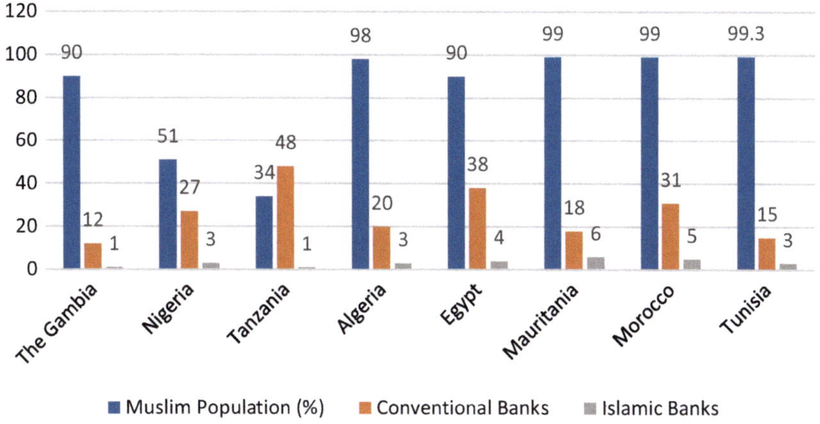

Fig. 7.1 Population & banks in Africa. (Source: Authors, data collected from various sources, 2022)

credit unions equals 54, and only 1 is Islamic.[5] In Nigeria, a country with a total population of about 206 million (about 51% Muslim), there are 27 banks, 3 of which are Islamic, and there is 1 Islamic banking window.[6] In Tanzania's semiautonomous state of Zanzibar, with a population of about 1.7 million, that is 99% Muslim, there are 13 banks, only one of which is fully fledged Islamic, and there are 4 Islamic windows. There is no takaful company on the islands.

North Africa portrays the same image: Algeria has a population of about 44 million, about 98% of which is Muslim, but has only three Islamic banks and no takaful companies at the moment.[7] In Egypt, with a population of about 104 million, about 90% of which is Muslim, there are 38 banks, 4 of which are Islamic.[8] Mauritania, with a population of about 3.8 million, about 99% Muslim, there are 18 banks, out of which 6 are full-fledged Islamic.[9] There are nine insurance companies, two of which are

[5] Central Bank of the Gambia website and various documents.

[6] Central Bank of Nigeria, website site, https://www.cbn.gov.ng/Supervision/finstitutions.asp#_last visited December 6, 2021.

[7] A. Benamraoui, "Islamic banking: the case of Algeria", International Journal of Islamic and Middle Eastern Finance and Management, 1 (2), pp. 113–131; "Algeria: Islamic insurance on the cards soon", *Middle East Insurance Review*, Oct 2020.

[8] Islamic Finance Development Report 2021, https://www.bcm.mr/; and BanksDaily.com.

[9] Central Bank of Mauritania website 2021, https://www.bcm.mr/.

takaful. Morocco, with a population of about 36 million, about 99% Muslim, there are 31 banks, 5 out of which are fully fledged Islamic and 3 are Islamic windows.[10] There are 23 insurance companies,[11] 6 of which are takaful, and Tunisia, with a population of about 11.6 million, about 99% Muslim, there are 15 banks, 3 of which are Islamic. There are 20 insurance companies, 3 of which are takaful.

7.3 Causes for the Slow Take-off and Growth

There are a number of causes for the very slow *overall* take-off and growth of Islamic finance in Africa over the years. Some have already been cited. In spite of the progress noted in recent years, actual achievements must not be taken complacently, because there is still much to be desired. Some of the causes are policy related, while others are structural. Policy constraints refer mainly to the lack of the regulatory frameworks in most African countries. The existing frameworks across the continent have historically catered for only conventional banks due to the colonial legacies of the countries.[12] Structural factors are broader and deeper. They include the lack of knowledge and skills that are vital for the growth of the Islamic finance sector, due to the nature of the syllabi of both the modern (Western) and Islamic educational systems in Africa. Whereas the former focuses on conventional banking and finance, the latter focuses on *ibadat*[13] and generally does not teach the main subjects that fall under *muamalat*[14] which can provide the skills that are vital to the rise and development of a

[10] Oxford Business Group, Morocco increases its sharia-compliant bank offerings", in *The Report: Morocco 2020*, OBG 2020.

[11] Oxford Business Group, Morocco increases its sharia-compliant bank offerings", in *The Report: Morocco 2020*, OBG 2019.

[12] Our focus in this section is regulatory support emanating only from the state in the forms of laws, rules, etc., which create an enabling environment for the Islamic finance sector. Islamic development finance institutions, such as the IsDB, do provide significant support to local Islamic banks, especially commercial banks, in their financial transitions with customers, but there seems to be, even in such much-needed instances, problems again of what we refer to as inadequate knowledge in this chapter because many potential beneficiary institutions do not seem to be aware of these opportunities.

[13] This focuses on acts of worship that are commonly referred to as the "Five Pillars of Islam": Monotheism (*shahada*), based on the conviction and pronouncement that: (1) "There is no god but God (Allah) and Muhammad is His Prophet and Messenger"; (2) prayer (*salat*); (3) fasting (*sawm*); (4) obligatory alms (*zakat*); and (5) pilgrimage (*hajj*).

[14] This focuses on business transactions, personal matters, inheritance and sanctions.

modern Islamic finance sector. Therefore, commonly the most influential local Sheikhs (Shuyukh—شيخ), with the biggest national followings, have no idea of Islamic finance.

Thus, one of the most important causes (if not the most important) for the lack of a vibrant Islamic finance sector in the continent has become the lack of even basic knowledge about Islamic finance and its essence among the majority of the population. For example, in the survey carried out by Sonko and Sonko (2020) in the urban elite areas of the Gambia, their hypothesis was found to be true when they discovered that about 96% of the population knew little or nothing about Islamic finance (refer to Fig. 7.2).[15] A similar survey in Libya by the World Bank (2020) revealed the same constraint. In spite of the advantages provided by Arabic as their official language and the level of training of the employees in the companies surveyed, the Bank found that much less than half of the firms in different regions of the country have significant knowledge of the workings of the Islamic finance system (see Fig. 7.3).[16] As the experience in the former Soviet Union illustrates, even outside Africa the power of

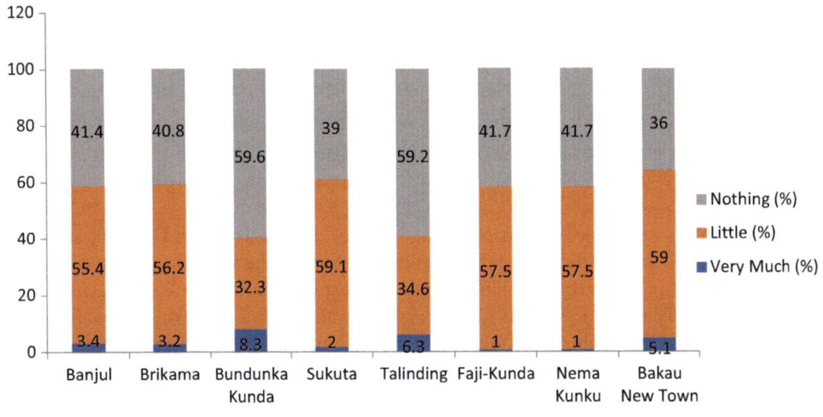

Fig. 7.2 How much do you know about Islamic banking. (Source: Sonko and Sonko 2020)

[15] Sonko and Sonko (ibid.).

[16] In World Bank, *Libya Financial Sector Review February 2020,* https://thedocs.worldbank.org/en/doc/288521600444837289-0280022020/original/LibyaFinancialSectorReviewEnglishFinal.pdf.

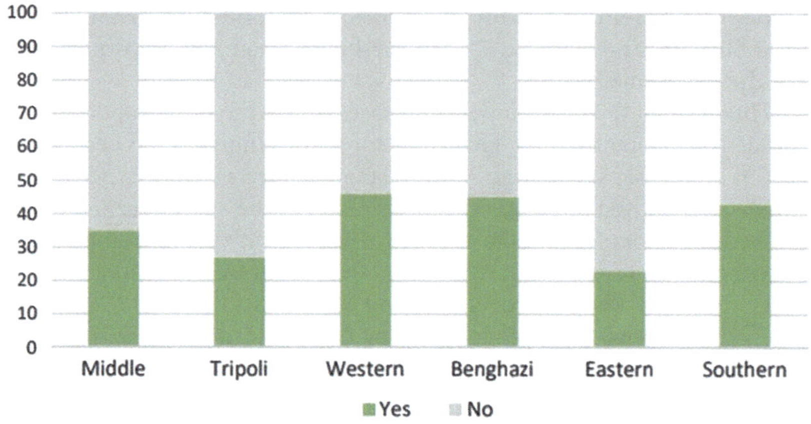

Fig. 7.3 Familiarity with Islamic modes of finance. (Source: World Bank 2020, table 47)

knowledge about the nature, potential and opportunities of Islamic finance can be used to create new or expand markets.[17]

However, in pointing out the lack of adequate knowledge as one of the most important causes of the very slow, overall, development of Islamic finance in Africa over the decades and the significant, but not enough, progress recently, we should also note that there are two opposite or mutually contradictory forces at work. Both of these dent the potential of

[17]The ITFC's experience in this regard in Uzbekistan is instructive. In 2018, at a time when the market was saturated with conventional financing, the Corporation did an experiment by providing a pilot Line of Financing to one bank (Asia Alliance Bank (AAB)). What followed was a pleasant surprise. As the news of the availability of credit on Islamic financing terms penetrated the market, through the Central Bank and ITFC's activities, customers started to go to their banks to request information on and apply specifically for Islamic financing. As a result of which Uzbekistan now has 13 banks with Islamic windows. The number is expected to increase to 16 by early 2024, more than half of the 31 conventional commercial banks (both state- and privately owned) operating in the country in 2023 (for IFTC in Uzbekistan, the interested reader may refer to IFTC, Annual Report 2022), https://www.itfc-idb.org/resources-center/publications. On the same subject of the importance of awareness (i.e., knowledge), Sukuk has rapidly risen in popularity, acceptance and hence transactions as the global market started to recognize that it is a particularly suitable instrument especially for financing infrastructure projects. Therefore, it has become better-known instrument and has found its way to even markets with minimal or no presence of Islamic finance institutions.

Islamic finance. They are the lack of adequate knowledge generally (discussed above) and the presence of ***sufficient*** awareness in some Muslim communities. Whereas the former undermines the potential of Islamic finance through conventional banks, the latter does so through the informal sector. Conventional banks get a boost from the lack of adequate knowledge because Muslims who do not know that *riba* is one of the major sins in Islam turn to these banks without hesitation, even in the presence of Islamic banks. On the other hand, the informal sector benefits due to sufficient awareness in *some* Muslim communities where those who have money and know about *riba* as a major sin (and do not have access to banks they consider Islamic or Islamic enough) decide to keep their money under their pillows instead of in the interest-bearing accounts of conventional banks.[18] Surveys of attitudes in North Africa have shown evidence of this saving behaviour.[19] See Fig. 7.4 for evidence from studies in Algeria, Morocco and Tunisia. In Algeria, for instance, the Central Bank has estimated that the informal sector thrives with $30–35 billion largely because of those who do not want to use conventional banks because of *riba* (Library of Congress 2020).

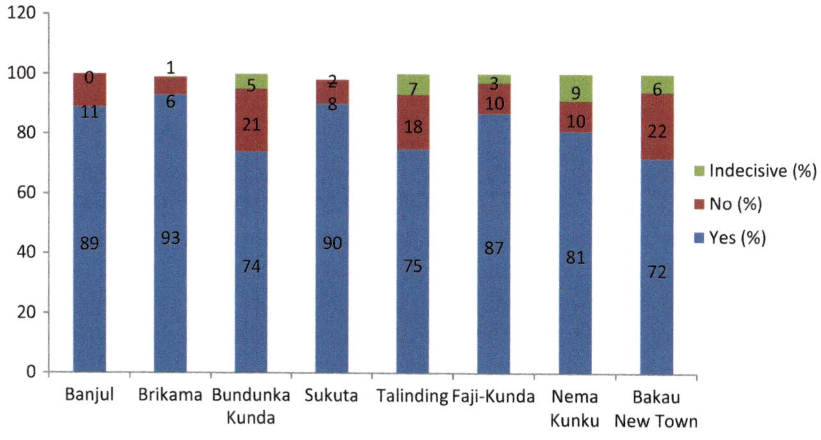

Fig. 7.4 Would you open an account in an Islamic bank if you have access to a new one? (Source: Sonko and Sonko 2020)

[18] This category of Muslims does not include those who know about *riba* but still use conventional banks because they do not care, have no choice or for some other reason(s).

[19] Cited in World Bank (2020).

Finally, until very recently North Africa, potentially the greater source of interest and growth of Islamic finance in Africa, because of linguistic (Arabic) and religious (almost 100% Muslim populations) advantages, tended to exhibit less interest in Islamic finance than Sub-Saharan Africa did. This is because of political problems with the so-called Islamists in the region, with whom Islamic finance tended to be wrongly associated with, potentially, because of, again, lack of understanding of the true principles of Islamic finance as argued and proven in this chapter. Many of the governments in North Africa were apprehensive about Islamic finance until very recently because of the civil wars, civilian uprisings and/or military takeovers in most of these countries, associated with the so-called Islamists, such as al-Qa'ida in the Lands of the Islamic Maghreb (AQIM), its offshoots and others not related to AQIM. These organizations have made the authorities in North Africa very cautious about activities that they consider to be outside the five pillars of Islam that their opponents, including violent groups, can use by stressing and exploiting their "Islamic" labels to mobilize public support against the governments. As a result, Islamic finance has not received the welcome and support one would expected it would or should in many North African countries for a long time and even now, when official attitudes seem to be changing positively, the word "Islamic" is sometimes removed from the "finance" and replaced with words such as "alternative", "participative" and "non-interest".[20]

Due to all the preceding explanations, the figures about Africa's contribution to the global Islamic finance sector and the situation on the ground throughout the continent mask the real potential of Islamic finance. In reality, the continent offers an immense potential for the promotion and growth of Islamic finance but the real harvest lies ahead. There are a number of reasons to demonstrate the real potential of Islamic finance in Africa. Some of these reasons are directly related to Islam and can have *direct* positive impact on Islamic finance and others are indirectly related to Islam and can have *indirect* positive impact on Islamic finance in the continent. The factors which can have direct impact are: (1) the very strong historical economic relationships between Africa and the Islamic world; (2) the

[20] These terminologies are not used only in North Africa; instead they tend to be preferable in countries where the word "Islam" raises eyebrows or outright concerns because of what the governments or public see or hear about Islam, rightly or wrongly. In Nigeria, for example, a country suffering from Boko Haram, the official name of Islamic finance/banking is "non-interest finance/banking".

number of Muslims in the continent; (3) the number of unbanked Muslims (mentioned earlier); and (4) the latent interest in Africa, generally, in Islamic finance. The factors which can indirectly benefit promotional efforts and the growth of Islamic finance are: (1) the population growth rate; (2) the composition of the growing population; (3) the continent's economic growth rate; (4) the rise of the middle class; and (5) poverty, the need and growing universal popularity of financial inclusion of the poor.

Regarding the first set of reasons (direct factors), Africa is the first continent that Islam spread to after the Middle East. In fact, formal Islamic banking has been reported in Africa (Egypt) in the 1960s, before the establishment in 1975 of the Dubai Islamic Bank, which is credited by many to be the first formal Islamic bank in the world.[21] Presently, the Sudan is one of the only two countries in the world where the entire financial system is 100% Islamic and it has been so since 1984.[22] Furthermore, international Islamic economic history illustrates a commendable (generally unknown even among Islamic scholars)[23] contribution of Africa to classical Islamic finance and trade long before formal colonialism. In West Africa, for instance, vibrant trade and financial relationships existed with the Middle East for centuries. These relationships began in the ninth century,[24] and were particularly strong in the thirteenth, fourteenth and fifteenth centuries, with transcontinental impacts in both Asia and Europe. Incidentally, most of this history was recorded by Arab travellers/writers, such as Ibn Batuta, Ibn Hawkal and Mahmud Kati, who also contributed significantly to European historical accounts about Africa. According to Ibn Batuta, some of the West African cities (including those which dated back to the first century BC) during these periods were engaged only in trade. Parts of this "golden era" of West African trade were contemporaneous with the heydays of some of the celebrated Islamic scholars, such as

[21] Sonko and Sonko (2020), p.51; Oxford Business Group (2020).

[22] The other country is Iran. In 1983, four years after the end of the revolution in 1979, the Iranian Government passed the Riba-Free Banking Act, forcing local banks into Shari'ah-compliant products. In the following year, the Sudan passed the Civil Transactions Act, making it mandatory for all financial institutions in the country to comply with Islamic laws (Sonko and Sonko (ibid.)). Following the political changes in 2019, Sudan has now officially switched to dual banking, as part of its efforts to rejoin the international financial community and attract financiers and investors, but conventional banking in the country is yet to be started in practice.

[23] Because of the common lack of coverage of this history in the academic literature.

[24] Mihoub Mezouaghi, "Sub-Saharan Africa and the Arab world: disconnected agricultural regions", in Cosimo Lacirignola, MediTERRA 2014, Presses de Sciences Po, Paris, 2014.

Ibn Taymiyyah, Ibn Qayyim and Ibn Khaldoun.[25] However, Africa could not bank on this history for the benefit of the Islamic finance sector. Consequently, the momentum was lost in the modern era.

Next, the growth of the Muslim population in Africa augurs well for the potential of Islamic finance in the continent. In 2020, Sub-Saharan Africa (excluding North Africa, a region which is almost entirely Muslim) had about 311 million Muslims (out of a total population of about a billion) and the fastest growth rate of Islam in the world. This has been projected to reach 385.9 million in 2030.[26] It has been forecasted that by the year 2060, 27% of the global population of Muslims would be living in Sub-Saharan Africa and this would be the largest conglomeration of Muslims in the world, outside of the Asia Pacific region.[27] It has further been projected that "the portion of the world's Muslims living in sub-Saharan Africa is projected to rise; in 20 years, for example, more Muslims are likely to live in Nigeria than in Egypt".[28]

7.4 Immense Potential and Continuing Progress

Although the knowledge of the population, generally, about Islamic finance is limited in Africa, as outlined here, there is a latent interest in discovering and using Islamic finance services in Africa. The case of the Gambia clearly demonstrated this in a survey by Sonko and Sonko (ibid.). As shown in Fig. 7.5, an average of about 83% of respondents in the urban

[25] For more historical evidence of this relationship and the form it took, the reader may refer to D. T. Niane, ed. General History of Africa: Volume IV. Africa from the Twelfth to the Sixteenth Century. California: Heinemann & UNESCO, 1984; Mark Cartwright, "Mali Empire", World History Encyclopedia, March 1, 2019. Retrieved from https://www.worldhistory.org/Mali_Empire/; and Karamo NM Sonko, "Learning Business from our Ancestors", African Business, January 2003; and Murat Çizakça, "Economic Systems of Muslims in History", Arab Law Quarterly, Volume 35 (2021): Issue 1–2 (Nov 2020).

[26] Pew Research Center, "The Future of the Global Muslim Population", Report January 27, 2011, https://www.pewresearch.org/religion/2011/01/27/the-future-of-the-global-muslim-population/.

[27] For this forecast refer to David Mcclendon, "Sub-Saharan Africa will be home to growing shares of the world's Christians and Muslims", Pew Research Centre, April 19. 2017, available at https://www.pewresearch.org/facttank/2017/04/19/sub-saharan-africa-will-be-home-to-growing-shares-of-the-worlds-christians-and-muslims/

[28] For this projection refer to Pew Research Center, Report, January 27, 2011, https://www.pewresearch.org/religion/2011/01/27/the-future-of-the-global-muslim-population/.

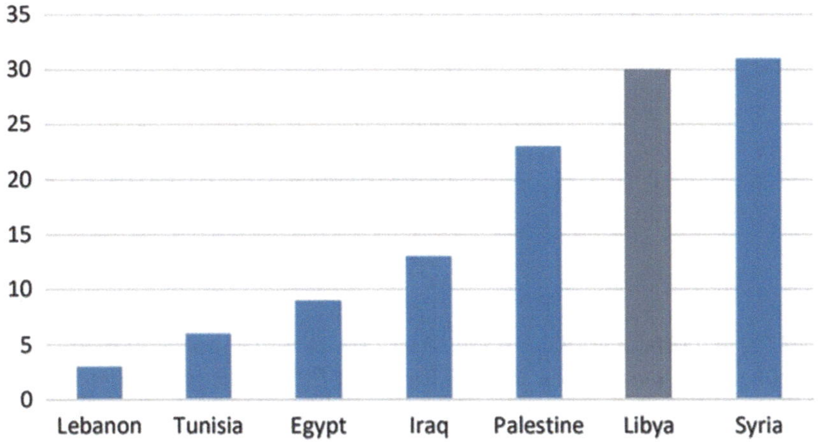

Fig. 7.5 Share of firms unwilling to borrow with interest (%). (Source: World Bank 2020, Table 46)

areas of the Gambia said they would open an account in an Islamic bank if they had access to a new one. The percentages may be different, but the evidence points to the same situations in other parts of Africa, as the World Bank found in studies of the Middle East and North Africa (MENA) region, including Egypt, Libya and Tunisia.[29]

In addition to the above causes for optimism, there is a set of factors indicating the immense potential of Islamic finance in Africa that can be *indirectly* beneficial to the sector's expansion. First among these is that the total African population (Muslims and non-Muslims) has now reached about 1.3 billion and growing faster than that of any other continent. It has been projected to double by 2050.[30] Second, the median age in 2020 was 19.7 and most of the population are under the age of 35—in other words, the youth (Table 7.5). In 2020, this age cohort amounted to almost a billion people in all of Africa and about 22.7% of the world's youth population. This youthful population has been projected to reach

[29] World Bank (ibid.).

[30] United Nations, "Global Issues. Population", https://www.un.org/en/global-issues/population, last visited December 4, 2021; and https://www.pewforum.org/2011/01/27/future-of-the-global-muslim-populationregional-sub-saharan-africa/ last visited 02/12/21.

Table 7.5 Median age by region in 2020 and 2100

Africa	*2020*	*2100*
Africa	19.7	34.4
Asia	32.0	46.7
Europe	42.5	48.2
Latin America & Caribbean	31.0	49.3
Northern America	33.4	42.6
Oceania	38.4	45.6

Source: Data from Rocca and Schultes (2021), and UN (2021)

47.7% in 2100, overtaking Asia's share of 37.8% (the second highest).[31] By 2100, Africa's youth will account for about 50% of the total population of the world's youth and be equivalent to twice the entire population of Europe.[32] Relatedly, as the IMF concluded, based on its own projection that one out of five workers in the world would come from Africa by 2050, the continent is headed for a demographic dividend, which many sectors (including Islamic finance) can benefit from.[33]

Third, during the period prior to the COVID-19 pandemic, seven out of the ten fastest growing economies in the world were in Africa. In 2019, the continent's average growth rate was about 3.4%, after consistent growth of more than a decade. With the improved economic performance of the continent, the middle class has also been rising in Africa. Although COVID-19 and political instability in some states have slowed down the continent's growth, and continue to seriously threaten several countries, the positive overall trends are expected to continue.[34]

Finally, as the population increases and the numbers of young persons and women[35] increase as well, concerns about poverty and, hence, finan-

[31] Camilla Rocca and Ines Schultes, "Africa's youth: action needed now to support the continent's greatest asset", Mo Ibrahim Foundation, available at https://mo.ibrahim.foundation/sites/default/files/202008/international-youth-day-research-brief.pdf, last visited 12 December 2021.

[32] Rocca and Schultes (ibid.).

[33] IMF, "Building Tomorrow's Workforce: Education, Opportunity, and Africa's Demographic Dividend", *Regional Economic Outlook: Sub-Saharan Africa Analytical Note* by Michele Fornino and Andrew Tiffin (AFR), April 2024.

[34] International Monetary Fund (IMF), *World Economic Outlook*, January 2023. This point was also made in Sonko and Sonko (2023), p. 74.

[35] More than 50% of the African population are female, according to McKinsey and Company, *The power of parity: Advancing women's equality in Africa*, November 2019.

cial inclusion grow simultaneously. These concerns create an opportunity for Islamic finance because the need to address such issues is an inherent part of the Islamic mode of financing due to the Islamic principles it is based upon. There may not be a better time than now because financial inclusion has become a global concern. There is no better indication of this trend than the fact that all the world's leading and most influential financial institutions, especially non-Muslim ones, have taken the lead in promoting inclusion.

Since the 2010s, developments in Islamic finance in both North and Sub-Saharan Africa have been encouraging. The Algerian government approved Regulation No. 02-20 of March 2020 authorizing Islamic banking and in August, the same year, the National Bank launched the first state-owned Islamic bank.[36] It also approved the Finance Law (Article 103) of 2020, which allows conventional insurance companies to provide takaful. In February 2021, the draft decree regulating takaful was completed.[37] In Libya, as the country continues with efforts to revive its stock market, two Islamic banks are preparing for listings. The government is also preparing to issue sukuk. Earlier, following the overthrow of Gaddafi, two laws were passed—Law No. 1 of 2013 on the prohibition of interest on deposits and loans in all civil and commercial transactions and Law No. 4 of 2016 on sukuk. A World Bank (2020) study of Libya painted a very positive picture of Islamic finance in the country:

"Libya has demonstrated a relatively high demand for Shari'ah compliant financing. The demand appears greater than in other Arab states. Surveys have typically put the Libyan population at the higher end of the scale, significantly higher, for example, than its far more secular neighbour Tunisia".[38] In Egypt, Islamic banking is slowly gaining momentum with its market share exceeding 5% by June 2021. Morocco legislated Shar'iah-compliant banking in 2017, issued its first sukuk in 2018 and legislated takaful in 2019.[39] Takaful can be boosted by the rapid growth of

[36] Library of Congress, "Algeria: National Bank Officially Launches Islamic Banking", November 23, 2020, https://www.loc.gov/item/global-legal-monitor/2020-11-23/algeria-national-bank-officially-launches-islamicbanking/, last visited December 12, 2021.

[37] *Islamic Finance Development Report 2021.*

[38] World Bank, Libya Financial Sector Review, Washington, D.C.: World Bank, February 2020, https://thedocs.worldbank.org/en/doc/288521600444837289-0280022020/original/LibyaFinancialSectorReviewEnglishFinal.pdf.

[39] Oxford Business Group (ibid.).

participative banking and property financing, which (according to the Central Bank of Morocco) accounts for most of Islamic financing in the kingdom.[40]

In Sub-Saharan Africa, Uganda opened discussions with the Islamic Corporation for the Development of the Private Sector (ICD) of the Islamic Development Bank (IsDB) Group to set up an Islamic bank for the first time in the country. Salaam Bank, a subsidiary of the Salaam Bank Group in Djibouti, became the country's first fully fledged bank, with the issuance of a licence from the Bank of Uganda on September 8, 2023. Elsewhere in Sub-Saharan Africa, according to the Islamic Finance Development Indicator (IFDI), in 2020, South Africa was listed among the Top Ten Islamic finance jurisdictions in the world, Top Ten for Islamic funds and also among the Top Ten countries by average Financial Reporting Disclosure Index (FRDI) scores.[41] In 2020, ZamZam, the first fully fledged Islamic bank was established in Ethiopia.[42] In 2021, Nigeria was included among the top markets for Islamic finance according to the IFDI, ranking number 13th in the list, while Sudan was ranked number five in the quantitative development sub-indicators (Refinitiv 2021).

Islamic banks in Africa are demonstrating significant levels of resilience, innovation and profitability and, as revealed earlier, they did so even during the COVID-19 pandemic. Jaiz Bank in Nigeria is an example. Despite the challenges caused by the pandemic, Nigeria's first Islamic bank was able to offer a positive return to its shareholders in 2020 (Jaiz Bank Plc 2021).[43] The financing and investment assets of the bank recorded a growth of 54% in 2020, from N166.00 billion in 2019 (Jaiz Bank Plc 2021).[44] The deposits of the bank also grew by 38% in 2020 from N127.193 billion in 2019. The total assets of the bank grew 40% in 2020 from N167.27 billion in 2019 (Jaiz Bank Plc 2021). Furthermore, it was announced in 2020 that regulators approved the bank's proposal to pay 30 Kobo per share as dividend for the year 2020, subject to the approval of the shareholders. In 2021, the bank accelerated its strides in delighting customers with technologically driven services, relevant financing and empowerment in impact-making sectors (Jaiz Bank Plc 2021; p.12).

[40] *Islamic Finance Development Report 2021.*

[41] *Islamic Finance Development Report 2021.*

[42] *Islamic Finance Development Report 2021.*

[43] Jaiz Bank Plc, *Annual Report and Accounts 2021* at https://jaizbankplc.com/investor-relations/annual-report-and-accounts/

[44] Average exchange rates are NGN360.0 = US$1(2019) and NGN380.3=$1 (2020).

Abu Dhabi Islamic Bank (ADIB), Egypt, is another pacesetter in the African Islamic finance scene. It is the biggest Shari'ah-compliant lender in Egypt. ADIB's financial performance saw positive growth again in 2020 when the total assets of the bank grew by 22.5% reaching EGP73.9 billion from EGP60.3 billion in 2019 (Abu Dhabi Islamic Bank-Egypt 2021).[45] The net financing of the bank grew by 30% reaching EGP40.2 billion in December 2020, due to increases in corporate finance by 29.7%, reaching EGP28.7 billion, and in retail banking by 30.7% to EGP11.5 billion. Positive growth of deposits has also been evident in 2020 when corporate deposits increased by 26% to EGP23.3 billion and individual deposits grew by 20% reaching EGP23.3 billion. The assets under treasury management saw growth too, with the portfolio growing by EGP3.8 billion or 17.7% to reach EGP25.3 billion in 2020. The net standalone profit after taxes increased by 4% and reached EGP1151 million in 2020 from EGP1103 million in 2019.[46]

When it comes to expansion and innovation, ADIB has created a very strong presence in the Egyptian banking industry and became a prominent landmark in the country's financial ecosystem. It has established two new companies during the pandemic: ADIB Consumer Finance and ADIB Microfinance—with the objective of providing services more conveniently to its customers using digital finance technology. The digital finance progress it has made in the midst of the COVID-19 outbreak include: "Beat"—the bank's first contactless wearable payment gadget; Contactless Debit Cards to help reduce the risk of the spread of the COVID-19 virus; Dynamic E-Statements (the first of its kind in the Egyptian market) to allow customers to interactively search by date, transaction and description, with the option of creating graphs; and, finally, the Meeza Contactless Prepaid Cards which are offered to both the banked and unbanked customers with easy onboarding and minimal documentation (Abu Dhabi Islamic Bank-Egypt 2021; p.5).

[45] Average exchange rates are EGP16.81= US$1(2019) and EGP15.8 =$1 (2020).

[46] See ADIB-Egypt, Annual Reports 2020 & 2021 and Annual Financial Statements 2021 at https://www.adib.eg/media/172834/ADIBEG_Annual%20Report_English_2020.pdf and https://www.adib.eg/investor-relations/financial-results. For the latest reports refer to Abu Dhabi Islamic Bank Egypt (ADIB Egypt). 2025. Financial Reports, Cairo. https://www.adib.eg/investor-relations/financial-results.

7.5 Resource Mobilization and the Way Forward

7.5.1 Resource Mobilization

According to the African Union Commission (AUC) and the Organisation for Economic Co-operation and Development (OECD), Africa's sustainable financing gap until 2030 is about US$1.6 trillion or US$194 billion per annum to reach the United Nations Sustainable Development Goals (UNSDGs) by 2030.[47] The European Centre for Development Policy Management (ECDPM) has put it much higher by estimating that in the area of climate action alone the gap is between $200 and $400 billion annually until 2030.[48] The potential for domestic resource mobilization through Islamic finance has been dealt with elaborately in this chapter. With regard to external resource mobilization, the potential is also very significant. As data we already provided in our introduction to this chapter shows, the total value of global Islamic finance assets in 2022 grew by 11% from 2021 to US$4.5 trillion and are projected to reach $6.7 trillion in 2027. This trend is most likely to continue and Africa stands to gain for two major reasons: (1) because of the very high rates of return on investments in Africa as proven by evidence from several studies on the performance of private equity funds and other investments in Africa;[49] and

[47] AUC/OECD (2023), Africa's Development Dynamics 2023: Investing in Sustainable Development, AUC, Addis Ababa/OECD Publishing, Paris, https://doi.org/10.1787/3269532b-en, https://www.oecd-ilibrary.org/docserver/3269532b-en.pdf?expires=1716697602&id=id&accname=guest&checksum=4B09A5EBDC1E8100F1A0620898C31F08, last visited May 26, 2024.

[48] Karaki, Karim, Medinilla, Alfonso, and Bilal, San, "Three ways to scale up debt-for-climate swaps", European Centre for Development Policy Management (ECDPM), 10 November 2023; and Landry Signé and Munyati, Chido, "COP28: Bridging the climate finance gap in Africa and beyond", Dec 6, 2023, COP28 Dubai, UAE, https://www.weforum.org/agenda/2023/12/cop28-bridging-the-climate-finance-gap-in-africa-and-beyond/#:~:text=Given%20the%20limited%20climate%20finance,adverse%20impacts%20of%20climate%20change, last visited May 26, 2026.

[49] For instance, the United Nations Development Programme (UNDP) (2022) has reported that for the Investment Opportunity Areas (IOAs) reporting internal rates of return (IRRs) in Africa, the services sector accommodates the IOAs with the highest IRR, where 80% of the IOAs provide an IRR of above 15%, followed by the infrastructure and healthcare sectors, where 69% and 67%, respectively, of the IOAs are projected to have an IRR of above 15%. See UNDP, *UNDP Africa Investment Insights Report 2022*, New York, NY: UNDP, 2022, https://www.undp.org/sites/g/files/zskgke326/files/2023-07/undp-africa-investment-insights-en-2022.pdf, last visited May 5, 2024; Chatham House has emphasized:

(2) because of poverty, underdevelopment, infrastructural, climate and other challenges calling for impact and responsible investments in Africa. In this regard, Lagarde (former Managing Director of the IMF) (2015) has emphasized that "Islamic finance has the potential to contribute to higher and more inclusive economic growth by increasing access of banking services to underserved populations. ... In addition, Islamic finance's risk-sharing features and the strong link of credit to collateral means that it is well-suited for Small and Medium-Sized Enterprise (SME) and startup financing—which we know can promote inclusive growth".[50]

Yousif and Ibrahim (2017) have also argued that "Islamic finance can increase access to finance and can help bridge the infrastructure gap in Africa."[51] Best-selling author, Chang (2022) in his latest book, a creatively tasty academic cuisine, highlights the immense potential of Islamic finance positing the compatibility of its Islamic base with economic development: "Lots of its elements suit economic development ... Malaysia and Dubai both illustrate that Islam is compatible with economic progress".[52]

Africa needs clear and effective policy directions in order to consolidate gains made so far and develop its huge potential for Islamic finance, sustainably.[53] We provide some recommendations for this purpose under six main topics—legal, governance, dispute resolution, technology, sustainability and inclusion (Fig. 7.6).

"The rate of return on foreign investment is higher in Africa than in any other developing region, and the continent is fast developing its commercial future" (Chatham House, "Investment in Africa: Examining Africa's increased economic momentum, as soaring prices for oil, minerals, and other commodities have helped lift GDP since 2000," London: Chatham House, n.d., https://www.chathamhouse.org/topics/investment-africa, last visited May 26, 2024).

[50] Lagarde, Christine, "Unlocking the Promise of Islamic Finance," Speech by Christine Lagarde, Managing Director, International Monetary Fund at the Islamic Finance Conference, Kuwait City, Kuwait; November 11, 2015.

[51] Yousif, Adnan Ahmed and Ibrahim, Ali Adnan, "Islamic finance could be the answer to Africa's growth problems", World Economic Forum, Geneva, October 4, 2017, https://www.weforum.org/agenda/2017/10/islamic-finance-could-be-the-answer-to-africas-growth-problems/, last visited May 25, 2024, https://www.imf.org/en/News/Articles/2015/09/28/04/53/sp111115, last visited May 25, 2024.

[52] Chang, Ha-Joon, *Edible Economics: A Hungry Economist Explains the World*, Milton Keynes, UK: Penguin Random House, 2022.

[53] For a pioneering work on sustainability, encompassing both Islamic and non-Islamic entities, within the context of Environmental, Social and Governance (ESG), the interested reader may refer to Karamo N.M. Sonko and Mariama Sonko, *Demystifying Environmental, Social and Governance (ESG): Charting the ESG Course in Africa* (Palgrave Macmillan, 2023).

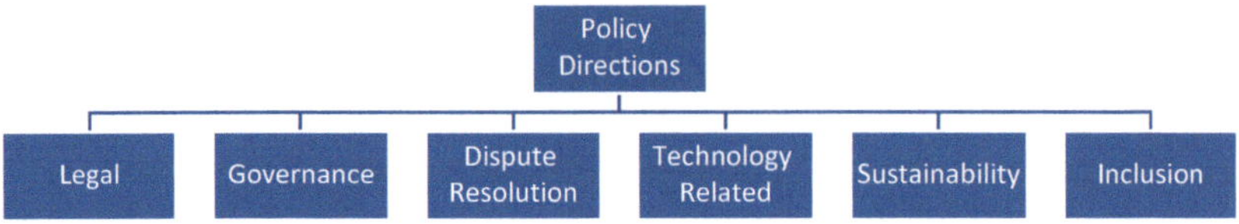

Fig. 7.6 Islamic finance in Africa: policy directions. (Source: Authors)

7.5.2 *Legal Policy Directions*

Government policies are critically needed in encouraging Islamic finance. It is clear, from the huge differences between the African central banks' annual issuances of T-Bills and those for Sukuk, where the governments' priorities actually lie. Even in African countries where there is Islamic financing, there are Islamic finance institutions and the majority of the populations are Muslims, when comparisons are made between conventional and Islamic finance instruments it becomes glaringly visible that the governments prefer T-Bills. This is a historical fact attributable to colonialism and the colonial legacies in African countries. Even after the attainment of independence in the continent, the situation did not change because of the nature of the global financial apparatus, the convenience of the status quo and the challenges of transformation from one system to another for African policy makers and customers. Therefore, the financial systems continued as they were. Naturally, it is much easier to simply maintain well-established conventional financial institutions and follow well-laid out conventional financial practices, as opposed to setting up or nurturing nascent and "complicated" Islamic finance systems.

There is currently no regulatory framework (specific laws and/or organized rules) in most African countries, even some of those with Islamic finance institutions. In most countries, such as the Gambia, there is one banking law and one set of licensing rules for banks. The existing requirements were designed for conventional banks and now applied to Islamic banking. Whilst this simplifies things, it does not provide the attention necessary to regulate, encourage and structure the Islamic banking industry better.

The lack of the regulatory frameworks has restricted or diverted attention from the possibilities of establishing Islamic finance institutions and hence the promotion of investment in the sector in most African countries. An effective regulatory environment is an important pre-requisite for the development of Islamic finance in any jurisdiction. As the *lex loci* applicable to Islamic finance is Sharia'h, financing can only be properly encouraged to be Sharia'h-compliant if the law (preferably) or rules applicable to Islamic finance transactions enables them to be Sharia'h-complaint. As such, it is imperative to develop a better environment that is compliant with Sharia'h for the development of Islamic finance.

The central banks and other relevant departments of the ministries of finance, in Muslim-majority countries in particular, should be more active in Islamic finance policy formation and the promotion of Islamic finance. The governments, through the ministries of education, should integrate Islamic business education into the curricula of national educational institutions. This would encourage private institutions to follow suit. Government officials, especially in the ministries of finance, should be more receptive to Islamic finance and have trained specialists to assist potential and actual investors interested in the sector. Government officials should also know that, in spite of its name, Islamic finance is about business and provides a legitimate means of doing so for *both* Muslims and non-Muslims.

To some extent, this is already happening in the United Kingdom, for example.[54] The United Kingdom's leadership in Islamic finance in Europe, the surge of attraction of Europeans towards Islamic finance and what Sadoveanu observes as the "attractive market for expansion for the Islamic banks" started at about the year 2000 (Sadoveanu 2011; p. 594). What spurred the interest in Britain, France and Germany (the biggest European Islamic finance markets) was the attractive potential generated by the interests of Muslims as well as non-Muslims to do business *together*. Whilst the UK example, in particular, shows a positive non-Muslim reaction to Islamic finance, through the acceptance of Islamic finance by non-Muslims and their governments, it also shows that Muslims must not try to force Islamic finance down the throats of the former as all the European experience was and still is voluntary.

[54] Refer to Ahmed Belouafi and Abdelkader Chachi, "Islamic Finance in the United Kingdom: Factors Behind its Development and Growth", *Islamic Economic Studies*, Vol. 22, No. 1, May, 2014 (37–78) DOI No. 10.12816/0004130; Diana Sadoveanu, "Islamic banking in European union countries: challenges and opportunities", CES Working Papers, III, (4), 2011.

7.5.3 Sukuk

Just as the lack of an established regulatory framework can and does inhibit the growth of Islamic finance, its existence can and does help African countries to tap into the wider variety of Islamic finance asset classes. One of these assets is Sukuk. As the global surge of Sukuk (encompassing many developed and influential non-Muslim economies) shows, Islamic finance can and does offer faith, ethics and profitability, depending on who you are and what your investment motive is. All of these are or should be attractive to Muslims and the latter two would be most likely appealing to non-Muslim investors anywhere as well. Therefore, at a time when Islam, in general, is associated with so many negative impressions, Islamic finance can be used to build bridges across the Muslim and non-Muslim worlds. This is indeed a great opportunity for Islamic finance and financial inclusion!

7.6 Governance Policy Directions

Governance is the backbone of any financial institution. Numerous scholars have pointed out its roles and importance at great length in the case of the conventional financial system.[55] In addition to Sharia'h governance, there is the corporate governance that ought to be adhered, even in the cases of Islamic finance institutions. Good governance helps in risk mitigation. Sharia'h risk refers to the risk that arises due to non-compliance with

[55] For very useful references on governance, the reader may refer to Andrei and Robert W. Vishny (1997), "A Survey of Corporate Governance", Journal of Finance, L11, pp. 737–783; Webb, David (1998); Haider A. Khan, "Some Institutional Issues in Corporate Governance and Finance", Paper presented at The Asian Development Bank, Manila; Haider A. Khan, Global Markets and Financial Crisis: Towards a Theory for the 21st Century (2004), Ch.6. "Corporate Governance: A New Theory", Macmillan/Palgrave; Haider A. Khan, "Corporate Governance of Family Businesses in Asia: What's Right and what's Wrong?" (1999) Tokyo: ADBI paper no. 3; Haider A. Khan, "Corporate Governance in Singapore and Hong Kong" (1999). Tokyo: ADBI paper no. 12; Berglöf, Erik (1997), "Reforming Corporate Governance", Economic Policy 24, pp. 91–123; Aoki, Masahiko and H.K. Kim (eds) (1995), Corporate Governance in Transitional Economies: Insider Control and the Role of Banks, Washington D.C.: The World Bank; World Bank (1998), East Asia: The Road to Recovery, Washington D.C.: The World Bank; and Aoki, Masahiko, H.K. Kim and Masahiro Okuno-Fujiwara (1996), The Role of Government in East Asian Economic Development: Comparative Institutional Analysis, Oxford: Clarendon Press.

Sharia'h. Due to non-compliance with Sharia'h, there could be three major undesirable consequences or risks that could arise facing Islamic finance institutions: non-financial, such as reputational consequences; forbidden consequences, such as not giving out the non-compliant income to charity; and statutory consequences, as in Malaysia, where the statute expressly states the punishment that has to be meted out for breaches of Sharia'h compliance. With regard to improper corporate governance, if good practices are not followed the situation could lead to unethical outcomes which can eventually cause the financial institution to go into difficulties. Good corporate governance has the opposite effects and that is why it is essential, whether the institution is Islamic or not.

7.7 Dispute Resolution Policy Directions

Commercial transactions, including those in Islamic finance, must not be expected to be free from disputes. As such, dispute resolution mechanisms are required to play an important role in protecting the rights of the parties involved in the transactions. In some countries in Africa, the courts that have the jurisdiction to hear Islamic finance disputes are the civil courts rather than Shari'ah courts (Mustapha et al. 2019; Hikmany and Oseni 2016).[56] This results in problems arising from the inabilities of judges, even if they are Muslims themselves, to decide on religious matters related to Islamic finance transactions, due to their lack of the required knowledge. In turn, this makes the case for alternative dispute resolution mechanisms that need to be created for arbitration and mediation and managed by those well trained in *Shari'ah*. However, to apply the alternative dispute resolution mechanisms, the contracts made between the parties should include clauses that show the common and consensual intentions of the parties to use the chosen mode of alternative dispute resolution mechanism before, or instead of, taking the matter to the courts.

[56] Z. Mustapha, S. Kunhibava, and A. Muneeza, "Court referral and Nigeria's Financial Regulation Council of Experts (FRACE)" *ISRA International Journal of Islamic Finance*, 11, 2, 2019, pp. 206–225; Hikmany, Abdel-Nasser, H.R., and U.A. Oseni, "Dispute resolution in the Islamic banking industry of Tanzania: Learning fron other jurisdiction", *International Journal of Islamic and Middle Eastern Finance and Management*, 9, 1, 2016, pp. 125–142.

7.8 Technology-Related Policy Directions

Ironically, as shown in this chapter, the COVID-19 pandemic has accelerated the pace and adoption of technological innovations by Islamic finance institutions in order to ensure that there is no interruption in the services they provide to their customers. As such, unlike the time before the COVID-19 pandemic when such services were provided by choice, now all Islamic financial institutions have been forced to find, or at least consider, the most suitable and convenient technology solutions to switch all, or a significant part of, their offline services to online services. Such innovative services, on- and offline, should not stop because they attract, enlarge the numbers and protect the customers whilst enabling the institutions to benefit from emerging opportunities. Due to the Fourth Industrial Revolution, different types of technology, such as blockchain and artificial intelligence, are gaining momentum very fast in the global financial sector. Tapping and regulating these technologies in the context of Shari'ah compliance should continue to be explored for the sustainable implementation of Islamic finance transactions in Africa.

7.8.1 Fintech

On the matter of banking and financial technology, specifically, generally Islamic finance institutions in Africa have very few options in the market for the platforms that can bring the desired satisfaction to customers. The technology options available are weakest when it comes to corporate banking and treasury management, but the most urgent and challenging are probably found in departments handling structured Islamic trade finance (SITF), which started very recently in most countries. The International Islamic Trade Finance Corporation (ITFC) (a member of the Islamic Development Bank Group) and other Islamic financiers had to improvise for themselves by working with information technology service providers to "build a platform as you go" and, in addition, take on all the inherent operational risks present in such ad hoc approaches.[57]

Salyani and Sonko (2022) found that Islamic Fintech in Africa is picking up with the growth of conventional Fintech in the continent. In order

[57] Information on ITFC's Islamic financing programmes around the world can be obtained from its Annual Reports, Annual Development Effectiveness Reports through its website (https://www.itfc-idb.org/resources-center/publications) or directly from the Corporation itself.

to sustain the momentum, they pointed out that efforts to tap the potential of Fintech have to be nationally coordinated, meaning that African governments and Fintech start-ups should work together. In this regard, governments should create the enabling environments for the Fintech ecosystems through policies and practices which encourage innovation and financial inclusion. The African Islamic Fintech companies can also, on their own, develop customer-focused marketing strategies, educate stakeholders about Islamic Fintech, especially products that target the massive rural populations, and design customer-friendly applications and websites with useful and attractive contents. Finally, they also recommended that Fintech companies must be able to form strategic alliances with parties that can enhance the efforts of these companies in growing their businesses. Primary among such partners should be Islamic finance institutions with common objectives and challenges.[58]

7.9 Sustainability

We refer to sustainability in this chapter in relation to the United Nations' 17 Sustainable Development Goals (UNSDGs). Yousif and Ibrahim (ibid.) argued that four of the principles of Islamic finance (prohibition of riba, prohibition of speculation, prohibition of financing illicit businesses, and profit and loss sharing) can tackle the following 12 out of the 17 SDGs shown in Fig. 7.7:[59]

1. No poverty;
2. Zero hunger;
3. Good health and well-being;
4. Quality education;
5. Decent work and economic growth;
6. Reduced inequalities;
7. Responsible consumption and production;
8. Peace, justice and strong institutions;
9. Clean water and sanitation;

[58] Salyani, Mohamed Shakeel, and Karamo NM Sonko, "Innovations in Islamic Fintech: A Focus on Africa", in M. Kabir Hassan, Aishath Muneeza, and Karamo N.M. Sonko, *Islamic Finance in Africa: The Prospects for Sustainable Development.* Northampton, MA, USA: Edward Elgar Publishing (2022).

[59] As can be seen in Fig. 7.7, some of these goals are repetitive and they overlap. However, they are universally accepted and referenced.

Fig. 7.7 The United Nations (UN) sustainability development goals. (Source: https://www.un.org/sustainabledevelopment/. This figure has been officially approved by the UN, but the contents of this publication have not been approved by the UN and does not reflect the views of the UN or its officials or Member States)

10. Affordable and clean energy;
11. Industry, innovation and infrastructure;
12. Sustainable cities and communities.

Yousif and Ibrahim did not explain how Islamic finance tackles the above and did not focus on the SDGs that Islamic finance can be used to directly target because of its principles and the financial resources it attracts and can attract. To be more precise, we present below the most directly targetable goals and how they can be targeted are:

1. No poverty—Islamic finance does not seek to make every man or woman rich on earth but aims to economically empower through profit and loss financing instead of debt financing with interest. Additionally, *Zakat* (obligatory alms or tax for the poor and one of

the five pillars of Islam) and *sadaqah* (charity) are for shared prosperity and eradicating poverty ***as much as possible***. ***Zakat*** is obligatory for Muslim investors, traders and employees/contractors in Islamic finance and voluntary, but highly recommended, for both Muslim and non-Muslim investors, traders and employees/contractors;

2. Zero hunger— This can be targeted directly with shortest term/immediate effects through *Zakat* and *sadaqah* are means of sharing prosperity and eradicating poverty as much as possible;
3. Good health and well-being—In the same way as in points 1 and 2. The eradication of poverty as much as possible would result in good health and well-being;
4. Quality education—Islamic finance has been widely recognized for its ability to attract large-scale infrastructure financing, particularly through sukuk, discussed earlier. The infrastructure projects does and should include schools;
5. Reduced inequalities—This is related to points 1–4; hence the answers are the same;
6. Responsible consumption and production—Although unknown to most, protection of the natural environment is one of the precepts of Islam. The environment is considered one of the uncountable Blessings of *Allah* (the One and Almighty God) to His creatures for consumption, production and sharing. In the process, anything with life has to be treated with mercy, even the animals we ate at the time of slaughter. Farming/agriculture and the cultivation of plants are considered to be good deeds because they enable other creatures, such as birds, to feed from the plants sown. Thus, given Africa's huge food deficit reflected in the numbers of the malnourished and food insecure, Islamic finance can be a major source of agricultural finance and good business too;[60]

[60] Africa is not on track to meet the food security and nutrition targets of UNSDG Number 2 and the Malabo Declaration on ending hunger and all forms of malnutrition by 2025. After ten years of improvement, hunger has worsened since 2010. In 2022, about 282 million Africans were undernourished, an increase of 57 million after the COVID-19 pandemic. In the same year, an estimated 868 million people were moderately or severely food-insecure and more 342 million people among them (more than a third) were severely food-insecure (FAO, AUC, ECA and WFP. 2023. *Africa—Regional Overview of Food Security and Nutrition 2023: Statistics and trends*. Accra, FAO. https://doi.org/10.4060/cc8743en).

7. Clean water and sanitation—Such projects may be financed relatively easy through sukuk (discussed earlier) than conventional finance;
8. Affordable and clean energy—Related to point 7;
9. Industry, innovation and infrastructure—Related to points 7 and 8. Enhanced resource mobilization (both domestic and external) can benefit industry, innovation and infrastructure;
10. Sustainable cities and communities—Related to points 1–5 and 7–9;
11. Climate action—Related to points 6–8;
12. Life below water—Related to points 6–8 and 10–11;
13. Life on land—Related to points 6, 7, 11 and 12;
14. Partnership for the goals—Islamic finance provides a great opportunity to build bridges between Muslims and non-Muslims through business. It has a huge and untapped potential, particularly in or for Africa, to boost development finance beyond conventional finance and to forge partnerships between Muslim and non-Muslim investors.

7.10 Inclusion

7.10.1 Financial Inclusion

We have already pointed out in this chapter that as the population and the numbers of young persons increase, concerns about poverty and, hence, financial inclusion in Africa will also increase. These concerns will augur well for Islamic finance because the need to address poverty is a principal concern of *authentic* Islamic finance. We add "authentic" to Islamic finance in this section because Islamic finance (banks especially) has come under criticism for sometimes emulating conventional finance by being expensive and forgetting its basic principles mentioned in this chapter. Therefore, for Islamic finance to be truly Islamic and live up to expectations, it has to be truly Islamic, by providing affordable financing where it matters the most and to those for whom it matters the most—that is, the poor, needy and vulnerable which includes the sick, women and children. It also means that financing should target those parts of the world and countries which are victims of imbalanced development, such as the rural areas and other places that are victims of imbalanced development.

7.10.2 Religious Inclusion

In this chapter we use "religious inclusion" to mean the willingness of Muslims and non-Muslims to do business with each other (specifically in Islamic finance) in the interest of humankind and the environment, both of which are at the "heart" of authentic Islamic finance. A unique feature of Islamic finance is that it does not advocate that business must be charity but that business must be charitable for better relations between human beings and between them and their Creator (the One and Almighty God referred to as *Allah* in Islam). Are Muslims allowed to do business only with Muslims? Apart from the obvious "No" in our contemporary world, the Holy Qur'an and the history of Islam provide the justifications for trans-religious business as far as such business is fair to the parties concerned. An ignored or unknown verse from the Holy Qur'an states:

> For you is your religion, and for me is my religion. (109:6)

Another verse states:

> (There is) no compulsion in the religion. (2:256)

The potential of Islamic to build bridges between Muslims and non-Muslims has been almost completely ignored in the literature. In fact, there is a popular tendency to treat the subject as if it covers and is only for the benefit of only Muslims, although non-Muslim governments and investors are already significant contributors to and advocates of Islamic finance. Ironically, some non-Muslim countries have shown warmer attitudes towards Islamic finance than some Muslim-majority countries as reflected in the number and diversity of Islamic finance institutions, a point that has also been raised earlier and shown in the case of the United Kingdom. In our modern world, money comes before anything (or almost anything). By proving to the world that business and care for the poor and needy are authentically part of Islam, Islamic finance can make Islam more appealing to both Muslims and non-Muslims, contradicting misconceptions and false representations of the religion that have now become only too common.

7.11 Conclusion: The Strategy-Knowledge Mix

The importance of a strategic approach by the key actors/practitioners and knowledge of Islamic finance by potential customers, especially but not limited to Muslims, cannot be over-emphasized. For the success of Africa's next and sustainable leap in Islamic finance post-COVID-19, both are essential. Therefore, this chapter ends on these two themes.

7.11.1 *Strategic Management*

Islamic finance institutions must be proactive in both their marketing and investment strategies.[61] By going after clients rather than clients going after them and constantly and boldly seeking attractive financing opportunities, they can improve their customer bases and services, build networks and contribute to product development and the development of the private sector. These will in turn increase the visibility of the institutions and their market penetration. If the large and increasing number of conventional banks across Africa can do these surmountable tasks and prosper,[62] even among African Muslim populations, then the African Islamic finance institutions should be able to do so too, especially given their scarcity and the little or no intra-sectoral competition among them. These (even intuitively) indicate that there is very significant potential for Islamic finance in the continent that remains untapped—a point reiterated throughout this chapter.

As observed by Sonko and Sonko in their study cited earlier, "A strategic approach to Islamic banking, based on innovation and education, would be the best way of boosting Islamic banking in The Gambia and other Sub-Saharan African countries. Innovation here refers to the ability to introduce creative and competitive products and services that can attract

[61] The case for this was first made by the first author in Karamo N.M. Sonko, "Modern Strategic Management and Islamic finance institutions in Africa: Facing the competition and promoting economic progress", paper presented to the Seventh Islamic Finance Summit, July 8, 2022, Hyatt Regency Hotel, Dar es Salaam, Tanzania.

[62] For the performances of conventional banks in Africa, see, for example: the Gambia (Sonko and Sonko, ibid.); Morocco (Abdelkader Derbali, "Determinants of the performance of Moroccan banks", *Journal of Business and Socio-economic Development*, Vol. 1 No. 1, 2021, pp. 102–117); Tanzania (https://www.tanzaniainvest.com/banks); and Nigeria and South Africa compared to the United States (Ozili, Peterson, "Bank profitability determinants: comparing the United States, Nigeria and South Africa", MPRA Paper No. 105638, posted 02 Feb 2021).

the existing clientele of conventional banks. It also, and perhaps equally or more important, refers to the ability to tap into the wealth of the largely unbanked Muslim population by encouraging them to save and bank according to Islamic principles" (Sonko and Sonko 2020, p. 82).

7.11.2 *Knowledge*

Finally, it is necessary to conclude with emphasis on another point that has also been observed in this study, asserting the need for an essential ingredient for the sustainable growth of Islamic finance in Africa—knowledge. In their extensive discussion of the way forward in promoting Islamic finance in the continent, Sonko and Sonko (ibid.) have reiterated and shown that knowledge is critical in the sustainable development of Islamic finance among Muslims and non-Muslims anywhere in the world. This point has also been demonstrated in this study, with practical examples. In addition to the business opportunity, it is essential for Muslims to know that Islamic finance is a matter of faith, which is far more important than business as usual for them. In other words, in reality it is not a matter of choice but an obligation for Muslims, because *riba* is not permissible for Muslims and, in fact, it is among the major sins in Islam. This knowledge can be the biggest booster of the potential of Islamic finance anywhere there are Muslims. Although the overwhelming majority of Muslims around the world use conventional banks, it is fair to assume that not all or most of them do so out of choice or in spite of the knowledge that it is forbidden in their religion. We doubt if any practising Muslim, aware of, or convinced about, the gravity of the sin of *riba*, would *willingly* and *happily* choose to bank conventionally (borrow/lend with interest) given the choice, or with the availability, of Islamic banking alternatives. The evidence in different parts of Africa (Northern and Sub-Saharan) presented in this study does prove this point correct. For non-Muslims seeking ethical and inclusive finance, authentic Islamic finance offers very appealing options. Like Muslims, non-Muslims need to know what Islamic finance is actually about—business, including profit-making, but based on Islamic principles that are beneficial to both Muslims and non-Muslims; again, this highlights the importance of knowledge.

Related to knowledge is informed policy making in Islamic finance. The renamed Islamic Research and Training Institute (IRTI), which awarded a research grant in Islamic Economics and Finance to the principal author of this chapter (2017), is now called the Islamic Development Bank Institute (since 2021). The challenge in name is not just in name we hope, as it is now being modelled on the IMF and World Bank Institutes using the vast financial resources of the Triple A-rated Islamic Development Bank in Jeddah, Saudi Arabia. In efforts to promote policy-oriented research the Bank has reformulated its Prize for Impactful Achievement in Islamic Economics into the: (1) Prize for Achievements in Development Solutions in IsDB Member Countries; and (2) Prize for Knowledge Contributions in Areas Related to Islamic Economics that have the potential of addressing major development challenges in the bank's member countries.[63] Khan (2020) has demonstrated the importance of rigorous policy-oriented research by introducing computable general equilibrium (CGE) modelling into the field.[64] In addition to the IsDB's efforts, research in academic institutions in Islamic finance is now moving at a fast pace in specialized and non-specialized academic institutions around the world, in both developed and developing countries, Muslim-majority and Muslim-minority countries. However, research in Africa is yet to catch up with the increasing pace.[65]

References

Abu Dhabi Islamic Bank Egypt (ADIB Egypt). Consolidated financial results for the financial year ending December 31, 2020, Cairo, March 2021.

Benamraoui, A. "Islamic banking: the case of Algeria", *International Journal of Islamic and Middle Eastern Finance and Management*, 1 (2020) (2), pp. 113–131.

Chang, Ha-Joon, *Edible Economics: A Hungry Economist Explains the World*, Milton Keynes, UK: Penguin Random House, 2022.

Çizakça, Murat. "Economic Systems of Muslims in History," *Arab Law Quarterly*, Volume 35 (2021): Issue 1–2 (Nov 2020).

[63] IsDB, "Islamic Development Bank Prize for Impactful Achievement in Islamic Economics", IsDB, Jeddah, Saudi Arabia, undated, https://prize.isdbinstitute.org/wp-content/uploads/2023/08/IsDB-Prize-Brochure_2023_EN_2.pdf, last visited May 29, 2024.

[64] Khan, Haider A., "Chapter 2: Islamic Banking in General Equilibrium: A Structural CGE Model for Policy Making within a Complex Socio-economic System", in Khan, Haider A., and Sonko, Karamo NM (eds.), *Islamic Finance as a Closed System: New Insights*, Lanham, MD: Lexington Books, 2020.

[65] The first volume addressing Islamic finance and sustainable development in Africa was co-authored by the first author of this chapter. See Kabir, Muneeza and Sonko (ibid.).

Derbali, Abdelkader. "Determinants of the performance of Moroccan banks," *Journal of Business and Socio-economic Development*, Vol. 1 No. 1, 2021, pp. 102–117.

Gelbard, Enrique, Mumtaz Hussain, Rodolfo Maino, Yibin Mu, and Etienne B. Yehoue. "Islamic Finance in Sub-Saharan Africa: Status and Prospects." *IMF Working Paper*, 14/149 (2014).

Hassan, M. Kabir. "Future of Islamic Finance in the Post-COVID Era in Africa," 8th Islamic Finance Summit, Banjul, the Gambia, March 21, 2022.

Mcclendon, David. "Sub-Saharan Africa will be home to growing shares of the world's Christians and Muslims", Pew Research Centre, April 19. 2017.

Mezouaghi, Mihoub. "Sub-Saharan Africa and the Arab world: disconnected agricultural regions", in Cosimo Lacirignola, *MediTERRA* 2014, Presses de Sciences Po, Paris, 2014.

Middle East Insurance Review, "Algeria: Islamic insurance on the cards soon", *Middle East Insurance Review*, Oct 2020.

United Nations, "Global Issues. Population", https://www.un.org/en/global-issues/population, last visited December 4, 2021.

Niane, D. T. ed. *General History of Africa: Volume IV. Africa from the Twelfth to the Sixteenth Century*. Paris, London and Berkeley, California: UNESCO, Heinemann & University of California, 1984.

Oxford Business Group, "Morocco increases its sharia-compliant bank offerings", in The Report, *Morocco 2020*, Oxford: OBG 2020.

Ozili, Peterson, "Bank profitability determinants: comparing the United States, Nigeria and South Africa," MPRA Paper No. 105638, posted 02 Feb 2021.

Refinitiv. 2021. *Islamic Finance Development Report 2021*, retrieved from https://www.refinitiv.com/content/dam/marketing/en_us/documents/gated/reports/report-2021-all-color2.pdf.

Rocca, Camilla, and Ines Schultes, 2021. "Africa's youth: action needed now to support the continent's greatest asset," Mo Ibrahim Foundation, available at https://mo.ibrahim.foundation/sites/default/files/202008/international-youth-day-research-brief.pdf, last visited 12 December 2021.

Salyani, Mohamed Shakeel, and Karamo NM Sonko, "Innovations in Islamic Fintech: A Focus on Africa," in M. Kabir Hassan, Aishath Muneeza, and Karamo N.M. Sonko, Islamic Finance in Africa: The Prospects for Sustainable Development. Northampton, MA., USA: Edward Elgar Publishing (2022).

Sonko, Karamo N.M., and Mariama Sonko. "Promoting Islamic finance in Africa: "Top-bottom" or "Bottom up"? a Case study of Banking in the Gambia", in Haider A. Khan and Karamo N.M. Sonko, Islamic Finance as a Complex System, Lanham, MD: Lexington Books, 2020.

Sonko, Karamo NM. "Learning Business from our Ancestors," *African Business*, January 2003.

World Bank, *Libya Financial Sector Review*, Washington, D.C.: World Bank, February 2020.

CHAPTER 8

Combatting the Social Cankerworm of "Tribalism" in Africa: Causes, Consequences and How, with a Gambian Case Study

8.1 Introduction

Ethnic conflict is one of the major threats to international peace and security. [1]

As used by Africans, tribalism in postcolonial Africa refers to the abhorrence for the abuse of common opportunities and public goods (that is, those owned in common by various ethnic groups) through manifestation of undue preferences for persons of one's own ethnic grouping. Tribalism has also been used as a term of opprobrium to denote objectionable activities of individuals who threaten the integrity of the nation and yet favor its specialized ethnic fragments.[2]

From Cape to Cairo, ethnic conflict, described here as tribalism, continues to be the cankerworm which bites into the economic, political and social well-being of Africa. Levels and forms may be different, but the ramifications are similar across nations—from non-violent expressions of superiority or hatred to violent outbursts which lead to deadly bloodshed. In this chapter, we will look at the causes, consequences and solutions of tribalism

[1] Reuter, Tina Kempin. "Ethnic conflict". *Encyclopedia Britannica*, 29 May. 2023, https://www.britannica.com/topic/ethnic-conflict. Accessed 6 July 2024.

[2] Ekeh, Peter, "Social Anthropology and Two Contrasting Uses of Tribalism in Africa", Comparative Studies in Society and History, Vol. 32, No. 4 (Oct. 1990), pp. 660–700, https://www.jstor.org/stable/178957, retrieved 13/12/2024.

K. N. M. Sonko et al., *21st Century African Development Strategies*, https://doi.org/10.1007/978-3-031-93079-9_8

in Africa, definitional differences between ethnicity and tribalism, examples from different parts of Africa, and present original in-depth statistical field evidence from a revealing path-breaking Gambian field and case survey. Then recommendations for policy makers, organizations and ordinary citizens in the Gambia and rest of the continent follow. In addition to the originality of the approach and data in this chapter, the analysis is also in relation to development policies, an approach and coverage which are rare in the large existing literature on ethnicity/tribalism in Africa, dominated by scholars in political science, anthropology, sociology and history and by journalists.

Next, we look at, and attempt to clarify, the differences between ethnicity and tribalism, a very difficult task to undertake an issue that is unclear and remains a major shortcoming in the literature. Then, thirdly, we carry out an exploration of the theories of tribalism or tribal conflict. Fourthly, we discuss the consequences of tribalism, especially in relation to economic development. Fifthly, we highlight major tribal incidents across Africa and, sixthly, their causes. Seventhly, we present our Gambian findings. Finally, we offer recommendations for dealing with the consequences of tribalism in an Africa that desperately needs peace, unity and all the ingredients of stability for the effective tackling of poverty and the achievement of shared prosperity for its people in the twenty-first century.

8.2 Difference Between Ethnicity and Tribe

Ethnicity and tribe are commonly taken to be the same and used interchangeably. Even in the academic literature, as shown by Welsh (1996)[3] they are associated or taken as one because of their similarities. Not many disassociate them because of differences that are not obvious (Posner 2005).[4] Therefore, there is a lack of clarity and some confusion even in the literature. In this study they are not taken as the same and an attempt is made to spot a few, but very important, differences.

First, we see one as more or less natural or inevitable and the other as artificial or political, functioning more like an interest group than a natural identity. One is mainly descriptive and the other tends to be more action-oriented for specific and, historically, ulterior motives. In other words, the ethnic group is somewhat natural or historically made so and descriptive,

[3] Welsh, D., 'Ethnicity in Sub-Saharan Africa', IA, Vol. 72, No. 3 (1996).

[4] Posner, D.N., Institutions and Ethnic Politics in Africa (Cambridge, 2005), pp. 1 (fn. 1) and 119–128.

whilst the tribe is artificial and can be used for the benefit of the fabricated tribe even, as it happens too often, at a cost to outsiders and/or the tribe itself. It is action-oriented in the sense that the tribe can be specifically or deliberately set up for the interest of the tribal group, whatever that interest may be, and whatever the cost of chasing that interest may be to outsiders. More illustratively, ethnicity is typically acquired at birth, although there are exceptions. It is directly related to the language spoken and to well-established customs and values of the group, the history and, commonly, even a rationale of which group members themselves cannot tell. Therefore, an ethnic group cannot be easily created whilst a tribe can be and by any group of people who comes together for a specific purpose, calling themselves a tribe and appointing their leader. The tribe can also be created by an external force or party that has influence over the group, as we will see later in this chapter when we explain the origins of tribalism in Africa. The latter is in fact the most common form of a tribe historically, because the existing literature overwhelmingly attributes tribalism to colonial policies. Thus, an ethnic group can be converted into a tribe and become tribalistic due to exogenous forces (external parties) or endogenous influences (internal sources). Some political scientists have already observed that the root causes of tribal conflicts do not always involve ethnicity per se but grow out of institutional, economic and political factors.[5]

As Ekeh (1990) reported, many of the earliest works Gluckman (1960), Mayer (1961), (Mitchell (1960), and Lee (1971)) on tribalism were on South Africa. These refer to the "folkways" that tribesmen took with them into the new urban areas as tribalism. In an effort to clear the air, his observations showed a distinction:

"Such an anthropological meaning of tribalism is dramatically different from its modern sociological uses in postcolonial Africa. In this latter context, tribalism refers to obnoxious modes of behavior in multiethnic circumstances that threaten and endanger normal coexistence among persons from different ethnic groups." (1990, p. 688). In also observing differences between the ethnic group and the tribes, others have also negatively portrayed the tribe as opposed to the ethnic group. For examples, Lonsdale associates the ethnic group with morality and the tribe with political

[5] Refer, for example, to Lijphart, Arend (2001). "Constructivism and Consociational Theory". *Newsletter of the Organized Section in Comparative Politics of the American Political Science Association*; and Giuliano, Elise (2011). *Constructing Grievance: Ethnic Nationalism in Russia's Republics.* Cornell University Press.

mischiefs.[6] Generally tribal identity was viewed as marks of primitiveness, savagery, inertia, corruption, small and degenerative (Mkenda, Gathara 2019).[7]

On the other hand and related to common usage of tribalism and ethnicity as one, "the term 'tribe' retains association with primary aggregates of people held together through kinship, living under headmen or chiefs, with compact cultures and largely self-sufficient economies, and often bereft of a national character".[8]

8.3 Theories of Tribalism/Tribal Conflict

There is a large amount of academic literature on factors that underlay tribal conflicts and tensions in Africa, including theories of such tensions and conflicts. For a continent that has over 3000 different groups identified as "tribes", with more than 1000 distinct languages, the diversity and importance of these social groups and their interactions have attracted a vast amount of scholarly and journalistic investigations, debates and controversy. What is evident from, and throughout, the research on the subject is that ethnic conflicts surfaced in nearly most parts of the African continent before, during and after colonial rule, although colonialism has aggravated it through weaponization and sophisticated divide-and-rule policies.

Before the formal settlement of the colonial powers in Africa, they seemed to have already studied and understood the dynamism and importance of social groups in the continent and, thus, were able to plan a system of control over Africans, using already established ethnic or pseudo-tribal groups.

Colonialism instigated deeper sources of ethnic-cum-tribal problems as the groups violently struggled for dominance over one another and competed for access to imperial powers and privileges. Upon arrival, the

[6] Lonsdale, j., 'Moral Ethnicity and Political Tribalism', in P. Kaarsholm and J. Hultin (eds.), Inventions and Boundaries (Roskilde, 1994).

[7] Also see, for instance, Mkenda, Festo, "On Tribes and Nations: Biology and Ideology in the Study of African Nationalism," undated, retrieved 14/12/2024; and Patrick Gathara, "What Is Your Tribe? the Invention of Kenya's Ethnic Communities, "What Is Your Tribe? the Invention of Kenya's Ethnic Communities," published by The Elephant, 2019, https://www.academia.edu/73675463/WHAT_IS_YOUR_TRIBE_The_Invention_Of_Kenya_s_Ethnic_Communities?email_work_card=title retrieved May 22, 2025.

[8] Mkenda, Festo (ibid.).

colonial powers relied on their historians, anthropologists, priests, scientists and military officials to advise them on or execute tribal policies. Some of these European civil servants and associates drew spatial maps that arbitrarily delineated the territorial areas of various tribal groups, with the intent to divide, or further divide, and isolate the groups.

Thus, in Uganda, for example, the British were able to exploit the longstanding divisions between the Baganda and Banyoro ethnic groups. Before the arrival of the British and their colonization of Uganda, battles were common for land and livestock between the Baganda, Banyoro and other ethnic groups, as they were between different ethnic groups in other parts of Africa. The British took advantage of such age-old conflicts as welcomed opportunities to exploit and they did so deliberately and successfully. The pre-existing conflictual situations provided the ideal opportunities for the British to further divide the ethnic groups when the British colonized Uganda. Thus, by aggravating the pre-colonial tensions and utilizing them in the dependent relationships with the African colonists, tribalism became real, official and a socially destructive weapon of colonialism. Whenever the colonialists were threatened by one group, they sided with another and created a common enemy when needed. For instance, when the British faced resistance against their rule by the leaders of the Banyoro, they conspired with the Baganda to wage war against the Banyoro. In return, the Baganda were given Banyoro land as their reward.

With such evidence, researchers tried to understand the nature of tribal issues that have afflicted Africa. In trying to do so, they focused on how the arrival of the colonial powers determined tribes, the relationships between tribes, and what is tribalism as defined by the colonial experience. Whilst their focus is justifiable because colonialism almost completely transformed ethnic relations by politicizing these relations in Africa, we are left with little knowledge about the subject of ethnic differentiation in pre-colonial Africa.

Consequently, most of the existing literature consists of discussions by anthropologists, sociologists and political scientists who have researched the underlining causes of tribal conflicts. Their radars scan mostly the colonial and post-colonial periods. Different theories have been postulated in their efforts to understand the factors that have ostensibly caused, and continue to cause, tribalism. The theories are useful, to different extents, in understanding tribalism, its causes and our findings in this study. The most elaborated and apposite ones in relation to contemporary

Africa are the primordialist, the instrumentalist and constructivist theories or schools of thought. A brief explanation of each of these is provided below.[9]

8.3.1 Primordialism

Proponents of the primordialist theory believe that ethnic identities are derived from nature. According to them, ethnicity is a quasi-natural creation that deserves utmost protection and defence against external threats, particularly (as in most cases) from other ethnic groups themselves. According to them, ethnicity is viewed from the lens of shared cultural history, language, a collective name, inherited human characteristics and territorial boundaries. They argue that ethnic identities are assigned at birth and handed from one generation to another. The theory explains the causes of some of the conflicts in Africa, such as in Uganda, based on ancestral myths and traditional beliefs that differentiate ethnic groups.

Ethnic identities are believed to be derived from nature (biologically determined or built by individuals in the past) and were passed down to present generations. In this way, everyone becomes a part of one ethnic group or the other.[10] Group consciousness is developed on the basis of the common language, culture, traditions, history and practices of members of an ethnic group. The group identity and consciousness emerge overtime from rituals, symbols and myths.

Primordialists maintain that ethnic conflicts are natural phenomena which are the results of cultural differences. These differences make ethnicity and tribe relational concepts of "in-groups" and "out-groups" or, in other words, insiders and outsiders when people view each other. Primordialists argue that the conflicts between ethnic groups are inevitable due to their conflicting group goals.[11] Primordialists attribute ethnic

[9] Also refer to Yeghiazaryan for a summary and application to Eastern Europe (Yeghiazaryan, Laura, " Which of the three main ethnic conflict theories best explains the Ethnic violence in the post-soviet states of Azerbaijan, Georgia, and Moldova?" *Undergraduate Journal of Political Science*, Vol. 3, No. 1, Spring 2018, Pp. 46–64; and Ngarachu, Fiona, "Applying Pierre Bourdieu's concepts of Habitus and Field to the study of ethnicity in Kenya," *Journal of Language, Technology & Entrepreneurship in Africa*, Volume 5. No. 1 2014, pp. 57–64.

[10] These identities, once acquired, remain fixed over time (Kanchan Chandra, "Cumulative Findings in the Study of Ethnic Politics," *APSA-CP Journal*, Volume 12, Issue No. 1, 2001).

[11] Jesse, Neal G. and Kristen P. Williams. *Ethnic Conflict: A Systematic Approach to Cases of Conflict*, Washington, CQ Press, 2011; and Dawisha, Adeed. "Nation and Nationalism:

conflicts to memories of past atrocities and the feeling for revenge, making violent retributions almost inevitable from one generation to another.[12]

The origins of primordialist theory go back to European thinkers, specifically German Romanticism, as shown in the works of Johann Gottlieb Fichte and Johann Gottfried Herder.[13] German primordialist philosophers argued that the embedment of life experiences and group identities in specific languages and ethnicities persists and does not change with time. They stress the importance of languages in ethnicities and point out that languages emerge from dispersed geographical spaces and distinguish ethnic groups, reflecting the unique circumstances of each. Thus, as the ethnic group's language continues from generation to the other, the spirit of each group is transmitted through the language.

8.3.2 Arguments Against the Primordialist Theory

Critics of this theory argue that it offers a myopic view of ethnic rivalry as it refuses to explain non-historical factors that contribute to ethnic conflict. For example, it is said to ignore factors such as political manipulation of the ethnicity card which was a central factor behind the "divide and rule" policies of the British during the colonial era and a commonly used policy in contemporary politics. Furthermore, primordialism takes ethnic groups as homogeneous entities although, in reality, they interact and co-exist with other groups instead of live in isolation.

Primordialism has also come under criticism for being too simplistic in explaining the causes of ethnic conflicts. Critics point to their inability to explain the differences in the levels of conflict between ethnic groups at different times and in different places. They question the theory on why the reasons for the lack of conflicts between the French and the English until the year 1066, for instance, and why the French and the English became allies after fighting each other in wars for centuries. Secondly, the

Historical Antecedents to Contemporary Debates," *International Studies Review* (2002): 3–22, 2017.

[12] Sambanis, Nicholas, "Ethnic Partition as a Solution to Ethnic War: An Empirical Critique of the Theoretical Literature," (September 1999), https://papers.ssrn.com/sol3/papers.cfm?abstract_id=623960#:~:text=Nicholas%20Sambanis,-Department%20of%20Political&text=Partition%20theorists%20argue%20that%20when,The%20empirical%20evidence%20suggests%20otherwise, retrieved April 17, 2025.

[13] Jacquin-Berdal, Dominique, *Nationalism and Ethnicity in the Horn of Africa: A Critique of the Ethnic Interpretation ELewiston*, New York: Edwin Mellen Press, 2002.

critics give examples of situations where people prefer to assimilate into other ethnic groups instead of waging wars against them.[14] Thirdly, the theory has been criticized for not taking into account ethnic groups that have ceased to exist or have changed their character over time.[15] Finally, the theory has been criticized for espousing fictional ethnic or tribal identities the origins of which cannot be attributed to nature. Examples in Africa are the "Tutsi" and "Hutu" so-called ethnic groups we have already cited in this chapter. These groups were the subjects of what might be the continent's worst case of tribal violence and genocide in the post-colonial period. Their tribal differences were fabricated by the Belgians during their colonial rule in Rwanda. The Rwandan case is of particular interest in this chapter because it illustrates the pertinence of our definition of a tribe and hence tribalism. Besides, it shows the deliberate role of colonialism in fermenting tribal hatred as pervasively argued in the existing literature. It shows too how gullible Africans (or humans) can go to extreme extent of destroying each other on the basis of invented tribal differences.[16]

8.3.3 Instrumentalism

Instrumentalists argue that tribalism is solely created for political purposes. In essence, the proponents of this thought posit that powerful leaders create the concept of tribal groups in furtherance of their political goals. The

[14] For example, sometimes, when people move to another country, they choose to disregard their old cultural practices and, instead, choose to adopt the beliefs and rituals of the new group that they belong to (Andersen 240).

[15] Jesse, Neal G. and Kristen P. Williams. Ethnic Conflict: A Systematic Approach To Cases of Conflict. Washington: CQ Press, 2011.

[16] In other words, these ethnic identifications did not exist in Rwanda prior to the Belgians moving into the region. Instead, these labels were the results of myths that the Belgians invented about the people living in the territory in order to create a polarized society, which would make it easy for them to conquer and control them. According to this myth, the "Tutsis", who appeared to be taller, lighter skinned and have longer faces, were a lost tribe from Egypt, which supposedly makes them higher up in the racial hierarchy than the "Hutus". Despite the fact that there were no actual differences between "Hutus" and "Tutsis", the Rwandan people came to believe the stories of the Belgians and have been using these ever since the colonial period as the basis of tribal discrimination. Refer to Fearon, James D., and David D. Laitin, "Review: Violence and the Social Construction of Ethnic Identity," *International Organization,* Vol. 54, No. 4, Autumn, 2000, pp. 845–877); McGarry, John, and O'Leary, Brendan, *The Rwanda Crisis: History of a Genocide*, Columbia University Press, New York, 1995.

leaders rely on the homogeneity of ethnic groups as a source of exploitation for the mass mobilization in their pursuit for political power and access to resources. This is because tribalistic card has proven to be more successful than other social classes. Exploiting tribalistic sentiments, the leaders who can amass unparalleled support within their ethnic groups can also get their followers do "anything" and "everything" to defend their tribal identities or the interests of the leaders against perceived or real opponents. This theory is very visible in most parts of Africa, where leaders manipulate their followers in pursuit of political control and dominance within and outside their tribe. While doing this, they create the narrative of "us" against "them" or the mentality whereby everyone outside the sphere of the "us" group is considered to be an enemy. According to our observations, it is such political manipulations that result in the transformation of the ethnic to the tribal group, the endogenous character of the ethnic group to the exogenous outlook of the tribe, and the "us" to the "us versus them".

According to instrumentalism, ethnicity is a tool that is deliberately used by some people to achieve their divisive objectives. They do so because of their awareness that shared ascriptive ethnic identities can be used successfully to influence and mobilize public policies and resources in their favour. Therefore, individuals who believe that ethnic divisions can help them obtain access to valuable public resources and services may try to use these differences anyway they can, in or outside the normal political processes, in order to achieve their objectives. As members of ethnic groups generally tend to feel the urge to stick to each other, this cohesive inclination becomes exploitable by "ethnic activists" and "political entrepreneurs" so as to mobilize their groups to commit violence or other acts, especially under real or imagined circumstances of threats or injustice against their in-groups by the out-groups. This is done by amplifying the differences, threats or injustices by the out-groups, blaming them for the misfortunes of the in-groups. Even when such blames may not be true, the accusers can justify them and attract sympathy from their ethnic groups or tribes.[17]

[17] To explain this phenomenon, Horowitz argues that a lot of the tension between ethnic groups comes from people evaluating their abilities and their situations in life relative to the lives and the abilities of people who have other ethnic ties (Horowitz 143–144). In other words, if one group of people believe that the people from another ethnic group are better off than them, they might perceive the other group as a threat to them, which can sometimes be an enough reason to resort to violence.

8.3.4 *Arguments Against the Instrumentalist Theory*

Instrumentalism has come under attack for a number of reasons. Principal among them is that it has been described as incomplete for not taking into account, enough, the possibility or otherwise of an ethnic conflict in a diverse society. Critics observe that even when extreme ideas and conditions exist, ethnic conflict may be unlikely to naturally evolve from political protest. This is because sometimes certain considerations, such as costs, probability of winning or losing, risks and the potential duration of a conflict may influence the actual outcomes under rationally assessed scenarios of potential conflict.[18] Thus, rational decision making may reduce the chances of opportunistic ethnic elites to stir tribal violence.[19]

8.3.5 *Constructivism*

The constructivist approach asserts that ethnic conflict is the result of social constructs based on experiences, knowledge and perceptions of one group as they see others. This knowledge may be the result of a misunderstanding or misinterpretation of certain events, which are subject to a variety of interpretations. The misunderstanding may be due to selectiveness

[18] Scholars generally argue that this is sometimes the case because rebel groups face collective action problems and rebellions are very expensive. For example, the Tamil Tigers, an ethnic group which makes up about 12% of Sri Lanka's population, spent between $200 and $350 million per annum in order to maintain their control over the Northeast part of Sri Lanka for which they sought a political secession which ended up in failure (Collier et al. 5). As civil wars between ethnic groups typically last for many years, causing large numbers of displacements and deaths, and rarely result in rebel victories, rebellions are not likely to be rational choices that are easy to make. See Collier, Paul, and Nicholas Sambanis, "Understanding Civil War. A New Agenda," *Journal of Conflict Resolution*, Vol. 46, No. 1 (February 2002), pp. 3–12; Collier, Paul, and Anke Hoeffler, "Greed and Grievance in Civil War", Collier, Paul and Hoeffler, Anke, Greed and Grievance in Civil War (May 2000). Available at SSRN: https://ssrn.com/abstract=630727; Nicholas Sambanis, "Ethnic Partition as a Solution to Ethnic War: An Empirical Critique of the Theoretical Literature," (September 1999). Available at SSRN: https://ssrn.com/abstract=623960; Collier, Paul et al., "Duration of Civil War," Journal of Peace Research, Vol 41, No. 3, 2024, pp. 253 – 273; and Nathan, Laurie, "The causes of civil war: The false logic of Collier and Hoeffler," South African Review of Sociology, Volume 39, 2008 - Issue 2, pp. 262–275.

[19] Lake Davd A., and Donald Rothchild, *The International Spread of Ethnic Conflict: Fear, Diffusion, and Escalation*, Princeton University Press, 1998; Lake Davd A., and Donald Rothchild, "Containing Fear: The Origins and Management of Ethnic," *International Security*, Vol. 21, No. 2 (Autumn, 1996), pp. 41–75.

in the retained knowledge. The Rwandan genocidal experience is considered by the constructivists to be a prime example.

Constructivists argue that individuals do not belong to a single ethnic group. Some of the theorists maintain that when analysing an ethnic group, one may notice that the ethnic group under scrutiny is in fact a mixture of several cultural identities. In other words, they believe that an ethnic group is made up of numerous identities that are unified under one primary category but goes (or may go) beyond it. According to constructivists, a concept described as "security dilemma" can be used to predict the probability of a conflict amongst various ethnic groups. The concept relates to situations in which ethnic conflicts are likely to occur due to the collapse of political regimes in the midst of the breakdown of law and order. In such situations, politicians leave behind various non-cohesive cultural groups who are then forced to compete with each other for acquiring senses of security. Secondly, constructivists argue that ethnic conflicts can result from elections that are based on politically defined or exploited differences created by ethnically defined political parties. Minority ethnic groups can be particularly gullible and vulnerable to political manipulations, because they can easily see competitive elections as threats to their identities or interests. Finally, and related to the preceding point, constructivists argue that ethnic conflicts can take place during periods of modernization when an ethnic group perceives that its expectations will not be met because it is at a disadvantage compared to others.[20] However, constructivists also maintain that ethnic groups are not always conflictual. In fact, they assert that most ethnic groups accomplish their objectives legally and peacefully through political avenues. Thus, ethnic groups can show that they are not inherently conflictual, although they can descend into conflict. This last point of constructivism validates our definitions of ethnicity and tribe as it indicates how, why and when the transition from the ethnic to the tribe and from ethnicity to tribalism takes place.

The original propagators of constructivism were British and French philosophers who argue that ethnic identities are constructed, reconstructed and used as mixtures of social and political factors. They point out, for instance, that the English language is a result of the linguistic influences of various groups of people (the Celts, the Danes, the Romans)

[20] Ellingsen, T., "Colorful community or ethnic witches' brew?" Journal of Conflict Resolution 44 (2) (2000): 228–49.

who conquered and lived in England.[21] The constructivists explain that ethnic groups are social constructs or creations, based on dominant cultural values (noted earlier in this section).[22] As a result, ethnic groups are made up of different identities that are combined into salient categories each of which becomes an ethnic or tribal group.[23]

8.3.6 Arguments Against Constructivism

Several flaws have been found by critics in the constructivist theory. These include an observation that it cannot explain how some ethnic groups remain static even during changing political and social times.[24] Secondly, constructionism does not recognize that literacy reinforces the identities of ethnic groups, making it very difficult for these identities to be reconstructed. Finally, the theory has come under attack for not explaining why some ethnic groups continue to exist even when they become more harmful than beneficial to their membership.[25]

[21] Dawisha (2002).

[22] For example, in 1992, 31% of the population living in Britain considered themselves to be English; however, less than a decade later, this number increased to 41% of the population even though there were no exceptional rates of fertility or migration in the area ("Constructivist Theories of Ethnic Politics" 4). To put this another way, the increase in the number of English people in Britain was due to the fact that the number of people who identified themselves as English increased. Constructivists also argue that individuals do not belong to only one ethnic category. Chandra, for example, maintains that when analysing a single ethnic group, one notices that this supposed single ethnic group is actually a mixture of several other cultural identities (Refer, for instance, Kanchan Chandra, *Why Ethnic Parties Succeed. Patronage and Ethnic Head Counts in India*, Cambridge University Press, 2017; and Winfried Ellingsen, "Social integration of ethnic groups in Europe…," Working Paper No. ISSN 15032701, Nr. 255, 2003; and Ebou Taal, "Senegambian Ethnic Groups: Common Origins and Cultural Affinities Factors and Forces of National Unity, Peace and Stability," *The Point*, Apr 22, 2010, https://thepoint.gm/africa/gambia/article/senegambian-ethnic-groups-common-origins-and-cultural-affinities-factors-and-forces-of-national-unit, retrieved April 3, 2025.

[23] Chandra (ibid.) Moreover, Cerulo supports this claim by brining to attention the idea that there are individuals who have mixed ancestries; and thus, they can choose which ethnic identity they want to stress based on the circumstances that they find themselves in (Refer, for instance, to Karen A. Cerulo, "Identity Construction: New Issues, New Directions," *Annual Review of Sociology*, Vol. 23 (1997), pp. 385–409, https://www.jstor.org/stable/2952557, retrieved April 2, 2025.

[24] Jesse, Neal G. and Kristen P. Williams. Ethnic Conflict: A Systematic Approach To Cases of Conflict. Washington: CQ Press, 2011.

[25] Jesse, Neal G. and Kristen P. Williams. Ethnic Conflict: A Systematic Approach To Cases of Conflict. Washington: CQ Press, 2011.

8.4 History

Whenever and wherever human beings live together in groups they would find a reason to discriminate against each other. Even if we have everything in common except height, we would invent a basis of discrimination called "heightism"! This is a reality and fact. Such discrimination often leads to tensions or outright conflicts, although it does not always reach the level where conflict would ensue. Therefore, tribalism and tribal conflicts have existed in Africa as long as ethnic groups or tribes existed in one form or another, real or imagined. However, general belief and significant evidence show that tribalism took another form and intensity during the colonial period, deliberately because of specific political reasons, leading to the type of tribalism that is prevalent in Africa today. There is general agreement among African scholars who wrote on the subject that this tribalism was designed by colonial political architects to meet their goals of divide and rule. The colonialists were so successful in implementing their colonial designs that the effects can still be felt and seen across Africa in complex contemporary realities.

8.5 Incidents of Tribal Violence in Africa

The number of tribal conflicts in Africa in recent decades tends to be on the rise, with the exact number of major and minor incidents impossible to list. However, the countries where the levels of the violence have attracted international attention include Burundi, Chad, Ethiopia, Ghana, Guinea, Ivory Coast, Kenya, Mali, Niger, Nigeria, Rwanda, Senegal, Somalia, South Africa and the Sudan. Some of these countries are relatively stable in spite of tribal violence. Of all the incidents of violence, the Rwandan genocide is the most well known because of its number of victims and intensity (the number of days and casualties, level of organization, use of heavy weapons, involvement of armies and extent of media coverage) as well as the role of the international community (especially the United Nations) in pre- and post-conflict peacekeeping. However, it is only one among other brutal and destructive ones.

In 1990, the Rwandan Patriotic Front (RPF), a group considered at the time to be a little known about, mainly Tutsi, rebel movement based in Uganda, invaded the northern part of Rwanda, starting what became known as the Rwandan Civil War. The fighting got into a stalemate. Under pressures from regional leaders, the warring parties entered into negotiations and ended up signing the Arusha (Tanzania) Accords on August 4,

1993. However, instead of ushering in peace, the Accord was followed by the assassination of President Juvénal Habyarimana (who signed it) on April 6, 1994. In the power vacuum that ensued, Habyarimana's assassination became the catalyst for the worst period of reported violence in the country's recorded history (in line with constructivism), precipitating the Rwandan genocide. The majority Hutu ethnic group, led by those in the military and police, supported by armed militia, massacred the minority Tutsi (mainly), the Twa and their sympathizers (moderate Hutus), wherever they could find them. The uncontrolled bloodshed took place from April 7 to July 15, 1994, igniting the most monstrous atrocities committed since the civil war began. According to the Rwandan Constitution, written after a Tutsi-dominated government took over, the death toll was more than a million victims.[26]

The Burundian civil war was related to the Rwandan civil war and started after the Rwandan genocide in October 1993. It followed the first multi-party Presidential elections in Burundi since independence from Belgium in 1962. It continued until at least May 2005. As in Rwanda, the war was the result of age-old ethnic divisions between the Hutus and Tutsis, going back to the colonial days. Another phase of the longstanding conflicts started after the multi-party elections. It was generally considered to be formally ended with the swearing-in of President Pierre Nkurunziza in August 2005. The estimated death toll in what is also considered a genocide was 300,000, including children, who were widely abused by both sides in the violence.

The Nigerian Civil War, also known as the Biafra War, is one of the most infamous examples of ethnic conflict in Africa and their colonial origins. It started in 1967, after Nigeria's independence from Britain in 1960. In Nigeria colonialism was epitomized by both ethnic and regional segregation, in addition to differentiation in economic opportunities created or aggravated by the colonial government. For example, the northern Muslim region was secluded from the eastern and southern regions.

[26]The actual number of fatalities is unclear, and some estimates suggest that the real number killed was likely lower. The most widely accepted scholarly estimates are around 500,000 to 800,000 Tutsi deaths.

Income distribution was skewed in favour of the Igbos of the southeast region who prospered from palm oil and petroleum. In spite of their wealth, however, the Igbos were also geographically isolated. "As a result of their decentralized location, wealth, and religion, the Igbo people were marginalized and labeled as outsiders."[27] These differences reinforced ethnic divisions and allegiances rather than national unity in Nigeria, despite federalism after independence. As a result, the segregation produced the conditions for a brutal civil war in the country in 1966, following the so-called the Coup of the Five Majors.[28] As Williams (2024) observed, the coup was seen as a Christian Igbo coup against Northern Muslims and worsened anti-Igbo sentiments in the North. Consequently, a massacre of Igbos took place in 1966.[29] The federal government, dominated by Hausas during the civil war, embarked on brutal measures which were viewed as means of deliberately eliminating the Igbo population, who had decided to secede from the rest of Nigeria into Biafra. The civil war led to the first, or one of the earliest cases of, ethnic cleansing in post-colonial Africa,

[27] Violence in Twentieth Century Africa, Wiki Round 2 – Causes of Conflict, https://scholarblogs.emory.edu/violenceinafrica/wiki-round-2-causes-of-conflict/ethnicity-and-ethnic-conflict/#:~:text=In%20contrast%20to%20the%20Hausa,marginalized%20and%20labeled%20as%20outsiders, last visited 13th June 2024.

[28] See Abubakar Ibrahim (29 July 2008). Rose, Esther; Aziken, Emmanuel; Ba, Amadou Mahtar (eds.). "Nigeria: The Forgotten Interim President". AllAfrica. Lagos, Nigeria: AllAfrica Global Media; Kirk-Greene, Anthony Hamilton Millard (1971). Crisis and Conflict in Nigeria: A Documentary Sourcebook, 1966–1969. Vol. 1 (1st ed.). New York City, New York: Oxford University Press; Bolashodun, Oluwatobi (2016). Akinrujomu, Akinyemi; Ebhomele, Eromosele; Ishaq, Mudathir (eds.). "50 Years After: 8 Facts to Know about the January 15, 1966, Coup D'état". Legit.ng. Lagos, Nigeria: Naij.com Media Limited Read, https://www.legit.ng/697216-50-years-8-facts-know-january-15-1966-coup.html, last visited, June 26, 2024; Khadija Thabit (January 15, 2016), "8 Facts To Know About The January 15, 1966 Coup D'état", https://www.legit.ng/697216-50-years-8-facts-know-january-15-1966-coup.html https://www.legit.ng/697216-50-years-8-facts-know-january-15-1966-coup.html; for an insider's account see Ben Gbulie (1981), *Nigeria's Five Majors: Coup D'état of 15th January 1966, First Inside Account*. Lagos, Nigeria: Africana Educational Publishers, 1981.

[29] Ogechukwu E. Williams, "The Biafran War", published online: 27 February 2024," https://doi.org/10.1093/acrefore/9780190277734.013.272.

during which more than one million of the Igbo population were reported to have died through systematic starvation measures by the federal government referred to as Kwashiorkor.[30]

8.6 The Causes

The real-life causes beyond theoretical postulates of the above and other incidences of large-scale ethnic conflicts in the form of warfare at national levels in African countries are several. None of the theories outlined above can fully explain all of them but some of their explanations are apposite. These relate to certain aspects of tribal conflicts which are common causes and features of all of these conflicts, such as their colonial origins, political influences by tribal and political leaders, fear of other tribes and pursuit of whatever the tribes consider to be in their interest no matter the costs to outsiders. These causes can be found partly in each of the discussed theories in this chapter.

8.7 The Consequences

Tribalism has many undesirable consequences. First, it can be deadly and destructive, in its worst or most aggressive forms. As clearly evident from tribal violence in numerous African countries, some of which are mentioned in this chapter, it has resulted in the deaths and injuries of millions and unquantifiable losses of properties and livestock. The brutality with which the multitude of tribal violences have taken place is shocking and illustrative of the worst of human misbehaviour, such as we have seen during devastating wars in other parts of the world, not only in Africa. In addition to its impacts on lives and properties, tribal violence directly

[30] The literature on the Biafran War is vast. The interested reader to refer to, for example, Al J. Venter (2016), *Biafra's War 1967–1970: A Tribal Conflict in Nigeria That Left a Million Dead*. Warwick, UK: Helion and Company, https://www.everand.com/book/353717479/Biafra-s-War-1967–1970-A-Tribal-Conflict-in-Nigeria-That-Left-a-Million-Dead, last visited June 26, 2024; Korieh, Chima J., and Ifeanyi Ezeonu (2010), *Bookshelf: Remembering Biafra: Narrative, History and Memory of the Biafra-Nigeria War*, Glassboro, N.J.: Goldline & Jacobs Publishers, synopsis available at https://www.ambroseehirim.com/2012/08/bookshelf-remembering-biafra-narrative.html; and Lasse Heerten & A. Dirk Moses (2014) The Nigeria–Biafra war: postcolonial conflict and the question of genocide, Journal of Genocide Research, 16:2–3, 169–203, DOI: 10.1080/14623528.2014.936700.

affects economic progress by the mass displacement of people and the destruction of established means of income and employment. It can take decades or generations for a country or region to recover from violence, not only from the economic impacts but from the social and psychological effects.

Deadly violence and destruction are the worst and clearest manifestations of tribalism and inhumanity. Below these, a country or community can also have a non-violent form of tribalism, which, although often manifested in subtle manners, can nevertheless have very serious unobvious negative effects on talent acquisition in human resources and productivity in the economy. This form of tribalism is based on discriminatory attitudes or policies, which favour one tribe over another. Examples in the public (the state) sector are when the head of state surrounds himself/herself with mainly members of his/her tribe and the civil service positions are filled on the basis of appointments which favour his/her tribe. Public services and infrastructure may also be unevenly distributed, with the head of state's hometown or region benefiting the most.[31] In the private sector, it is demonstrated when access to finance, land and infrastructure is dominated by the head of state's tribe. Furthermore, it can take the form of discrimination in employment with preference for members of the head of state's tribe in private companies, resulting in incompetence in the workforce.

The lowest level at which tribalism may be manifested, which is also of a non-violent character, is at the community level. Here different tribes may deliberately develop sarcastic behaviours towards each other, reflected in their attitudes towards and comments about each other. They may discourage deep and blood interactions, such as joint communal activities and intermarriage, which go beyond casual and unavoidable relations. Such tribalism may find its way into other spheres, such as religion. In the case of religion, it becomes easy to see the expression of tribalistic behaviour when churches, mosques and other places of worship are obviously built along tribal lines and the faithful choose where to go on tribal basis.

[31] For example, in a study of why public service reforms have continued to fail in Nigeria, Balogun found out that nepotism is one of the causes or "performance disablers" in what he describes as "the traditional, exceptionalist, entitlement-oriented, anything-goes, 'hard' environment" (M. J. Balogun, "Why reform sometimes fails to cure performance disorders: multiple fiefdoms theory and lessons from a recent study, IIAS Conference on "Next Generation Administrative Reforms: Empowering Citizens and Reaching the Last Mile.", New Delhi, February 2025.

8.8 The Gambia: A Statistical Survey and Case Study

8.8.1 Background and Objectives

The Gambia is a small West African country with a population of approximately 2.4 million people, comprising diverse ethnic groups such as the Mandinka, Fula, Wolof, Jola, Sarahule, Aku, Manjago and Bambara. Since the rise and fall of the country's former ruler (Yahya A.J.J. Jammeh, 1994–2016) the Gambia, despite its size and diversity, has been plagued by tribalism which has often resulted in low-level violence and other forms of confrontation in the country. Jammeh was a forceful populist and clientelist ruler who set up one of the most successful kleptocracies in Africa and ruled the Gambia with an iron fist for 22 years. His violent reign was evidenced by the numbers of political murders and imprisonments during his rule. According to popular view in the Gambia, tribalism was fostered by him for political gains, although, as the early part of his rule showed, he might not have been a tribalist at the personal level or prior to becoming a politician. The intensification of tribalism in the second part of his rule might have been caused by the pitting of the Mandinkas (the country's largest ethnic group) or a section of Mandinkas, Jammeh himself and other ethnic groups against each other because of uncompromising confrontational stances by each party. Other (non-Mandinka) ethnic groups motivated by the divisive pronouncements and actions of the head of state himself and fearful of the Mandinka majority, because of what we refer to as "the ethnic minority syndrome", became victims of Jammeh's eventual post-colonial divide-and-rule behaviour and policies.

Such ethnic tensions in African countries have been blamed on, and are exacerbated by, historical colonial factors noted earlier. However, in the post-colonial era we should also take account of political and economic factors (the struggle for power and resources and the manipulations of political leaders), and the lack of education and awareness about the negative impact of tribalism on all. In the case of the Gambia, the state machinery under the full control of one individual (Jammeh, with the support of his enablers) successfully used, abused and misused ethnic sentiments for political goals. Hence, we refer to this kind of tribalism in our study as "political tribalism", a classic case of how ethnic differences can be transformed into outright tribalism for political reasons.

In the case of Gambia, it would be difficult to hold colonialism accountable or mostly accountable for the tribalism of the Jammeh and the post-Jammeh eras. The reason is that in spite of the Gambian experience with the British colonial administrative system of "indirect rule", Gambian ethnic groups have co-existed in peace and harmony after independence in 1965 until the Jammeh era. Tribalism had never been able to find its way, in any noticeable or disruptive manner, into the public and private domains.[32]

The aim of this case study is to investigate the extent and impact of ethnicity and tribalism in Gambian society. For this purpose, we carried out a survey with the hope of gaining deeper insights into the dynamics of tribalism, in particular, and contributing to a better understanding that can inform policy interventions and academic research, aimed at promoting national unity and social harmony.

Specifically, the objectives of the Gambian study are to:

(1) Identify the level of ethnic identity and tribal consciousness among Gambians;
(2) Gauge how ethnicity has been converted into tribalism and assess the prevalence and impact of tribalism in the country;
(3) Detect the insights that can help understand interpersonal and social relations better;
(4) Explore the causes and consequences of tribal tensions and conflicts;
(5) Assess the attitudes of Gambians towards each other and national unity and the role of tribalism in economic, political and social affairs and
(6) Provide recommendations for addressing the negative impacts of tribalism on the promotion of social cohesion in Gambian society.

The Gambia study is intended to present a novel, refreshing and insightful approach to tribe and tribalism, capable of exposing and understanding the complicated motivations which make the subject very intricate,

[32] For relations between the various ethnic groups, refer to Ebou Taal, "Senegambian Ethnic Groups: Common Origins and Cultural Affinities Factors and Forces of National Unity, Peace and Stability," *The Point*, Apr 22, 2010, https://thepoint.gm/africa/gambia/article/senegambian-ethnic-groups-common-origins-and-cultural-affinities-factors-and-forces-of-national-unit, retrieved April 3, 2025, and colonial administrative systems refer to Michael Crowder West Africa under Colonial Rule, Hutchinson, London, 1968 and his related works.

sensitive and controversial. This is done in the study through an in-depth investigation, in a rigorous manner, into what Gambians as groups and individuals feel about tribalism and why they feel about it the way they do. The study shows, among other things, how ethnic identity can be utilized for political reasons by a clientelist and populist leader and politicians. In addition to revealing how people feel about each other as ethnic groups or tribes, we go further to reveal what they think about their attitudes towards each other. The analytical and empirical case study of tribalism in Gambian society unravels how a majority ethnic group and minority ethnic groups can be made to dislike each other because of politics (mainly) and some social stereotyping or finger-pointing.[33] The study conveys the beliefs and voices of those who are directly concerned, affected and involved throughout the Gambia.

Fieldwork throughout the Gambia, using a well-designed questionnaire, was conducted by the African Youth Entrepreneurship Academy (AYEA) from December 22 to February 17, 2023. The survey enlisted the assistance of 40 research assistants and two supervisors, alongside statistical advisors.[34] Through this rather rare type of field survey of tribalism, we were able to gain practical and valuable insights into the subject in the Gambia, which are revealing for the rest of the continent. It should be noted that although the threat of tribalism in the Gambia is real, on the rise and a major concern to most Gambians, it is, so far, far from the violent types/levels experienced in many countries. Nevertheless, it requires

[33] Ethnic violence is part of the incredible, but real, brutality of man on man and humanity. It must not be limited to Africa alone, although Africa's post-colonial experience deserves special attention in the context of its economic struggles and the search for peace in the continent. For explanations of the causes of "acts of great inhumanity" globally and historically, refer to Esses, Victoria, and Richard A. Vernon, *Explaining the Breakdown of Ethnic Relations: Why Neighbors Kill.* Blackwell Publishing Ltd., 2008, http://ndl.ethernet.edu.et/bitstream/123456789/44150/1/14.pdf, retrieved April 15, 2025; and Glover, J. *Humanity: A moral history of the twentieth century*, Pimlico, London, 2001.

[34] For the Gambia study, the authors are grateful to Mamadou Jallow, Adjunct Lecturer, University of the Gambia (who served Principal Statistical Adviser of the survey); Abdoulie D. Bah, Executive Director of AYEA; and Omar cham, Technical Assistant and Board Treasurer, AYEA; and the survey team of AYEA. We are also grateful to the Advisory Group for the Study, in particular those who commented on the proposal and methodology—Dr Bakary Sonko, Director of Healthcare Services, Center for Immigrants and Immigration Services (Denver, CO); Dr Tamsir Cham, Adviser, International Monetary Fund (IMF), Washington, DC; C. Omar Kebbeh, Economist, Washington, DC; Dr Ebrima Ceesay, Senior Research Fellow, University of Birmingham; Dr Neneh Sallah, Lindau Nobel Laureate; and any others we might have forgotten.

the serious attention we have given it in this study in order to nip it in the bud, or not too far away from the bud, before it grows into torn trees or turns into a cankerworm.

8.8.2 *Data Collection and Interviews*

The data collection process was conducted through face-to-face interviews with the participants. We used a formalized list of questions to ensure consistency and coverage of all the key areas of interest. The interviews were conducted in the local languages spoken by the participants to facilitate better communication and understanding.

Thus, the survey methodology encompasses qualitative interactions. Typically, the interview method is an effective way of collecting in-depth and detailed information from individuals, allowing interviewers to gain a deeper understanding of the interviewees' opinions, experiences, attitudes and perspectives. In addition to the quantitative data, the survey team listened to the stories of the respondents and interacted with them informally during the interviews, so as to further enrich our reports and understanding. At the beginning of the project, we used the formalized list of questions which we drafted and then circulated them to members (Gambians and non-Gambians) of our teams (led by an Advisory Group and their networks as far as Denver, Colorado) for comments. The questions were simple but carefully constructed and attracted numerous comments from the teams, which generated a very lively debate. The interviews were then carried out in the field by the research assistants.

8.8.3 *Data and Thematic Analysis*

Thematic analysis is a qualitative research method used to identify, analyse and report patterns (themes) within a data set. In the context of our survey, thematic analysis is used to systematically examine the responses and narratives obtained from participants to identify recurring themes related to ethnicity and tribalism. This process helped in organizing and interpreting the qualitative data, allowing our survey team to gain insights into the perspectives and experiences of individuals on the chosen topic. Alongside this, the visual description of data involved representing information through graphical or visual presentations. Visual representation enhances the communication of findings, making complex data more accessible and understandable for both researchers and a broader audience.

Thematic analysis generally helps identify recurring patterns in qualitative data, allowing researchers to uncover commonalities or variations in participants' views on ethnicity and tribalism. It also provides a structured approach to understanding the narratives shared by participants, contributing to an understanding of the issues under investigation. The analysis, when combined with visual representation, provides a holistic insight into both the qualitative and quantitative aspects of the research, offering a comprehensive understanding of the phenomenon being studied.

8.8.4 *Participatory Mixed-Method Project*

This survey in the Gambia was conducted using mixed-method research. The survey consisted of face-to-face interviews, as mentioned above. As explained already, the interview method is an effective way of collecting in-depth and detailed information from individuals, allowing the researchers to gain a deeper understanding of their experiences, attitudes and perspectives.

As stated earlier too, the methodology for the Gambian case study benefited from the detailed comments of Gambian and non-Gambian statisticians and scholars (scientists and social scientists) in the Gambia and abroad. They are thoroughly discussed and debated the preliminary proposal and questionnaire and later the results. Their inputs helped in increasing the rigor and completeness of the methodology and results, as discussed further next.

8.8.5 *Sampling*

Both purposive and random sampling techniques were utilized to select participants for the survey. Participants were randomly identified based on local government areas, ethnicity, age (youth, elder) and gender. We ensured diversity and representation of different ethnic groups in the Gambia. A sample frame encompassing individuals aged 15–64 years, constituting approximately 53.5% of the Gambian population (GBoS Census 2013),[35] was employed. With a target population of approximately

[35] Gambia Bureau of Statistics (GBoS), Population and Housing Census 2013, Banjul, The Gambia: GBoS, 2013.

1,029,526, a confidence interval of 95% and a 5% margin of error, the sample size is approximately 9907.[36]

The parameters measured in this survey included ethnic group/tribe, age, gender, local government area, youth and elder. The ethnic groups include Mandinka/Jahanka, Fula/Tukulor/Lorobo, Wollof, Jola/Karoninka, Sarahule, Serere, Creole/Aku Marabou, Manjago, Bambara and others.

Sample sizes were allocated based on the percentage distribution of each group in the Gambia from the target population. The percentage distributions of ethnic groups by population for Mandinka, Fula/Tukulor/Lorobo, Wollof, Jola/Karoninka, Sarahule, Serere, Creole/Aku Marabou, Manjago, Bambara and others are 34.4%, 24.1%, 14.8%, 10.5%, 8.2%, 3.1%, 0.5%, 1.9%, 1.3% and 1.2%, respectively (GBoS Census 2013). Additionally, the percentage distributions of local government areas by population are 1.6%, 19.9%, 38%, 4.3%, 11.7%, 5.1%, 6.6% and 12.7% for Banjul, Kanifing, Brikama, Mansakonko, Kerewan, Kuntaur, Janjanbureh and Basse, respectively (GBoS Census 2013). The survey encompasses males and females aged 15–64, accounting for the population distribution by gender (GBoS IHS 2015/2016). The sample size was proportioned into males and females for each local government area. All the eight local government areas in the Gambia were included in the study: Banjul, Kanifing, Brikama, Mansakonko, Kerewan, Kuntaur, Janjanbureh and Basse. To ensure an unbiased survey, questionnaires were distributed according to the proportion of each of all eight regions in the total population as in the cases of the other categories in the sample. The matrix used to disaggregate tribes is presented in the Appendix.

8.8.6 Population

The survey covered and focused on two distinct age groups: the youths and elders. The youths, aged between 15 and 29, represent the future of the Gambia and are often the most involved or used in tribal tensions and conflicts. The elders, aged 30 to 64 in the Gambia, have lived through a

[36] With the change in the Gambia's total population, reported in the latest census (GBoS, 2024), these figures would be different if viewed in the new context. However, as the attitudes being tested take time to develop and change, our findings here maintain their validity. Furthermore, our sample is big enough even with the reported population growth. Nevertheless, it would be worthwhile for a future study to ask the same questions with a bigger sample based on the new census data.

longer period of significant economic, social and political changes in the Gambia and can provide valuable insights into the causes and consequences of tribalism in the country. Furthermore, like the youths, they can express their own personal viewpoints.

The statistical survey was carried out and completed across all regions of the Gambia, with participants randomly selected. We made sure that the sample was diverse and representative of the different ages, local government areas, ethnicity and gender, as explained above.

The statistically large sample size and data collected from responses to our carefully designed and targeted questions provided a wealth of information. The large sample size enabled our research assistants to reach a diverse and truly representative sample of Gambians, encompassing all the various ethnic, gender and age groups targeted.

8.9 National Findings

8.9.1 Ethnicity

According to the data collected, the Mandinka/Jahanka emerge as the predominant ethnic group, constituting 34.35% of the data, trailed by the Fula/Tukulor/Lorobo group at 24.12% and the Wollof ethnic group at 14.78% (Table 8.1 and Fig. 8.1).

Table 8.1 Ethnicity

Ethnicity	*Count of ethnicity*	*Percentage*
Mandinka/ Jahanka	3403	34.35%
Fula/Tukulor/Lorobo	2390	24.12%
Wollof	1464	14.78%
Jola/Karoninka	1042	10.52%
Sarahule	811	8.19%
Serere	308	3.11%
Manjago	191	1.93%
Bambara	131	1.32%
Other	116	1.17%
Creole/Aku Marabou	51	0.51%
Grand total	**9907**	**100.00%**

Source: Authors

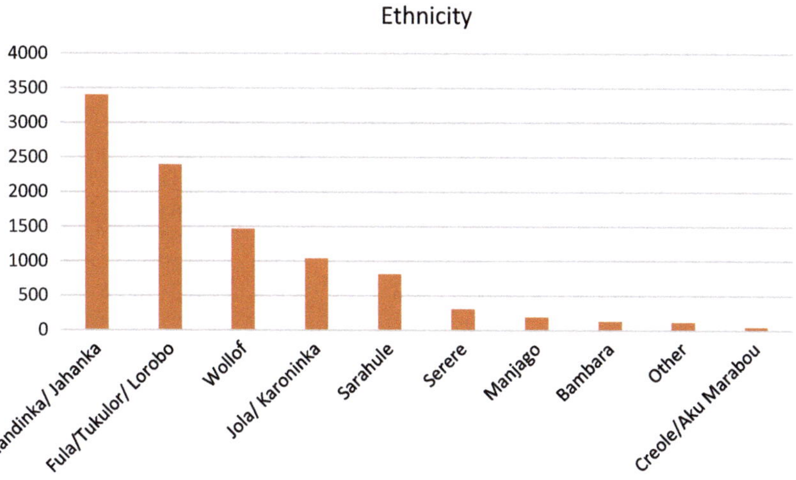

Fig. 8.1 Ethnicity. (Source: Authors)

8.9.2 *Gender and Age Range*

The data gathered reveals that the majority of participants surveyed fall within the age bracket of 25–29, comprising 18.01% of the total. Notably, a significant portion of this group consists of females, as illustrated in Table 8.2. Following closely behind are the age groups of 20–24, accounting for 17.40%, and 30–34, representing 17.14% of the respondents, respectively (Fig. 8.2).

8.9.3 *Occupation*

The data also indicates that the largest group among participants comprises students, making up 23.79% of the total. Following closely behind are business owners, constituting a significant portion with 15.45% of the total. Conversely, 13.31% of the total represents individuals who are unemployed. The smallest percentage belongs to those employed in academia, accounting for only 4.59% of the total (Table 8.3 and Fig. 8.3).

Table 8.2 Gender and age range

Gender and age range						
Age range	*Female*		*Male*		*Total*	*Percentage*
15–19	846	60.1%	561	39.9%	**1407**	14.20%
20–24	954	55.3%	770	44.7%	**1724**	17.40%
25–29	968	54.3%	816	45.7%	**1784**	18.01%
30–34	870	51.2%	828	48.8%	**1698**	17.14%
35–39	550	49.2%	569	50.8%	**1119**	11.30%
40–44	404	48.3%	433	51.7%	**837**	8.45%
45–49	223	45.1%	271	54.9%	**494**	4.99%
50–54	202	50.0%	202	50.0%	**404**	4.08%
55–59	88	43.1%	116	56.9%	**204**	2.06%
60–64	87	36.9%	149	63.1%	**236**	2.38%
Total	**5192**		**4715**		**9907**	**100%**
	52.41%		**47.59%**			

Source: Authors

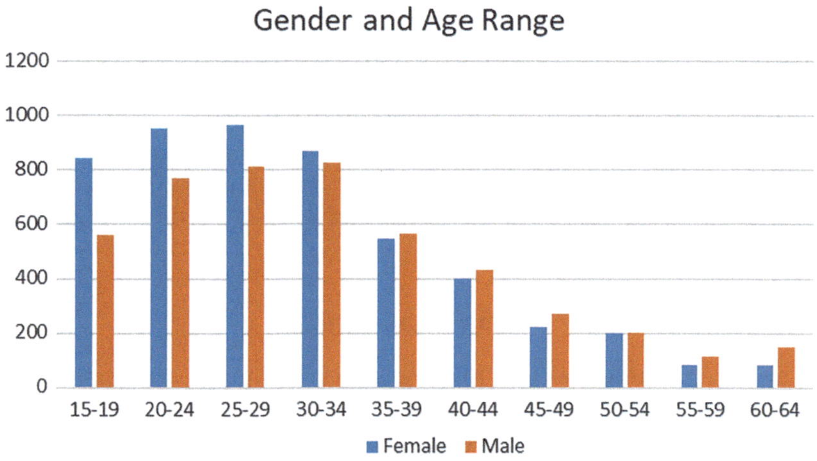

Fig. 8.2 Gender and age range. (Source: Authors)

Table 8.3 Occupation

Occupation	*Total*	*Percentage*
Student	2357	23.79%
Business owner	1531	15.45%
Unemployed	1319	13.31%
Driver, mechanic, carpenter or other manual worker (employed or self-employed)	1258	12.70%
Business employee	908	9.17%
Government employee	873	8.81%
Farmer	714	7.21%
Private sector, NGO or international NGO	492	4.97%
Academic	455	4.59%
Total	9907	100.00%

Source: Authors

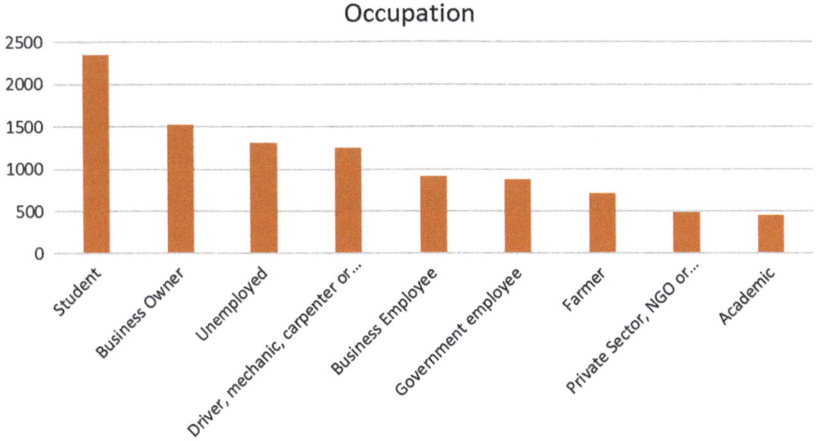

Fig. 8.3 Occupation. (Source: Authors)

8.9.4 Attitudes Towards Other Ethnic Groups

The data shows that majority of participants, comprising 97% of the total, exhibit positive attitudes towards other ethnic groups. Conversely, only a small fraction, representing 3% of the total participants, display negative attitudes towards other ethnic groups (Table 8.4 and Fig. 8.4).

Table 8.4 Attitudes towards other ethnic groups

Attitude towards other ethnic groups	*Total*	*Percentage*
Positive	9578	96.68%
Negative	329	3.32%
Total	**9907**	**100%**

Source: Authors

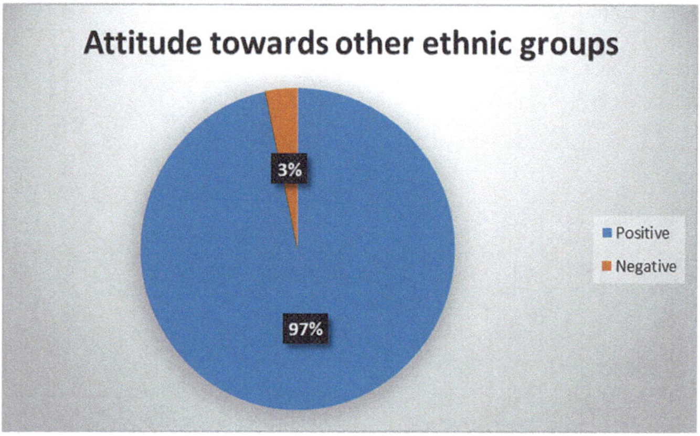

Fig. 8.4 Attitudes towards other ethnic groups. (Source: Authors)

8.9.5 Are You a Tribalist?

Regarding the inquiry into whether the interviewed participants identify themselves as tribalists, the data reveals that the majority, constituting 90.46%, stated that they are not tribalist. However, 9.29% of the participants confirmed that they are tribalist, while a small fraction, comprising only 0.25%, remained undecided on the matter (Table 8.5 and Fig. 8.5).

8.9.6 Is Tribalism Bad?

Regarding the question of whether tribalism is perceived to be bad or not, the vast majority of participants, representing 94.25% of the data, affirmed that it is bad. Conversely, 5.75% of participants expressed the view that tribalism is not inherently bad (Table 8.6 and Fig. 8.6).

Table 8.5 Are you a tribalist?

Are you a tribalist?	*Total*	*Percentage*
No	8962	90.46%
Yes	920	9.29%
Undecided	25	0.25%
Total	**9907**	**100.00%**

Source: Authors

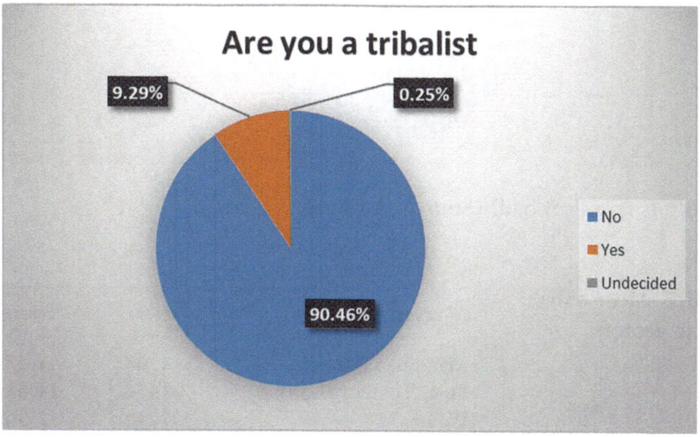

Fig. 8.5 Are you a tribalist? (Source: Authors)

Table 8.6 Is tribalism bad?

Is tribalism bad?	*Total*	*Percentage*
Yes	9337	94.25%
No	570	5.75%
Total	**9907**	**100%**

Source: Authors

Nationally, therefore, these suggest that it is the "loud minority" who are planting the seeds of tribal discord in the Gambia, assuming that there are none of those whom we would refer to as "closet tribalists" --? tribalists who do not confess it, except, perhaps, privately to those they are most comfortabel with.

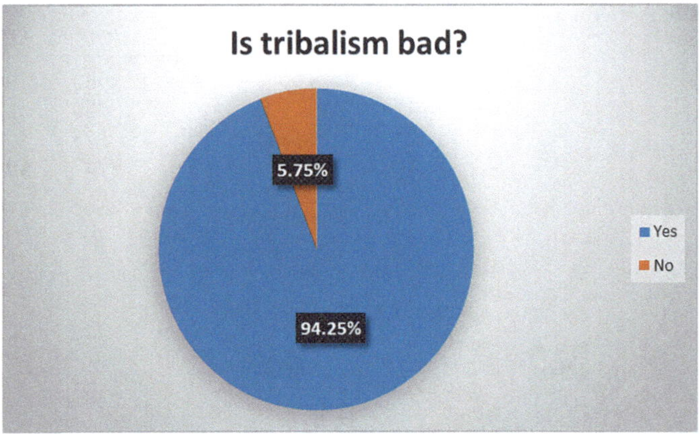

Fig. 8.6 Is tribalism bad? (Source: Authors)

Table 8.7 Most tribalistic ethnic group

Most tribalistic ethnic groups	*Total*	*Percentage*
Mandinka/Jahanka	4108	41.47%
Fula/Tukulor/Lorobo	1454	14.68%
Wollof	1244	12.56%
Jola/Karoninka	1054	10.64%
None of the above	887	8.95%
Sarahule	729	7.36%
All of the above	320	3.23%
Serere	54	0.55%
Bambara	29	0.29%
Creole/Aku Marabou	27	0.27%
Manjago	1	0.01%
Total	**9907**	**100%**

Source: Authors

8.9.7 *Most Tribalistic Ethnic Group*

On the delicate matter of identifying the most tribalistic ethnic group, there was a lot of finger-pointing. Multiple tribes were accused of being tribalistic at varying extents, from 41.47% of total respondents saying the Mandinka/Jahanka are to lowest number of respondents (0.27%) saying that the Creole/Aku Marabou are. Therefore, every ethnic group tends to have some share in the blame for tribalism to different extents (Table 8.7 and Fig. 8.7). The pattern of the results suggests that the bigger the ethnic

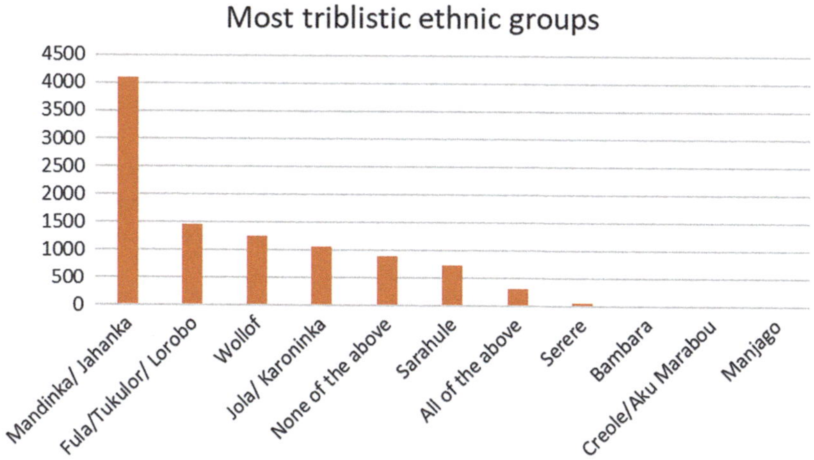

Fig. 8.7 Most Tribalistic Ethnic Group. (Source: Authors)

group the more attention it attracts in the tribalism debate. This may be due to a number of reasons, such as the majority/bigger ethnic groups being more prevalent, vocal and/or the existence of a sense of intimidation (justified or unjustified) among the minority groups. It is this justified or unjustified sense of intimidation among the smaller groups/ ethnic minorities that we refer to as “the ethnic minority syndrome”. Another possible cause may be due to another syndrome we refer to “they think they are better than us syndrome” because of which ethnic groups accuse each other of tribalism based on assumptions or stereotypes. This latter syndrome can be used by ethnic groups or individuals to justify their own tribalism. It is important to note that these are perceptions; whether they are justifiable or not is not an objective of this study, but that may be the subject of future research. Further research may also disaggregate responses by gender.

8.9.8 Whom to Blame for Tribalism

Regarding the responsibility for tribalism in the Gambia, the majority of respondents, accounting for 34.32% of the total data collected, attribute blame to politicians. This is closely followed by individuals, with 28.37% of participants assigning blame to them, while 26.02% blame the ethnic groups themselves. However, a small fraction, 0.44%, believes that everyone shares some degree of responsibility for the issue of tribalism in the Gambia (Table 8.8 and Fig. 8.8).

8.9.9 Solutions to Tribalism

The responses of survey participants regarding the approaches to combating tribalism are categorized into four main solutions: intermarriage, dialogue, public sensitization and formal education. These solutions were

Table 8.8 Whom to blame for tribalism

Whom to blame for tribalism	*Total*	*Percentage*
Politicians	3400	34.32%
Individuals	2811	28.37%
The ethnic groups	2578	26.02%
The government	1006	10.15%
None of the above	68	0.69%
All of the above	44	0.44%
Total	**9907**	**100%**

Source: Authors

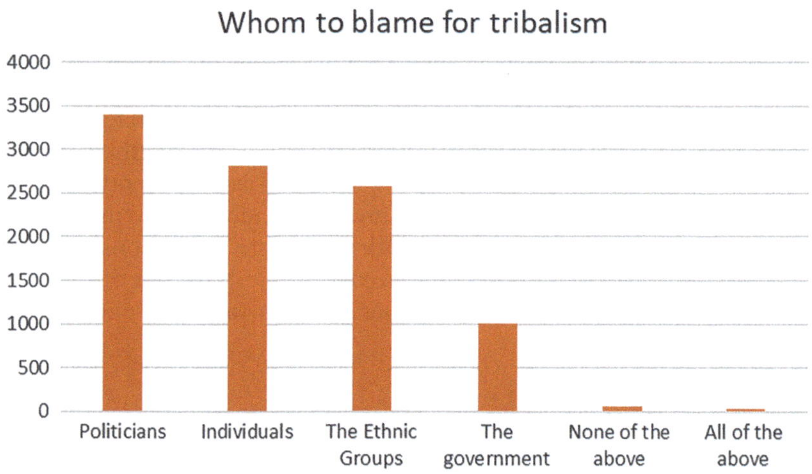

Fig. 8.8 Whom to blame for tribalism. (Source: Authors)

evaluated using a weighted scale: Strongly Agree (5), Agree (4), Neither Agree nor Disagree (3), Disagree (2) and Strongly Disagree (1).[37]

According to the data collected, the majority of participants preferred intermarriage as the primary solution to tribalism. Based on the data, intermarriage has 26.11% support. This is closely followed by public sensitization at 25.20%, dialogue at 25.11% and formal education at 23.59%. On a national scale, therefore, the majority of participants favoured intermarriage as the primary solution to tribalism.[38]

[37] The weighted scale is a well-known research in decision making and survey evaluations. According to Siegel (2011), it allows the allocation of varying degrees of importance (weights) to different outcomes or issues, making sure that factors that are more critical are captured in a greater in the total score. Hanneman (2012) calculates the formula for a weighted average and offers a detailed analysis of how to understand data better by highlighting the significance of the more essential elements. Mantero et al. (2020) examine how attitudes towards mathematics can be measured through Likert scale surveys and emphasized the effectiveness of the weighted average approach. Taherdoost (2019) emphasizes that the five-point Likert scale is a widely used tool in survey research by offering a balance between depth and simplicity. Typically, the responses range from 1—Strongly Disagree, 2—Disagree, 3—Neither Agree nor Disagree, 4—Agree and 5—Strongly Agree. His studies show how well the five-point scale captures respondents' attitudes without overwhelming them, thus increasing the quality of the collected data. The design of the scale further reduces the response bias and increases the reliability of the results. Johns (2010) highlights that the key to accurate attitude measurements using a Likert scale. In conclusion, using the weighted scale model in conjunction with the five-point Likert scale offers a robust framework for ranking and assessing the solutions based on our survey data. This technique ensures that the study accurately captures both the intensity of responses and the relative significance of every solution. For further information, the interested reader may refer to: Taherdoost, H. (2019). What is the best response scale for survey and questionnaire design; review of different lengths of rating scale/attitude scale/Likert scale. International Journal of Academic Research in Management (IJARM), 8; Johns, R. (2010). Likert items and scales. Survey question bank: Methods fact sheet, 1(1), 11–28; León-Mantero, C., Casas-Rosal, J. C., Pedrosa-Jesús, C., & Maz-Machado, A. (2020). Measuring attitude towards mathematics using Likert scale surveys: The weighted average. Plos one, 15(10), e0239626; Siegel, A. F. (2011). Practical business statistics. Academic Press; and Hanneman, R. A., Kposowa, A. J., & Riddle, M. D. (2012). Basic statistics for social research. John Wiley & Sons.

[38] Despite its popularity among our survey respondents, a number of participants in a webinar on the results of the survey pointed out that intermarriage may be complicated as marriage is by choice. Therefore, no one should be forced to marry outside their ethnic group if they do not want to. Similarly, no one should be prevented from marrying out of their ethnic group if they want to. Such should be the case even in the broader context of interracial marriages, which also has its challenges worldwide. Refer to the Report of "The Presentation of the Findings of the Gambia Ethnicity & Tribalism Survey", a Webinar organized by Heeno International, 1st of March, 2025.

The overall findings of the survey underscore the significant role of ethnicity and tribalism in Gambian society. The majority of respondents acknowledged the existence of tribalism and recognized the need for solutions, given its detrimental effects on community living and political relations. Notably, 34.32% and 28.37% of respondents attributed blame to politicians and individuals, respectively, for the prevalence of tribalism in the Gambia.

Moreover, the survey highlighted the adverse impact of tribalism on national unity and development. A striking 94.25% of respondents expressed the belief that tribalism impedes national progress, emphasizing its detrimental effects on societal cohesion. Additionally, nearly 90.46% of respondents identified themselves as non-tribalist. Ultimately, the survey underscores the urgent need for concerted efforts to promote social cohesion and address the negative impact of tribalism on Gambian society.

These findings underscore the importance of proactive measures aimed at fostering inclusivity, understanding and unity within the society, thus paving the way for a more harmonious and cohesive national landscape. Considering the findings, we recommend the need for dialogue and awareness campaigns that promote tolerance and unity among ethnic groups. We urge political leaders and policy makers to prioritize national unity over ethnic divisions and work towards addressing the root causes of tribalism in the Gambia (Tables 8.9, 8.10, 8.11, 8.12, and 8.13 and Fig. 8.9).

Table 8.9 Solutions to tribalism: intermarriage

	Intermarriage	*Count of intermarriage*	*Percentage*
5	Strongly agree	4961	50.08%
4	Agree	3323	33.54%
3	Neither agree nor disagree	869	8.77%
2	Disagree	426	4.30%
1	Strongly disagree	328	3.31%
		9907	**100.00%**

Source: Authors

Table 8.10 Solutions to tribalism: public sensitization

	Public sensitization	*Count of public sensitization*	*Percentage*
5	Strongly agree	3714	37.49%
4	Agree	4075	41.13%
3	Neither agree nor disagree	1387	14.00%
2	Disagree	479	4.83%
1	Strongly disagree	252	2.54%
		9907	**100.00%**

Source: Authors

Table 8.11 Solutions to tribalism: dialogue

	Dialogue	*Count of dialogue*	*Percentage*
5	Strongly agree	3864	39.00%
4	agree	3852	38.88%
3	Neither agree nor disagree	1322	13.34%
2	Disagree	533	5.38%
1	Strongly disagree	336	3.39%
		9907	**100.00%**

Source: Authors

Table 8.12 Solutions to tribalism: formal education

	Formal education	*Count of formal education*	*Percentage*
5	Strongly agree	2923	29.50%
4	Agree	4017	40.55%
3	Neither agree nor disagree	1475	14.89%
2	Disagree	1065	10.75%
1	Strongly disagree	427	4.31%
		9907	**100.00%**

Source: Authors

Table 8.13 Solutions to tribalism: comparative solutions

Public sensitization	*Intermarriage*	*Dialogue*	*Formal education*
187.45	250.40	195.00	147.50
164.52	134.16	155.52	162.20
42.00	26.31	40.02	44.67
9.66	6.62	10.76	21.50
2.54	3.31	3.39	4.31
406.17	**420.80**	**404.69**	**380.18**
25.20%	**26.11%**	**25.11%**	**23.59%**

Source: Authors

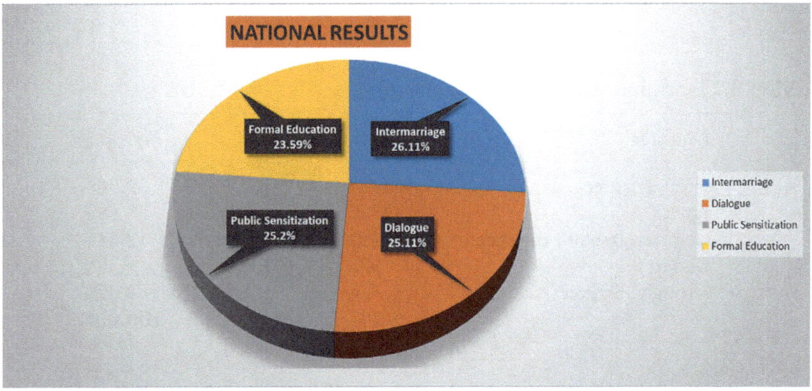

Fig. 8.9 Solutions to tribalism: comparative solutions. (Source: Authors)

8.10 Summary

The survey of ethnicity in the Gambia aimed to investigate the extent and impact of tribalistic opinions and tensions in Gambian society. The survey used mixed method research (qualitative and quantitative), consisting of face-to-face interviews with youths and elders, representing the future and the history of the Gambia, respectively. The interviews were conducted in the local languages spoken by the participants to facilitate better communication and understanding.

The survey focused on identifying the level of ethnic identity and awareness among Gambians, determining the prevalence and impact of tribalism in the country, exploring the causes and consequences of tribalistic tensions and conflicts, assessing the attitudes of Gambians towards tribalism and providing recommendations for addressing the negative impact of tribalism in order to promote social cohesion. In doing these, we let the people speak for themselves, resulting in a rather rare and unique approach to the study of ethnicity/tribalism in Africa.

Qualitative analysis involves interpreting non-numerical data, such as interviews or open-ended survey responses, to understand the nuances of participants' experiences. On the other hand, quantitative analysis deals with numerical data and statistical methods (visual description of data), useful for identifying patterns or trends in structured survey responses. The integration of both approaches provides a comprehensive understanding, with qualitative data offering depth and context, and quantitative data providing breadth for generalizations.

The rationale for employing both methods lies in their complementary strengths. Qualitative exploration is suitable for understanding personal experiences, while quantitative examination is effective for determining prevalence rates. The convergence of qualitative and quantitative results strengthens the validity of research outcomes, offering a more holistic investigation. This dual approach enhances credibility and rigor, minimizing limitations associated with relying on a single method. Policy makers often require both qualitative insights and quantitative evidence, making the research more relevant to policy development. The diverse and nuanced context of ethnicity and tribalism is aptly captured through qualitative analysis, while quantitative analysis identifies broader trends across demographic groups. The combination of both analysis types ensures a robust, nuanced exploration of the research topic, as demonstrated in our report here.

The data collected from the interviews are analysed using thematic and descriptive analyses to identify common experiences, attitudes and perspectives related to ethnicity and tribalism in the Gambia. The survey found that tribalism exists in the Gambia, and many point fingers at political leaders and individuals. The survey also found that there was a need for interventions aimed at promoting national unity and social harmony, such as education and awareness campaigns, inter-ethnic dialogue and policies that promote inclusive governance and resource allocation.

The survey highlights the significant impact of ethnicity and tribalism in Gambian society. Although its existence must not be exaggerated, most respondents acknowledge tribalism's existence and its negative effects on community life and political relations. Politicians and individuals are primarily blamed for tribalism, with 34.32% and 28.37% of respondents attributing responsibility to them, respectively. Additionally, tribalism is seen as detrimental to national unity and development by 94.25% of respondents, with nearly 90.46% identifying themselves as non-tribalists. Respondents recommend intermarriage, public sensitization, dialogue and formal education as essential measures to combat tribalism, emphasizing the need for proactive efforts to foster inclusivity, understanding and unity in Gambian society. Overall, the survey provides rare and valuable insights, based on primary evidence, into the dynamics of ethnicity and tribalism in the Gambia and can inform policy and interventions aimed at promoting social cohesion and national unity.

8.11 Policy Implications and Recommendations for Gambians and Africans

In any environment of latent or blatant tribalism, the first thing is to admit that it exists and then to take the bull by the horns. Commonly and unfortunately, both do not take place until the situation erupts. Through appropriate measures, tribalism can be reined in or nipped in the bud. However, being a very complicated and sensitive issue, it needs to be addressed in any African country through joint and coordinated measures and efforts at different levels.

The most important prerequisite, apart from the admission of its existence, before the measures are designed and actions are undertaken, is to understand the extent of tribalism and the tribal threats at the national, regional, communal and settlement (city/town/village) levels. Another prerequisite is the willingness to act (take the bull by the horns, as we put it above). With about a quarter of the twenty-first century gone, at least half a century of independence and post-colonialism in most of Africa, African political leaders and policy makers must be ready and able to stem all cacophonous behaviour, which can create conflict-generating divisions. Such conflicts, in turn, restrict or reverse economic progress. Evidence in Africa shows that tribalism may be the most serious of these behaviours.

Although there are academic proposals for managing tribalism through, for instance, federalism[39] and consociationalism,[40] they have largely failed so far to have enough practical positive impact on tribal conflicts in modern Africa. Our Gambian statistical survey has enabled us to hear from the African people themselves, directly and on the ground, and get their first-hand recommendations on how the social cankerworm of tribalism can be dealt with.

Appendices

Appendix 1: Interview Questions

1. What is your last name?
2. Which ethnic group do you belong to?
    1. Mandinka/Jahanka
    2. Fula/Tukulor/Lorobo
    3. Wollof
    4. Jola/Karoninka
    5. Sarahule
    6. Serere
    7. Creole/Aku Marabou
    8. Manjago
    9. Bambara
    10. Other

[39] See, for instance, Bednar, Jenna (2011). "The Political Science of Federalism". *Annual Review of Law and Social Science.* 7: 269–288. doi:10.1146/annurev-lawsocsci-102510–105522; Brancati, Dawn (2009). *Peace by design: Managing intrastate conflict through decentralization.* Oxford University Press. doi:10.1093/acprof:oso/9780199549009.001.0001; and Hale, Henry E. (2004). "Divided We Stand: Institutional Sources of Ethnofederal State Survival and Collapse". *World Politics.* 56 (2): 165–193. doi:10.1353/wp.2004.0011.

[40] For the debate on consociationalism see, for instance, O'Leary, Brendan (2005). "Debating consociational politics: Normative and explanatory arguments". In Noel, Sid JR (ed.). *From Power Sharing to Democracy: Post-Conflict Institutions in Ethnically Divided Societies.* Montreal: McGill-Queen's Press. pp. 3–43; McRae, Kenneth D. (September 1979). "Comment: Federation, Consociation, Corporatism—An Addendum to Arend Lijphart". *Canadian Journal of Political Science.* 12 (3): 517–522; and Du Toit, Pierre (July 1987). "Consociational Democracy and Bargaining Power". *Comparative Politics.* 19 (4): 419–430 at 425. doi:10.2307/421815.

3. What is your gender?

    1. Male
    2. Female

4. What is your age?

    1. 15–19
    2. 20–24
    3. 25–29
    4. 30–34
    5. 35–39
    6. 40–44
    7. 45–49
    8. 50–54
    9. 55–59
    10. 60–64

5. Which municipality/local government area do you live in?

    1. Banjul
    2. Kanifing
    3. Brikama
    4. Mansakonko
    5. Kerewan
    6. Kuntaur
    7. Janjanbureh
    8. Basse

6. What is your occupation?

    1. Government employee
    2. Business owner
    3. Farmer
    4. Business employee
    5. Academic
    6. Student
    7. Driver, mechanic, carpenter or other manual worker (employed or self-employed)

   8. Private sector, NGO or international NGO
   9. Unemployed

7. **Confidentially**, how would you describe your attitudes towards other ethnic groups in the Gambia?
   1. Positive
   2. Negative
8. **Confidentially**, do you consider yourself a tribalist or not?
   1. Yes
   2. No
9. **Confidentially**, which of the following Gambian ethnic groups do you think are mostly tribalistic?
   1. Mandinka/Jahanka
   2. Fula/Tukulor/Lorobo
   3. Wollof
   4. Jola/Karoninka
   5. Sarahule
   6. Serere
   7. Creole/Aku Marabou
   8. Manjago
   9. Bambara
   10. None of the above
   11. All of the above
10. Do you think tribalism is bad?
    1. Yes
    2. No
11. Whom do you blame for tribalism in the Gambia?
    1. The government
    2. Politicians
    3. The ethnic groups
    4. Individuals
    5. All of the above
    6. None of the above

12. Please answer and rate (on a scale of 1–5) which of the following can be used to manage tribalism in the Gambia: 1 (Strongly Disagree), 2 (Disagree), 3 (Neither Agree nor Disagree), 4 (Agree) and 5 (Strongly Agree).

    1. Formal education
    2. Intermarriage
    3. Public sensitization
    4. Dialogue
    5. Other—what?

Appendix 2: Survey matrix for participants aged 15–64 years

Regions	*Gender*	*Total*	*A*	*B*	*C*	*D*	*E*	*F*	*G*	*H*	*I*	*J*
Banjul	**Total**	158	55	38	23	16	13	5	1	3	2	2
	Male	81	28	19	12	8	7	3	0	2	1	1
	Female	77	27	19	11	8	6	2	1	1	1	1
Kanifing	**Total**	1978	679	476	293	208	162	62	10	38	26	24
	Male	924	317	222	137	97	76	29	5	18	12	11
	Female	1054	362	254	156	111	86	33	5	20	14	13
Brikama	**Total**	3766	1295	907	557	396	309	117	19	72	49	45
	Male	1827	628	440	270	192	150	57	9	35	24	22
	Female	1939	667	467	287	204	159	60	10	37	25	23
Mansakonko	**Total**	423	143	105	62	45	34	13	2	8	6	5
	Male	198	65	51	29	21	16	6	1	4	3	2
	Female	225	78	54	33	24	18	7	1	4	3	3
Kerewan	**Total**	1162	399	280	172	122	96	36	6	22	15	14
	Male	545	187	131	81	57	45	17	3	10	7	7
	Female	617	212	149	91	65	51	19	3	12	8	7
Kuntaur	**Total**	507	175	123	75	54	40	15	3	9	7	6
	Male	235	81	57	35	25	18	7	2	4	3	3
	Female	272	94	66	40	29	22	8	1	5	4	3
Janjanbureh	**Total**	656	226	158	97	69	54	20	3	12	9	8
	Male	308	104	74	46	32	25	10	2	6	4	4
	Female	348	120	84	52	37	29	11	2	7	5	4
Basse	**Total**	1256	432	303	185	132	103	39	6	24	17	15
	Male	598	206	144	88	63	49	19	3	11	8	7
	Female	658	226	159	97	69	54	20	3	13	9	8

The matrix used in the survey to disaggregate ethnic groups is presented above as:

A = Mandinka/Jahanka
B = Fula/Tukulor/Lorobo
C = Wollof
D = Jola/Karoninka
E = Sarahule
F = Serere
G = Creole/Aku Marabou
H = Manjago
I = Bambara
J = Other

References

Gambia Bureau of Statistics. (2013). *Population and Housing Census 2013*. Banjul, The Gambia: GBoS.

Gambia Bureau of Statistics. (2016). *Integrated Household Survey 2015/2016*. Banjul, The Gambia: GBoS.

Gluckman, Max. 1960. "Tribalism in Modem British Central Africa." *Cahiers d'Etudes Africaines, 1*(1): 55–70.

Lee, Pamela Reynolds. 1971. *Tribalism*. New York: American-African Affairs Association.

Mayer, P. 1961. *Townsmen or Tribesmen?* Capetown: Oxford University Press (for the Institutefor Social and Economic Research, Rhodes University).

Mitchell, J.C. 1960. *Tribalism and the Plural Society*. Inaugural Lecture at the University College of Rhodesia and Nysaland. London: Oxford University Press.

CHAPTER 9

Strategies for African Development in the 21st Century Beyond the East Asian Model: Integrating Markets and the Enabling Developmental State

9.1 Introduction

The starting point for a reasonable approach to development as freedom for the African countries is a critical assessment of the capabilities theory and its extension to what I have called the *Socially Embedded Intersectional Capabilities Theory or SEICT* (Khan 2020a, b, 2021a, b, c). My earlier critical assessment of human development and capabilities exercise in Africa includes the following areas for achieving capabilities enhancement: (i) *Macroeconomic framework component*, analysing the evolution and nature of macroeconomic policies and their inter-relationships with trade policy and their effects on SDGs and human development; (ii) *Fiscal component*, examining the effects of trade reform and policies on the fiscal position of the countries and its relation with SDGs' expenditure needs and potential constraining effect on the application of flanking policies; (iii) *Institutional component*, assessing institutional capacity and performance of trade- and finance-related institutions in particular and their effect on economic, social and political outcomes; (iv) *Dynamic effects component*, undertaking specific studies to assess spillovers and externalities brought about by various policies, particularly trade, financial and investment policies; and (v) *Intellectual property rights (IPR) component*, assessing the effects of more stringent protection of IPRs on SDGs and human development indicators. I have evaluated critically the neoliberal approach to these aspects of development and capabilities in Africa

K. N. M. Sonko et al., *21st Century African Development Strategies*,
https://doi.org/10.1007/978-3-031-93079-9_9

generally and with special case studies of Kenya and South Africa (Khan 2011, 2020a, b, 2021a, b, c). Khan and Sonko (2020) contain several relevant studies of similar nature with emphases on the financial development.

Amartya Sen's pioneering contributions contra utilitarian welfarism and more recent extensions including the controversial listing issue are discussed in Appendix as part of a partial historical background to capabilities approach.[1] I put particular emphasis on social and political aspects of capabilities both because of their general relevance and also because of their particular relevance to Africa in light of political and social upheavals, particularly in Central African Republic, Ethiopia, Nigeria, most of North Africa, Sahel countries, South Africa and most recently the Sudan, among others, which exemplify many of the common problems of the African countries. Of course, each country and the region as a whole exemplify in their own specific ways the law of uneven development within an uneven world capitalist system. Therefore, for Africa as for other geographical regions in the Global Political Economy (GPE), there is no substitute for specific country studies and sub-national region studies within this WCS using the framework of Evolutionary Ecological Global Political Economy (EEGPE). In the second, third, fourth—and particularly in the fifth—parts of this chapter, I endorse a country-by-country model approach advocated by Amsden and others by discussing some lessons from the East Asian development experience in creating structures of learning and capabilities enhancement. However, whilst learning from the East Asian experience in the analysis, I also discuss the limitations of the East Asian Model

[1] Major references to the capabilities literature—particularly Sen's pioneering contributions—are also given separately as references to the appendices at the end of Khan (2011). See also in particular about the thin and thick conceptualizations of capabilities—M. Quizilbash, Interpreting the Capability Approach: Thin and Thick Views" *Human Rights Defender* 19 (1): March 2010, pp. 5–7. See also the special issue of Journal of Human Development, Vol.7, No.3, Nov. 2006 on capabilities and Quizilbash's introduction. Appendix (Section "Model of a Complex Financial Economy with Multiple Equilibria, Possibilities of Crisis and BRICS-Like Facilities in Africa") of the present chapter shows the links between a fully social concept of capabilities and the building of deep democracy in the North African region. Also see, Haider A. Khan, *Technology, Development and Democracy,* Edward Elgar 1998, chs. 6 an7 in particular and Khan (2003a). Technology and Modernity: Creating Social Capabilities in a POLIS. In Misa T ed. *Technology and Modernity*, Cambridge: The MIT Press, Chapter12. A recent piece linking human development and Arab spring is by Kuhn (https://onlinelibrary.wiley.com/doi/abs/10.1111/j.1728-4457.2012.00531.x). On SEICT, see Khan (2020a, b, 2021a, b, c).

and identify further conditions for development as freedom that should be part of one's analytical apparatus in studying the regions and countries within Africa. In my previous empirical work I have focused critically on assessment of human development and capabilities exercise in Africa in the five broad areas mentioned in the first paragraph here—and their components—concretely in order to highlight the ambiguities of the neoliberal approach and its real costs for the African economies in human capabilities terms. Out of this exercise and my further thinking on development I have extended Sen's approach described later to include both social embeddedness institutionally and historically with further emphasis on intersectionality—particularly the intersectionality of class, race/ethnicity and gender.

My approach integrates poverty and social impact analysis (PSIA) techniques, economic and technical tools of ex-ante and ex-post assessment, and monitoring and evaluation methodologies in a comprehensive approach. Accordingly, the strategic features highlighted here can be concretized in empirical applications. Tactical questions can be posed by identifying interested stakeholders and asking questions regarding facilitating and coordinating their participation as well as building institutional arrangements that will assure sustainability of the human development process through concrete multidimensional SEIC enhancement. A related aspect is the need for documenting and analysing local historical settings. Finally, progress towards collecting data and building a database of relevant indicators, and developing tools of monitoring and evaluation along with the development of the institutional and technical capability of stakeholders is examined. Building on other experiences of participatory assessment of different policies, the approach I advocate, besides producing empirical analysis, is intended to engage all actors involved (government, business, labour and civil society institutions representing different segments of the population, in particular women) in active participation.

In Doha, Qatar, at the 2012 meeting of UNCTAD, a fight broke out with respect to language that actually echoed back to a paragraph in the final document of UNCTAD XII in Accra in 2008. More specifically, paragraph 115 of that document read:

> Developing countries should pursue development strategies that are compatible with their specific conditions within the framework of an Enabling Developmental State, which is a State that deploys its administrative and political means for the task of economic development, efficiently focusing human and financial resources. Such a State should also provide for the positive interaction between the public and private sectors.

There was a conflict at the Doha meeting over the ratification of the Accra Accord four years earlier when the idea of an Enabling Developmental State became a contentious issue. The neoliberals from the Global North wanted a more neoclassical view, calling for a "neoliberal effective state". Such a state would work with private and NGO sectors in order to "help forge a coherent development strategy and provide the right enabling environment for productive economic activity".[2]

As is usually the case under such circumstances, the final document was a compromise. The relevant part of the Doha document reads:

> Each country has the primary responsibility for its own economic and social development, and national development efforts need to be supported by an enabling international economic environment. The State, having an important role to play, working with private, non-profit and other stakeholders, can help forge a coherent development strategy and provide an enabling environment for productive economic activity.
> (Doha Mandate, Paragraph 12)

In retrospect, it does appear that the major achievement was the unity of G77 and China, and despite the confusing incorporation of both sides, the idea of an Enabling State survived the political storm. It is up to the progressive scholars to give the idea a more coherent conceptual shape so that it can guide social movements and policies for progressive change in the twenty-first century. This chapter can be seen as an attempt to do this. The main purpose of the chapter is to explore a fairly comprehensive strategy for development as freedom. Accordingly, I try to find a way to integrate useful markets with the key characteristics of the Enabling Developmental State for the 21st Century in order to build a growing ecologically sustainable economy with equity in terms of capabilities in Africa.

In what follows, I first try to define development a bit more precisely. In particular, I ask what people-focused development means, whether in Africa (the focus of this chapter) or elsewhere. It turns out that answering this question rigorously requires elaboration of Sen's concept of freedom as capabilities in an explicitly social and political direction. Then I proceed to ask what are some of the strategic questions we must ask when we wish

[2] UNCTAD, Draft President's negotiating text for UNCTAD XII, Thirteenth Session, Doha, Qatar 21–26 April 2012.

to enhance capabilities over time. This leads us to a view of an Enabling Developmental State that includes many features from the East Asian Developmental State model, but it is crucially augmented by considerations of deepening of democracy during the developmental process. Building on other experiences of participatory assessment of different policies, the approach I advocate, besides producing empirical analysis, is intended to engage all actors involved (government, business, labour and civil society institutions representing different segments of the population, in particular women) in active participation. Thus, this chapter presents a novel approach for Africa. Appendix (Section "The Model on a Lattice") on deepening of democracy deals with some of the deeper theoretical issues involved in this process.

9.2 Development as a Complex Social-Economic-State Systemic Process

Writing in 1926, in a biographical essay on Edgeworth, Keynes underlined some of the problems of complex human systems:

> We are faced at every turn with problems of organic unity, of discreteness, of discontinuity—the whole is not equal to the sum of the parts, comparisons of quantity fail us, small changes produce large effects, the assumptions of a uniform and homogeneous continuum are not satisfied.[3]

If anything, the developing part of the world economy today shows to even a greater degree the kind of complexity captured in Keynes's words above. Fortunately, systems theory and economic theory have both made some progress since those dark days. Although we are far from a genuinely complete theory of complex economic systems, efforts are underway that have already borne some interesting fruit in several limited areas.[4] A review of even partially successful set of country experiences such as that contained in Fosu (2013) can be seen as case studies that reveal many facets of complex developing economies—each with its own sub-systemic characteristics to be sure, but also sharing some common strategic features. The purpose of this chapter is to synthesize from a strategic perspective—to the extent it is possible to do so—the development experiences of East Asia in

[3] Keynes (1971–1979), Vol. X, p. 261.
[4] See, for example, Khan (1997a, b, 1998, 2003a, 2004a, b) and the references therein.

particular and draw some appropriate lessons for Africa. The claim is that such an approach can lead to a theoretical view of an Enabling Developmental State that includes many features from the East Asian Developmental State model. But in my theory, I go beyond that model. In particular, it turns out that the theoretical basis of the East Asian Developmental State model must be crucially augmented by considerations of deepening of democracy during the developmental process. Furthermore, the systemic crises of accumulation and the deepening ecological crisis impose new challenges that the old East Asian Model did not address (Arrighi 1994, 2007, 2010; Khan 2003b, 2010; Khan and Liu 2008; Li 2008). A distinguishing feature of this book is that it draws attention to the latest developments in international business, development and political economy in relation to Africa.

However, at this point in my discussion, some clarification of the key term "development" is necessary in order to avoid ambiguities and confusions. In the rest of this chapter, I will be referring to three concepts of development that are implicit in much of the discussion in the political economy of development literature. The first is the idea of development as growth with some structural change or at least the idea that this type of growth is the most crucially necessary condition for development. The second concept is derived by adding explicit distributional elements to growth—particularly inequality and poverty. Both these ideas are shared by many development economists—for example, many of the authors of the chapters in Fosu (2013)—at least implicitly. Fields was one of the earliest in being explicit in discussing all three—growth, absolute poverty and inequality—and his thoughtful model in *The Quarterly Journal of Economics* (Fields 1979) article alerts the reader to the performance of a developing economy in all three areas and derives—at least partly—a logic of further necessary reforms following from his cogent analysis of the three aspects of development in this sense. Warr (2008) is a more recent example. For the case of Thailand he concludes:

> Not all aspects of the Thai development strategy have been similarly successful. Inequality has increased at the same time as absolute poverty has declined. The underlying causes of this increase in inequality are still not well understood. (Warr 2008, p. 11)[5]

[5] See also Warr (1993, 1999, 2005) for nuanced analyses of the various aspects of Thailand's development experience and Jomo (1995, 2007) for Malaysia.

The third—and the broadest approach to development discussed here—is in terms of Sen's idea of capabilities and its further extensions. In this view, development is really an extension over time and space of freedom, particularly the positive freedom to lead a certain type of life an individual has reasons to value. Sen and his co-authors have, of course, used this idea, and following Sen, many others have done so as well (Sen 1992, 1999, 2009; Nussbaum 1995, 2000; Khan 1998, 2014). Yet, in so far as there is a normative aspect about development being a "(public) good" that is a premise for the whole project such a view is consistent with the analyses of the East (and to some extent Southeast) Asian Development. Warr's essay on Thailand again is quite explicit in mentioning both the positive achievements and the shortcomings of Thailand's record and its strategy which can fit into this broad systemic capabilities approach. For Korea, Keun Lee has gone further. In fact, Keun Lee's perceptive comments on the possible role of democracy in development extend considerably the terrain of discussion in the direction of the "development as freedom" perspective when he writes:

> We see obvious advantages in democracy, amongst which is the convenient feature that citizens are not subject to arbitrary arrest and torture. Truly strong states get it wrong more often than they get it right. Thus the military dictatorships of Latin America left little in the way of legacy, whereas the military dictatorships in Korea and Taiwan (while not on anything like the same scale of brutality) left a powerful legacy of development. The difference lies clearly in strategic orientation and in institutional capacity in formulating and implementing a program of national industrial development. Our point is that this is an option available to the political leadership of any developing country today. On top of this, the key to the Korean or Asian success was institutional longevity. (Lee 2008, p. 13)

It would seem, therefore, that there is an implicit agreement that development is "growth plus" other things (Khan and Weiss 2006). While the list of "other things" may vary somewhat, none of the thoughtful scholars of development would want to equate growth and development. Yet, as the East Asian experience shows, generating high growth may be a useful means towards development. But one must also pay careful attention to what can be called "the political economy and the well-being consequences of growth". Consideration of these factors leads inevitably to the role of the state. The East Asian experience suggests that the role of states in their developmental process was "enabling", but the transition from an authoritarian to more democratic forms of state was slow. In terms of class character, these states are still bourgeois with accommodations for popular interests that are the results of long and hard struggles by the masses from below.[6] This suggests a change in strategic orientation for the progressives in the twenty-first-century Africa for the benefit of their people. Such an approach necessarily will need to take differences—particularly class, gender, racial-ethnic differences—seriously in a critical theory of equalizing capabilities (Khan 2009, 2012a, b, 2014). Chapter 4 of this book deals specifically with the ethnic issue.

What precisely can be the character and role of such an "Enabling" Developmental State in the twenty-first century? I try to answer this question in the next section.

9.3 An Enabling Developmental State for the 21st Century

At least since the classic work by Johnson (1982) on the Ministry of International Trade and Industry (MITI) and the Japanese economy, the role of the developmental state has received much attention. Woo-Cumings (1999) is a good collection of papers that explore various aspects of developmental states. Meredith Woo-Cumings (1999, p. 1) presents the theory of the developmental state as the explanation for the East Asian industrialization. Earlier, Chalmers Johnson had stated: "it is a shorthand for the seamless web of political, bureaucratic, and moneyed influences that structures economic life in capitalist Northeast Asia" (Johnson 1982). Johnson in his book *MITI and the Japanese Miracle* had coined this term for analysing Japanese industrial policies. According to Woo-Cumings, the concept of the developmental state was originally used to analyse a plan-rational capitalist system like Japan, "conjoining private ownership with state guidance" (Woo-Cumings 1999, p. 2). Johnson explains in his contribution to the history of the developmental state debate that "one of [his] main purposes in introducing the idea of capitalist developmental state [...] was to go beyond the contrast between the American and Soviet economies" (Johnson 1999: 32). At least one part of the theory is drawn from the history and the theory of mercantilist intervention of the state in

[6] Prashad (2014) presents a history of the Global South. More importantly, the last chapter of Prashad (2014) discusses critically the details of the emerging movements in the Global South and their transformational potential.

the economy. But in the fashion of Hamilton and List, the developmental state theory is applied to late capitalist development in the sense of building industrial capitalism within a world capitalist system (WCS) where early starters are already in a more advanced stage of industrialization. Historically, in Bismarck's Prussia and in Japan during the Meiji era the developmental states carried the burden of starting and then (contrary to the experiences of most African countries) sustaining the industrialization process. Scholars such as Reinert have traced the history of interventionist states all the way back to the Renaissance (Reinert 2007).

After World War II, Japan, Korea and Taiwan were particularly successful in building both the developmental state and industries that were export-oriented. The debate picked up speed after the work of Amsden (1989) and the World Bank Study of 1993. Wade (1990) studied the Taiwanese economy in detail from a "governing the market" perspective. Chang's study of Korean industrial policies was important to develop the thesis further. Khan (1983, 1997a) discussed the technology policies of Korea and advanced a variant of a theory of state-market interaction in multiple dualisms within a developing economy. Khan and Thorbecke (1988, 1989) had applied a similar theory to study the choice and diffusion of technologies for Indonesia by using a social accounting matrix (SAM). Khan (2002, 2003a, b, 2004a, b) developed nonlinear models of "governing the market" and innovation and applied these to both Korea and Taiwan.

As many have emphasized (Amsden 1989; Chang 1994, 2003, 2007, 2008; Evans 1995, 2007; Ghosh 2009, 2010; Jomo 2007; Khan 1983, 1985, 1997a, b, 2002, 2003a, b, 2004a, b, 2012a, b, 2013; Wade 1990;Weiss 1998), a set of encompassing institutions where the state is both an initiator of development policies and a builder of development institutions is a crucial determinant of development success. The state is also a settler of conflicts before they became disabling as in many African countries. This Enabling Developmental State shows "embedded autonomy" (Evans 1995). It also analyses state capacity as a special form of infrastructural power (Mann 1988; Weiss 1998) and states can use this power to lead structural transformation of the economy. Weiss calls such a state-business class relationship one of governed interdependence. In East Asia such interdependence has been important and should be important to take into account in the case of Africa too.

More specifically, a dynamic picture of the leading role of the Enabling Developmental State emerges over time. The state provides disciplined support for export-oriented sectors through directed credit and other subsidies. The state also coordinates investment across sectors and within industries. It invests itself in areas where private risk absorption capacity is too low. This is important in building up a national system of innovation in particular. The state also steps in to manage sectoral and macroeconomic crises ensuring a relatively smooth accumulation process to proceed. However, the distributive conflicts were lessened for Japan, Korea and Taiwan through US-imposed land reforms after the war. In China on the other hand, an egalitarian society with a Gini coefficient between 0.25 and 0.28 in the 1970s became highly unequal from 1990s onwards with a Gini index over 0.45.

Given the capabilities perspective in Sect. 9.2, we need to include among the characteristics of the Enabling Developmental State for the 21st Century its capacity to build an egalitarian development strategy from the beginning. In addition, democracy must be deepened also from the beginning, as I have already stated. Khan (2008a, b, 2009, 2010, 2012a, b) has attempted to build a theory where *egalitarian distribution and deepening of democratic institutions* and practices along with the standard industrial, trade, monetary-financial and other developmentalist policy making of the state have theoretical salience. Furthermore, given the deepening ecological crisis in Africa and the world at large, this type of state will have to devise policies for *at least mitigating the ecological crisis.*

It is such a state that we can call it an *Enabling Developmental State for the 21st Century*, which is suitable for Africa. It is both technically and socially efficient. Egalitarian innovation systems are set up throughout, but particularly after the middle-income stage they become crucial in terms of enhancing people's capabilities rapidly and widely.[7] Khan (2012a) has therefore replaced the idea of a national innovation system (NIS) with that of an augmented national innovation system (ANIS). A thoroughly innovative Enabling Developmental State for the 21st Century will augment both efficiency and capabilities of people in an egalitarian manner. It is clear that the state of this kind cannot be formed unless popular forces can launch movements and programmes of their own. Is there any hope of this being achieved in the next few decades? Prashad (2014) discusses the complex processes underway in the Global South now—particularly in

[7] Refer to Mugabe (2011) https://www.acode-u.org/uploadedFiles/PRS44.pdf in Chap. 2 on African innovation systems.

Latin America. Although by no means guaranteed, the achievements of people's movements in Argentina, Brazil, Chile, Bolivia, Venezuela and elsewhere give us some room for optimism (Peet 2007; Peet and Hartwick 2009). But the project has barely been started. A new theory of an Enabling Developmental State for the 21st Century that both nurtures and is nurtured by these movements will be of a kind that can play a counterhegemonic role. We are at the beginning of this process. Such a process already shows a multidimensional nonlinear complex system of WCS breaking down with a combination of ecological-economic, political, social and ideological crises. We cannot predict the forms resistance and transformational movements will ultimately take. However, the emerging self-organization of people's movements will undoubtedly take multiple forms ranging from anti-capitalist local resistances to national-regional-international political parties and broad-based social movements and new social formations.[8]

[8] Thus, without falling into self-refuting relativism, there is a way to accept epistemic limits, resist imperial power-knowledge-discourse schemes and formulate positive pro-people programmes that are internationalist but local and regional at the beginning and with time passing, ultimately, global in scope. Prashad (2014) presents a good case for the local-regional-global sequence in the current context. I along with others have argued to accept the proposition that capitalism will not be able to solve the currently unfolding ecological crisis as well as the other crises endogenous to the WCS. If not the other crises, the ecological crisis itself, left unchecked, will destroy human civilization. Thus capitalism which is a complex exploitative system must be transformed into a more harmonious people and nature-oriented system. It has to be understood that capitalism which has created the ecological and other crises is a *global* system and ultimately can only be defeated by *a democratic global movement*. Thus although I am critical of their insufficient appreciation of the political economy of complex exploitative global capitalism, I accept much of the postdevelopment school's criticism of development as expressed, for example, by the work of Escobar, Rahnema and others. In fact, I have tried to make many of these cultural and ecological criticisms in addition to the critical political economy analysis of global capital, starting with Khan (1983) and continuing till now, without falling into the epistemological and ethical-political impasse of the postdevelopment school. See Khan (1998, 2009) for a sympathetic critique of poststructural and postmodern turns and their application in postdevelopment thought, and an alternative critical positive construction of a dynamic democratic-participatory counterhegemonic development from below that can deepen with time. Richard Peet and Elaine Hartwick (2009) present a very fair summary of the various poststructuralist and postdevelopmentalist positions, ending with a thoughtful critique and defence of "critical modernism". It may be that when the new pro-people and deeply democratic dynamic system is more visible than it is now, we could describe the emergent features more fully and find a term which is more adequate than "development". I would like to keep that possibility open. On ecological crisis and capitalism in the twenty-first century, see Li (2008), Khan and Lippit (1993, 2007) and Khan (1997a, b, 1998, 2010).

I now ask this question: how do we conceive of an initial strategic plan that draws from the best experiences of the East Asian Developmental States and augments these with mainly egalitarian and democratic elements for the twenty-first century, especially in Africa?

9.4 An Eleven-Point Characterization of a Strategic Approach Towards Integrating Useful Markets with an Enabling Developmental State for African Development in the 21st Century

Synthesizing the experiences of the East Asian countries further reveals some common strategic orientations as well as the effects of changes in the external environment and shifts in policies over time. This is consistent with the characteristics of complex economic systems which are nonlinear with multiple equilibria and path dependence. Over time, one may observe the emergence of structural shifts in some cases, stagnation in other cases depending on initial conditions, strategies, policies and external environment among other things. For the cases discussed in the vast literature, there are many specific variations within each. However, they also share to various degrees many specific features listed below. It must be kept in mind that in the twenty-first century, ecological sustainability with justice to the poor people and their needs will have to act as a constraint. But this applies particularly to the duty of the developed countries to curtail their consumption in general, and of nonrenewable energy consumption in particular.

9.4.1 Strategic Openness

Openness is to various degrees with Thailand being the most open and Vietnam[9] the least. But in all cases there is a strategic commitment to export promotion and further goals of moving up the value-added ladder. It should be kept in mind, however, that there can be a "fallacy of composition" (Cline 1982; Khan 1983; Mayer 2002; Razmi and Blecker 2006) in claiming that all that developing countries need to do is to pursue an export-led growth policy. Reciprocal demands may not exist sufficiently,

[9] However, see Thoburn et al. (2007) for an insightful and nuanced discussion of Vietnam's trade-orientation and policies for the textiles sector.

and the ensuing competition for export markets in developed countries may create winners as well as losers. Therefore, what may be needed in the future for Africa and other aspiring countries is a strategic approach including the development of national and regional markets and the creation of dynamic comparative advantage along with a number of other policies and institution-building processes described below.

9.4.2 *Heterodox Macroeconomic Policies for Stability*[10]

Japan, Korea and Taiwan and many Southeast Asian countries such as Malaysia, Vietnam and Singapore display more of a mix of heterodox policies. It seems that the rigidity of the Washington Consensus particularly in this area is rejected by the experiences of developing economies like Japan, China, Korea, Taiwan and Vietnam. In particular, use of fiscal policy, monetary policy and exchange rate policy together with trade and selective industrial policies can build an industrialized sustainable economy with good jobs and decent incomes for the people both in rural and urban areas. Further discussion of this last item can also be found under points 4 and 5—Agricultural Development, and Industrial Development and Structural Change, respectively.

9.4.3 *Creation of Institutions for Productive Investment*

This exists in all cases, but Korea seems to have gone much further than the others much earlier. Starting with the reforms in the 1960s, it moved through several successive stages and is now trying to find appropriate technological niche in a world that is moving towards a convergence of information, bio- and nano-technologies by 2050. The role of state in the creation of these institutions is still very prominent. China has followed with its own plan for building an innovation system (Gabriele and Khan 2010).

9.4.4 *Agricultural Development*

Earlier, in the immediate post-World War II (WWII) Keynesian-liberal and Social Democratic Spirit Japan, Korea and Taiwan carried out land reforms. China followed a revolutionary socialist path and land is still legally held

[10] See Jomo and Nagaraj (2001) for a good discussion of heterodoxy in this context.

collectively even with the current responsibility system. In Africa the opposite is the case—either land is undervalued because it is not productive as in most countries or overvalued and became a source of major confrontation, as in the cases of South Africa and Zimbabwe. Among the poor Asian countries Vietnam probably put through the most egalitarian pro-peasant development policies after its victory in the national liberation war in the 1970s. Warr (2008, p. 12) describes the importance of agriculture in the Thai case:

> The results of the analysis indicate that agriculture's contribution to economic growth in Thailand included impressive rates of TFP growth. But its main contribution occurred through releasing resources which could be used more productively elsewhere, *while still maintaining output*, rather than through expansion of agricultural output. It is seriously wrong to characterize Thai agriculture as 'stagnant', based merely on the fact that output growth is slower in agriculture than in other sectors. If agriculture had really been 'stagnant' economic growth would have been substantially lower because it would not have been possible to raise productivity significantly within agriculture or to release resources massively while still maintaining moderate growth of output.

Vietnam's reforms in agriculture are evaluated by Thoburn (2008) in the following words:

> Rice, indeed, is the great success story of the agricultural reforms. Vietnam changed from being a net importer of rice in the 1980s to the world's third largest exporter (after the US and Thailand) in the mid-1990s, though there has been little further export growth since the late 1990s, particularly compared to other products .... This lack of growth is not necessarily surprising or a sign of failure. In the late 1990s, when rice export growth was peaking, less than 15% of output was being exported .... In an economy where around 70% of households were both consumers and producers of rice, rises in rice output were important primarily for raising rural incomes and for food security, with the surplus available for export varying with fluctuations in domestic production.
>
> The state has played a role in encouraging new crops such as cashew, and later coffee .... Coffee is not straightforwardly a success story, though, as the expansion of Vietnam's coffee exports in the mid-1990s was a factor in causing a substantial fall in the world price.

9.4.5 *Industrial Development and Structural Change*

The strategic perspective in this important area suggests that the successful Asian countries, to various degrees, pursued a continuously unfolding and dynamic set of policies with much trial and error. The retrospective attempts to tell a coherent story have often led to an overly deductive picture where good performances supposedly follow from a few, usually neoclassical economic principles. The Malaysian case study is a good and convincing counterexample.

Jomo and Wee (2008, p. 10) describe some changes in strategy and policy for Malaysia within specific time-sensitive contexts:

> Over the years, the government has changed its industrialization strategy. In response to problems and new priorities, the government announced the Second Industrial Master Plan (IMP2) for 1996–2005 in December 1996 to replace the (first) Industrial Master Plan (IMP) for 1986–1995. In September 1996, the government had set up the Multimedia Super Corridor (MSC) to promote certain information technology investments. The government committed over RM50 billion for infrastructure development to support this initiative. At the same time, the government strengthened intellectual property laws to reassure foreign investors and provided more generous incentives for new investments in this area.

Thus, the policy changes of the mid-1980s appeared successful in reviving growth and industrialization. Confirmation of the new policy direction from the mid-1980s came with the 1991 enunciation of Vision 2020, favouring growth, modernization and industrialization. Although FDI began levelling off in the mid-1990s, increased domestic investments—inspired by greater domestic investor confidence—sustained the momentum of rapid economic growth until the 1997–1998 regional crisis. The gravity of the crisis and the difficulties of recovery were exacerbated by injudicious policy responses, compromised by cronyism, though there is little persuasive evidence that cronyism itself precipitated the crisis.

They also point out changes in the 1960s and 1970s in response to changing global economic environment:

> The decline of rubber prices in the 1960s must surely have affected economic performance and policy. Malaysia's experiment with import-substituting industrialization under foreign (principally British) auspices was quite different from most other developing countries where state-owned

> enterprises played leading roles as well as Northeast Asian experiences where effective protection was conditional on export promotion. Malaysia's transformation from net oil importer to exporter in the mid-1970s, when petroleum prices rose sharply, allowed the government to spend much more, while the recycling of petrodollars later allowed it to borrow from abroad at low cost until the Volcker intervention of 1980 raised real interest rates and precipitated a global recession, bringing commodity prices down. (Jomo and Wee 2008, p. 14)

The case study of Vietnam also confirms the suspicion that there is much that is improvised and ad hoc during the earlier phases of apparently successful development cases. The lesson here is perhaps to avoid major resource allocation distortions (as documented by the Thai case also) and constant monitoring and policy revisions when existing policies do not work well. The political preconditions for this are in the background even in the Malaysia and Vietnam papers which are more explicit in these regards than the other two papers.

9.4.6 *Creation of Technological Capabilities*

Here the Korean case stands out as a very apt illustration of creating technological capabilities throughout the entire growth and development trajectory in definite stages.[11] As Lee (2008, pp. 4–5) points out:

> Among various aspects of capacities, emphasis should be on technological capabilities because without these, sustained growth is impossible. In this era of open market competition, private companies cannot sustain growth if they rely upon cheap products; they need to be able to move up the value-chain to higher-value added goods based on continued upgrading and improvement and technological innovation. Furthermore, private companies had better be "local" companies, whenever possible, including locally controlled JVs, not foreign controlled subsidiaries of the MNCs. MNCs subsidiaries are always moving around the world seeking cheaper wages and bigger markets. Therefore, they cannot be relied upon to generate sustained growth in specific localities or countries although they can serve as useful channels for knowledge transfer and learning.

[11] See also Lee (2006) for a contrast of Korean experience with the Washington consensus and Khan (1997, 1998, 2002, 2008a) for a discussion of the Korean (and Taiwanese)case(s) in the context of a distributionally sensitive growth model for positive feedback loop innovation system.

The Malaysia paper by Jomo and Wee also recognizes this essentially strategic aspect of creating technological capabilities during medium- to long-run development. It is also clear from the Thailand and Vietnam cases that strategic concerns with the creation of appropriate technological capabilities have been and continue to be very important. Khan (2002, 2004a) has discussed the interventionist role of the state in Taiwan in this area.

9.4.7 *Technological Learning and Innovation*

Creating national innovation systems in particular requires the creation of specific institutions and technological learning over time. Ultimtely, if development is to continue beyond the catching-up phase, this may present the most crucial set of policy challenges. Here, the paper on Korea is an admirable attempt to sum up the lessons (also refer to Chang 2022).[12] There are specific features here to which Lee (2008, p. 5) draws our attention:

> Therefore, while the ultimate goal and criterion of development is to raise the capabilities of local private companies, the process needs pilot agencies to guide and coordinate the whole process. Such needs exist because key resources are so scarce, and thus had better ... be mobilized for uses in sectors or projects with greatest externalities. As understood by Gerschenkron, who analysed the latecomer industrialization of Germany and Russia, and identified latecomer agencies, such as large state-owned investment banks to drive the process in these countries, it is such agencies that can make up for gaps or lacunae in the country that is seeking to industrialize. All the east Asian countries built specific state-agencies that played a role of guiding the process of industrialization. In Korea the institutions established in the 1960s under the Park regime included the Economic Planning Board to set economic plans; the Ministry of Trade and Industry to support industrial policy and export; and the Ministry of Finance to finance economic plans.

Both state and civil society have to play important roles. At an earlier stage, the state necessarily plays a large and activist role. At a later stage, however, the creation of technological capability has to rely on a private-public partnership at both the precompetitive and the competitive phases

[12] Chang, Ha-Joon, Edible Economics: A Hungry Economist Explains the World, Milton Keynes, UK: Penguin Random House, 2022.

of innovation (Khan 2004a). For China, Gabriele and Khan (2010) present an analysis that points out the key role of the state in building an innovation system.

9.4.8 Direct Foreign Investment and Foreign Aid

These factors have played a role for all East Asian economies but perhaps more so for countries like Thailand, Vietnam and Malaysia. Investment from abroad has perhaps been more significant than aid per se. However, internal generation of investible funds and public sector support have also played a crucial role—particularly in Korea. Direct Foreign Investment (DFI) in manufacturing sector can be important as the Vietnam (and also the Thai and Malaysian cases) case shows:

> Sectorally, manufacturing has been the most important area for DFI, with 51% of accumulated registered foreign capital over the 1988–2006 period, followed by transport, storage and communications (9.6%), mining and quarrying (8%) and real estate (8%). (Thoburn 2008, p. 8)

Not everything has to be of the best practice genre for DFI to come in as Thoburn shows for Vietnam:

> Paradoxically, Vietnam scores badly on conventional measures of competitiveness and investment climate, yet is highly regarded by foreign investors who operate in the country. The World Bank's *Doing Business 2019* survey ranks Vietnam as 104th out of 175 countries as a good place to do business. In contrast, the *WDR* for 2007 claims that Japanese inward investors see Vietnam as the third most attractive investment location in the world. It seems that Vietnam's stable macroeconomic environment, high quality and low cost labour, and low levels of crime are more important considerations for investors than the details of bureaucratic procedures which are often included in international surveys. (Thoburn 2008, p. 9)

Foreign aid—particularly Japanese aid—has played a role in the development of Thailand and Malaysia, but in the Asian cases the leveraging of aid for domestic development has perhaps been more important than the actual quantity of aid.[13]

[13] This is not to say that the quantity does not matter. Also for very poor countries today, aid can fill crucial financing gaps. See Khan (2003b) on these issues. However, surrendering domestic decision-making capability and flexibility to foreign experts in exchange for aid is not strategically helpful. If there is such a pressure then it may be necessary to forgo aid.

One must be aware that in many cases aid and DFI can also lead to external dependence.

A developmental state cannot surrender its sovereignty in domestic decision-making capability and flexibility to foreign experts in exchange for aid. Khan (2003a, b) points out some of the pitfalls in aid and DFI regimes. Ultimately self-reliant domestic institution-building process is the key to sustainable development.

9.4.9 *Poverty Reduction Strategies*

These are a varied set of policies that are necessary in addition to growth. Although growth is a very important component of such a strategic approach to poverty reduction, in all cases specific policies targeting both rural and urban poverty were undertaken. In case of Thailand and Vietnam, it can be argued, such attention for some time to come is still a necessary part of a coherent pro-poor development strategy. This suggests a "growth plus" (Weiss and Khan 2006) strategy for development.

It must also be kept in mind that the move in 1999 by the International Monetary Fund (IMF) and the World Bank and other Northern Development organizations to make anti-poverty policies the core strategy for development is not credible. First, it was a political response to the crisis created by the failing and (after the 1997–1998 financial crises) disastrous neoliberal policies, observed by Khan and Sonko in the early 1990s.[14] Second, even without this political background, without overall sustainable development, anti-poverty policies are only palliatives. Poverty can only be ended globally when exploitative accumulation through dispossession can be ended.

In addition to the nine sets of factors discussed above, there are also somewhat random, historically contingent factors. The Jomo and Wee paper on Malaysia acknowledges the presence of such factors explicitly. But even a quick look at several other cases will reveal historically contingent factors ranging from momentous events such as wars and revolutions to more usual changes in domestic and international political factors and

[14] See, for example, Haider A. Khan, and Sonko, Karamo NM, "A Multidimensional Approach to Designing Effective Adjustment Programs," in G.W. Shepherd, Jr., and Karamo N.M. Sonko, *Economic Justice in Africa Adjustment and Sustainable Development*. New York, NY: Bloomsbury Publishing, 1994; and Karamo NM Sonko, "Debt in the Eye of a Storm: The African Crisis in a Global Context," *Africa Today*. 4th Quarter, Vol. 37, No. 4, 1990.

changes in policies that depended on crucial personalities such as that of President Park in Korea in the 1960s. As Jomo and Wee (2008, p. 14) indicate in summing up the lessons from at least five different policy periods in Malaysia:

> It is difficult to evaluate policy success or failure simply in terms of subsequent economic performance. Malaysia's very open economy has often been subject to circumstances not of its own choosing or making.
>
> The decline of rubber prices in the 1960s must surely have affected economic performance and policy. Malaysia's experiment with import-substituting industrialization under foreign (principally British) auspices was quite different from most other developing countries where state-owned enterprises played leading roles as well as Northeast Asian experiences where effective protection was conditional on export promotion. Malaysia's transformation from net oil importer to exporter in the mid-1970s, when petroleum prices rose sharply, allowed the government to spend much more, while the recycling of petrodollars later allowed it to borrow from abroad at low cost until the Volcker intervention of 1980 raised real interest rates and precipitated a global recession, bringing commodity prices down.
>
> The Plaza Accord of September 1985 led to the strong yen just as Malaysia's sovereign foreign debt became yen-denominated. The mid-1980s' recession precipitated a banking crisis, which led to the 1989 banking reform to the seeming success of earlier deregulation facilitated financial liberalization, culminating in the 1997–98 crisis. The late 1980s' regulatory reforms encouraged further limited private foreign borrowings from abroad before that, limiting vulnerability on that front. The East Asian economic recovery from the last quarter of 1998, following the Russian and LTCM crises, similarly does not allow proper evaluation of the impact of Mahathir's controversial measures of early September as he moved to politically eliminate his deputy.

The above observation underlines an important strategic consideration. I formulate this aspect as a two-point strategic proposal in addition to the nine points presented above. I submit that for a capabilities-enhancing Enabling Developmental State of the twenty-first century with the multiple ecological-economic, political, social and ideological crises facing the planet, the following two items are indispensable.

9.4.10 Income and Asset Distributional Equality

This is more of a challenge today than it was in post-WWII setting. Vibrant egalitarian anti-free market movements were widespread—even in the United States. A combination of cold war policies and then a revival of Hayekian and other varieties of neoliberalism in the 1980s, coinciding with the global crises of WCS, made Income and Asset Distributional Equality an anathema among the mainstream. However, the greatest reversal was in China in the 1990s. Today Chinese leaders are at least partially rethinking this policy.

But the greatest hope here comes from the people's movements from below all over the world and their partial successes in Latin America in particular. However, egalitarian goals need to be explicitly put on movement agendas and concrete strategies devised. When in power, the energies of such movements then can be largely directed towards making the objectives more concrete and solving practical problems of implementation. Through learning feedback mechanisms, mistakes can then be detected and corrected and further appropriate modifications can be made. Such a process cannot be anything but deeply democratic. This is my final point.

9.4.11 Deepening of Democracy

The theory of deepening democracy is derived from a history of efforts from below. In the uneven world of twenty-first century described by Prashad (2014) and many others, the pursuits for democracy take many forms and will differ from one place to another. But the struggles for basic needs such as food, clothing, shelter, healthcare and education are important everywhere. With ecological destruction, movements to save the global commons are crucial. In both these movements the voices of women, minorities, workers and peasants are important. One group whose role needs to be underlined is the indigenous peoples of the world. Their increasingly progressive and leading role in places like Bolivia is exemplary. Movements of indigenous peoples everywhere can learn from them. New forms of deliberative democracy and advancing human rights for the people can be discovered only through these movements. Even when state power is held by the minority dominant classes, such efforts can lead to some democratic deepening. Alternatively, they can lead to minority exploiting classes being forced to share some state power with the popular classes. Thus, even without complete hegemony and state power, popular movements can influence infrastructural aspects of state power in particular.

Schneider (2015) contrasts these two scenarios for contemporary India and Brazil:

> India and Brazil have both emerged in the international political economy, but their paths to emergence show important variations. Indian democratic deepening incorporated a cross-cultural coalition of caste, regional and other identity-based groups, providing enhanced state capacity to embed itself in key sectors to promote their technological upgrading and international competitiveness. This type of capacity provided room for an intensive strategy of international insertion, assisting domestic firms to insert themselves into global value chains and pursue strategies to capture more value. This type of insertion coincided with a national positioning as a voice for non-Western countries in the international system, leading to patterns of international behavior by which Indian governments sought to triangulate their position between Western and Non-Western powers, with India acting as mediator and voice of a more accountable and tolerant world system with greater respect for the sovereignty of poor countries.
>
> Brazilian democratic deepening incorporated a cross-class coalition of working class and middle sectors, providing enhanced state capacity for public collective action borne out domestically in increased revenues and efforts to expand social protection. Internationally, this type of capacity provided room for an extensive strategy of international insertion, led by government assistance to national champions seeking to scale-up activities they dominated nationally into international markets. This type of insertion coincided with a national positioning as a voice for poor countries in the international system, leading to patterns of international behavior by which Brazilian governments sought first to build alliances among poor countries and then bargain more forcefully with rich countries, with Brazil acting as mediator and voice of the poor in favor of a more accountable and equitable world system with greater respect for the sovereignty of poor countries. (pp. 45–46)

Clearly, both in India and Brazil—perhaps particularly in India—the democratic deepening needs to go much further. But the successes, however limited in these two cases, underline the role of mass progressive movements from below. These also point to the need for organizing under a coherent transformational strategic perspective and tactical programme not only in Africa but beyond.

9.5 Dual Observations

Two observations follow logically from the above identification of both the necessary and the more contingent factors that have played a role in East Asia, and my additional crucial strategic factors (egalitarianism and deepening of democracy for the twenty-first century) enabling the Developmental State and a strategy for development as freedom in Africa. The first is the need for taking a historically grounded pragmatic and diagnostic approach to the technical problems of development on the one hand. The second is that at the same time we must make democratic deepening and egalitarianism the strategic centrepieces of any progressive social movement. It is important to make these last two factors the most salient identifying criteria for an innovative Enabling Developmental State that integrates useful markets with developmental objectives to increase the capabilities. It is at least theoretically plausible that in practice opportunities for implementing such a strategy with further ongoing learning will arise as a result of efforts from below that are unfolding. Adapted to specific historical domestic conditions, along these lines, African countries can learn and apply useful lessons from the East Asian experience.

It is necessary to identify distortions from the perspective of deepening democracy and egalitarianism and correct these quickly. It is also equally necessary to identify market failures and other institutional failures. Instead of taking a grand, presumptive approach to development, the role of a mix of heterodox policies with the willingness to revise policies before the cost gets too high seems to be the best recipe for avoiding failures. However, I believe that compromising on democracy and egalitarianism will be strategic mistakes. Therefore, the people's movements must avoid these even if it means slowing down growth within acceptable limits for some time. In general, with careful participatory planning and implementation, deepening of democracy will not conflict with growth and other goals of development.

Clearly, in order to promote equitable growth and broad development in Africa we must build institutions that can supply social insurance and safety nets, and create a democratic space for voice and accountability. But there is no one-size-that-fits-all for any of these functions.[15] Here the role of the history of popular movements and institution building will be cru-

[15] See Chang (2007) for a number of thoughtful contributions on this topic among other things.

cial. While movements in different parts of the world can certainly learn from each other and have ties of solidarity, each part will need to have specific strategic orientation and tactical and organizational forms for both building the movement and building the egalitarian and democratic institutions in every sphere according to its particular historical trajectory. No predetermined futures for African countries are foreordained in this complex twenty-first-century world.

But it must be admitted honestly that the WCS which has been crisis-ridden by its own contradictions throughout its history has now created an additional and, under its own terms, an irreversible ecological crisis. The only sustainable future for human civilization is ultimately a non-capitalist world which is not the same as a purely nonmarket world. There is truly a race against time for creating such a world, and for this reason, all movements that are potentially capable of contributing to the creation of a non-capitalist world are promising and worthy of support. Even a partial but thoughtful diagnosis of specific problems in particular regions relatively early on may suggest solutions which can be implemented before it is too late. This chapter is written with the hope of making a modest contribution to the evolving counterhegemonic movements in our world by suggesting some pathways towards an egalitarian, deeply democratic and ecologically sustainable Global South.

For Africa in particular a new cooperative community of African nations following their own rhythm to reach their own dynamic trajectories towards development as freedom will be possible if they cooperate regionally on the basis of equal sovereignty and mutual respect. One precondition is to pragmatically unite to end the European Union (EU) and United States (US) hegemony in Africa. For this a decolonization of the African mind is also necessary. A new nonaligned pan-African movement in Africa can then begin for dealing with the Global North on the basis of equality and mutual respect.

From a mathematical point of view, the propositions developed in this essay can be formalized in a multisectoral model with integrated finance. Based on some formal work of Jumarie and others in mathematics of entropy, a dynamic relativistic information theory-based systems approach to development can be developed. Although this ongoing research is preliminary, the combination of nonlinear multiple equilibria systems with entropy minimization in developing economic systems can be shown to exhibit a wide range of dynamics from stagnation to rapid growth and transformation. It is particularly applicable to BRICS economies (Brazil,

Russia, India, China, South Africa, Iran, Egypt, Ethiopia and the United Arab Emirates). A bridge to empirics via successive Social Accounting Matrices (SAMs) can be developed for empirical applications in Africa and other developing countries.

Appendix

Model of a Complex Financial Economy with Multiple Equilibria, Possibilities of Crisis and BRICS-Like Facilities in Africa

A number of African countries, including South Africa, are members of the BRICS. In order to give the reader some idea of the problem of formalizing global and regional complex financial cum real economic systems (GRFS and RRFS) we summarize here the basic structure of a "simple" nonlinear model embodying distinct financial architectures which can be applied to analyse the BRICS-like financial facilities cum real sectors, and therefore applicable to South and other African countries. At any single point in time, the model can be presented as a Social Accounting Matrix (SAM) and flow-of-funds representation of the socio-economic system. We will indicate the first m sectors as real and the next n as financial. There are p households and q other institutions including global and regional governance institutions.

The key distinction here is the explicitly nonlinear nature of the economy-wide functional relationships. The key theorem shows the existence of multiple equilibria. Some further considerations of complexity and increasing returns prospects for development show that multiple equilibria are indeed the "natural" outcomes in such models. Thus, there would seem to be some role for domestic policy in guiding the national economy to a particular equilibrium among many. Likewise, such policy space in a Regional Complex Financial cum real Economic System (RCFES) within a Global Complex Financial cum real Economic System (GCFES) can only be possible under some hybrid Global Financial Architecture (GFA) of which BRICS-like multi-regional financial architectures can be an integral and desirable part.

The virtue of a global economy-wide approach to technology systems is the embodiment of various intersectoral linkages within and across regions. In a SAM, such linkages are mappings from one set of accounts to another. In terms of GRFS and RRFS, the production activities can be broken down into a production (sub-) system and a set of institutional innovative activities leading to the creation of BRICS-like multi-regional financial architectures.

Although the existence theorems for these global cum regional multi-sectoral models provide some structure for the equilibria as sequences of fixed points in the socio-economic structure with evolving technology systems, it is not specified a priori which equilibrium will be reached. The problem of equilibrium selection thus remains open and depends on global, regional and national institutions. The idea behind a BRICS-like multi-regional financial architecture can now be stated somewhat more formally. It is to reach a sequence of equilibria for developing economies so that in the nonlinear models of the entire economy the maximal fixed points that are attainable are in fact reached through a combination of market forces and policy manoeuvres over time. It is also to be understood that path dependence would rule out certain equilibria in the future. Thus, initial choices of projects and institutions can matter crucially at times. It has been argued in the chapter that BRICS-like multi-regional financial architectures matter precisely in this way.

The Model on a Lattice

Define X as a vector lattice over a subring M of the real field R. Let $x_+ = \{x|$ $x \in X, x \geq 0\}$

A nonlinear mapping N is defined such that $N: X_+ \to X_+, N_0 = 0$. Given a vector of exogenous variables d, the following nonlinear mapping describes a simultaneous nonlinear equations model of an economy, E:

$$x = Nx + d \tag{9.1}$$

for a given $d \in X_+$.

This nonlinear system represents a socio-economic system of the type described previously. In order to specify the model further, the following assumptions are necessary.

1. X is order complete
2. N is an isotone mapping
3. $\exists \hat{x} \in$ such that $\hat{x} \geq N\hat{x} + d$

In terms of the economics of the model, the nonlinear mapping from the space of inputs to the space of the outputs allows for non-constant returns to scale and technical progress over time. The three assumptions are minimally necessary for the existence of equilibrium. Assumption 3, in particular ensures that there is some level of output vector which can be produced given the technical production conditions and demand structure.

Existence of Multiple Equilibria

Theorem: Under the assumptions 1–3, there exists $x^* \in X_+$ so that x^* is a solution of $x = Nx + d$

Proof: Consider the interval $[0,x] = \{\hat{x} \mid, \hat{x} \in X_+ \mid, 0 \le \hat{x} \le x\}$ where $\hat{x}$ is defined as in assumption 3. Take a mapping F.

$$F : x \in X_+ \to Nx + d$$

F is isotone and maps $[0, x]$ into itself.

Define a set $D \equiv \{x|x \in [0, x], x \geq Fx\}$.

By assumption 3, D is non-empty.

I now show $x^* \equiv \inf D$ is a solution to $x = Nx + d$. $x^* \equiv \inf D$; therefore $x^* \leq x, \forall\ x \in D$. F is isotone; therefore $Fx^* \leq Fx \leq x$ for each $x \in D$ implying.

$$Fx^* \le x^*$$

From (2) I have $F(Fx^*) \leq Fx^*$. Thus $Fx^* \in D$; hence $x^* \equiv \inf D \leq Fx^*$ so, $Fx^* \leq x^* \leq Fx^*$. Therefore $x^* = Fx^*$.

This is an application of Tarski's and Birkhoff's theorem. The key feature to note here is that the equilibrium is not necessarily unique. It should also be noted that under additional assumptions on space X and the mapping N the computation of a fixed point can be done by standard methods (e.g. Ortega and Rheinboldt).

Multiple Equilibria on Banach Space

In this section the results for multiple equilibria are extended to functionals on Banach Space. I can define the model again for monotone iterations, this time on a non-empty subset of an ordered Banach space X. The mapping $f: X \to X$ is called compact if it is continuous and if $f(x)$ is relatively compact. The map f is called completely continuous if f is continuous and maps bounded subsets of X into compact sets. Let X be a non-empty subset of some ordered set Υ. A fixed point x of a map $N: X \to X$ is called minimal (maximal) if every fixed point y of N in X satisfies

$$x \leq y(y \leq x)$$

Theorem: Let (E, P) be an ordered Banach space and let D be a subset of E.

Suppose that f: $D \to E$ is an increasing map which is compact on every order interval in D. If there exists y, $\hat{y} \in D$ with $y \leq \hat{y}$ such that $y \leq f(y)$ and $f(\hat{y}) \leq \hat{y}$, then f has a minimal fixed point x. Moreover, $x \leq y$ and $x =$ lim $F^k(y)$. That is, the minimal fixed point can be computed iteratively by means of the iteration scheme

$$x_0 = y$$
$$x_{k+1} = f(x_k) \quad k = 0, 1, 2, \ldots.$$

Moreover, the sequence (x_k) is increasing.

Proof: Since f is increasing, the hypotheses imply that f maps the order interval $[\overline{y}, y]$ into itself. Consequently, the sequence (x_k) is well defined and, since it is contained in $f[\overline{y}, y]$, it is relatively compact. Hence it has at least one limit point. By induction, it is easily seen that the sequence (x_k) is increasing. This implies that it has exactly one limit point $\overline{x}$ and that the whole sequence converges to $\overline{x}$. Since f is continuous, $\overline{x}$ is a fixed point of f. If x is an arbitrary fixed point in D such that $x \geq \overline{y}$, then, by replacing y by x in the above argument, it follows that $\overline{x} \leq x$. Hence $\overline{x}$ is the minimal fixed point of f in $(\overline{y} + P) \cap D$. It should be observed that I do not claim that there exists a minimal fixed point of f in D.

I can also show that if $F: x \in X_+ \to Nx + d$ is an intersecting compact map in a non-empty order interval $[x, \hat{x}]$ and $x \leq Fx$ and $F\hat{x} \leq \hat{x}$ then F has a minimal fixed point x^* and a maximal fixed point x^{**}. Moreover, $x^* =$ lim $F^k(x)$ and $x^{**} = \lim F^k\left(\hat{x}\right)$. The first of the above sequences is increasing and the second is decreasing.

Complex Dynamics and Out-of-Equilibrium Behaviour: Possible Entropy and Information Theoretic Extensions

As is well known, nonlinear dynamic systems can display a wide range of dynamic behaviours. As Keynes perspicuously pointed out in the General Theory during the great depression, the capitalist economies with complex financial systems are unstable but within limits. However, as we know, dissipative systems with a big enough perturbation can move to a new basin of attraction with much disorganization during transition. Also, even with bifurcations, we do not know for certain which path it will follow. Furthermore, catastrophic singularities are also possible.

My argument can now be summarized in terms of dissipative systems dynamics in a world of multiple equilibria none of which may be reached. Instead, a neoliberal global economy may simply go through cycles of instabilities. A large part of my argument, therefore, has been that the recent global crisis is an example of a large accumulated perturbation that has created instabilities giving us a foretaste of what may become a pattern in the twenty-first century unless a new flexible hybrid GFA with sufficient liquidity and enforcement power is constructed soon. The BRICS bank and financial facilities are moves that can possibly dampen further instabilities in the global financial system and help promote growth with equity particularly in the poorer countries in the global system. With the creation of enough BRICS-like multi-regional financial architectures after the failures and crises in the twenty-first century, the world will have a chance to pursue appropriate capabilities-enhancing development strategies along with a deepening of civilized social democratic structures in the core countries.

Finally, based on some formal work of Jumarie and others in mathematics of entropy, a dynamic relativistic information theory-based systems approach to development can be developed. Although this current ongoing research is preliminary, the combination of nonlinear multiple equilibria systems with entropy minimization in developing economic systems can be shown to exhibit a wide range of dynamics from stagnation to rapid growth and transformation. It is particularly applicable to BRICS economies like South Africa. A bridge to empirics via successive Social Accounting Matrices (SAMs) can be developed for empirical applications.

On Creating a Deepening of Democracy in the North African Region

The main purpose here is to propose a somewhat novel theory of *deep democracy* from a political and social economy perspective which can serve as an analytical framework for setting an important part of the agenda for such substantive democracy in the North African region. For setting a practical agenda in the region, the cluster conditions in Table 9.1 and the subsequent discussion of clusters of political, economic and other conditions for deepening democratic capabilities in a network of appropriate institutions can be used.

In deep democracy, democratic practices have to become institutionalized in such a way that they become part of normal life in a democratic society. Ontologically, deep democracy overlaps with Barber's (1984) idea of *strong democracy*. There are, however, epistemological differences as well as differences of emphasis, particularly in the economic sphere. Cluster conditions for deep democracy include both cultural-political and socio-economic conditions.

My theory of deep democracy also fields sceptical challenges of post-modern philosophers. However, I restrict discussion here to matters as they relate to the moral agency of the democratic actors while developing the idea of moving towards deep democracy in the context of important failures of both capitalism and socialism in the last century (Frame 2007; Khan 1994, 1998, 2006, 2007). I begin by discussing the meaning of the political and social economy approach as I use this term. Next, I discuss in greater detail the economic and political dimensions of deep democracy. Finally, I take up the crucial task of defending the subjectivity of a deeply democratic individual. Conclusions follow in the political and social economy approach based on SEICT.

By *political economy* I mean the classical state and civil society and its interactions. By *social economy* I mean the underlying social basis of the political economy including the family structure. Khan (1994, 1998, 2007) presents deep democracy as a structure in addition to formal democratic apparatus, such that the practice of democratic life can be reproduced with the basic values intact. Change is not precluded. But all such changes should deepen democracy, not weaken it. Deep democracy in this sense is intimately connected with economic and social justice. In order to make economic justice tenable, however, at least a cluster of conditions

Table 9.1 Cluster conditions for deep democracy

No.	*Condition*	*No.*	*Condition*
01	Ending of economic and other status inequalities	13	Public funding of issue-oriented committees as well as parties
02	Public emphasis on furthering democratic autonomy, internationalism and individuality	14	Takeover of some security and civil judicial functions by neighbourhood or regional democratic associations; abolition of centralized, especially secret police powers and units
03	Adequate incomes for all socially recognized work, as well as for children, the handicapped, the aged and others not able to work in order to promote equality of capability	15	Universal public service, military or community; restructuring of armed forces in a defensive, civilian-oriented direction; removal of authoritarianism of rank and status, and institution of democratic unit organization, allowing serious discussion of policy
04	Respect for and articulation of differences in public life and within parties		
05	Downward democratic congruence of and within ordinary social institutions, including work place democracy	16	Proportional representation of parties
06	Debate over the history and future of the movement—the nature of deep democracy—in neighbourhood assemblies and schools	17	Abolition of patriarchy
07	Cultivation of respect for civil disobedience, strikes and other acts of protest on major public issues	18	Adoption of democratic child-rearing practices
08	Integration of local and national leaders into features of ordinary economic and political life and creation of arenas for criticism	19	Full freedom of social intercourse of diverse groups
09	Curtailment of all direct political intervention in the arts, religion and personal life	20	Full freedom of diverse cultural expression
10	Establishment of independent judicial, policy, communication and electoral review bodies	21	Encouragement of the arts and varying modes of expression so that every individual can experience and struggle with the challenge of non-dominating discourse
11	Diversity of perspective in communications and education	22	Practice of radical forms of individual and group subjectivity leading to what Guattari has termed the molecular revolution
12	Use of differential, serial referenda on central issues	23	Adoption of technology and innovation systems, which will reinforce the conditions above, rather than undercutting them

Source: Khan (1998, p. 101)

connected with deepening democracy must be realized (Khan 1994, 1998). Table 9.1 lists such cluster conditions.

It may be useful to elaborate upon the idea of social capabilities. I have summarized a list in Table 9.2, following Sen and Nussbaum (1993). However, I have tried to give a fully social interpretation of all the capabilities as in Khan (1998). Having summarized my approach to deep democracy from the political and social economy perspective, I now turn to the crucial problem of deepening democracy as a set of practices over time.

Towards a Deeply Democratic Society in Various Regions of Africa

Dialectical Relationships

Whether in Africa or any other place, the aim of any sane, progressive socio-economic system must go beyond the blind accumulation of capital or development at all costs. The goal of a just political and social economy is to guarantee each individual's freedom or ability to live the kind of life he/she chooses. Capabilities can be construed as the general powers of human body and mind that can be acquired, maintained, nurtured and developed.[16] Capabilities are economic, but they are also political, social, psychological and spiritual. A comprehensive development as freedom strategy for the North African countries will require us to objectively pay particular attention to the social, political and economic foundations for democracy in these countries taking into account their uneven development. Particularly, in Africa there are many regional path dependencies along with the common colonial and post-colonial factors. There will be no one-size-fits-all model—least of all superficial models exported by the US think tanks. Each regional or country model in Africa must be home grown without being provincial. To be sure, there are deep general principles to follow but these must be developed and grasped within the African geo-historical political context. It is in this spirit the rest of this essay should be viewed.

A deeply democratic society must take into account all forms of capabilities without the sacrifice of some over others. Further, no one capability can be substituted for another. All are irreducible. As Frame (2007)

[16]As interpreted by Khan (1998, p. 95). Here, Khan emphasizes the irreducibly social nature of certain capabilities.

Table 9.2 Summary of social capabilities[a] from a SEIC framework perspective

No.	*Condition*	*No.*	*Condition*
01	Being able to live to the end of a complete human life, as far as possible	15	Being able to live for and to others, to recognize and show concern for other human beings, to engage in various forms of familial and social interaction
02	Being able to be courageous		
03	Being able to have opportunities for sexual satisfaction (lawful and socially sanctioned)	16	Being capable of friendship
04	Being able to move from place to place	17	Being able to visit and entertain friends
05	Being able to avoid unnecessary and non-useful pain and to have pleasurable experiences	18	Being able to participate in the community
06	Being able to use the five senses	19	Being able to participate politically and being capable of justice
07	Being able to imagine	20	Being able to live with concern for and in relation to animals, plants and the world of nature
08	Being able to think and reason	21	Being able to laugh, to play, to enjoy recreational activities
09	Being acceptably well informed	22	Being able to live one's own life and nobody else's
10	Being able to have attachments to things and persons outside ourselves	23	Being able to live in one's very own surroundings and context
11	Being able to love, grieve, to feel longing and gratitude	24	Capability to have self-respect
12	Being able to form a conception of the good	25	Capability to appear in public without shame
13	Capability to choose; ability to form goals, commitments, values	26	Capability to live a rich and fully human life, up to the limit permitted by natural possibilities
14	Being able to engage in critical reflection about the planning of one's own life	27	Ability to achieve valuable functionings

Source: Sen & Nussbaum, as cited by Khan (1998, p. 95)

[a]Here the controversies regarding listing should be kept in mind. But this list without being definitive can nevertheless offer some guidance regarding the kinds of capabilities that are necessary for a deeply democratic society in the North African region keeping in mind the history and respect for the cultural specificities of the region as well

illustrates, there are significant challenges to this aim under the capitalist system. For all members of a society to develop freely, an individual's capabilities cannot infringe upon the capabilities of another. Any form of exploitation in society, no matter how legally construed, should infringe upon an individual's freedom. In addition, radical change without actual participation is impossible.

Economic Aspects for Deepening Democracy: A Dialectical Approach

For a deeply democratic society to exist, it must contain political and social conditions that foster the full development of individual capabilities. It must also contain economic conditions that provide the material base for egalitarian political and social participation as well as physical and psychological health. In economic systems that promote or sanction significant inequalities and/or alienating divisions of labour, deep democracy is impossible. Proponents of deep democracy must examine, therefore, which specific values and institutions within an economic framework would support or hinder democratic practices from taking root and flourishing.

I will, first, consider the principal values upon which an economic system conducive to deep democracy must strive to adhere to and, secondly, possible institutional changes that would abet the concrete realization of a deep democratic society. Can the economic ever be ranked before social? Such a fundamental question must be addressed if a humane economic system is to be constructed which is not merely sustained by the blind drive to accumulate, as in capitalism, or develop without regard to social relations, as in more vulgar forms of economic determinism.

Sen (2000) argues that in contrast to the utilitarian approach of maximizing GDP growth, the fundamental goal should be the development of substantive freedoms—capabilities—to choose a life one has reason to value. Thus, the aim of economic growth should be to enhance the freedom of the individual to choose the kind of life he/she desires. The question that needs further examination is precisely what values must drive, shape and ultimately determine an economic system so that the full capabilities of each individual are developed? What values must be given primary consideration so that the system itself does not perpetuate a feedback loop in which inequality, hierarchy and eventually exploitation and alienation come to dominate?

Albert and Hahnel (1991) suggest the evaluation of economic institutions based upon five moral and logical criteria: equity, efficiency, self-management, solidarity and variety. To this list, I add transparency in dealings with all those affected in respect of full social (and ecological) costs of every economic transaction. Capability deprivation can only be eliminated if the economic system is fundamentally equitable. Albert and Hahnel (1991) chose to define equity as based upon effort alone rather than accumulated private property or fortuitous individual talents. Gilbert (1990) suggests equal incomes for all socially recognized work.

The capabilities-enhancing viewpoint might maintain, in slight contrast, that equity is desirable only to the extent that it fulfils the individual's ability to partake socially on equal footing with other members of society. Such a viewpoint might break with the maxim equal pay for equal effort; in the case of the physically ill or mentally handicapped, for example, greater pay above the effort expended may be necessary. In any case, it would seem that the most vital components of equity would be the elimination of surplus-value extraction and compensation for the disadvantaged. This would include the elimination of all forms of surplus-value extraction currently found under the wage labour system of capitalism.

An economic system that eliminates the extraction of surplus value would greatly abet abolishing exploitation and hierarchy, and to some extent, class disadvantages. The increasing self-management of workers would further erode hierarchy, division of labour and class, as all members would gain experience in organizing and decision making. Through self-management alone can the dilemma of alienation in either hierarchal capitalist systems or top-down command structures of centralized planning be alleviated.

If we consider Sen's (2000) capabilities approach, which advocates the freedom to choose a work environment suitable to individual needs, it is hardly likely that any individual would choose less self-management over increased self-management. If the goal of deep democracy is indeed capabilities enhancement, the development of freedom and choice must not be excluded from the sphere of work. Solidarity through team effort, rather than competitiveness, is also crucial in the return of the individual to his/her social essence as envisioned by Marx and overcoming the alienation of species-being where economic transactions are a zero-sum game.

Work as a variety of tasks rather than repetition would help develop and unite the currently disparate emotional, physical, mental and spiritual aspects of the individual. Through a variety of tasks, the breakdown of the invidious division between manual and mental labour, which centralizes authority within the hands of the elite, could be eroded. Finally, a transparent, eco-friendly economic system that allows citizens full awareness of the social and environmental costs of economic transactions within that system is vital to full citizen participation and decision making.

Is such a seemingly utopian economic system possible? Numerous authors have written on alternative economic systems. Khan (1998) suggests furthering democratic practices through citizen participation in oversight, design, governance and evaluation processes of technological development; in a deep democratic society, research and development expenditures, for example, would be publicly debated, and some asset redistribution would be necessary so that the poor can have access to markets. Albert and Hahnel (1991) explored the theoretical feasibility of creating highly decentralized democratic economic model with a radically different system of production, consumption and allocation.

The participants in the planning process are worker councils and federations, consumer councils and federations, and an Iteration Facilitation Board (IFB). The IFB announces indicative prices for all final goods/services, capital goods, natural resources and categories of labour. Consumer councils and federations respond with consumption proposals. Worker councils and federations respond with production proposals listing the outputs they propose and the inputs they need to make them. The IFB then calculates the excess demand or supply for each input and output and adjusts the indicative price up or down. Using the new indicative prices, consumer and worker councils and federations revise and resubmit their proposals until other councils accept them.

The economic processes of production, consumption and allocation are determined by production, consumer and IFB councils, reaching from the micro level of the workplace, the meso level of the community, to the macro level of the nation. Democratic participation in all the councils is carefully regulated. Equal status inhibits centralization of power, which occurs in central planning. Workers' councils allow for democratic deliberation, and self-management. Solidarity is promoted through cooperation in decision making and non-hierarchal positions in the workplace, while a variety of tasks circumvents the ossification of traditional divisions of labour and hierarchy.

Concerning equity, Albert and Hahnel's (1991) economic model strikes at a very central issue. Can money as an exchange system remain as capital and not promote competitiveness, acquisitiveness and exploitation?

Equity, in the radical economic model, is insured through payment for effort, which is ultimately no more than equal exchange through effort for consumption goods as opposed to capital accumulation. However, the real problem is to go beyond treating labour power as a commodity. In terms of value theory, we need to go beyond the value form itself. This requires going beyond what Marx calls bourgeois rights (Khan 2006). This would indeed call for a radical restructuring of the current economic system.

Political Dialectical Aspects for Deep Democracy

Rights that enhance the ability of each individual to participate politically, equally and fully constitute a vital component of a deeply democratic society. The extent to which political rights are relevant can be argued from a variety of perspectives. From the Marxist perspective, political rights are reflective of the extent to which citizens are not alienated from the political processes. The theory of deep democracy does not separate political processes from all other forms of power (social, economic or ideological) in society.

Deep democracy criticizes the divisive characteristic of the state (such as tribalism in Chap. 8). Although citizen created, the state dominates its creators. Individuals have no direct control over the instruments they are being governed by. The processes of legislating, administering and governing are often beyond the reach of the average citizen. Hence, with the increasing power of the state, alien forces increasingly govern public life of the individual. Hence, political rights must be given priority.

Barber argues for political rights from a somewhat different but no less important vantage point. He criticizes liberal democracy as inherently limited in its conception of both the individual and the social contract between individual and state. The individual in liberal theory is no more than, "a creature of appetite, or of reason indentured to appetite ... incapable of bearing the weight of his ideals" (Barber 2003). The role of the state in liberal democracy, Barber claims, is no more than that of a zookeeper.

The conundrum which liberal democracy finds itself unable to resolve is the tension between the freedom of the individual and the power of the state. The state, a necessary apparatus to protect the freedom of the individual, ends up usurping the freedom of the individual itself. This dilemma arises because liberal democracy does not truly regard the citizen's role as a participatory one; hence the characteristic of the state as usurper of the citizen's natural freedom arises. Only a political system "with a civic culture nearer to the themes of participation, citizenship, and political activity" (Barber 2003) remedies political alienation and apathy found in formal democracies.

From the developmental and capabilities approach, Sen offers three different perspectives as to why political rights are necessary. First, political rights are inalienable rights. Self-determination, liberty and democracy are capabilities to be developed as any other. Second, the instrumental role of political rights is crucial in enhancing the hearing that people get in expressing their political and economic needs. Last, political rights are necessary in the constructive role that they play in the conceptualization of needs in a social context. Public debate, discussion and the civil liberties to engage in them shape how people conceptualize their own needs (Sen 2000).

The question which one must engage with then is not so much whether or not political rights are necessary. The question, then, is what hinders political rights as capabilities, whether it is the capability to engage politically on equal footing as another member of society, or the capability to engage in a political setting which fosters self-governance, fellowship of civic association, or mutual deliberation, decision and work (Barber 2003).

Progress in this direction, like the question of economic capabilities, must consider the complex issue of political alienation which arises, as radicals note, from the disparate capabilities of individuals caught in a class-based society. In the call for liberty and democracy, the difference between formal rights, which are possessed by both the poor and the rich, and effective rights, which are profoundly affected by hierarchy, division of labour, economic inequality and political elitism, cannot simply be ignored. In addition to the social and economic structures that hinder the political rights of individuals, deeply democratic societies must evaluate the institutional structures of formal democracy and critique their effectiveness in providing real political capabilities to citizens.

As Barber (2003) argues, liberal democracy is too limited in its concept of the individual, and lacks the necessary political institutions for truly participatory democratic processes. A deeply democratic society must strive to implement concrete institutions that promote democracy. Accountable institutions of representation and leadership, participatory political processes enjoined by a highly informed citizenry and progressive legislation are three areas of focus here.

A deeply democratic society seeks to enhance the political capabilities of each citizen in respect to self-governance, freedom, equality and justice. Certain features of formal democracy appear unable to fully provide political capabilities to citizens. The first feature that stands out prominently is the issue of representation. In cases of small communities, direct democracy may allow for equal representation and participation of each citizen; however, large regimes or nation-states necessitate some form of political representation. Yet formal democracy, or representative democracy, can be criticized as the political rule of electorally chosen elites, who are often biased with partisan interests.

Benjamin Barber criticizes the concept of representation itself as fundamentally flawed, "men and women who are not directly responsible through common deliberation, common decision, and common action for policies that determine their common lives are not really free at all ... citizens become subjects to laws they do not truly participate in making; they become the passive constituents of representatives who, far from reconstituting the citizens' aims and interests, usurp their civic functions and deflect their civic energies" (Barber 2003). To a great deal this can be attributed to the problem of class and economic inequalities.

With a more equitable socio-economic system, such as the participatory economic system envisioned by Hahnel and Albert, which decentralizes economic decision making and checks the usurpation of resources by elites, the partisan interest of politicians representing class-bias and political alienation of ordinary citizens would be greatly reduced. However, some institutional changes to formal democracy would be necessary that would limit the purely political power of representatives and leaders.

Gilbert recommends institutionalized possibilities of recall, criticism and restriction on pay of representatives (Gilbert 1990). Representatives at the local, state and national level could be subject to public evaluation and/or criticism and in cases of transgressions recall, allowing for greater accountability. Restrictions on pay comparable to salaries of other workers (in a society wherein roughly equal incomes are the norm) would discourage individuals from political involvement for monetary gains. In addition, measures taken to guard against the growth of a "political elite"—wherein certain individuals become professional politicians for life and can thereby manipulate political power for their particularistic interests—would be necessary.

Such measures would include a limit to one's time in office and a limit to one's involvement in politics overall. Additional measures might have to be implemented to avoid the development of political familial dynasties. The establishment of independent judicial, policy, communication and electoral review bodies would maintain a system of checks and balances. To check the monopoly of one or two powerful parties, Gilbert (1990) also recommends proportional representation of parties in accordance with the percentage by which the party is elected.

Beyond institutional checks and balances of representatives, a deeply democratic society must be as highly decentralized as possible. This would entail both a highly informed, active citizenry combined with institutions that delegate decision-making power directly into the hands of the people. Barber's (2003) strong democracy advocates unmediated self-governance through local, state and national institutions that allow for discussion, decision making and action at all three levels. At the local level, Barber (2003) recommends a national system of neighbourhood assemblies of one to five thousand citizens with deliberative eventually local legislative competence as well as selective local elections to local office by lottery with pay initiatives. At the national level, he recommends a national initiative and referendum process that permits popular initiatives and referenda on congressional legislation.

In contrast to current trends of political apathy, self-governance would call for a highly informed citizenry. Barber (2003) recommends such programmes as a civic videotext service and civic educational postal act that would promote full civic education, and a programme of universal citizen service. Khan (1998, 2007) and Gilbert (1990) call for the establishment of a universal public service that would involve either military or community service. Similar to the democratic, civilian-based ideals of the Chinese People's Liberation Army practised during the Chinese Revolution, Khan and Gilbert (1990) call for the restructuring of armed forces in a "defensive, civilian-oriented direction" along with the "removal of authoritarianism of rank and status, and institution of democratic unit organization, allowing serious discussion of policy".

In addition, deeply democratic governance would necessitate abolishing of all centralized, secret police powers and units as well as secret military interventions in foreign governments. Deep democracy, and the possibility of internationalism and solidarity, cannot exist when many foreign policies, some of a more nefarious nature, are regulated to elite decisions, as in the case of the United States, where many foreign military interventions circumvent both congressional and public oversight (Johnson 2004). The Appendix (Section "The Model on a Lattice") offers a full reprise of Barber's strong democratic programme for revitalizing citizenship.

Finally, the adoption of progressive legislation similar to the UN Charter on Human rights that calls for both the protection of individual rights and the explicit rights of women, minorities or other disadvantaged groups would ensure, beyond deeply democratic decentralized deliberation, a standard of human rights. Even if a decision settled through democratic deliberation, it must be invalidated in cases where that decision oppresses particular groups in society, or upholds exploitative norms. A deeply democratic society in all cases must seek to uphold the equal economic and political rights of all citizens.

Social capabilities from an intersectional dialectical perspective: Beyond economic and political preconditions in Africa, for a deep democratic society to be both sustainable and fully human, we need to question more deeply the meaning of well-being. The development of "social capabilities" is no less crucial but perhaps more difficult to define. Social capabilities are capabilities that can only be developed in relation to others. They consist of positive relations to other members of society as well as a healthy relationship to oneself.[17] List the capabilities to think and reason, to imagine, to be able to form a conception of the good, to be capable of having self-respect, to be able to participate in a community, among others.

If we conceive of social possibilities in the context of legislation, Khan includes as part of the set of cluster conditions for a deeply democratic society the abolition of patriarchy, the adoption of democratic child-rearing practices, the full freedom of social intercourse of diverse groups and the full freedom of diverse cultural expression (Khan 1998). A progressive legislation that ensures these basic rights would be the first step for the establishment of social capabilities.

Beyond progressive legislation, truly deep democracy would call for an end to the monopoly of intellectual, artistic, scientific and spiritual elitism. It is as impossible to judge scientifically, given this historical elitism, the extent to which the majority are capable of developing in these areas as it would have been to determine the intellectual/spiritual potential of women two hundred years ago under patriarchy. The bias of class-based societies towards these social capabilities has pervaded social norms to

[17] Or, to be more precise, an "interior monologue" where the unconscious processes are symbolized, interpreted and conceptualized.

such a profound extent that only an elite few are able, or even believe they are able, to develop in any of these areas.

The elite produce art and culture, the many simply consume it. At the same time, overwhelmingly art and culture portray a lifestyle and culture alien and inaccessible to lower classes. Science or other intellectual endeavours are equally inaccessible to the majority due to both the gulf between mental and manual labour, and the price of education. It may be argued that under the current capitalist society education is more widespread and accessible than ever before. Yet this, too, comes at a price. As already discussed extensively under the section on alienation, in a consumerist society, even the limited artistic, scientific, intellectual and spiritual fields are commodified, infringing upon the individual's ability to perceive anything without a price.

A deeply democratic society would have to both disentangle the elitism which typically surrounds these areas and distance material means from the decision to participate or not in these areas. This could be done by free, accessible, lifelong adult education with the reduced working hours available under participatory economics.

Within social institutions such as education, greater democratic practices are also necessary. Alternative systems of education have experimented with such practices with considerable success. Education centres built upon the philosophy of the Indian thinker Krishnamurti attest to this. His educational philosophy protests against the typical use of reward/punishment, competition and fear and hierarchy which, according to him, condition the individual so deeply that real self-discovery, questioning and creative thought is impossible. Instead, more emphasis is placed upon self-inquiry around such vital life questions as follows: Why do we fear? Why do we feel the need for power? What is love? Only by such expansive questioning free from authority, Krishnamurti maintains, can we become whole human beings. Only through understanding of issues such as the ego and separateness can the deeper aspects of the human psyche be developed healthily.

Democratic practices within the educational system could be expanded to include more spiritual institutions with similar democratic practices of non-elitism and non-hierarchy, and full participation in both thinking and interpreting spiritual script. Important studies by Frankl (1985) reveal that "will to meaning", the ability to find meaning in one's life, is an essential necessity to living. The capability to discover one's "will to meaning" is an irreducible social capability as much as proper clothing or political participation. Logotherapy helps patients find meaning in any given situation in their life, even in suffering. Therapy such as logotherapy, along with community, spiritual support and deeper education, would help provide members of a deeply democratic society with the psychological wherewithal to possess this capability.

While Frankl's (1985) logotherapy is primarily individualistic, Khan (1998) recommends continuous therapy available for all members of a deeply democratic society, which would include forms of group therapy. This would be an affirmation of the necessity of social healing in class-based societies where disparate groups are, by and large, alienated from one another. Most importantly, this could allow the development of empathy between individuals from disparate backgrounds. The point here is not to emphasize one form of education or social institution above all others, but to draw attention to the variety of alternative institutions that could help to positively develop the social capabilities of members in a deep democratic society.

The problem of moral agency in creating social capabilities for deep democracy: If indeed there were no real subjectivity for humans, as many postmodernists have claimed, then the task of theorizing about deep democracy and economic justice would seem completely hopeless. This is really the problem of agency or—as it is well known in the French postmodernist and poststructuralist circles—the problem of the subject. In France it was made popular by Althusser's discussions of ideology.[18] However, the deeper philosophical and psychoanalytic motivations for considering the subject problematic have been articulated by Lacan (1975). In Lacan's (1975) view, the subject has both conscious and unconscious motivations. The unconscious part is the source of the problem.

Lacan (1975) claims that the structure of the unconscious is the same as the structure of repressed. This chain of repressed signifiers hides the actual incoherence of the subject's subjectivity. However, the leap from a nuanced analysis of the unconscious aspects of the psyche to the conclusion that there is no subject with a moral capacity for action is illegitimate

[18] See, for example, Althusser's essays on ideology in *For Marx and Lenin and Philosophy*. Althusser seems to misconstrue Lacan's concept of the imaginary (and implicitly, the mirror stage) in the former.

for several reasons.[19] First, the idea of a subject can have a limited warrant even if the unconscious motivations are discerned as contradictory. The potential for moral capacity of such a subject is weaker. Nevertheless, even weakly constituted, quasi-juridical subjects can serve as putative agents of moral actions.

The second and more important objection to the Lacanian fallacy is that Lacan's position can actually be used to reformulate the view of a subject effectively. Recognizing the inevitable unconscious contradictions allows one to distinguish between two kinds of subjecthood in a dynamic sense.[20] On the one hand we have the (relatively) unaware subject who is the ideologically constructed individual. Such a person may be shored up by all the reassuring dogmas and ideologies of our contemporary society. The crack in the mirror where such a person observes himself is invisible as long as he is ignorant of his own inner turmoil at the conscious level. This is not to say that archaic thought-processes or emotions do not invade the person from time to time.

Cohen (1994) argues that a trained analyst can perceive both the moral capacities and moral failures of subjects. Conceptually, the argument simply establishes the possibility of the subjecthood of a person. The precise content of the subjectivity may indeed be unhealthy in a clinical sense. But such characterization only reestablishes the moral potential of the person as an agent. Denying this potential is itself an act of ideological repression.

Such considerations lead us to think of a second type of moral agent. This is a subject whose awareness has unfolded to such an extent that he/she is able to conceive of himself/herself as a moral agent. However, such awareness also encompasses the repression that accompanies our insertion into the symbolic. Thus his/her moral insights about himself/herself and the world also include a recognition of human vulnerability, epistemic shortcomings and the need for a twofold dialogue. This dialogue is, on the one hand, a conversation within oneself and, on the other, a dialogue with the outside world.

Depending on the state of the individual psychoanalytic therapy may or may not be necessary for such subjectivity to occur. However, Khan has argued elsewhere (Khan 1992, 1993a, b, 1995), in a just and democratic

[19] It is not clear if Lacan himself would go so far, but most postmodernists, French and non-French alike (e.g. Foucault and Rorty), have taken this position.

[20] We hope it will become clear in the following discussion that actually there is a continuum of subjects within this dynamic setting.

society, the resources for such therapy will be available to all. Here a further source of confusion may arise. There is a widespread view both within and outside of psychoanalysis that analysis "shrinks the realm of the moral responsibility". As Sherman puts it, "there is the surface paradox that while morality is ubiquitous, the clinical hour boasts of time and space that is morally neutral" (p. 1).

But as Wallwork (1991) has argued, psychoanalysis is uncompromisingly situated within an ethical perspective. Sherman follows and develops Aristotle's critique of the Socratic denial that one can know what is good and fail to act on it. Aristotle, of course, claimed that Socrates's denial of akrasia was simply "against the plain facts" (*ta phainomena*). However, Aristotle views akrasia as an intellectual failure rather than a failure of desire. In discussing Freud's own case of being afflicted by the "blindness of the seeing eye" in his struggle to understand the case of Miss Lucy R.'s knowing and not knowing her love for her employer, Sherman explains:

> The Socratic dogma that knowledge cannot be tyrannized by desire has long been abandoned. But against Kant, it is not simply the inner tribunal of conscience and moral judgment that will track down secret but motivating desires. Conflictual and concealed mental contents need a therapy of self-knowledge that does something other than continue to disavow them. They need to be heard from, in parliamentary fashion, and given their own voice as a part of coming to be united with avowed and endorsed interests. Therapeutically working through what is disavowed or repressed requires freedom from the stance of moral appraisal, even if the decision to submit to the analytic process might be thought of as a morally praiseworthy act in the most general sense of taking charge of one's character, and pursuing that project with courage. (Sherman, p. 13) But the outcome of the therapy when it succeeds is to produce a new type of agency. No longer split off from emotion's testimony, agency takes on a newer and bolder form. Psychoanalysis transforms the notion of moral agency by bringing the emotions to the center. In an ironic way, the "talking therapy" seems to be able to bring to moral agency those potential allies that moral theory, so often on its own, does not quite know how to train or enlist. (Sherman, pp. 22–23)

Therefore, for both types of subjects, it should be emphasized, the possibility of acting justly (or otherwise) remains open in Africa, as in other parts of the world. In an unjust economy and society, most people are victims of oppression and injustice. In a nearly just society, such institutionalized injustice disappears, but there could still be unjust actions by individuals for which they should be culpable. However, in a well-ordered society, the view towards crime and punishment may be very different from ours. Instead of responding to issues of guilt with conventional punishment, a more compassionate, therapeutic approach may be taken.

The point of this chapter, of course, is not to produce a blueprint for a future just society in Africa, but to open up the possibility of such a discourse even under the postmodern conditions of epistemic uncertainty and anti-foundationalism. Enough has been said to show that even a radical epistemic uncertainty is consistent with the two kinds of subjects discussed. The previous discussion of a Hegelian approach to foundationalism was intended to show that anti-foundationalism is also consistent with a systemic approach to economic and social justice. Thus, both at the level of large-scale social and economic structures and at the level of the individual's epistemological uncertainties, anti-foundationalism need not lead to scepticism, relativism and ultimately nihilism.

Conclusions

I have offered a somewhat novel theory of deep democracy from a political and social economy point of view. The theory of deep democracy presented here makes a distinction between formal aspects of democracy and the deeper structural aspects. In order for democracy to be deep, democratic practices have to become institutionalized in such a way that they become part of normal life in a democratic society. In this sense, ontologically, deep democracy overlaps with Barber's idea of strong democracy. There are, however, epistemological differences as well as differences of emphasis, particularly in the economic sphere. Cluster conditions for deep democracy include both cultural-political and socio-economic conditions.

My theory of deep democracy also answers important sceptical challenges of postmodern philosophers. Epistemologically, the postmodern dilemma arises from a correct critique of metaphysics and transcendentalism. However, the critique is partial and negative. It is partial in the sense that it does not take the challenge of Kant to develop normativity seriously enough to explore alternatives as Hegel did. It, therefore, pursues entirely the negative critical path leading to thoroughgoing scepticism and nihilism.

In my approach, a concrete set of institutions consistent with the development of self-determination can be seen as necessary for the idea of deep democracy and economic justice to have meaning. In the spheres of production, distribution, exchange, law and contracts among others, the development of appropriate political, economic and social institutions allowing this inter-subjective idea of freedom to unfold becomes the thematic development of economic justice and democracy.

An important problem in this context is the coherence of the concept of the moral subject. By carefully considering poststructuralist psychoanalytical theory of Lacan and others a dynamically oriented approach to the question of the subject becomes possible. Pre-Freudian thinkers such as Hegel or Marx did not see the formation of the individual in all its deeply problematic aspects. However, the "speaking subject", though not innocent (as Hélène Cixous wittily put it), is nevertheless capable of agency under specific social and economic conditions. A continuum of subjectivity ending with the fully liberated individual offers various possible levels of moral agency. In an economically and socially unjust setting radical, analytic and social interventions will be necessary for these possibilities to materialize.

Deep democracy and economic justice, therefore, can be presented as a coherent set of positive requirements. It is part and parcel of the need for rational autonomy in our world. The cluster conditions I give, together with the social capabilities perspective, offer a way of defending and advancing the justification for deepening democracy.

Specific References for Appendices

Albert, M., & Hahnel, R. (1991). *The political economy of participatory economics.* New Jersey: Princeton University Press.

Barber, B. (1984). *Strong democracy.* Berkeley: University of California Press.

Barber, B. (2003). *Strong democracy: Participatory politics for a new age.* Berkeley: University of California Press.

Cohen, J. (1994). A view of the moral landscape of psychoanalysis. *Journal of the American Academy of Psychoanalysis*, 22(4), 695–725.

Frame, M. (2007). *The political economy of deep democracy.* M.A. Thesis, GSIS, University of Denver, Denver, U.S.A.

Frankl, V. (1985). *Man's Search for Meaning* Washington Square Press, NEW YORK.

Gilbert, A. (1990). *Democratic individuality.* New York: Cambridge University Press.

Johnson, C. (2004). *The sorrows of empire.* New York: Henry Holt & Co.

Khan, H.A. (1992).Language and democracy. *Voice of Bangladesh*, October, __-__.

Khan, H.A. (1993a). *Democracy, markets and the new social movements.* Presented at the Conference on Democratization, Denver, U.S.A.
Khan, H.A. (1993b). Markets, structural adjustment and democracy. *Relaciones Internationales*, 45 (1): 1–16.
Khan, H.A. (1994). *The fragility of freedom.* Presented at the Democracy Conference, Denver, U.S.A.
Khan, H.A. (1995). *Economic justice and democracy.* Presented at the Democracy Conference, Denver, U.S.A.
Khan, H.A. (1998). *Technology, development and democracy.* ________: Edward Elgar.
Khan, H.A. (2006). *Value, social capability and alienation: The right to revolt.* Discussion Paper, CIRJE Series, University of Tokyo.
Khan, H.A. (2007). *A theory of deep democracy and economic justice in the age of postmodernism.* Discussion Paper, CIRJE Series, University of Tokyo.
Lacan, J. (1975). *Le seminaire.* Paris: Editions du Seuil.
Sen, A. (2000). *Development as freedom.* New York: Anchor Books.
Sen, A., & Nussbaum. (1993). *The Quality of Life.* Oxford: Oxford University Press.
Wallwork, E. (1991). *Psychoanalysis and ethics.* New Haven: Yale University Press.

Other References

Amsden, Alice H. 1989. *Asia's Next Giant.* New York: Oxford University Press.
Arrighi, Giovanni. 2010, 1994. The Long Twentieth Century. London: Verso
———. 2007. Adam Smith in Beijing. London: Verso
Chang, H.-J. ed.(2007) *Institutional Change and Economic Development*, UNU press, Tokyo.
———. 2003. *Globalisation, Economic Development and the role of the State*, London: Zed Books.
———. 2008. *Bad Samaritans*, London: Bloomsbury Press
———. 1994. *The political economy of industrial policy*, New York: St. Martin's Press.
Cline, William R. (1982). "Can the East Asian Export Model of Development Be Generalized?", *World Development*, Vol.10, no.2 pp. 81–90.
Evans, Peter. 1995. *Embedded Autonomy: States and Industrial Transformation.* Princeton, Princeton University Press.
———. 2007. "Extending the Institutional Turn: Property, Politics and Development Trajectories", in Chang (2007):35–52.
Fields, Gary S. 1979. "A Welfare economic approach to Growth and distribution in the Dual Economy", Quarterly Journal of Economics, August. volume 93, issue 3, pages 325-353
Fosu, Augustin K. ed. 2013. *Achieving Development Success*, Oxford University Press.

Gabriele, Alberto and Haider Khan.2010. *Enhancing technological progress in a market-socialist context: China's national innovation system at the crossroads*, Berlin: LAP LAMBERT Academic Publishing

Ghosh, Jayati. 2010. "Global crisis and beyond: Sustainable growth trajectories for the developing world", *International Labour Review*, July 2010. vol. 149(2), pages 209-225.

Ghosh, Jayati (2009). *After crisis: adjustment, recovery, and fragility in East Asia.* Delhi: Tulika Books

Johnson, Chalmers. 1982. *MITI and the Japanese Miracle.* Stanford: Stanford University Press.

———. 1999. "The Developmental State: Odyssey of a Concept", in Woo-Cumings, M.ed.(1999). The Developmental State in Historical Perspective. Ithaca, NY: Cornell University Press.

Jomo K. S. ed. (2007). *Malaysian Industrial Policy.* Singapore University Press, Singapore, and University of Hawaii Press, Honolulu.

Jomo K. S. ed. (1995). *Privatizing Malaysia: Rents, Rhetoric, Realities.* Westview Press, Boulder.

Jomo K. S. with Shyamala Nagaraj eds. (2001). *Globalization Versus Development: Heterodox Perspectives.* Palgrave, Houndmills.

Jomo, K.S. and Wee (2008) "Lessons From Post-Colonial Malaysian Economic Development", paper prepared for WIDER conference on Country Role Models for Development Success, June13–14, Helsinki

Keynes, J. M.(1971–1979), *The Collected Writings of John Maynard Keynes,* 29 vols., ed., D. E. Moggridge for the Royal Economic Society, London: Macmillan.

Khan, H.A. (2021a). Human Capabilities in Complex Global System and Financial Governance: A Theory with Application to the BRICS. in P. Anand et.al. eds. *BRICS Handbook*, (Oxford University Press: Oxford)

———. (2021b). A Sustainable Development Strategy for Bangladesh in the Post-COVID 19 Era: A Socially Embedded Intersectional Capabilities Perspective. *Journal of Bangladesh Studies.* January/February, Vol.22, No. 2:1-14.

———. 2021c, COVID-19 in South Africa: An Intersectional Perspective based on Socio-economic Modeling and Indigenous Knowledge Base, EconPapers https://econpapers.repec.org/paper/pramprapa/108321.htm

———. (2020a). "On Socially Embedded Intersectional Capabilities Theory (SEICT)—An Example from the Philippines" In H. A. Khan, *Women's Socially Embedded Capabilities and Development: A Theory-based Empirical Investigation of Some ASEAN Countries*, Background paper for the Cambridge University Project on Human Development in ASEAN, 2020.

———. (2020b) Economic Impact of COVID-19 On Bangladesh: Agenda for Immediate Action and Planning for the Future, EconPapers https://econpapers.repec.org/paper/pramprapa/100380.htm (last visited on Dec.6, 2020)

Khan HA. 2014. Development and Women's Rights as Human Rights: A Political and Social Economy Approach within a Deep Democratic Framework, *Denver Journal of International Law and Policy* Vol. 42, No. 3(Aug. 2014).

Khan HA 2013.Development Strategies: Lessons from the Experiences of South Korea, Malaysia, Thailand and Vietnam, in Augustin K. Fosu ed. *Achieving Development Success*, Oxford University Press:119–132.

Khan HA (2012a). "Enhancing Economic Integration in the Asia-Pacific through the Strengthening of National Innovation Systems - Challenges and Strategies", *Asia-Pacific Technology Monitor, March-April, 2012*

Khan HA (2012b). "Deepening Democracy During Crisis", *Cosmopolis*, Summer, 2012

Khan HA (2011). Human development and capabilities in MENA economies with special emphasis on Egypt, EconPapers.https://econpapers.repec.org/paper/pramprapa/39381.htm

Khan HA (2010). "China's Development Strategy and Energy Security", in Amelia Santos-Paulino and Guanghua Wan ed. *The Rise of China and India: Development Strategies and Lessons*, Palgrave/Macmillan, 2010

Khan HA (2009). "A Theory of Deep Democracy in the Age of Postmodernism" (2009), in *Readings in Law and Society Journal*, 1. (1), 47.

Khan HA (2008a). "Building an Innovative Economy through Managed Creative Destruction: A Theory with Applications to South Korea". Accessed April 2015 at: http://econpapers.repec.org/paper/pramprapa/7713.htm

Khan HA (2008b). "Democracy in Bangladesh: from Crisis to Sustainability" (2008), *Journal of Bangladesh Studies*, 9. (2): 13–25.

Khan HA (2004a). *Innovation and Growth in East Asia: The Future of Miracles*. Houndmills and New York: Macmillan/Palgrave.

Khan HA (2004b). *Global Markets and Financial Crisis in Asia: Towards a Theory for the Twenty First Century*. Houndmills and New York: Palgrave Macmillan.

Khan HA (2003a). Technology and Modernity: Creating Social Capabilities in a POLIS. In Misa T ed. *Technology and Modernity*, Cambridge: The MIT Press, Chapter12.

———. (2003b) "What can the African countries learn from the macroeconomics of foreign aid in Southeast Asia?", Aryeetey, E., Court, J., Nissanke, M. and Weder, B., *Asia and Africa in the Global Economy*, Tokyo, UNU Press.

Khan HA (2002). "Innovation and Growth in a Schumpeterian Model". *Oxford Development Studies* 30(3): 289–306.

Khan HA (1997a). *Technology, Energy and Development: The South Korean Transition*. Cheltenham, United Kingdom: Edward Elgar.

Khan HA (1997b). "Ecology, Inequality and Poverty: The Case of Bangladesh" *AsianDevelopment Review*, 15 (2), 164–179

Khan HA. 1985. "Technology Choice in the Energy and Textile Sectors in the Republic of Korea" (1985), in A.S. Bhalla (ed.) Technology and Employment in Industry, 3rd ed. ILO

Khan HA (1983)"Technology, Energy, Distribution and Balance of Payments: A Macroeconomic Framework", Unpublished dissertation, Cornell University, Ithaca, New York.

Khan HA and Victor Lippit. 1993."The Surplus Approach to Environment" (1993), *Review of Political Economy.*

Khan HA and Victor Lippit. 2007. "Sustainability and Surplus ", Storrs, Ct.: Econ Papers http://econpapers.repec.org/paper/tkyfseres/2007cf464.htm (Last accessed on Sep. 15, 2015).

Khan HA and Yi-bei Liu (2008). "Ecological Economics of Water Management in China" in I. Usha ed. *Global Law and Economics of Sustainable Development*, IFCAI Press.

Khan HA and Erik Thorbecke (1989)."Macroeconomic Effects of Technology Choice: Multiplier and Structural Path Analysis", *Journal of Policy Modeling*, 11 (1): 131–156

Khan HA and Erik Thorbecke (1988), *Macroeconomic Effects and Diffusion of Alternative Technologies Within a Social Accounting Matrix Framework: the Case of Indonesia*, Gower Publication, CO. Aldershot, U.K.

Khan HA and K. Sonko (2020) *Islamic Finance as a Complex System.* Lanham, Md. And London: Rowman and Littlefield.

Khan HA and John Weiss 2006. "Poverty Strategies in Asia: growth plus", in Weiss, John and H. A. Khan eds.(2006) *Poverty Strategies in Asia: A Growth Plus Approach*, Cheltenham: Edward Elgar and ADBI. 1–40.

Lee, Keun (2008) "Can Korea be a Role Model for Development? A "Capability-based View" on Korea", paper prepared for WIDER conference on Country Role Models for Development Success, June13–14, Helsinki

Lee, Keun, 2006, "The Washington Consensus and East Asian Sequencing: Understanding Reform in East and South Asia," J. Fanelli and G. McMahon, eds. *Understanding Market Reforms* Vol. 2: Palgrave, 2006.

Li, Minqi. 2008. *The Rise of China and the Demise of the Capitalist World Economy.* New York: The Monthly Review Press.

Mann, Michael. 1988. "The Autonomous Power of the State: Its Origins, Mechanism and Results", in Mann, M. *States, War and History*, Oxford: Blackwell.

Mayer, Jörg (2002). "The Fallacy of Composition: A Review of the Literature", *The World Economy*, Vol.25,pp.875–94.

Nussbaum, Martha (1995). "Human capabilities, female human beings." In M.C. Nussbaum, and J. Glover (eds.), *Women, culture and development* (pp.61–104). Oxford: Clarendon Press.

———. (2000). *Women and Human Development: the capabilities approach.* Cambridge: Cambridge University Press.

Peet, Richard.2007. *Geography of Power: Making Global Economic Policy.* London: Zed Press

Peet, Richard and Elaine Hartwick. 2009. *Theories of Development: Contentions, Arguments, Alternatives.* London: Guilford Press.

Prashad, Vijay. 2014. *The Poorer Nations: A possible history of the Global South.* London: Verso.

Razmi, Arslan and Robert Blecker (2006). "Developing Country Exports of Manufactures: moving up the export ladder to escape the fallacy of composition?", *Journal of Development Studies*, Vol.44, No.1, January:21–48.

Reinert, Erik S. 2007."Institutionalism ancient, old and new: A historical perspective on institutions and uneven development", in Chang, H.-J. ed.(2007) *Institutional Change and Economic Development*, UNU press, Tokyo. 53–74.

Schneider, Aaron (2015). "Democratic Deepening and International Insertion: The Emergence of Brazil and India", unpublished paper, JKSIS, University of Denver.

Thoburn, J.T. (2008), "Viet Nam", paper prepared for WIDER conference on Country Role Models for Development Success, June13–14, Helsinki

Sen, Amartya. 2009. *The Idea of Justice.* Cambridge, Ma.: The Belknap Press of the Harvard University Press.

———. (1999). *Development as Freedom.* Oxford: Oxford University Press and New York: Alfred A. Knopf, Inc.

———. (1992). *Inequality Reexamined.* Oxford: Oxford University Press.

Thoburn, J.T., K. Sutherland and Nguyen Thi Hoa (2007), 'Globalisation and restructuring in the textiles sector on households in Vietnam: impacts on households', *Journal of the Asia Pacific Economy*, vol.12, no.3, August,: 345–366

Wade, Robert 1990. *Governing the Market.* Princeton: Princeton University Press.

Warr, Peter (2008) "Thailand's Development Strategy and Growth Performance", paper prepared for WIDER conference on Country Role Models for Development Success, June13–14, Helsinki

Warr, Peter (1993) 'The Thai Economy' in Peter Warr (ed.) *The Thai Economy in Transition*, Cambridge University Press, Cambridge, 1–80.

Warr, Peter (1999). 'What Happened to Thailand?', *The World Economy*, 22 (July), 631–650.

Warr, Peter (2005) 'Boom, Bust and Beyond' in Peter Warr (ed.) *Thailand Beyond the Crisis*, Routledge, London, 3–65.

Weiss, Linda.1998. *The Myth of the Powerless State.* Ithaca: Cornell University Press.

Weiss, John and H. A. Khan eds.(2006) *Poverty Strategies in Asia: A Growth Plus Approach*, Cheltenham: Edward Elgar and ADBI.
Woo-Cumings, M. ed.(1999). *The Developmental State in Historical Perspective*. Ithaca, NY: Cornell University Press.
World Bank. 1993.The East Asian Miracle. New York: Oxford University Press.

CHAPTER 10

Conclusions: Towards an African Renaissance

10.1 Synopsis

Throughout this book, we have observed that Africa is a continent with numerous opportunities for, but problems too of, development. We have argued that a new approach towards optimal solutions for the problems in Africa needs to be outlined. We have suggested specific policy agendas at the continental level within an overall strategic shift in the emerging multipolar world based on cooperation among the African countries and their partners in the Global South. We have gone into some country-specific details and suggested policy perspectives that take into account local specificities as well. Such specificities range from agriculture and extraction to industrial and service sectors covering inter alia productive activities, factorial and household incomes and income distributions and household incomes and well-being.

We have also dealt with crucial functional areas such as corporate governance, innovation and distribution of wealth in addition to income, to mention just a few significant exemplifying issues. Here in this concluding chapter, we want to be forward looking and ask what a renaissance for Africa would look like. Of course, we can only offer the barest outline of a possible future for Africa in a short concluding chapter. But with a realistic refutation of Afro-pessimism in the substantive chapters in specific areas some broad discussion here is at least possible. Hence, we focus on strategic aspects of creating a new prosperous and peaceful Africa where the

K. N. M. Sonko et al., *21st Century African Development Strategies*,
https://doi.org/10.1007/978-3-031-93079-9_10

social capabilities of ordinary Africans are guaranteed to be enhanced. In keeping with realism, we also present our perspectives within geoeconomic and geopolitical realities that are emerging in a multipolar world in the making.

This chapter covers these key future strategic problems and argues for a sound strategic horizon for African development with flexible tactics appropriate for specific time periods and definite African geography of space. We start with the critical problems related to how Africa can move beyond rent-seeking towards a genuine people-oriented development. We then move into some related methodological issues and defend our approach from the perspective of causal depth and scientific realism. In a natural way, such a quest for analytical depth leads us to stress the common good for Africa and the well-being of the African people.

It has been recognized for some time that uneven development under unchecked capitalism leads to harmful inequalities and polarization with violations of the common good—particularly in Africa. In the previous chapters we have attempted deep structural explanations for maldevelopment in Africa.

Based on such an approach we now ask: what can a deep structural causal explanation for uneven development in Africa deliver on the epistemological, ontological and ethical sides? To answer a set of questions for Africa, we must further ask: how are relatively deeper scientific explanations to be distinguished from superficial or shallower ones in the African case? Furthermore, what roles can scientific counterfactual analysis play in social sciences and policy making which can help overcome uneven and unequal development in Africa? For a competent, morally motivated scientific policy maker in development economics for Africa, it is important to avoid inflicting harm and promote the common good of the African people. Related geopolitical and geoeconomic considerations lead to a further critical argument for a future non-aligned Africa in general with multi-alignments in specific circumstances.

While the above areas of critical analyses do not exhaust all issue areas for Africa, we argue that strategic steps in these areas will give the African people and their leaders a fighting chance to build towards a prosperous and equitable future. This is the essence of prospects for an African renaissance in the twenty-first century.

10.2 Africa Beyond Rent-Seeking and Towards Genuine Development as Freedom

In the substantive chapters of this book, we have presented and analysed a number of deep structural-institutional and policy problems for Africa. The African people and their leaders need to solve these problems at various levels in all sectors. The key unifying thematic problem would appear to be that of rent-seeking and draining of surplus from Africa (Khan 1997; Jomo and Khan 2000 and Khan 2012). Concentration of wealth and income, class and ethnic divisions, struggling educational systems, persistent poverty, inequality, etc. are characteristic complex webs of mutually reinforcing vicious cycle linkages in Africa, made possible by continuous rent-seeking and draining of surplus from Africa.

More generally, these rent-seeking activities also reinforce and regenerate, inter alia, uneven development in Africa (Khan and Sonko 2020; Khan 1997, 1999; Kingdon et al. 2005). The vicious cycles make uneven development an almost inevitable relentless process unless some of the countries bravely break away from neocolonial dependence. Here the external and internal relations are indeed dialectically related. Only key internal political and economic changes linking up with progressive external forces can repudiate the neocolonial relations. Only such a renewal of a commitment towards genuine African sovereignty can make the prospects for people-oriented African development a reality. As difficult as such a renewal may seem, we can argue that for Africa in the future this can happen. Among other things, the governance (including corporate) for sustainable development which is a challenging task in Africa can begin to happen finally under such an African renaissance. A new rebirth of African freedom as African capabilities can make this continent a powerful pole in the emerging multipolar world.

Here, the steps taken by South Africa towards creating a multipolar world via the expanded BRICS are a good beginning. But it is only a beginning. Other leading African countries must come forward and help develop a genuine agenda and plan of action for enhancing the capabilities of the African people, especially by Africans first and foremost, a recurrent theme throughout this book. All key areas including political, economic, ecological, social and cultural priorities should be part of this agenda for African renaissance.

Therefore, African countries at different levels of development must work together cooperatively. Accordingly, in this book we have tried to find multiple pathways to integrate useful genuine need-fulfilling markets with the key characteristics of the African enabling developmental states for the twenty-first century that must be constructed in order to build a growing ecologically sustainable African political economy with equity in terms of capabilities. This is urgent both for theoretical clarification and for aiding the strategies of popular democratic movements in Africa, as I have argued in Chaps. 6 and 9. A few tentative steps have been taken in this book to serve this dual purpose. Proceeding from a critical capabilities perspective that is fully grounded in social reality of deepening structural and ecological crises of the world system, on which I have done substantial work, I discover that such a perspective leads to the need to include among the characteristics of the enabling developmental states in Africa for the twenty-first century, their capacity to build an ecologically sustainable egalitarian development strategy from the beginning. The specific theoretical approach I follow has been developed during the last few decades by ecological scientists and social scientists.

My own particular version can be called Evolutionary Ecological Global Political Economy or EEGPE for short. In addition, democracy must be deepened from the beginning, for the sake of not only democracy but yielding concrete benefits for the people. For Africa in particular, a new cooperative community of African nations following their own rhythm to reach their own dynamic trajectories towards development as freedom will be possible if they cooperate regionally on the basis of equal sovereignty and mutual respect. One precondition is for Africa to pragmatically unite for a common economic strategy, as called for in this book by my co-authors and me. For this a decolonization of the African mind is also necessary.

To this end, methodologically I have followed a critical scientific realist approach that is evolutionary. Without being a naïve Social Darwinist, I apply the real insights of Darwinian selection principles (Darwin 1859, 1871, 1883; Romanes 1883, 1893; Barrett et al. 1987; Dennett 1995; Archer 1995, 1996; Bhaskar 1975; Boyd 1973, 1992; Hodgson 2001, 2002, 2003, 2004; Khan et al. 2021; Khan 1982, 1998, 1999, 2004, 2006, 2020, 2021a, b, c, 2022, 2023, 2024a, b, c; Khan and Rahman 2022; Khan and Thorbecke 1988, 1989; Sen 1992, 1999, 2009; UNCTAD 2006; Wilson 1994). I have done this methodological exercise via substantive work in historically evolving societies in the African continent. In order to do this work, I needed to develop some novel concepts and theoretical perspectives that have been discussed in the earlier chapters. The novel approach is also evident in the ideas offered by my co-authors in their chapters.

10.3 Causal Depth, Counterfactuals and Common Good in African Political Economy Poverty Reduction in the Counterfactuals via the Dual-Dual Structural Model as an Exemplar

"Had Cleopatra's nose been shorter, the whole face of the world would have changed", so speculated Blaise Pascal in 1669. This is an example of a counterfactual thought. Leaving aside the truth value of Pascal's speculation, the method of counterfactuals in history has been known at least since Thucydides's famous history. Khan (2024a, b, c) shows that Thucydides's history also contains germs of the idea of what scientific realists today call "causal depth". Putting the idea of counterfactuals together with the scientific realist concept of causal depth helps us explore different states of the African socio-economic institutions in causally salient ways. We have demonstrated for Africa this type of scientific realist analysis in the previous chapters. In fact, the realist interpretation of randomized controlled trials which are being done in Africa now is precisely that of specifying counterfactuals in a precise enough manner in order to draw conclusions by realizing alternate—factual and counterfactual—states of the world in specific trials. Structural models for Africa by Khan and others follow the same logic. More importantly, such realism for Africa has the significant normative implications for identifying and pursuing African common good in addition to avoiding harm to the African people.

As an example of avoiding harm and pursuing the common good of capabilities enhancement by reducing poverty within the dual-dual model can be mentioned. The neoliberal model claims deductively that since "free markets" lead to the most efficient and *Pareto optimal state* of the economy, there is no logical case for increasing well-being via interventionist poverty reduction policies. The counterfactuals' pursuit in causally deeper structural dual-dual model shows at least two common good-related results empirically (Khan 2006).

First, the free trade argument that tariff reduction is sufficient for poverty reduction turns out to be largely wrong. Even under the most favourable counterfactual conditions, the results do not carry through below 20% tariff. Furthermore, even in the quantitatively effective range, the actual quantitative poverty reduction is miniscule. Even within that "achievement", I find that urban poor groups actually fare worse than before. Thus, a nuanced scenario analysis requires a possibility for posing detailed counterfactual conditionals in a critical scientific realist manner.

Second, the structural model shows that counterfactual experiments involving structural changes such as asset redistribution can lead to a vastly more favourable situation for the poor and an unambiguous improvement in well-being. From an ethical point of view, such an outcome can be defended either through the Rawlsian difference principle or better yet through the socially embedded extensions of Amartya Sen's capabilities theory.

Furthermore, we should consider the question of causal mechanisms in light of causal depth. Neoclassical theory postulates mechanisms that are mathematically consistent with optimizing agents' calculus. However, ontologically salient causal mechanisms in any mature scientific field require more depth than just the consistency with the optimizing calculus. Among other things, there must be concrete causal pathways—diagrammable according to the principles of mathematical graph theory—showing the elementary paths, causal loops and multiple pathways that are all causally salient. This looms as an important future task for analysing and ultimately realizing the common good in Africa.

Therefore, for Africa in particular, causal depth and realist counterfactual thought experiments are not mere scientific arcana. In reality, these are tools of causal analysis for crucial experiments for policy formulations for avoiding the harm that unreflective neoliberalism can inflict and indeed has inflicted on the most vulnerable groups in Africa. More broadly and positively, the approach defended here can lead to advancement of common socio-economic good leading to a real African renaissance. Such a search for discovering the common good for Africa and implementing appropriate policies including policies for building institutions to enhance African common good can be seen to be also deeply connected with the great African thinker and writer Ngugi wa Thiongo's idea of "Re-membering" in/of Africa. To recover Africa's proud, although little known, history and to reconnect the dismembered parts of today's politically and economically deformed Africa through real regional cooperation based on pan-African unity are urgent tasks for which Africa also needs to redefine its priorities in international relations. I now turn to this crucial area in the final section of this concluding chapter.

10.4 A New Non-aligned Africa for Genuine Development

For such a strategy to succeed, Africa should stay away from aligning with one geopolitical or geoeconomic camp or another. Indeed, given its resources, under proper regional leadership Africa can do so. India has declared a "multi-alignment" strategy. Africa can pursue a similar multi-alignment that preserves the freedom of non-alignment. Essential for this to happen is African sovereignty that can preserve its independence under pressures from the great powers pushing Africa towards aligning itself with only one camp. As the African proverb famously points out, when elephants fight, it is the grass that gets trampled. Africa has suffered enough from this during the first cold war after WWII. Learning from that experience, wise African leaders can try to follow a different non-aligned and multi-aligned developmental trajectory in the twenty-first century. Within such a strategic framework, genuine human development and capabilities enhancement can indeed happen in Africa in this century.

My critical assessment of human development and capabilities exercise in Africa includes the following areas for achieving capabilities enhancement: (i) *macroeconomic framework component*, analysis of the evolution and nature of macroeconomic policies and their inter-relationships with trade policy and their effects on SDGs and human development; (ii) *fiscal component*, the effects of trade reform and policies on the fiscal position of the countries and its relation with SDGs' expenditure needs and potential constraining effect on the application of flanking policies; (iii) *institutional component*, assessing institutional capacity and performance of trade- and finance-related institutions in particular and their effect on economic, social and political outcomes: (iv) *dynamic effects component*, undertaking specific studies to assess spillovers and externalities brought about by various policies, particularly trade, financial and investment policies (Khan et al. 2023 for example); and (v) *intellectual property rights (IPRs) component*, assessing the effects of more stringent protection of IPRs on SDGs and human development indicators. I have evaluated critically the neoliberal approach to these aspects of development and capabilities in Africa generally and with—for instance—special case studies of Kenya and South Africa (Khan 1989, 1887, 2005, 2020a, b, 2021a, b, c, 2011). Khan and Sonko (2020) also contain several relevant studies of similar nature with emphases on the financial development.

Amartya Sen's pioneering contributions contra utilitarian welfarism and more recent extensions including the controversial listing issue have been discussed by me elsewhere as part of a partial historical background to capabilities approach.[1] I put particular emphasis on social and political aspects of capabilities both because of their general relevance and also because of their particular relevance to Africa in light of political and social upheavals, particularly in South Africa, which exemplifies many of the common problems of the African countries. Of course, each country and the region as a whole exemplify in their own specific ways the law of uneven development within an uneven world capitalist system. Therefore, for Africa as for other geographical regions in the Global Political Economy (GPE), there is no substitute for specific country studies and sub-national regional studies within this world capitalist system using the framework of Evolutionary Ecological Global Political Economy (EEGPE).

In the substantive chapters, we thus argue for looking at Africa as a complex system of national economies and polities where both the system and its components matter. We have developed our arguments theoretically and have at least partially illustrated this approach methodologically and substantively through concrete analyses of concrete conditions within Africa. We have emphasized experiential learning by discussing some lessons from the East Asian development experience in creating structures of learning and capabilities enhancement. I have carried out extensive earlier on this experience. However, I have also discussed the limitations of the East Asian Model and have identified further conditions for development as freedom that should be part of one's analytical apparatus in studying the regions and countries within Africa. In my previous empirical work I have focused critically on assessment of human development and capabilities exercise in Africa in the broad areas analysed in this book. I also have analysed their various components concretely in order to highlight the ambiguities of the neoliberal approach and its real costs for the African economies in human capabilities terms. Out of this exercise and further thinking on development I have extended Sen's approach described in several chapters to include social embeddedness institutionally and historically with further emphasis on intersectionality—particularly the intersectionality of class, race/ethnicity and gender in Africa.

[1] See Haider A. Khan, *Technology, Development and Democracy,* Edward Elgar, 1998, chs. 6 and 7 in particular. On Socially Embedded Intersectional Capabilities Theory, see Khan (2021a, b, c, d) and Khan (2020, 2022).

My approach integrates, among other things, poverty and social impact analysis (PSIA) techniques, economic and technical tools of ex ante and ex post assessments, and monitoring and evaluation methodologies in a comprehensive analytical setting. Accordingly, the strategic features highlighted here can be concretized in empirical applications and tactical questions can be posed by identifying interested stakeholders. They can be asked questions regarding facilitating and coordinating their participation as well as building institutional arrangements that will assure sustainability of the human development process through concrete multi-dimensional Socially Embedded Intersectional Capabilities enhancement.

I have suggested the construction and use of social accounting matrices (SAMs) for African countries, regions and Africa as a whole to enable the policy makers to gather appropriate data and build appropriate structural models for Africa using such SAMs. This research area needs to be a task of highest priority and resources need to be mobilized to enable Africans to make quick and substantial progress in the next few years on this strategic task. Here, given that South Africa has already produced a number of SAMs covering both the national and sub-national socio-economic data in a consistent framework, there is much room for pragmatic cooperation, led by this pioneering country, with other African nations.

A related aspect is the need for documenting and analysing local historical settings including the construction of sequential historical SAMs. Finally, progress towards collecting data and building a database of relevant indicators and developing tools of monitoring and evaluation along with the development of the institutional and technical capability of stakeholders can be addressed for appropriate African capacity building. Building on other experiences of participatory assessment of different policies, the strategic approaches I advocate, besides producing empirical analysis, can be used to engage all actors involved (government, business, labour and civil society institutions representing different segments of the population, in particular African women) in active participation for development as genuine freedom.

Given that such genuine development is a complex social-economic-state systemic process, only many forces working together in clear and flexibly strategic and tactical alliances can get this systemic process going in the right direction. I have suggested that deepening BRICS-like alliances might be a good, flexible start. But further complexities only unfold with such a beginning. Even with the best political will all African countries—particularly those at the low level of development—will need to mobilize internal and external resources. My co-authors and I have suggested various strategies for such resource mobilization in this book. For further success institutions should be built once this mobilization process gets started. But constant monitoring, evaluation and fresh thinking must be pursued continuously. Only in this way can mistakes be caught and corrected in time to minimize losses and enable all African countries to tackle the systemic problems that inevitably arise in large, nonlinear, complex systems in nature and society.

Therefore, Africa cannot just follow any externally supplied model mechanically. The list of such externally supplied models includes not just the neoliberal model but also the old East Asian model. Inter alia, the systemic crises of accumulation and the deepening ecological crisis impose new challenges that the old East Asian Model did not address (Khan 2024a, b, c). African policy makers must learn from multiple crises and develop an appropriate African model of development. Our substantive chapters develop some ideas that point towards this ambitious but absolutely necessary task. We have made some modest progress towards this goal. But much more work remains to be done, particularly in areas of cooperative pan- and trans-African institution building for genuine African development. My co-authors and I have provided this book for further discussions on more genuine and sustainable human-centred African development.

References

Archer, M. S. (1995). *Realist social theory: The morphogenetic approach*. Cambridge: Cambridge University Press.

Archer, M. S. (1996). Social integration and system integration: Developing the distinction. *Sociology, 30*(4), 679–699.

Barrett, Paul H., Gautrey, Peter J., Herbert, Sandra, Kohn, David and Smith, Sydney (eds) (1987) *Charles Darwin's Notebooks, 1836–1844: Geology, Transmutation of Species, Metaphysical Enquiries*, Cambridge: Cambridge University Press.

Bhaskar, Roy (1975) *A Realist Theory of Science*, 1st edition, Leeds: Leeds Books.

Boyd, Richard N. (1973) "Realism, Underdetermination, and a Causal Theory of Evidence," *Nous*, pp. 1–12.

———. (1992) "Constructivism, Realism, and Philosophical Method," in J. Earman, ed. *Inference, Explanation, and Other Philosophical Frustrations*. Berkeley: University of California Press.

Darwin, Charles R. (1859) *On the Origin of Species by Means of Natural Selection, or the Preservation of Favoured Races in the Struggle for Life*, 1st edn, London: Murray.

Darwin, Charles R. (1871) *The Descent of Man, and Selection in Relation to Sex*, 1st edn, 2 vols, London: Murray and New York: Hill.

Darwin, Charles R. (1883) *The Variation of Animals and Plants Under Domestication*, 2 vols., 2nd edn, London and New York: Murray and Appleton.

Dennett, Daniel C. (1995) *Darwin's Dangerous Idea: Evolution and the Meanings of Life*, London: Allen Lane.

Hodgson, Geoffrey M. (2001) 'Darwin, Veblen and the problem of causality in economics', *History and Philosophy of the Life Sciences* 23: 383–422.

———. (2002) 'Darwinism in Economics: from analogy to ontology', *Journal of Evolutionary Economics* 12(2): 259–81.

———. (2003) 'The mystery of the routine: the Darwinian destiny of *An Evolutionary Theory of Economic Change*', *Revue Économique* 54(2): 355–84.

———. (2004) *The Evolution of Institutional Economics: Agency, Structure and Darwinism in American Institutionalism*, London and New York: Routledge.

Jomo, K.S. and Mushtaq Khan. 2000. *Rents, rent seeking and economic development*. Cambridge, UK: Mushtaq University Press.

Haider A. Khan, Shahryar Ghorbani, Elham Shabani and Shahab S. Band. 2023. Enhancement of Neural Networks Model's Predictions of Currencies Exchange Rates by Phase Space Reconstruction and Harris Hawks' Optimization. *Computational Economics*. February. DOI: https://doi.org/10.1007/s10614-023-10361-y

Haider Khan. 2022. November: Afterward: Where do we go from Crisis, Inequalities and Poverty. In *Crisis, Inequalities and Poverty*, Francesco Schettino and Fabio Clementi. Leyden, The Netherlands: Brill Publishers, November, 2022. pp.: 141–182.

Haider A. Khan and S. Rahman. 2022. The Political Economy of Development: Bangladesh From Its Emergence toward the Future. In H. Khondker et al. eds. *The Emergence of Bangladesh*, Springer, 2022

Haider A. Khan, 2021a. Governing a Complex Global Financial System in the Age of Global Instabilities and BRICS: Promoting Human Capabilities through Global Financial Stability and Growth with Equity, Chapter 37 in P.B. Anand, Shailaja Fennell and Flavio Comim eds. *Handbook of BRICS and Emerging Economies*, Oxford University Press, 2021:940–979 https://global.oup.com/academic/product/handbook-of-brics-and-emerging-economies-9780198827535?cc=us&lang=en&#

Khan, H.A. 2021b. Towards a New Socially Embedded Intersectional Capabilities Theory (SEICT) in the 21st Century: Analysis of COVID-19 Policies in South Africa through Socio-Economic Modeling and Indigenous Knowledge Base. *Journal of Applied Economic Sciences*, Volume XVI, Summer, 2(72): 162–178. http://cesmaa.org/Docs/Summer%202021/3_KhanHaider.pdf

Haider A. Khan. 2021c AI, Deep Machine Learning via Neuro-Fuzzy Models: Complexities of International Financial Economics of Crises. *Int Journal of Computation and Neural Engineering*. 2021; 7(3):122–134 DOI:https://doi.org/10.19070/2572-7389-2100016

Khan, H.A. (2021d) Women's and Minorities' Rights, Socially Embedded Intersectional Capabilities and ASEAN Identity, *Cambridge University (Department of Land Economics) Monograph*, October, 2021

———. (2024a), 21st Century Accelerated Dedollarization, Multipolarity and The Global South Beyond Modern Money Theory: Governance of a Complex Global Financial System in the Age of Global Instabilities. Econpapers. https://econpapers.repec.org/paper/pramprapa/119650.htm

———. (2024b). Development Orders and Disorders: Real Competition in Complex Global Capitalist System, China's Ambiguous Case, and the Need for Democratic Socialism in the 21st Century. Econpapers. https://econpapers.repec.org/paper/pramprapa/119640.htm

———. (2024c). Dialectics of Emergy in a Social Accounting Matrix. Econpapers https://econpapers.repec.org/paper/pramprapa/119651.htm

———. (2023). Towards a New Non-aligned Movement(NNAM) and a New International Economic Order: A Strategy for Comprehensive Non-capitalist Development in the 21st Century. EconPapers. https://econpapers.repec.org/paper/pramprapa/117143.htm

Khan, H. A. (2020)Islamic Finance as a Complex System: A Mathematical Model with Human Capabilities in Complex Global System and Financial Governance in H. Khan and K. Sonko eds. Islamic Finance as a Complex System, Cambridge, MA: Lexington Press: 11–46. https://rowman.com/ISBN/9781793608666/Islamic-Finance-as-a-Complex-System-New-Insights

———. (2006). "Poverty Analysis in a Dual-Dual Model" in J. Weiss and H.A. Khan (eds.) *Poverty Strategies in Asia*, Edward Elgar.

———. (2004). "Using Macroeconomic CGE Models for Analyzing the Poverty Reduction Impact of Structural Adjustment Policies", Asian Development Bank Institute Discussion Paper No. 12, Tokyo.

———. (1999). "Sectoral Growth and Poverty: a multiplier decomposition analysis for South Africa, *World Development*, March.

———. (1998). *Technology, Development and Democracy*, Cheltenham: Edward Elgar,

Khan, Haider A. 1997. *African Debt and Development: Policies for a New Partnership with Africa*. New York: Phelps-Stokes Fund.

———. (1982). "Energy, Technology and Income Distribution: A Social Accounting Matrix for Energy Modelling," *Applied Simulation and Modelling*, Calgary, Canada, ACTA

Khan, H. A. and K. Sonko (2020)Islamic Finance as a Complex System, in H. Khan and K. Sonko eds. Islamic Finance as a Complex System, Cambridge, MA: Lexington Press: 1–10. https://rowman.com/ISBN/9781793608666/Islamic-Finance-as-a-Complex-System-New-Insights

Khan, H.A. and E. Thorbecke (1988) *Macroeconomic Effects and Diffusion of Alternative Technologies within a Social Accounting Matrix Framework: the Case of Indonesia*, Gower Publication, Co., Aldershot, U.K.

Khan, H.A. and E. Thorbecke (1989). "Macroeconomic Effects of Technology Choice: Multiplier and Structural Path Analysis," *Journal of Policy Modelling*, Vol. 11, No. 1

Khan, Mushtaq. 2012. Governance and growth challenges for Africa, in A. Norman, K. Botchwey, H. Stein and J. Stiglitz eds. *Good Growth and Governance in Africa: Rethinking development strategies.* Oxford: Oxford University Press.

Kingdon, G., J. Sandefur and F. Teal (2005). "Labour market flexibility, wages and incomes in sub-Saharan Africa in the 1990s", Center for the Study of African Economies, Department of Economics, University of Oxford, UK.

Romanes, George John (1883) *Mental Evolution in Animals*, London: Kegan Paul, Trench.

——— (1893) *Darwin and After Darwin: An Exposition of the Darwinian Theory and a Discussion of Post-Darwinian Questions*, vol. 1, 2nd edn, London: Longmans, Green.

Sen, Amartya. 2009. *The Idea of Justice*. Cambridge, MA: The Belknap Press of the Harvard University Press.

———. (1999). *Development as Freedom*. Oxford: Oxford University Press and New York: Alfred A. Knopf, Inc.

———. (1992). *Inequality Reexamined*. Oxford: Oxford University Press.

UNCTAD (2006). *The Least Developed Countries Report: Developing Productive Capacities*, Geneva and New York

Wilson, Robert A. (1994). Causal Depth, Theoretical Appropriateness, and Individualism in Psychology, *Philosophy of Science*, Vol. 61, No. 1 (March), pp. 55–75

Index[1]

[1] Note: Page numbers followed by 'n' refer to notes.

K. N. Sonko et al., *21st Century African Development Strategies*,
https://doi.org/10.1007/978-3-031-93079-9

GPSR Compliance

The European Union's (EU) General Product Safety Regulation (GPSR) is a set of rules that requires consumer products to be safe and our obligations to ensure this.

If you have any concerns about our products, you can contact us on ProductSafety@springernature.com

In case Publisher is established outside the EU, the EU authorized representative is:

Springer Nature Customer Service Center GmbH
Europaplatz 3
69115 Heidelberg, Germany

Batch number: 10755348

Printed by Printforce, the Netherlands